BRAZILIAN NARRATIVE

IN A COMPARATIVE

WORLD LITERATURES REIMAGINED

MODERN LANGUAGE ASSOCIATION OF AMERICA

Brazilian Narrative Traditions in a Comparative Context.
Earl E. Fitz. 2005.

BRAZILIAN NARRATIVE TRADITIONS IN A COMPARATIVE CONTEXT

Earl E. Fitz

THE MODERN LANGUAGE ASSOCIATION OF AMERICA

NEW YORK 2005

For information about obtaining permission to reprint material from MLA book publications, send your request by mail (see address below), e-mail (permissions@mla.org), or fax (646 458-0030).

LIBRARY OF CONGRESS CATALOGING-IN-PUBLICATION DATA

Fitz, Earl E.
  Brazilian narrative traditions in a comparative context / by Earl E. Fitz.
      p. cm. — (World literatures reimagined ; 1)
  Includes bibliographical references and index.
  ISBN 0-87352-587-6 (hardcover : alk. paper) — ISBN 0-87352-588-4 (pbk. : alk. paper)
  1. Brazilian fiction—History and criticism. 2. Literature, Comparative—Brazilian and American.
3. Literature, Comparative—American and Brazilian. 4. American fiction—History and criticism.
I. Title. II. Series.
  PQ9597.F58 2004
  869.3'009981—dc22   2004017526
  ISSN 1553-6181

Cover illustration for the paperback edition: *Estrada de Ferro Central do Brasil.* 1924. By Tarsila do Amaral. Oil on canvas. Collection of Museu de Arte Contemporânea da Universidade de São Paulo, Brazil

Published by The Modern Language Association of America
26 Broadway, New York, New York 10004-1789
www.mla.org

CONTENTS

World literature: for many years, this concept has been little understood and even less agreed upon. Since Goethe's invention of the term *Weltliteratur* in 1827, readers have tended to invest world literature with both an impossibly ideal character and an inconceivable material scope. For some, it is a highly selective canon of works that transcend their national literatures and languages. For others, it is everything—the sum of all the national literatures considered together. For still others among a spate of recent theorists who have embraced the topic, world literature is the outcome of a confrontation between received forms and local conditions, a mode of reading and exchange between works of different times and places, or a metropolitan construction that ensures the maintenance of categories such as "major" and "minor" literatures.

Meanwhile, world literature has become increasingly prevalent in departments of literature, as the rubric for a kind of course that—despite its name—usually reflects local institutional notions of what might be relevant. While the concept has been undergoing considerable intellectual revision in recent years, little has changed for the teacher or student who seeks to expand his or her reach.

The series World Literatures Reimagined, sponsored by the MLA's Publications Committee, seeks to redress this gap by exploring new conceptions of what world literature—or literatures—might mean. Written by specialists but addressed to a wide audience, books in the series consider particular literatures in an international context. The books seek to develop new articulations of the connections among literatures and to give a sense of the ways in which literatures and their cultures might be like and unlike one another. Volumes in the series look afresh at works that might expand or complicate our notions of world literature; make comparisons between less-known works and their better-known counterparts; and deal forthrightly with translation, showing the teacher and student what is (and what should be) available in English. A shelf of these volumes should go far to encourage the reimagining of world literatures in our consciousness as well as our classrooms.

Roland Greene
Series Editor

This book could not have been completed without the constant love and support (technical and otherwise) of the following wonderful people: Julilaya (who continues to know and understand), Zinho, Snabby, Chiller, and el señor G. *Muito obrigado!*

I would also like to thank my editors, Roland Greene, whose vision, sage counsel, and meticulous readings kept the project on track and headed in the right direction, and Sonia Kane, whose organizational sense, professionalism, and good humor overcame innumerable manuscript and schedule problems. Thanks, too, go to Elizabeth Holland and her staff, whose efforts made my text more readable. To the extent that this work succeeds, it does so largely as a result of all your efforts. *Muito obrigado!*

Finally, and in the spirit of giving credit where credit is due, I acknowledge the writers whose studies comparing Brazil and the United States have made this volume possible. In particular, I call attention to Samuel Putnam's *Marvelous Journey*, which exerted a powerful influence on my early sense of Brazilian literature and its place in the world and which, in many ways, remains the prototype for this type of comparative scholarship. To Putnam, then; to the farsighted intellectual innovators Gregory Rabassa and Raymond Sayers; and to the pioneering scholars E. Bradford Burns, Gilberto Freyre, Vianna Moog, Sérgio Buarque de Holanda, Renata Wasserman, Nelson Vieira, Robert Stam, Randal Johnson, Oscar Fernández, Mary Daniel, David Haberly, David Jackson, and Roberto DaMatta (among many others), I say, in great admiration and in all sincerity, *Muito obrigado!*

CHAPTER 1

Introduction:
Brazil and the United States

A COMPLEX RELATIONSHIP

With both nations possessing powerful, diverse, and innovative narrative traditions, Brazil and the United States are beginning to realize how extensively they parallel each other in historical and cultural development and how much they can learn from each other. Indeed, we can gain a more thorough understanding of the literature of the United States by studying it in comparison with that of Brazil, the hemispheric nation that offers some of the best opportunities for critical rethinking and interrogation. As the concepts American literature and American studies undergo reassessment of their definition and scope (see G. Jay; P. Jay, "Myth" and "Discipline"; Porter, "What"; Mulford)—and as the reconsideration takes place in the context of inter-American or Pan-American studies (see Miller; P. Jay, "Discipline"; and Fitz, "Theory")—the importance of Brazil will become evident. Although Brazil has long been more aware of its northern neighbor than the United States has been of Brazil, this aspect of the relationship has, fortunately, started to change. From the free play of international economics to the ebb and flow of cultural trends, from literature to politics, and from *futebol* to music, Brazil is making its presence felt, not only in the United States but in the world at large. Ample evidence from a number of fronts suggests, in fact, that the relative absence of the South American giant from world affairs is coming to an end. Popularly known among its citizens, with a characteristic sense of self-deprecation, as *a terra de amanhã* ("the land of tomorrow"), Brazil at long last has arrived.

As to the question of why we would counterpose the narrative traditions of the United States and Brazil, we find several compelling reasons. First is the long tradition of influence and reception that has linked the two hemispheric neighbors.[1] Although the literary tie between Brazil and the United States has been dominated by the northern country, unexpected connections are being revealed at an increasing rate. For example, the debt that John Barth owes the Brazilian master Machado de Assis has been clearly established (Fitz, "Influence" and "John Barth's Brazilian Connection"; Barbosa), as have John Updike's interest in Brazil and its writers, and, more recently, the role Brazil plays in the fiction of Gayl Jones and Toni Morrison (see R. Jackson), while the poststructural and feminist fictions of Clarice Lispector are becoming permanent fixtures in many programs in Spanish and Portuguese, women's studies, and comparative literature. Second is the provocative argument that Brazil and the United States possess the two strongest narrative traditions in the Americas. Brazil's, in fact, may well be "the most independent, and perhaps most original, national literature in the New World."[2] Finally, comparative studies on Brazil and the United States, though still relatively few, are growing rapidly, in both sophistication and quantity (see, e.g., Putnam, *Marvelous Journey*; Wasserman, *Exotic Nations* and "Re-inventing"; Edinger, "Hawthorne" and "Machismo"; Valente; Stam). This trend is likely to continue as the nations and cultures of the Americas learn more about one another. So while at first glance we might be skeptical about comparing the history of narrative in the United States and Brazil, closer consideration provides clear justification. Indeed, as even a cursory glance at the bibliography suggests, such a development is well under way.

Concerned about the way the study of the literature of the United States, in particular, is evolving into a "transnational mode of writing," for example, Paul Jay has written that a new model for American studies is emerging, one in which "a broad critique of the narrow, nationalist conflation of the American and the United States has sparked vigorous efforts to resituate the study of United States literature and culture in a hemispheric or Pan-American context" ("Discipline" 45). J. Hillis Miller underscores this point. A. Owen Aldridge, another early exponent of an integrated and comparative approach to New World literature, put it this way in 1982:

Many parallels exist between the literature of Latin America and that of English America before 1830. Both areas went through periods of conquest and exploration, colonial domination, struggle for political independence, and national recognition. Although these stages in development are completely parallel, they were widely separated chronologically on the two continents. Conquest and exploration in South America took place in the sixteenth century, but not until a hundred years later in North America. (209)

Aldridge then poses a question that anticipates by nearly twenty years the disciplinary sea change that Jay describes: "Should one conceive of Latin American literature and Anglo-American literature as two separate, more or less homogeneous zones or should an attempt be made to combine the two and consider them together as constituting a single comprehensive zone?" (211). The creation of such a zone would turn on improved literary and cultural relations not merely between the United States and Latin America but, specifically, between the United States and Brazil, the New World nation it perhaps most resembles in its historical development.

Arriving at a similar conclusion, Robert Stam maintains, first, that "for North Americans, the image of Brazil is both reassuringly familiar and disconcertingly alien" and, second, that

> Brazil and the United States are deeply interconnected in a specular play of sameness and difference, identity and alterity. The two countries offer distorting images of each other. Although in no way identical, the two countries are eminently *comparable*. The same elements exist, but reshuffled.

Stam then sounds a note of warning by declaring:

> As a vast, continent-size New World country, similar to the United States in both historical formation and ethnic diversity, Brazil constitutes a kind of southern twin whose strong affinities with the United States have been obscured by ethnocentric assumptions and media stereotypes. (1)

Thinking of Brazil's place in world literature may shed further light on the unexpected pairing of the two cultures. Too long ignored outside the ken of Brazilianists and Latin Americanists, Brazilian literature has much to offer specialists in other national literatures, in literary theory, and in literary history. Reminding us that Goethe's concept of *Weltliteratur* assumes "a reciprocal reading that progressively illuminates identity" and that "the literacy of world literature is consequently the ability to read for a new world in relation to the old: to construct new world views by comparing other systems of reality," Sarah Lawall validates the importance of interpreting Brazil and its literature in a larger, international context (48).

Undertaking this literary rapprochement entails a grasp of the complexity of Brazilian history and culture. Joseph A. Page writes that the varied images of Brazil

> cannot always be taken at face value. The former dominant perception of the country as a friendly playground or an exotic refuge in the tropics took no account of the social and economic inequities that consigned much of the population to lives of poverty, disease, and ignorance. It also missed the serious side of Brazil, the slumbering leviathan with the potential to become a great power, ever on the verge of awakening to claim its rightful place among nations. (3)

Discussing the diverse ways Brazil is perceived abroad, Page continues:

> Since outsiders have traditionally misinterpreted what they see in Brazil, it is conceivable that Brazil's current [mid-1990s] negative image abroad is yet another erroneous impression drawn by foreigners. This is certainly what Brazilians would like to believe. However, it also could be that at long last the real Brazil has begun to emerge from the romantic mists that have long clouded the judgement of nonnative observers. (3)

Because of its size and diversity, Brazil has long been compared—both by inhabitants and by outsiders—with the United States. Indeed, Page notes

> there was once a sanguine vision of Brazil that held that the nation possessed sufficient human and natural resources to enable it to overtake the United States as an economic power; that while the twentieth century [had] been the "American century," the twenty-first would belong to Brazil. (5)

In *The Brazilian People* Darcy Ribeiro states that his purpose in writing this controversial book is to explore why "North America, with less resources, colonized by people poorer than the Irish and the English, got it right and became rich, while a rich province like Brazil devolved" (x; Ribeiro qtd. in an interview with the *Jornal do Brasil*, 22 Apr. 1995).[3] An anthropologist and cultural commentator, Ribeiro explains that "we Brazilians . . . are a people in the making. . . . We are a mixed-blood people in flesh and spirit, for miscegenation here was never a crime or a sin. We were made through it and we are still being made that way." Asserting that "Brazilians are today one of the most linguistically and culturally homogeneous and . . . most socially integrated peoples on earth," that Brazil contains no groups "demanding autonomy or clinging to a past," and that Brazilians "are open to the future" (321), Ribeiro concludes his study on an optimistic note. Brazil, he insists, is

> the new Rome—a tardy, tropical Rome. Brazil is already the largest of neo-Latin nations in population size and it is beginning to be so in artistic and cultural creativity also. It must become so now in the domination of the technology of future civilization in order to become an economic power with self-sustaining progress. We are building ourselves in the struggle to flourish tomorrow as a new civilization, of mixed blood and tropical, proud of itself—happier because it is more enduring; better for incorporating within itself more humanities; and more generous for being open to all races and all cultures and because it is located in the most beautiful and luminous province of the earth. (322)

From the perspective of the United States, however, Brazil has a strong aura of the exotic about it. Its *mirage,* a term comparatists use to describe the impression one culture makes in the collective mind of another, is based on its vastness and natural beauty; its brilliant soccer tradition (it was the first nation to win the World Cup five times, in 1958, 1962, 1970, 1994, and 2002); its captivating music; the politeness, ebullience, and cordiality of its people; and, lamentably, its seemingly endless debt crisis, its death squads, its environmental depredations. At the same time, Brazil, to many people in the United States, has become invisible, lost, or misconstrued in the amorphous clutch of nations known, vaguely, as Latin America. This turn of events is ironic because we can observe in the Brazilian experience "not only American history repeating itself but also what might lie ahead for American society" (Page 7). As Page argues:

> [T]he homelessness that has become a feature of life in American cities has been endemic in Brazil over the past decade or two. The poverty affecting ever-increasing numbers of American children has long afflicted large numbers of Brazilian children. . . . The "savage capitalism" that greatly exacerbated social and economic disparities in Brazil during the 1970s in certain ways foreshadowed the decade of the 1980s in the United States.

Indeed, it may not be too far-fetched for Brazilians to suggest to their neighbors to the north, "We are you yesterday, and we are you tomorrow." (7)

Misconceptions about Latin America in general and about Brazil in particular have long plagued outside observers, so much so that the misunderstandings

have become intertwined with sedimented prejudices that are at once *religious* (Christian condescension toward Africa and indigenous religions); *social* (poverty as a sign of degradation); *sexual* (the view of Latin women as sultry temptresses); and *racial* (reproducing Eurocentric hierarchies of white European over African "black" and indigenous "red"). (Stam 1)

By the standards and goals of the United States, Latin America is underdeveloped. Such an evaluation is compounded by the tendency of the United States to consider the southern continent to be an inferior social, political and economic system. Too often, people in the United States have viewed Latin America in simplistic, uninformed terms, as an ideological battleground between capitalism and communism rather than as a struggle "between reformers and counterreformers" (Burns, *Latin America* ix). As an unfortunate result of the misinterpretation, the United States has intervened in the internal affairs of a number of the sovereign nations of Central and South America—and all too often (as in Chile, Guatemala, and Brazil, three of the better-known examples) on the side of repressive, antidemocratic dictatorships. Understandably, the effect has been to alienate hemispheric neighbors and to make them leery of cooperating in any way with the United States. This abiding sense of mistrust, resentment, and animosity is the fundamental obstacle that prevents inter-American studies from developing as felicitously as it might.

Despite the failure of many in the United States to differentiate among the distinct cultures of Latin America, Brazil must be understood in all its contrasts and extremes. "In Brazil," as Chris McGowan and Ricardo Pessanha note,

the first world and the third world exist side by side. Brazil is highly industrialized in some areas and absolutely medieval in others. It is wealthy and miserable, chic Ipanema and mud-and-stick hut, high-tech engineer and Stone Age Indian, computers and bananas.

The authors go on to say that "another argument for Brazil's singularity is that nowhere else on earth do different races, cultures, and religions coexist as peacefully as they do there." While there is prejudice in Brazil, "it is rare to encounter overt racial or religious hatred of the kind that is common in many other countries" (9).

In both area and population, Brazil is the largest and wealthiest Latin American country. As of 2002, its national language, Portuguese, was the world's sixth most widely spoken tongue. With a population of 175 million, Brazil, a federal republic, has more people than the rest of South America combined; the country's 3,286,487 square miles occupy nearly half the continent. Brazil is the fifth largest country in the world (larger, in fact, than the continental United States) and ranks sixth among the nations of the world in population. It is the third largest democracy (after India and the United States). Rio de Janeiro and São Paulo are Brazil's two largest cities; São Paulo, the industrial and commercial heart, with a population of 7 million, is the world's tenth largest city. In 2003, Brazil's economy was the world's eighth largest. Driven by the two largest populations and economies in the Americas, Brazil and the United States are also generally urban, very mobile, receptive to new ideas and technologies (Brazil is second only to the United States in terms of Internet users), youth-oriented, and characterized by distinctive regional differences. Yet for all its size, abundant natural resources, and tremendous potential, Brazil has remained largely a mystery for people in the United States. If Brazil is thought of at all by its northern neighbors, in fact, it is likely to be regarded as a seductive enigma, a land of abject poverty and of a rain forest being systematically destroyed in the name of progress.

From the perspective of Brazil, however, the relationship with the United States has assumed, from the two nations' early days, significantly different proportion. Legend has it, for example, that the dentist and army lieutenant Joaquim José da Silva Xavier (better known by his nickname Tiradentes, or Tooth-puller), who in 1789 spearheaded Brazil's first independence movement, would read aloud from a copy of the Declaration of Independence that he kept in his pocket. Two years earlier a young Brazilian student, José Joaquim da Maia, met in Nîmes, France, with Thomas Jefferson to seek American support for Brazil's incipient revolt from Portuguese rule (Putnam, "Jefferson"; Carneiro). Although Jefferson was understandably cautious about committing the resources of his fragile nation to revolution in another New World country, dispatches to his superiors in Washington suggest enthusiasm for the idea of a free and independent Brazil. Indeed, as Afrânio Peixoto summarizes Jefferson's private view of the matter, "the United States would profit by an alliance with a great friendly power in the Southern continent" (3).

During the rest of the eighteenth century, American interest in Brazil was limited and sporadic. Becoming the first nation to do so, the United States finally recognized Brazil's independence in 1824, two years after Prince Pedro assumed the title Constitutional Emperor and Perpetual Defender of Brazil. In the nineteenth century, cultural relations between the two countries increased, in both number and complexity. A skilled diplomat and negotiator, the Baron of Rio-Branco (José Maria da Silva Paranhos, Jr.) gradually succeeded in shifting Brazil's primary focus away from England and toward the United States. By this time, the United States had begun to take note of Latin America's largest and, potentially at least, most powerful republic. What we could describe as consistently close relations between Brazil and the United States did not begin until the second half of the twentieth century, however. According to E. Bradford Burns,

> the years since World War II witnessed a burgeoning interest and concern on the part of the North Americans. U.S. investments in Brazil during [the twentieth] century rose spectacularly. When it became evident by the late 1950s that Brazil would exercise a major international role not only in the Western Hemisphere but on a global scale as well, United States government leaders, military officials, scholars, and businessmen rushed to learn more about the South American giant. President John F. Kennedy reminded his listeners that one had only to glance at a world map to appreciate the geopolitical importance of Brazil. (*History* [3rd ed.] 2)

Although we may agree that, as Burns suggests, the people of the United States are slowly gaining an awareness of Brazil, the American public does not know nearly as much as it might about its southern neighbor. Remedying the problem should be a stimulating and rewarding project.

BEGINNINGS OF THE NEW WORLD

"While the nations of the New World might not have a common history," Burns says, "they do share some common historical experiences." This connection constitutes the intellectual basis for inter-American study. In addition, Burns notes, the Europeans explored the Americas

> during an exciting era of rapid commercial expansion. Throughout this hemisphere, they encountered and confronted Indians whose civiliza-

tions varied widely. Exploration, conquest, and settlement challenged the English, Spanish, and Portuguese and elicited different responses from them. They transplanted European institutions to the Western Hemisphere, and their adaptation and growth here took various courses. The Europeans hoped to solve their pressing labor problems by coercing the natives to work for them and, where that failed, by importing legions of African slaves. (*History* [3rd ed.] 3)

In contrast to what happened in Spanish America, however, it is interesting to note that in neither colonial Brazil nor the colonial United States were Native Americans ever successfully enslaved and transformed into a significant labor force. The English, French, Spanish, and Portuguese crowns all sought, with varying degrees of success, to impose a mercantilist system on their American colonies. In the long run, however, none of the monarchies retained its power in the New World. From 1776 to 1824, Burns observes,

> colonies from New England to the Viceroyalty of the Plata revolted, threw off their European yoke, and entered the community of nations. The struggles to establish national states, to develop economically, and to assert their self-identity absorbed the energies of the newly independent peoples. (*History* [3rd ed.] 3)

Within the Western Hemisphere, however, Brazil's case merits special attention. Like the United States, the southern nation steadily expanded westward, claiming, in the process, territory settled by others, mostly Native Americans. Especially in the nineteenth century, as Marshall Eakin notes, "the cultural and technological disjuncture between Western and native civilizations produced a bloody and costly clash on the U.S. frontier. The Brazilians, on the other hand, have moved quickly and fitfully across their frontier in just a few decades." In both societies the concepts of frontier and hinterland have been fundamental in any attempts to characterize a national identity.[4] As Eakin points out, though, the planning and construction of the federal capital, Brasília, in the 1950s "signaled the opening" of the frontier; in the United States the frontier was effectively closed by the 1890s (100). Other significant dissimilarities between the two cultures exist as well. During the nineteenth century, Burns observes, Brazil evolved peacefully "from a colony to an independent empire, from a monarchy to a republic, and from a slaveholding society to a free society." Early on, the nation merged three diverse racial groups (Europeans, Native Americans, and Africans) into a single, homogeneous society that, in a variety of ways, exemplifies the concepts of miscegenation and cultural mixing. Moreover, Brazil epitomizes a developing nation "whose governments have been determined to 'modernize,' that is, to recreate their nation after the image of Western Europe or the United States" (Burns, *History* [3rd ed.] 4).

The problems associated with delayed development have had devastating consequences for Brazil. "Urbanization has outrun industrialization at a rapid pace," Eakin writes, "industry has not been able to absorb the flow of migrants into the cities," and "agricultural production has not kept up with the demand for food in the cities." Unlike Western Europe and the United States, which "industrialized in the eighteenth and nineteenth centuries in a world that was overwhelmingly agrarian," Brazil modernized

> in [the twentieth] century and faced not only the competitive challenges of highly developed industrial economies in Europe, the United States, and Japan, but also the challenges presented by other newly industrializing nations. As social scientists have often pointed out, the later the onset of industrialization, the higher the costs of entry into the club. (Eakin 212)

A unique element of the Brazilian experience derives from the Portuguese kings, whose virtual monopoly on the sea-lanes to Africa and India had made them wealthy merchants.[5] In Brazil the kings erected what was basically a commercial empire rather than a colonial one (Burns, *Latin America* 13). Trade, not settlement, thus became the primary motivation of the Portuguese monarchs; the situation differed considerably from that in Spanish America and, later, in the English colonies of North America, where pejorative views of the wilderness undercut the Edenic vision and where, as we see in John Smith, the entire concept of a New World Arcadia was "mainly a utilitarian utopia," one based on experience (*Harper American Literature* 1: 7).

One effect of the Lusitanian emphasis on commerce and trade rather than on conquest and colonialization is that the people who would eventually come to be known as the Brazilians had a colonial experience that was less rigidly organized and controlled than in Spanish America and less militaristic. A small, seafaring people long accustomed to dealing with cultures different from their own, the Portuguese, especially after Vasco da Gama's discovery of a sea route to India in 1499, were more concerned with their lucrative maritime trade routes to the Orient than with the development of a new civilization. The result was that in the beginning Brazil functioned largely as a supplier of fresh water and other goods for the Portuguese caravels headed for the eastern markets and as a kind of outpost for the western side of the expanding Portuguese commercial empire. Because Portuguese eyes were so fixed on the riches of the Orient, Brazil, as a developing colonial culture, was left largely to its own devices, a fact that, as seen in some of the satirical poetry of Gregório de Matos, led if not exactly to an early sense of nationalism then certainly to a sense of being different, of being a people and a culture in search of an identity.

At the dawn of the sixteenth century, the Portuguese explorers encountered between one million and two and one half million Native Americans who were, essentially, from two groups, the Tupi-Guarani and the Tapuya.[6] Because of their predominance along the Atlantic coast, the Tupi, among the indigenous groups, would have the greatest impact on Brazilian culture (Wagley 251–53). Loosely organized forest dwellers, the Tupi whom the Portuguese mariners observed in 1500 wore no clothing and seemed to the Europeans to possess a proclivity for music, song, and dance. As a result, they were quickly, but inaccurately, thought to be living the idyllic life of children of nature. The official chronicler of the Portuguese fleet, Pêro Vaz de Caminha, reported to the king that "the innocence of Adam himself was not greater than these people's" (qtd. in Burns, *History* [3rd ed.] 18). Such conclusions about the native people had an immediate effect on European thought. Montaigne, for example, in two famous essays on the New World, conceived his theory of the inherent goodness of natural man (Burns, *History*, [3rd ed.] 19; for a discussion of "Des cannibales," see Hoffman), despite the suggestion of ritual cannibalism (later so important to Oswald de Andrade) and the penchant for warfare that characterized the Tupi. The cultures of the Brazilian Indians, in fact, were substantially less developed than the extraordinary civilizations created by the Aztec, Maya, and Inca, the native peoples encountered by the Spanish. "The Brazilian Indians," Burns notes, "possessed no well-established tribal organization; their agriculture was simple; they did not know how to use stone to build; they lacked any animal for transportation; they had no written means of communication" (*History* [2nd ed.] 21). Although the Indians came to exert a significant influence on colonial Brazilian culture (Brazilian Portuguese, like American English, still features a high percentage of Indian words, for example), the Europeans soon realized that "the Indian would not provide the labor supply that Brazil needed" (Wagley 18–19). The situation, which became critical by the 1550s (when sugarcane had established itself as a source of wealth for the Brazilians), would expedite the importation of African slaves to Brazil.

Like the slaves brought to the southern United States, the Africans shipped to Brazil were generally from west Africa, in the region of the Senegal and Niger rivers (Wagley 19), but a number were from Angola and Mozambique, areas controlled by the Portuguese. Even though both Brazil and the United States were deeply marked by the legacy of slavery, a grasp of the substantial differences in the two nations' experiences of the institution is crucial in understanding modern Brazil. From the middle of the sixteenth century to the middle of the nineteenth, slave traders shipped some 3.6 million Africans to Brazil, making it "the final destination of more than one-third of all the African slaves brought to the Americas" (Eakin 114–15).[7] Although the first known shipment of Africans arrived in Brazil in 1538, some slaves may have reached the New World as early as 1502 (Burns, *Latin America* 20). The primary labor force for Brazil's colonial society, the slaves exerted a growing influence on Brazilian culture generally—so much so that, in the words of the historian Manuel Querino, "it was the black who developed Brazil" (qtd. in Burns, *Latin America* 22). Intermingling with both the Europeans and the Indians, the Africans significantly deepened the racial mix that characterized life in colonial Brazil. Racial mixing "took place throughout the hemisphere," Eakin observes, but "in Anglo America whites refused to accept racially mixed children in their world. Anglo Americans rarely acknowledged miscegenation, and when it occurred, they segregated racially mixed children with blacks in a bipolar society that recognized no middle ground between black and white" (19). It is thus a significant contrast between the two cultures that in Brazil the term *mestiçagem* ("miscegenation") does not carry the negative connotation that it does in the United States. A similar conclusion is reached by McGowan and Pessanha: the Brazilian "colony of mixed races" was "quite different from the civilization that would be created in North America by English Protestants and their families, who came to settle permanently, kept more of a distance from the natives, and maintained an air of moral superiority with regard to other races" (10–11).

The centrality, to Brazilian culture, of racial intermingling can be seen in the fact that by 1803, the city of Salvador da Bahia—the capital of colonial Brazil and therefore the heart of Brazil's African heritage—had a population of 100,000, of which 40,000 were black, 30,000 were European, and 30,000 were mulatto. Many, if not most, Brazilians could therefore claim "at least some African ancestry" (Burns, *Latin America* 22).[8] Brazil's racial mixture, moreover, has long had a cultural counterpart. The nation's music, art, and literature reflect contributions from the nation's diverse populations. Even the Roman Catholicism imported by the Portuguese (themselves attuned to the benefits of both racial and cultural blending) was quickly interwoven with African and Indian religious practices, to such an extent that, in Brazil, "Catholicism . . . coexists with other forms of religion, some of which are peripheral to Catholicism and others frankly antagonistic to it" (Wagley 213). Furthermore, as the cultural anthropologist Thales de Azevedo has pointed out, "Brazilian Catholicism inherited from Portuguese culture a certain softness, tolerance and malleability which an exalted, turbulent and hard Spanish religious character did not know" (qtd. in Wagley 214). (This argument begs referencing to the religious character of the Puritans and of the early French clerics as well.)

The theme of racial intermingling, in fact, is a defining motif of Brazilian literature, appearing in works as diverse as Santa Rita Durão's *Caramuru* (1781), José de Alencar's *Iracema* (1865), Euclides da Cunha's *Rebellion in the Backlands* (1902), Graça Aranha's *Canaan* (1902), Cassiano Ricardo's *Martim Cererê* (1928), Jorge Amado's *Tent of Miracles* (1969), and Helena Parente Cunha's *Woman between Mirrors* (1983). The theme has no equivalent presence in the literature of the United States (see Fitz, *Rediscovering* ch. 4), though certain writers (Faulkner, Baldwin, Silko) have cultivated it extensively. Nevertheless, the issue remains a particular point of comparison (see Marx) because, while Brazil and the United States have a similar racial history—characterized by the interplay of indigenous peoples, Africans, and Europeans—many North Americans have "[looked] to Europe for self-definition rather than to the multiracial societies of [their] own hemisphere" (Stam 10). In addition,

> it has become commonplace to see Latin America as a "mestiço" continent, [but] it is not always recognized that "United Statesian" culture is *also* mestiço, mixed, hybrid, syncretic. . . . Whereas the North American vision of national identity has been surreptitiously premised on an unstated yet nonetheless normative "whiteness," the Brazilian vision of national identity has usually been premised on the notion of racial *multiplicity*.

These are two variations on "the same racial theme." For Brazilian intellectuals, then, the issue of race has long been, in part, a function of the "primordial role" racial plurality has played, and continues to play, in the formation of a national identity (Stam 10–11). From its very beginnings, Brazil has allowed the intermingling of native peoples, Europeans, and slaves to develop as if it had been officially sanctioned policy.

The colonial period in the United States was relatively short—less than 170 years—while Latin America's colonial experience lasted some 300 years. Francis Fukuyama observes, moreover, that "the United States was settled primarily by British people and inherited not just British law but British culture as well, whereas Latin America inherited various cultural traditions from the Iberian peninsula"—as well as the extensive contributions of Amerindian and African peoples. Thus, Fukuyama maintains, radically different socioeconomic assumptions helped determine the development of North America and South America:

> The vitality of [Protestant and decentralized] American civil society was crucial both for the stability of the country's democratic institutions and for its vibrant economy. The imperial and Latin Catholic traditions of Spain and Portugal, in contrast, reinforced dependence on large, centralized institutions like the State and the Church, weakening an independent civil society. (59)

Fukuyama is not alone in his position. Samuel Eliot Morison writes that the "English colonists of North America were able to select the more vigorous and valuable features of English political institutions, and consciously adapt them to New World needs, rejecting the useless residue of feudalism" (38). A similar interpretation is offered by Henry Bamford Parkes. While "the peoples of Mexico and South America became accustomed to despotic rule, to an authoritarian church, and to an aristocratic social structure," Parkes says, the English colonies had the "freedom to develop their own way of life" (16). Colonial Latin America, to a large degree, "became an extension of Latin Europe," whereas settlers in the United States, benefiting from England's distinctive political experience, "created a new way of life that quickly acquired certain unique qualities" (5). And Eakin observes that "the political heritage of the United States emerged as a branch of the well-rooted traditions of limited government and individual rights that had been growing in England long before the English reached the shores of North America." Brazilians, in contrast, "trace the roots of their political traditions back to the statist and centralist political culture of Iberian monarchy that faced few checks on its power before overseas expansion, or during centuries of colonial rule" (166).

THE ERA OF NATION BUILDING

As Brazil moved toward independence, in the early nineteenth century, intellectual curiosity in the writings of Benjamin Franklin, Thomas Jefferson, and Thomas Paine was strong. As Eakin writes, "the Enlightenment . . . and the Age of Revolution (1770–1830) brought fundamental changes to the political cultures of the Americas, both North and South" (168). The social dynamics set in motion by the Enlightenment had appeared in Brazil as early as 1724 and the establishment of the nation's first academy. Yet the "progress of intellectual change," Burns notes, "from adherence to more traditional ideas to acceptance of much of the thought associated with the Enlightenment took place over generations." The shift in attitudes occurred much later in the century, when "many ideas of the Enlightenment penetrated the interior of Brazil sufficiently to arouse economic and political discontent" (Burns, *History* [3rd ed.] 109). In evaluating the impact of the Enlightenment on Brazil, writers contrast the southern nation's experiences with those of the neighbor to the north. In the United States, Eakin explains, the Enlightenment "reinforced the move toward limited government, challenged established authority, and provided the intellectual ammunition for the American Revolution," whereas in Brazil, "the influence of the Enlightenment did not produce a dramatic rupture with the corporatist, bureaucratic tradition" (168), which had happened in Spanish America (where bloody civil wars raged well into the nineteenth century). Although not as decisive in Brazil (which was less ready politically, economically, and civically to receive it) as it was in the United States, the Enlightenment, the Século das Luzes ("Century of Lights"), nevertheless encouraged Brazilians to explore both the history and the likely future of their land and its peoples—and to consider, at least, amending some of the nation's laws and institutions.

While progressive ideas from North America and Europe permeated nineteenth-century Brazil, and Brazilian intellectuals struggled to adapt them to local conditions, some social critics have, in recent years, reassessed the effects of imported social theories and sociopolitical systems on Brazil's development as a modern nation. Prominent among the revisionist thinkers is Roberto Schwarz, whose influential work continues the critique of Brazilian literature initiated in the 1960s by Antônio Cândido. Schwarz argues that the principles of European liberalism, crucial to nation-building efforts else-where, were perverted and miscast in nineteenth-century Brazil, where the continuing existence of slavery tainted all attempts to move forward as a lib-eral, progressive culture. So far was Brazil from benefiting from progressive notions that even the Declaration of the Rights of Man, which was partially transcribed into the Brazilian constitution of 1824, served only to "cast the institution of slavery into a sharper light" (the slave trade was outlawed in Brazil in 1850; slavery in 1888). Evoking comparisons with the United States (where slavery was formally abolished in 1863), Schwarz writes that Brazil, an agrarian society, was built on the latifundia (landed estates) and depend-ent on both slave labor and foreign markets. "Challenged at every turn by slavery," he contends, "the liberal ideology—the ideology of the newly eman-cipated nations of America—was derailed," supplanted by a hypocrisy and cynicism the human manifestations of which Machado de Assis would make a career of exposing and ridiculing (20, 21, 25–29).[9] So interested was Brazil in the United States at this time that the emperor, Dom Pedro II, who had visions of Brazil's becoming a major exporter of cotton, recruited some three thousand Confederate families to migrate to Brazil in the post–Civil War era. Although most eventually repatriated, some stayed to found the city of Amer-icana, which, located not far from São Paulo, today has a population of some 250,000, many of whom have English surnames.

During the nineteenth century, trade between Brazil and the United States was rapidly increasing. Although reflecting different social and politi-cal goals, commercial and cultural exchange was important to each country's struggle to achieve a sense of identity. Further economic and cultural inter-action was spurred by Pedro II's visit to the United States, in 1876, to par-ticipate in the centennial celebration in Philadelphia and to tour the country. (An admirer of Abraham Lincoln as well as an enthusiast of science and tech-nology, Dom Pedro was an early investor in the Bell Telephone Company and had phones installed in the emperor's private residence in Petrópolis.) By all accounts, the highly successful trip can be regarded as a turning point in relations between the two countries.

When, in 1822 (under the enlightened leadership of the crown prince, Dom Pedro), Brazil finally declared itself independent, it did so under cir-cumstances that involved the United States and its links to its New World neighbors. The Monroe Doctrine (1823), intended to close the Americas to further European colonization (and perhaps also to monopolize the markets of the newly independent Latin American nations), elicited a mixed reception from the Latin Americans, "some of whom had as much reason to suspect the North American motives as they did those of the Europeans" (Burns, *Latin America* 101). In contrast to the Spanish American nations, who never officially accepted the doctrine, Brazil welcomed it:

> Less than two months after its issuance, the Brazilian government recognized the new doctrine and spoke of an offensive and defensive alliance with the United States. Brazil, more than any other of the Latin American states, saw in the doctrine a defense of its newly proclaimed independence and protection from European aggression. (Burns, *Latin America* 102)

In essence, Brazil saw the doctrine as the endorsement of its independence movement, which the student revolutionary José Joaquim da Maia had sought from Jefferson in 1787.

Because of what the United States viewed as Brazil's economic and strategic importance, the southern nation played a major role in the first Inter-American Conference, held in Washington, DC, in 1889–90. Called by the American secretary of state, James G. Blaine, the parley sought to strengthen hemispheric solidarity by stimulating commercial and economic ties and, eventually, by creating a kind of American common market (in which Latin America would supply the raw materials and the United States the finished product). Rapid industrialization in the United States had intensified the demand for new markets, "and none seemed more promising than Latin America, long the domain of European salesmen" (Burns, *Latin America* 148). Although Brazil was poised to benefit, at least in the short run, from the arrangement, acrimonious debate about the need for the United States to respect the sovereignty of Latin American nations came to dominate the conference.

Having established itself as a republic in 1889, Brazil relied heavily on the Constitution of the United States in preparing its own document of governance in 1891. The United States, by this time, was fast replacing Britain as Brazil's primary trading partner, and Brazil's leaders sought to imitate its rapid industrial progress after the Civil War. Brazil, they felt, was destined to become the United States of South America. Advocates of this position failed to recognize that Brazil faced social, political, and economic obstacles "far more formidable than those the United States had to surmount in its climb to adulthood" (Page 5). Between 1870 and 1900, for example,

> when North Americans opted to industrialize, technology was relatively simple and inexpensive, and hence easy to acquire or replicate. Brazil's commitment to large-scale industrialization did not occur until well into the twentieth century, at a historical moment when technology had become exceedingly complex, costly, and difficult to import. Moreover, although social and economic disparities existed in the United States in the late nineteenth and early twentieth centuries, they were minor compared with the yawning chasm that now separates Brazil's "haves" and "have-nots." (Page 5)

In November 1889, the opening of the United States consulate in Rio de Janeiro helped certify the legitimacy of the recently created Brazilian republic. Within a few years the United States would also play a decisive role in quelling the first major challenge to the still-weak government—a naval revolt in and around the capital. "In Washington," as Burns explains, "the Brazilian minister, Salvador de Mendonça, a dedicated, historic Republican, importuned the government of President Grover Cleveland to come to the aid of the fledgling sister republic." The United States, dispatching additional cruisers to Guanabara Bay, instructed them "not to allow the rebel ships to interfere in any way with commerce in the port" (Burns, *History* [3rd ed.] 243–44). Assessing the volatile situation, the American commander deployed warships between the rebel vessels and Rio itself. The Brazilian navy—if it chose to open fire—would thus have to lob its shells over the American forces. The danger in this strategy apparently persuaded the rebellious admirals not to bombard the city, and the revolt collapsed. The Brazilian republic had survived its first crisis.

The early twentieth century saw increasing connections between Brazil and the United States. One notable event during this period was Theodore Roosevelt's 1914 expedition to the Amazon basin, a trip that allowed Roosevelt to strike up a friendship with Colonel Cândido Rondon (later the head of Brazil's Indian Protection Service and the man who took care of Roosevelt after he fell seriously ill with malaria). Roosevelt and his group explored the uncharted River of Doubt, a thousand-mile-long tributary of the Amazon later renamed the Rio Roosevelt in his honor. United States business investments in Brazil were also on the rise; by 1919, the Ford Motor Company had begun to assemble the Model T in Brazil. A few years later, in 1927, Henry Ford himself would select the Tapajós Valley, located in the lower Amazon, as the site of what he hoped would become a successful supplier of rubber for his automobile-production lines.

Overall, the decades before the Great Depression marked a period of growth in the commercial, cultural, military, and political ties between Brazil and the United States. North American investment in Brazil expanded; by 1930, the United States surpassed England as Brazil's number one foreign investor. As early as 1927, the United States, Brazil's largest single trading partner, "owned about 35 percent of Brazil's entire federal debt" (Burns, *History* [3rd ed.] 341). (In the second half of the twentieth century, the situation would become a source of conflict as nationalistic political groups emerged.)[10]

CLOSER HEMISPHERIC TIES

During the 1930s, a decade of economic crisis and sociopolitical challenges, the destinies of the two countries became more closely entwined. As Morison writes, "The main trend of New Deal foreign policy until 1940 was to continue to avoid European commitments, but to cultivate New World solidarity." From the perspective of the United States government at least, the Latin American aspect of this plan, commonly known as the good-neighbor policy, enjoyed significant success (967).[11] At meetings in 1933 (Montevideo), 1936 (Buenos Aires), 1938 (Lima), 1939 (Panama City), 1940 (Havana), and 1942 (Rio de Janeiro), Brazil gradually established itself as a growing hemispheric force and as a major ally of the United States. In 1944, Brazil would deploy more than twenty-five thousand men to fight alongside the United States Fifth Army in the Italian campaign. Beyond the political realm, however, Brazil was beginning to exert a strong cultural attraction in the United States. In the 1920s and 1930s, for example, Latin American artists and intellectuals, especially in Cuba and Brazil, explored black culture and history and their impact on national identity. Stam believes:

> The currently fashionable talk of postcolonial "hybridity" and "syncretism" often elides the fact that artists and intellectuals in Brazil and the Caribbean were theorizing hybridity over half a century earlier. In two manifestos—"Manifesto of Brazilwood Poetry" (1924) and "Cannibalist Manifesto" (1928)—Oswald de Andrade pointed the way to an artistic practice "at once nationalist and cosmopolitan, nativist and modern,"

and called (in the "Cannibalist Manifesto") for an intellectual and cultural revolution that ultimately would be "greater than the French revolution." (70; see also Johnson, "Tupy")

A number of writers, like João da Cruz e Sousa, Jorge de Lima, Raul Bopp, José Lins do Rego, and Jorge Amado, portrayed the black presence in their country's evolution. In Amado's novel *Jubiabá* (1935), widely regarded as one of his finest books and much admired by Albert Camus, the proletarian theme is enhanced by credible symbolism and heightened technical control (see app. C). Bopp's *Poemas negros* (1932) contrasts the vitality of a free black Africa with the degradation of enslaved Africans in the New World (see app. C, Tapscott). And in 1928, Lima published one of his most influential poems, "That Black Woman Fulô."

Another important development of the early 1930s had to do with the status of women. Although in the United States the Nineteenth Amendment granted women the right to vote in 1920, in Brazil women gained suffrage in 1934, which was several years before such European nations as France, Belgium, and Switzerland took this step.

Yet another indication of the shared interests of America and Brazil in mid-century was the number of Hollywood movies about Brazil. *Flying Down to Rio*, a prime example of the popular genre, as Sérgio Augusto observes, enjoyed a long run at New York's Radio City Music Hall. Brazil's appeal grew significantly when Nelson Rockefeller, then the coordinator of the Council of Inter-American Affairs, redirected the council's project from commercial transactions to cultural endeavors. The result, Augusto says, was a series of good-neighbor animated films, notably *The Three Caballeros* (1944), featuring the affable Brazilian parrot Zé Carioca (Johnson and Stam 357–59), who became a close friend of Donald Duck's. Titles such as *Nancy Goes to Rio* (1950), *The Steel Trap* (1952), and *Holiday for Lovers* (1959) suggest the romantic, even stereotypical, image of Brazil with which Hollywood captivated American audiences. To some critics, the appearance of *Black Orpheus* (1959) marked the advent of a less frivolous depiction of Brazil on the screen.

Perhaps the most intriguing story of this fecund cultural period concerns the American filmmaker Orson Welles, charged by Rockefeller with promoting the good-neighbor policy, with "countering Nazi propaganda" in the region, and with improving relations between Latin America and the United States in an honest fashion, a task that gave rise to "the ill-fated Pan-

Americanist documentary *It's All True*" (Stam 107; Johnson and Stam 360). Arriving in Brazil in February 1942, Welles, who would become enamored of Brazilian folk culture, apparently found life in Rio de Janeiro congenial to his "sybaritic tastes" (Page 8). Although Rockefeller and RKO felt that *It's All True* should begin with an examination of Carnival in Rio, the film's most dramatic footage deals with the 1,650-mile sea voyage on a wooden raft, or *jangada,* from the Northeast to Rio undertaken by four fishermen seeking economic reforms from Getúlio Vargas, the country's leader. Tragically, one of the men fell overboard and drowned. "Welles," according to Augusto, "was unfairly blamed" for the accident, "and the film never recovered from the shock" (Johnson and Stam 360). In seeking to pay homage to the *jangadeiros,* it is clear that "Welles was honoring both African and indigenous traditions in Brazil since the *jangadas . . .* were an Indian invention, examples of the *caboclo* culture that sprung from the intermingling of black slaves with indigenous groups, and since the *jangadeiros* themselves were black and mestiço" (Stam 108). Responding to criticism of Welles and of *It's All True,* Stam counters that Welles's detractors were driven by the "implicit racial conventions of ethnocentric discourse" and that the attacks on Welles were really attacks on Brazilian culture itself, especially its very prominent African heritage (110). "*It's All True* was never finished and most of the footage was dumped into the Pacific. . . . Around 30,000 feet of excerpts survived, however, enough to convince Charles Higham . . . that *It's All True* was 'the cinematic equivalent of the treasure of King Solomon's mines or the lost city of the Incas'" (Johnson and Stam 360). Although coming to fruition "within a highly racist context," Stam observes,

> *It's All True* was animated by a democratic, antiracist spirit. The emphasis was to be not on elite individual history but rather on collective heroism and creativity. Welles wanted to show *Brazilian* heroes, not North American heroes against Brazilian backdrops. The pivotal characters . . . were black . . . and mestiço. . . . The approach in *It's All True* was neither miserabilist nor idealized; his intention was to show people who are poor but dignified, energetic, hardworking, and who transform their lifes through art and activism. . . . Welles in this sense was too good a "neighbor." (131–32)

Rediscovered in 1985, *It's All True* ranks as "one of the famous 'lost' films of cinema history" (Stam 107).[12]

POSTWAR YEARS TO THE PRESENT

In Brazil, where art and politics are rarely separated, the 1950s and early 1960s were characterized by ferment and unrest. In 1954, the democratically elected Vargas committed suicide, whereas 1961 saw both the election and unexpected resignation of Jânio Quadros and the reestablishment of parliamentary government. Problems surrounding the interference of the United States in Brazil's economy and politics came to a crisis in March 1964, when, with the support of the United States government and the CIA, President João Goulart was deposed by the military. Alarmed, no doubt, by events in Cuba since 1960, Washington had viewed the left-leaning Goulart as a foe of foreign investors and a destabilizing force in the region. "Clearly involved in the military overthrow of the constitutional and democratic government of Brazil," Burns concludes, "the United States government became intimately associated with the military dictatorship which followed" (*History* [3rd ed.] 444). Economically and culturally, however, the United States remained active in Brazil, even after the reestablishment of civilian rule in 1985. From the perspective of the United States, Brazil, since the election of Luis Inácio Lula da Silva as president in 2002, has emerged as the linchpin of Latin America and as a nation that has a major role to play in the stability and prosperity of the Americas as a whole.

Brazil's literary history is most usefully approached from three closely related perspectives: as a rich and diverse national literature, as a major New World literature, and as a distinctive, if egregiously understudied, Latin American literature. Long overlooked as a New World literature and often ignored as a Latin American literature, Brazilian literature has followed a path that diverges in many ways from that of eleven other New World literatures.[13] We should distinguish the development of Brazilian literature from that of Spanish American literature (see Merquior; Rabassa, "Comparative Look"), because Brazilian literature—like Brazil generally—is often lost in the vague "Latin American" context. Indeed, some critics have argued that there is no cohesive Latin American literature, that what exists is an intercontinental literature in the process of self-formation. Although this argument is more difficult to sustain now, in the early years of the twenty-first century, than it was in 1977, when it was advanced by Emir Rodríguez Monegal (see Monegal, *Borzoi Anthology* 1: xiii), it is still plausible. What Latin American literature is only now developing and what—as Monegal, José Donoso, and

Octavio Paz have noted—it lacked until the early 1960s is a network of communication between authors in the eighteen Spanish-speaking republics, Haiti, and Brazil. In the 1950s, according to José Donoso in *The Boom in Spanish American Literature: A Personal History*, few of the writers were aware of developments in the other countries. Thus a novelist in Chile might know less about literary events in Argentina or Mexico than in Europe or the United States. Worse, writers in Brazil were little known in Spanish America. "Despite their common peninsular origin," Monegal reminds us, "Spanish America and Brazil have always been separate and apart, since the first days of the discovery and conquest of the New World" (*Borzoi Anthology* 1: xiii).

Indeed, contacts between the two cultural traditions have been minimal to nonexistent, with the result that Brazilian literature evolved in almost complete isolation from Spanish American literature. Even Jorge Luis Borges, who seems to have read everyone else, never mentions the Brazilian master Machado de Assis, who did as much to revolutionize Brazilian narrative as Borges did for its Spanish American counterpart. Although Sor Juana Inés de la Cruz, the brilliant author and nun of colonial Mexico, caused a controversy by criticizing a sermon by the Brazilian intellectual and visionary Father Antônio Vieira, we can say that "Spanish American and Brazilian literature progressed in parallel but separate lines of development" (Monegal, *Borzoi Anthology* 1: xiii). In later decades of the twentieth century, a number of points of influence and reception emerged. The poetry of Pablo Neruda and Borges's *Ficciones* became well known in Brazil; Paz enjoyed a fruitful relationship with the Brazilian concretist poets. Brazilian music and film, in addition to the hugely popular *telenovelas* (romantic series on TV), have wide audiences throughout the Americas and the world.

In terms of significant reception in the United States, however, Brazilian literature has had to wait longer than Spanish American literature has. Although a number of translations appeared during the 1940s and 1950s, it would take another ten years before Brazilian writers began to make their mark in the lucrative American market and to catch the attention of the intellectual community. During the Boom period of the 1960s, the work of such Spanish American masters as Borges, Julio Cortázar, Carlos Fuentes, Neruda, and Gabriel García Márquez won accolades from readers and critics alike and, almost immediately, influenced fiction writing and poetry in the United States (see Barth, "Exhaustion" and "Replenishment"; Payne). Brazilian literature started to emerge in the United States during the same period—most prominently, the works of Jorge Amado. His comic novella *A morte e a morte de Quincas Berro D'Água* (1961; *The Two Deaths of Quincas Wateryell* [1965]; see app. C) is regarded by many as his finest work. No Brazilian author (and, indeed, no Spanish American author) rivaled the popularity of Amado, who, until García Márquez won the Nobel Prize in 1982, was perhaps the most widely known and translated Latin American author.[14] Unfortunately, however, the few Brazilian works translated during the Boom years were overwhelmed by the avalanche of dazzling material coming from Spanish America. The result is that, although Machado de Assis's major novels appeared in the United States in the 1950s and other Brazilian writers were published in English in the late 1960s and early 1970s (e.g., Érico Veríssimo, Clarice Lispector, João Guimarães Rosa, Antônio Olinto; see app. C), the widespread recognition of Brazilian literature in the United States on aesthetic grounds would be delayed for some years.[15]

Not until the 1980s (Putnam's pioneering 1948 investigation aside) were studies linking Brazilian and American literature undertaken, and not until the 1990s did readers in the United States fully appreciate Brazil's writers and the richness of the country's literary heritage. Although, as Bobby J. Chamberlain points out (604–05), we must be skeptical of the standards that critics in the United States use in evaluating a less well known, chronically undervalued literature like Brazil's, comparisons between the two literatures are becoming more common. As the trend develops, both nations will benefit—the United States, from increased exposure to the historical context of the Americas and the American experience, will gain a deeper understanding of itself (see Clemons; R. Jackson); Brazil, by breaking out of its longstanding cultural isolation, will bring its literature to the attention of the world.

Despite its myriad social, political, and economic problems, Brazil continues to evolve. And we should not allow the problems to obscure Brazil's many successes. The nation has, in fact,

> maintained its unity in the face of every obstacle, emancipated its slaves without civil war, evolved from a monarchy to a republic without bloodshed, and laid the foundations for a modern industrial society. The ever-diversifying economy is no longer a simple extractive one. The illiteracy rate has fallen gradually. The nation has shown it can exercise greater independence in international relations. The population in general is becoming aware of those advancements, is proud of them, and is enticed by

the mystique of a greater Brazil that will provide a fuller life for all. (Burns, *History* [3rd ed.] 7)

In literature, too, Brazil is asserting itself in the international arena. Its writers are gaining the respect and admiration of readers and critics alike throughout the Americas and the world. Leavened linguistically, literarily, and culturally and by several rich and varied traditions—including the European-Portuguese, the African, the Amerindian, and the Asian—Brazilian literature deserves recognition "for its original, vital, and creative position as a contributor to the international context of comparative literature." Famous among its devotees as "an intriguing case of literary hybridization" (Jackson and Miller 7, 8), a heady mixture of native and foreign influences, Brazilian literature— with its affinity for irony, parody, formal experimentation, and political engagement—takes its well-deserved place among the literatures of the world.

NOTES

1. In history, anthropology, and the social sciences, studies comparing the United States and Brazil are neither new nor rare. Initiated in the main, not surprisingly, by Brazilians, these comparative approaches have proliferated. Three outstanding titles are Vianna Moog's *Bandeirantes and Pioneers* (1955; trans. 1964), Darcy Ribeiro's *As Américas e a civilização* (*The Americas and Civilization*) (1988), and Roberto DaMatta's *Carnivals, Rogues, and Heroes: An Interpretation of the Brazilian Dilemma* (1978; trans. 1991). Moog's study, beyond comparing the cultural archetypes of the pioneer and *bandeirante* (the approximate Brazilian equivalent), examines several American incursions into Brazil, including Henry Ford's failed rubber plantation of the 1930s and 1940s in the Amazon basin and the fate of the colony, also in the Amazon valley, founded by Confederate families fleeing the United States after the Civil War. Ribeiro, concerned about Brazil's social inequities, argues that Brazil should be seen as a violent, unjust society that only revolution can make livable. DaMatta, focusing on race and on Carnival, rejects Gilberto Freyre's thesis that the Portuguese were more open and humane in their approach to interracial relations. In Brazil, DaMatta believes, "the White and the Negro each had a fixed and unambiguous place within a well-established hierarchical totality" (79; qtd. in Skidmore, "Essay" 362).
2. González Echevarría and Pupo-Walker 3: 1.
3. As Elizabeth Lowe notes, *The Brazilian People* "generated considerable controversy among critics when it first appeared in Brazil." While some derided the book for what they felt was its fanciful and unrealistic presentation of Brazil, others called the author vain, simplistic, and authoritarian (Ribeiro x).
4. The preeminent historian of the colonial period, João Capistrano de Abreu, propounded,

in a seminal essay (1889), the importance of Brazil's interior to the formation of a national identity. For Abreu, the interior is the authentic Brazil, while the densely populated coastal regions are poor imitations of European culture. The theme of Euclides da Cunha's masterpiece, *Rebellion in the Backlands*, echoes Abreu's thesis. The viewpoint recalls Frederick Jackson Turner's assertion, in "The Significance of the Frontier in American History" (1893), that the frontier is not a fixed line but a fluid process, contested by groups whose interests, goals, and resources differ.

5. When Vasco da Gama, for example, returned to Lisbon after his 1497–99 voyage to India (establishing an East-West water route), his cargo repaid the cost of the expedition more than sixty times over. The Treaty of Tordesillas (1494) allowed the Spanish to pursue their conquest of the Americas (Brazil excepted) and freed Portugal to concentrate on its lucrative trade routes to the East. Conflict between Spain and Portugal in the New World was thus minimized.

6. More recent population estimates vary, however, as do theories concerning the Native Americans' relation to their environment. In the lower Amazon basin, for example, researchers have discovered great "swaths of *terra preta*—rich, fertile 'black earth' that anthropologists increasingly believe was created by human beings. . . . Faced with an ecological problem, . . . the Indians *fixed* it. They were in the process of terraforming the Amazon when Columbus showed up and ruined everything" (Mann 52).

7. Eakin calculates that about 750,000 Africans, or 6% of the total slave traffic, were transported to the United States (115).

8. Corroborating Burns's point, Eakin estimates that in Brazil generally, "some 65 million people (about 45 percent of the country) have African ancestors," while in Salvador da Bahia the percentage of those of African descent may run as high as 80% (19).

9. Schwarz also sees a significant parallel between the Russian novels of Gogol, Dostoyevsky, Goncharov, and Chekhov and the work of Assis: "The system of ambiguities growing out of the local use of bourgeois ideas—one of the keys to the Russian novel—is not unlike the one we described for Brazil" (*Misplaced Ideas* 29).

10. According to Burns, investments in Brazil from the United States "jumped from $28 million in 1914, to $577 million in 1950, to $1.5 billion in 1960—about half of the total foreign investment in Brazil. . . . In several respects . . . the nationalists depicted the United States as an enemy whose influence and presence had to be challenged and defeated if nationalism was to triumph. They cultivated anti-Americanism as a convenient and certain means to arouse national feeling" (*History* [3rd ed.] 399).

11. The historian Alonso Aguilar believes that the good-neighbor policy involved serious internal contradictions. "While, on the one hand," he writes, "it showed respect, previously non-existent, for the Latin American nations, on the other hand it manifested itself as an effort to further subordinate them to United States economic needs" (qtd. in Johnson and Stam 358).

12. For a more complete discussion of Welles's sojourn in Brazil and the obstacles Welles encountered in the making of the film, see Stam 107–32.

13. To avoid confusion, the term *Latin America* should be used only when speaking of both

Spanish America and Brazil. New World literature too often ignores both Brazil and Canada and focuses only on relations between the United States and Spanish America.

14. The marketing strategies promoting Amado's work in the United States must be taken into consideration in explaining his singular popularity. As critics have noted, after the tremendous success of *Gabriela, Clove and Cinnamon* in the early 1960s, Amado was picked up by Avon, a publisher whose book covers emphasized the more titillating aspects of his work.

15. To account for the difference in their impact on the American reading public and the intelligentsia of the 1950s and 1960s, we might consider Amado's impact as primarily cultural (in his depiction of Brazil as the sexy, exotic other) and that of writers like Machado de Assis, Lispector, and Rosa as aesthetic (an evaluation stressing technical innovation and thematic exploration).

CHAPTER 2

An Overview of Brazilian Literature and Culture: The Americas and Beyond

THE COLONIAL ERA

Historically speaking, Brazilian and American literature begin under analogous—though far from identical—circumstances.[1] Both are derived from established European literatures and heritages; both were driven by an unstable mixture of religious, political, and commercial imperatives; both struggled to define themselves, first as cultures and then as unique national literatures; and both eventually developed distinctive generic, ethnic, and thematic traditions. Important differences, of course, existed from the outset, and they would affect the ways the two New World literatures evolved. Focusing on the disparities, Darcy Ribeiro, in *The Brazilian People*, depicts the English settlers as cautious and industrious, eager to turn the New World into a new England; they made common cause with smugglers and other unsavory characters. Later on, "through the mechanism of mercantile exchange," they would become major beneficiaries of the Atlantic trade. "The Iberians, by contrast, . . . landed without illusions, ready for new worlds, aiming to rule them, rebuild them, convert them, and mix racially with them." Nowhere in the New World would the process be more apparent than in Brazil, where "Portugal's colonial work with the Indians and blacks was . . . something radical" and where its "real product was not the gold so eagerly sought . . . , or even what so much wealth permitted to be built in the Old World. Its real product was a nation-people forged principally here through racial admixture" (38, 39).

By the late sixteenth century, England, realizing that it was behind in the race to colonize the New World, was forced to compete with Spain, Portugal, and France. Spain, especially, and Portugal had erected a vast colonial empire in North, Central, and South America, while France, holding a virtual monopoly on the lucrative fur trade, controlled Canada and much of the Mississippi River valley.[2] The three countries' domination of the colonies would engender a cultural legacy as well. In 1607, while Captain John Smith "struggled with a disorganized band of lazy colonists in Jamestown to erect a dingy fort," Spain, France, and Portugal (whose first permanent New World settlement dates from 1532) were using the narratives of conquest and appropriation to create a vibrant if inchoate New World literature. A potent cultural pluralism, including the distinctive African and Native American dimension, thus "characterized the New World from the start" (*Harper American Literature* 1: 9).

A related distinction between England's aspirations in the Americas and those of Spain, France, and Portugal was that adventurers from the three nations sought, generally, to return to Europe after profiting from the trade in gold, silver, and furs (or, in the case of Brazil, in lumber—brazilwood—sugar, and dye). Because they were essentially feudal social structures, in which nobles ruled their fiefdoms as if they were monarchs, the three continental nations developed their colonies more as garrisons for soldiers, priests, and traders than as self-sustaining communities. The English, as we know, came with families, intending to form a new civilization—a Puritan citadel—in the wilderness. Their determination led to an early emergence, in the English colonies, of a sense of social and political identity. If the Puritans, who had sought a reformed or "purified church-state" back in England, "could not compel the Old World to yield to their vision, they could interpret the New in their own image." Thus they adapted "the European images of America (land of gold, second paradise, utopia, 'primitivism' as moral regeneration) to fit the Protestant view of progress," replete with a Protestant apocalypse now (Bercovitch, "Puritan Vision" 36, 37–38).

In colonial Latin America, the great obstacle to the development of political self-determination was the "enforced inability to govern themselves" (Oliveira Lima 50–51)—a weakness bequeathed them by the social and political institutions implanted by the Spanish and Portuguese in the early sixteenth century (see Vianna). Ribeiro locates the roots of the problem in the early economic structures that defined Brazil and that would determine its future: the slave trade, particularly in the harvesting of sugarcane and the extraction of gold; "the communal enterprise of the Jesuits, based on Indian slave labor"; subsistence farming and ranching; and "the coastal nucleus of bankers, ship owners, and export-import entrepreneurs," the "most lucrative component of the colonial economy." Ribeiro further argues that the "dominant commercial-bureaucratic-ecclesiastical class" that sprung from this economic base became "the guiding force in the formation of the Brazilian people," who would see themselves reduced from a "civic and political entity into an offering of servile labor" (122–24).

Another fundamental difference is the still-contentious religious issue. New Spain, New France, and Brazil were generally Catholic (often driven by Jesuit theology and sociopolitical organization), whereas England was not merely Protestant but—during the Puritan regime of the mid-seventeenth century—of a conservative stripe. Exacerbating the theological differences were the long-standing animosities between the colonial powers in Europe— antagonisms that were being woven into the inter-American fabric from its creation. Thus Cotton Mather and his Puritan brethren, troubled by the wealth, influence, and opulence of colonial Mexico, were eager to supplant both its religion and its power. Samuel Sewall suggested "the bombing of Santa [sic] Domingo, the Havana, Porto Rico, and Mexico itself" with a Spanish-language Bible. In 1699, Mather set out to master Spanish in hopes of expediting this plan, which he believed would hasten "the evangelization of Latin America and the creation of a Puritan continent" (Sewall qtd. in Chevigny and Laguardia x–xi; see also Williams 17–18).

Entangled in the agencies of both the military and the civil government, religion played a major role in the formation of colonial Brazil, where "spiritual needs were placed on the same footing as the demands of civil life." Pervasive in its power and influence, the Portuguese Catholic church was, from the beginning, an equal partner of the state and, as such, wielded authority over such secular concerns as the economy, education, and what Caio Prado, Jr., describes as colonial social policy. One could even argue that in colonial Brazil the Portuguese Catholic church, itself deeply marked by the Counter-Reformation, sought to build an idealized Catholic culture in ways that parallel what the English Puritans would later seek to do in New England. As the church "vied with civil authorities," the line between the religious and the secular became blurred, a condition that led, perhaps more than in early New England, to "frequent conflicts between civil and ecclesiastical authorities" (Prado 385–87).

To some extent, religious teachings determined how the Europeans would interact with the Native Americans they were encountering and whose cultures they were destroying. In general, the Catholic countries assiduously sought from the beginning to convert the Native Americans, while the Puritans, whose attitude toward the wilderness and the people who inhabited it was distinctly pejorative, were less committed to conversion, an engagement with others that might well have troubled the Puritans' claim to religious exclusivity.[3] Samuel Eliot Morison reports that while such missionaries as John Eliot (who translated the Bible into Algonquin), John Cotton, and Richard Bourne "made great efforts to teach the Indians to read their own language, printed the Bible and other books for them, and trained native preachers," by 1675 "the total number of converted Indians did not exceed 2,500, out of about 10,000 in southern New England" (107, 108). Ned Landsman is of a similar mind. Because "most English colonists assumed there could be no true Christianizing without prior civilizing," he writes, "the efforts of English Protestants to convert Indians were notably less successful than those of their French or Spanish Catholic neighbors" (15). Two other scholars interpret the colonial treatment of the indigenous peoples somewhat differently. In the north, according to Ribeiro, "the Indian was a detail who soiled the landscape that had to be Europeanized" or eliminated, whereas the Iberian peoples, who exercised a different style of colonization, tended to view the Indians as a labor force that could easily be denied its rights (40). Making an important distinction, however, between the Spanish and the Portuguese in their attitudes toward the Native Americans, Roberto González Echevarría concludes that

> by remaining close to the coast, the Portuguese did not engage in large-scale, epic campaigns and mass migrations like the Spanish. From the start, perhaps given the character of the Portuguese, Brazil was more open to European influence and less confrontational in its contact with native populations. Unlike Spain, Portugal, where the Arabs had been defeated much earlier, was not absorbed by questions of doctrinal and racial purity. Hence, it did not apply itself to the conversion of the Indians with the same zeal. (*Oxford Book* 10)

Parkes, too, argues that for the Puritans, who saw themselves as exemplars of "civility" and Christianity (Landsman 15), the dark and foreboding American forest was closely associated, morally and sexually, with the figure of the witch and that it was indeed "the devil's own territory" (207)—an attitude that may well have poisoned relations between the English and the Native Americans for generations to come. Given all this, it is easier to understand how, as William Bradford gazed out at it from the cold, pitching deck of the *Mayflower*, this New World—in sharp contrast to the warm, sunny Caribbean beach that greeted Columbus in 1492 and Cabral in 1500—seemed to the English settlers to be a "hideous and desolate wilderness, full of wild beasts and wild men" (qtd. in *Harper American Literature* 1: 4), a place to be entered only for purposes of contrasting one's own civilization to it.

Overall, however, as Sacvan Bercovitch observes, making reference to English-speaking North America:

> The discovery of America was preeminently a secular venture, a process of exploration and appropriation empowered by what scholars have come to call the forces of modernization: capitalist enterprise, state nationalism, the expansion of Western European forms of society and culture throughout the world. So considered, "America" meant the triumph of European imperialism. ("Puritan Vision" 34)

A comparative reading of the colonial period also reveals that while the sociopolitical and economic organization of the Spanish, French, and Portuguese colonies was largely medieval, the English, as evidenced by the Pilgrims' Mayflower Compact, in 1620 (and even earlier by Magna Carta, 1215), held a more democratic and entrepreneurial view of government and self-rule. The heritage of the colonial era influenced the way the Americas would evolve as political entities, organize themselves as societies, and relate to each other as sovereign nations and as hemispheric neighbors. Although colonial Brazil did not attain the levels of wealth of Spanish America, it was able to generate a robust economy. The Brazilian economist Celso Furtado has described the importance of the sugar trade in colonial Brazil. As Brazil developed its sugar production, it sent the raw commodity to the Netherlands, where it was refined and shipped to other European countries. Colonial Brazil also benefited from an active commerce in precious metals and from "the existence of a lively trade in agricultural commodities," in which "Dutch and later English interests participated in substantial form," a situation that made it "impracticable to exercise any firm control over a gold production which came entirely from alluvial sources and extended over a vast territory" (148, 153). While it is true, as González Echevarría contends, that Latin America "is a Western culture that reaches back to the Middle Ages" (even as its nations have been enriched by indigenous and African heritages), we should not underestimate the fact that "Latin American colonial culture, in many ways medieval, is so distant from that of the United States that gross distortions and misreadings are bound to occur unless substantial study of it is required in the curriculum" (*Oxford Book* 51).

In many ways (the tradition of self-government notwithstanding), colonial Brazil resembled the "vale of plenty" (as John Smith put it) of the southern colonies in what would become the United States. Both the early Brazilians and the early southern writers saw their bountiful land as a natural paradise, a land of milk and honey. In Brazil, this epithet, a refrain that echoed from the colonial period through the twentieth century, helped define the nation's identity as a rich and fertile land and as a distinct cultural entity (see B. Nunes). The colonies of Brazil and the southern United States both had labor-intensive, single-crop agricultures (cotton and, to a degree, tobacco in the United States; sugarcane, cotton, and, later, tobacco in Brazil); both developed an agrarian-based aristocracy; and both were sustained by slave labor. By the 1820s and 1830s, both were worried about the prospect of a general slave rebellion; in Brazil the explosive issue was central to the country's drive toward independence. "The elites' commitment to slavery," Costa argues, "constituted a major obstacle to their full acceptance and implementation of liberal ideas. . . . Their distrust of the masses, their fear of a slave rebellion, and their desire to preserve the slave system led the elites to repudiate democratic procedures" (7–8). Still, as Prado notes, while "the English-settled temperate colonies (New England, New York, Pennsylvania, New Jersey, and Delaware)" tended, with some exceptions, to practice "the small peasant-type system of land-holding, south of Delaware Bay . . . in the hot and humid coastal plains where the physical environment is already subtropical in nature, we find that the system established is that of the large estate worked by slaves, the Southern plantation." This latter structure, based on the "large estate and the one-crop system," was the one that came, on the strength of slave labor, to be implanted in Brazil (Prado 136; Furtado 151–53, Pereira 14).

Mention must be made of yet another fundamental difference between colonial Brazil and colonial New England: from the beginning, Brazil's was a racially and culturally mixed population, much more so than in New England. Almost no Puritan writers consider the possibility of racial mixture or extensive cultural exchange. An exception, Roger Williams, an advocate of

reason and religious tolerance, concerns himself with "the tragic consequences of colonial settlers' behavior and their influence on Native Americans" (Scheick 94). Several of his poems from *A Key into the Language of
America* (1643), for example, show Williams breaking from convention "in
significant ways" and, indeed, even suggesting that "the Indians are morally
superior to many of the English" (Elliott, "Poetry" 229–30). "Rich in paradox, word play, and sometimes satire" (Scheick 94), these poems, if they do
not approve or advocate sexual contact between the Indians and the English,
demonstrate that Puritan writing was not wholly devoid of sensitive, reflective meditations on the troubling issue of cultural interaction.

E. Bradford Burns, by way of contrast, stresses the centrality of racial
mixing in colonial Brazil: "The Portuguese . . . evidenced a flexibility, both
physical and psychological, that seemed to make them sufficiently malleable
to learn from the conquered. In Brazil, the blending of the Lusitanian and
Amerindian cultures was facilitated by the favorable attitudes of both toward
miscegenation" (*History* [3rd ed.] 37–38). By about 1820, Brazil had a population of 3.5 million. Fewer than a third were European, 2 million were
black, and half a million were Indian African or Indian European. Because of
the significant representation of blacks, one Portuguese observed that "Brazil
has the body of America and the soul of Africa" (47). As a result of the country's demography, there appeared in Brazil a "new race" of people, one made
up of Europeans, Indians, and Africans (38).

Nevertheless, we should recognize that the myth of Brazil as a racial paradise is a greatly exaggerated and often highly selective view—one that, according to Ribeiro and many others, may actually prevent Brazilians from
seeing the "deep abysses" that separate its social strata and that cripples its
progress and development as a modern nation (5). In Ribeiro's view, Brazil
cannot move forward until it addresses the social, political, and economic divisions that currently rend it. Inequities involving class, race, economic status, gender, and education, which date back to Brazil's colonial formation,
must be eradicated if Brazil is to escape the shackles of its past (1–6).

Writing of "the vast commercial enterprise" that was the colonization of
Brazil and that bound "white Europeans, African Negroes, and the indigenous peoples of the continent," Prado argues that the resulting admixture

> was composed of highly diverse ingredients: three different races and cul-
> tures, of which two . . . whose original culture traits were to be smothered

in the process, supplied colonization with its largest contingent; races brought together by force and incorporated into colonization by violence, without any preliminary attempt to prepare them for their contact with an alien society; races whose only "school" was to be the field and the slave hut. (399)

Imperfect though it is, the early Brazilian racial experience contrasts vividly with that of the colonial United States, where no comparable "new race" was formed and where racial separation was the norm. This separation established a pattern that would torment the United States for generations, even as the nation has steadily become a more racially tolerant society.[4]

In comparing the colonial periods of Brazil and the United States and the prevailing social myths that derive from them, we are struck by the primacy of two in particular, both of which came to define their cultures: the American myth of the self-made man and the myth of Brazil as a racial paradise. As Emilia Viotti da Costa observes, the myth of the self-made man, "so pervasive in American society," simply "did not have the same appeal" in Brazil. Well into the nineteenth century (except among a few immigrant petit-bourgeois groups), "it remained alien to the experience of most Brazilians, upper and lower class alike, who believed instead in the myth of racial democracy." In the United States "the myth of the self-made man helped to blind Americans to class differences. In Brazil the myth of racial democracy obscured racial differences. In both cases the 'truth' of past generations became the myth of today" (235).

DEVELOPMENT OF EARLY LITERATURES

What we see, then, in comparing the emergence of the United States and Brazil, first as European colonies and then as independent countries, is that they share broad patterns of development, as Herbert Bolton and others have argued. Inevitably, of course, the substantial dissimilarities in their emergence as societies have played a role—certainly in the evolution of their national literatures. The colonial literature of the United States has its origins in the Protestant Reformation, specifically in the doctrines of John Calvin (1509–64). As Claude Hulet points out, Brazil's early writing was marked, aesthetically and conceptually, first (1500–1650) by the intellectual outlook and the poetics of the Renaissance, later (1650–1750) by the baroque. Thus, even as the early English settlers were struggling to survive in the New World, the Portuguese in Brazil were creating a rich and complex national literature, characterized, particularly in its baroque stage, by

> its insistence on wit, conceits, and the use of such devices as aphorisms, analogies, anaphoras, antitheses, and paradoxes. Everywhere there are unexpected contrasts in language, in thought and in themes: realism-idealism, flesh-spirit, world-heaven, reason-faith, life-death, tranquility-ecstasy, pain-pleasure, worldliness-asceticism. The rational and the irrational become fused, sensualism and the emotions are exaggerated, egomania becomes the law, hyperbole is the rule, movement is constant, loneliness becomes a fetish, and man flees from reality into illusion or wallows in animality. (1: 40–41)

From their quite different critical and aesthetic perspective, the "New England Puritans radically distrusted the senses and the imagination and were highly suspicious of all forms of art." There is a clear discordance, however, "between Puritan theory and poetic practice." In the mid-seventeenth century, in fact, "a major shift had become evident authorizing writers to use sensual imagery more freely and even to strive for eloquence" (Elliott, "Poetry" 226, 227, 228); both had earlier been discouraged as affronts to the word of God. While the Puritan style has traditionally been "condemned for its plainness" and its "subservience to theology," the English settlers' "literary taste was flexible enough to accommodate pagan models, scatology, erotica, ambiguity, and personality," and their simple style was not "arid" or "artless" (Bercovitch, *Puritan Imagination* 4). Although the didactic quality of Puritan verse remained, the post-1650 change in artistic sensibility apparently placated the apprehensions even of John Cotton. Among the intellectual leaders of the time, he most feared the "idolatry" that he believed would result from "the use of figurative, imagistic, or symbolic language" (Elliott, "Poetry" 228, 226).

The two stars under which Brazilian literature was born—the Renaissance and the baroque—help explain why Brazil's colonial literature differs so sharply from that of the Puritan United States. Moreover, its origins demonstrate why, from the outset, Brazilian colonial literature was more complex and expansive, more worldly and imaginative.

No less significant, however, is the fact that Brazil's New World adventure may well have been an accident, a by-product of Portugal's fifteenth-century expansion around Africa and on to India, Japan, and China. For the English, the conquest of parts of the New World was primarily a function of the Enlightenment, with its embracing of science and reason, its belief in the improvability of humankind and in the concept of progress. For the Portuguese, deeply influenced by the Renaissance (Hulet 1: 2), conquest was one facet of an era of extraordinary exploration and growth, which would put them into contact with cultures quite different from their own. The first settlers in Brazil, arriving in the New World without wives, were adventurers, "penniless noblemen," exiles, not a few criminals, military men, Jews and "new Christians," missionaries, and "a sprinkling of artisans to perform the manual toil" (Putnam, *Marvelous Journey* 8). According to Gilberto Freyre, the Portuguese colonizers became perhaps the most adaptive of all European conquerors (185; see Abreu 29, 47). Famously (or, as some commentators would have it, infamously), Freyre asserted that the Portuguese who came to the New World in 1500 were "less ardent in their orthodoxy, than the Spaniards and less narrow than the English in their color prejudice and Christian morality."[5] This argument led to one of Freyre's most influential and controversial conclusions: "Hybrid from the beginning, Brazilian society is, of all those in the Americas, the one most harmoniously constituted so far as racial relations are concerned" (81, 83). Long regarded as orthodoxy, this overly optimistic sense of Brazilian race relations—an issue long contested in Brazilian literature—came under attack, beginning in the 1950s, with scholars such as Darcy Ribeiro, Emilia Viotti da Costa, Celso Furtado, and Roberto DaMatta leading the reaction. DaMatta especially has been critical of Freyre's thesis and has argued instead that "any easy intimacy of inter-racial relations had been possible only because" in Brazil nonwhites were trapped in a social and economic system based on a "profound inequality" in which formal segregation was not necessary (qtd. in Skidmore, "Essay" 361–62).

Concentrating on the "cultural *métissage*" that "global circulation, mutual influence, and cross-breeding" engenders (and Freyre typifies), Stephen Greenblatt advocates a new kind of literary history, one that "does not inevitably betray the aleatory, accidental, contingent, random dimensions of literary creativity" and that stresses not "the dialect of the tribe" (the theoretical basis for traditional literary histories) but "the daring intersection of multiple identities" (59, 60, 61).

Scholarly attitudes about colonial literature have been undergoing significant change in recent years, in both Brazil and the United States. In the view of Emory Elliott, "there is hardly a statement one can make about the Puritans today without arousing controversy" (*Columbia Literary History* 183). Although scholarship on colonial Latin American letters does not generally elicit such contentiousness, the revised critique has provided Brazilians and Spanish Americans with a stronger sense of origin and of the "density" of their literary history (González Echevarría and Pupo-Walker 1: xiv–xvi, xv). For the United States the scholarly shift has resulted in the discovery of a literary heritage that is more complex and variegated than it appeared to be. The moment is propitious, then, to undertake a rapprochement and to consider how the early literatures of Brazil and the United States, as New World cultures in the process of formation, differ and what they have in common.

To examine colonial literature in the two nations properly, we should be aware of significant historical disparities. In the United States the colonial period was short—lasting from 1607 and the founding of Jamestown, the first permanent English settlement in the New World, to 1775 and the beginning of the Revolutionary War. In Spanish America and Brazil, however, the colonial period lasted for more than three hundred years, from 1492 (Columbus's voyage) and 1500 (Cabral's landing in Brazil) to the early decades of the nineteenth century, when political independence came to the continent. Brazil's colonial period also began more than one hundred years earlier than did that of the United States. In Brazil and in Spanish America, moreover,

> literature began to flourish almost concurrently with settlement, and it reached a high level of development before the establishment of the first printing press in New England. Highly sophisticated examples of the epic, the satire, and the lyric were produced in Spanish America during the first century of European occupation, but very little of comparable quality can be claimed for the first century of the English colonies, during which nearly all writing was religious or utilitarian. (Aldridge 210)

While recent scholarship might question Owen Aldridge's evaluation of colonial literature in the United States (see, e.g., Mulford), his description of cultural developments seems accurate enough: if the New World literature of the seventeenth century was dominated by Latin America, then by the eighteenth century, with the breakthroughs of the English Enlightenment taking hold, the situation was largely reversed. As he suggests, the movement for independence in the northern colonies brought about literary flowering. Spanish America and Brazil, in the meantime, "fell behind in literature concerned with independence and political organization" (210).

In his *Description of New England* (1616), John Smith, his imagination fired by rumors of the New World's abundance, envisioned it as an earthly Utopia or Canaan. (This image, as we have noted, was also used to characterize Brazil.) As many scholars have pointed out, the basic motives for the English incursion into the New World can be divided into four categories: the patriotic, the economic, the sociopolitical, and the religious.[6] In conflict with Spain and France for domination, the English, their national pride at stake, could not sit idly by while their continental rivals benefited significantly from their New World colonies. In the early 1570s, at Queen Elizabeth's command, English sea captains like Francis Drake began to raid the Spanish galleons, laded with gold and silver from Mexico and Peru, on their way back to Spain. England now recognized the strategic necessity of possessing a New World colony itself, to check the power of the Spanish, the French, and (to a lesser extent) the Portuguese.

By the late sixteenth and early seventeenth centuries, English trading companies, such as the Virginia Company, were set up to capitalize on the New World adventures. The companies organized groups interested in colonizing the New World and participating in what was expected to be a financial windfall. Thus from the beginning English exploration of the New World was primarily a real estate and trade venture, although to be sure, other issues were at stake. One was the need to defuse what many in the government viewed as the severe social problems afflicting England. Social and economic disruption were causing widespread unemployment; political unrest was rife; urban overcrowding had become epidemic as people fled the countryside in search of largely nonexistent industrial jobs; and crime was on the rise. The prospect of relieving these troubles by exporting people to the New World—where they just might provide a new source of wealth for England as well—must have been appealing to England's leaders. Perhaps most important (at least in terms of the social, political, and intellectual development of the United States) was the religious question. Beset by a growing religious fervor among reformers of the Church of England, government officials saw the New World as a convenient way to avoid what might turn into an explosive situation. The Puritan challenge to the church had been gaining strength since the sixteenth century, and it would, of course, become bound up in the politics of Oliver Cromwell and the English Civil War (1642–49).[7]

Historically, then, the rise of the Puritans in England parallels and, to a degree, follows the Spanish and Portuguese conquest of the New World.

The most radical of the Puritan separatists, the forty-one Pilgrims who arrived in Cape Cod in 1620, knew they were seeking to establish a civilization in a part of the world already controlled by Spain, France, and Portugal. Realizing the need to create a "civil body politic" to govern themselves, the Pilgrims, with William Bradford as their leader, undertook to write the Mayflower Compact, a political document unique in postconquest America.[8] Battle-hardened from the internecine religious conflicts in England, the Pilgrim separatists were determined not to "found a democracy" or "establish a free state" but to create, on their terms, a religious society and to bar from their "new Jerusalem" any who might differ with them (Foerster, Grabo, Nye, Carlisle, and Falk 6–7). As Henry Bamford Parkes puts it, "In their dealings with the Indians and with certain rival groups of colonists who attempted to settle in New England a few years later," the Pilgrims "showed themselves suspicious, self-righteous, and capable on occasion of acting with real cruelty" (32–33).

Ironically, although in the Spanish, French, and Portuguese New World colonies there was little sense of democratic self-rule (see Oliveira Lima 50–54; Vianna), neither was there the degree of intolerance sometimes exhibited by the English separatists. The issue would be crucial in encounters between the colonists and, first, the Native Americans[9] and, second, the African slaves who were soon to be imported as the primary labor force.[10] Widespread recognition of the contributions of blacks and Indians did not come, in Brazil, until the 1870s, when the literary critic Sílvio Romero and the historian João Capistrano de Abreu, together and individually, called attention to their efforts. Romero contended that Brazil's development owed more to the blacks than to the Indians because, he believed, the blacks had penetrated more extensively into all aspects of European Brazil's social strata. Abreu, focusing on the social and economic contributions of the African slaves, would eventually make much the same argument (Burns, *History* [3rd ed.] 211; Abreu 18).

The Puritans who arrived in Massachusetts Bay in 1630 were less separatist than the *Mayflower* Pilgrims a decade earlier. With John Winthrop as their leader, the later group declared that their purpose was not to amass wealth, as had been the objective of the Virginia Company, but "to worship God in their own fashion—to establish a 'true' religious society," "a city upon a hill" (Foerster, Grabo, Nye, Carlisle, and Falk 7). For all its self-described godliness, however, this city would be remarkably receptive to the worldly ways of commerce. Following John Cotton's admonition that a religious soul could be achieved by godly (but profitable) labor in the secular world, Puritan theology forged an advantageous alliance between the attainment, on the one hand, of wealth and power and, on the other, of a sense of righteousness. As Morison expresses it, "These Puritans had a definite mission—to establish a community rather than a mere colony, where they could put their ideals into practice. New England, to them, was a New Canaan which the Almighty had set apart for an experiment in Christian living," where, they believed, they could "lead the New Testament life, yet make a living" (65).

This approach to the role of religion in public life, one that blends the desire for wealth with the quest for personal sanctimony, would have a lasting impact on American society. By facilitating an uneasy union between those who professed to do only God's will (as they interpreted it) and those who prayed at the altar of Mammon, Puritanism's dream of a holy commonwealth, free from the corrupting temptations of the outside world, became increasingly difficult to maintain (Foerster, Grabo, Nye, Carlisle, and Falk 8). "Perhaps," Robert Spiller explains, "in the beginning of American civilization can be found a clue to the incongruous mixture of naive idealism and crude materialism that produced in later years a literature of beauty, irony, affirmation, and despair" (5)—a literature that would show Americans advocating "an unrestrained drive toward domination and exploitation, in spiritual as well as in material things" (Parkes 192). Although Brazil suffered from many shortcomings in its colonial formation, this particular marriage of religion, sociopolitical vision, and commerce was not one of them. The Catholic Church, in fact, played a fairly limited role until 1549, when the first of 128 Jesuits arrived. Still, because "to be Portuguese was to be Roman Catholic," issues of religion, politics, and economics were intertwined (although not as inextricably as in Spain or as materialistically as in the United States). As a consequence, the church and the state effectively functioned as one entity (Burns, *History* [3rd ed.] 31; see also Prado 384–89; Abreu).

By 1750 the American colonies had become a reasonably sophisticated society, one increasingly empowered by the ideas of the Enlightenment. Spanish America and Brazil, with some 250 years of colonial experience behind them, had, with a few notable exceptions (particularly in Brazil, where arcadianism had produced polished and subtle poetry), entered a period of turmoil and decline, their "heroic" ages having long since passed. Again the exception, Brazil, by the 1750s, was reaching the zenith of its first expansion into its vast interior (see map). An epic undertaking in which the three primary racial groups participated, the journey anticipated, to some extent, the westward expansion of the United States; it also had, in the figure of the *bandeirante* ("pioneer" or "flag bearer"; see Moog), much in common with the Canadian *voyageur* of the same period (Burns, *History* [2nd ed.] 64–70).

Several generations earlier, Brazilian and Spanish American literature had arisen, both from within the colonies and as influenced by the creative period of Spanish and Portuguese literature associated with the European baroque. The celebrated Spanish poets Francisco de Quevedo and Luis de Góngora were especially influential in Spanish America and Brazil. Their work spawned servile imitations and—as with Mexico's Sor Juana Inés de la Cruz, who, as a poet and thinker, had no equal in colonial America (for a comparison with Anne Bradstreet, see Aldridge 25–52)—some brilliant prose, poetry, and drama. At the same time, the rich English literary tradition was exerting a considerable influence on New England letters, imparting a diversity we might not expect. Edward Taylor (1645?–1729), for example, whose best lines (Aldridge's views notwithstanding) seem more similar to Sor Juana's than to Bradstreet's, shows a clear connection to John Donne and the other metaphysical poets, who have much in common with Góngora and Quevedo. When we assume a comparative inter-American perspective, however, we see that the Puritan heritage, with its practicality, its embrace of civic responsibility, its strong theological roots, and its frequently apocalyptic tone, produced a literature that differed profoundly, in its sense of purpose (which we will explore shortly), from the elegant, inventive, and often profane literature that was emanating from Spanish America and Brazil. The Iberian baroque had energized and liberated Latin American colonial writing, enabling it to become the most sophisticated body of literature in the Americas.

The same Puritan heritage that may have inhibited imaginative writing put a much greater emphasis on general literacy than did the settlers in Latin America, especially Brazil, which has long suffered from an inadequate educational system and which did not gain its first modern university until 1920, when, in Rio de Janeiro, three hitherto separate colleges—law, medicine, and engineering—were reorganized under a central administration (Burns, *History* [3rd ed.] 364). For the Puritans, reading and writing represented access to the holy scriptures, the source, in Puritan ideology, of all true knowledge. For the Puritans, to be illiterate—to be unable to interpret the word of God—was to fall prey to Satan himself (Foerster, Grabo, Nye, Carlisle, and Falk 11). With a sense of mission deriving from an "extraordinary reliance on texts"

Western Boundaries of Brazil, 1600, 1780, and the Present

Legend
--- Western Boundary, 1600
Western Boundary, 1780
Brazil, 2004

This map tracks the expansion of European settlement in Brazil that took place following the arrival of the Portuguese in 1500. By 1600, Europeans, mainly the Portuguese, controlled a narrow strip of land along the Atlantic coast. By 1780, following the territorial expansion of the sixteenth and seventeenth centuries and a series of treaties between Spain and Portugal, Brazil's interior boundary lay thousands of miles to the west. The present-day boundary reflects additional expansion in the twentieth century.

and on a commitment to their scrutiny, the New England Puritans became, in the New World,

> a self-declared people of the Book. They were a community that invented its identity *ex verbo*, by the word, and continued to assert that identity through the seventeenth century, expanding, modifying, and revising it in a procession of sermons, exhortations, and declarations, histories and hagiographies, covenants and controversies, statements and restatements of purpose—a stream of rhetorical self-definition unequaled by any other community of its kind (and proportionately, perhaps of any kind). (Bercovitch, "Puritan Vision" 34)

In addition to founding colleges like Harvard and Yale, the Puritans, many of whom had university training, instituted a system of public and private schools.[11] In Spanish America and Brazil, only a privileged few had a formal education. We can only speculate what would have happened if the highly literate Puritan had had an opportunity to read the extraordinary sonnets and epistles of Sor Juana or the often scabrous satires of colonial Brazil's Gregório de Matos (see app. C), who moved easily between "the world of the bureaucracy, the church, and the upper class" and the "underworld of slums and slave quarters, bars and brothels" (Haberly, "Colonial Brazilian Literature" 57).

Scholars have long sought explanations for the ways in which colonial American letters developed. One theory has stressed the fact that the original English settlers, who would implant their society's attitudes about imaginative writing, were born before the golden age of English literature (Foerster, Grabo, Nye, Carlisle, and Falk 15). Moreover, and unlike the early Spanish and Portuguese arrivals (who came to the New World both during and after the golden age of Iberian literature), the Puritans represented a new middle class that did not particularly appreciate nondidactic writing. Furthermore, most writing in New England in the seventeenth century consisted of a brief discussion of a simple topic, not the comprehensive grappling with ideas and the intellectual rigor that mark serious literature (12–15). There is little in the literature of the colonial United States that approaches the power and complexity of Sor Juana's *First Dream* (arguably the finest poetic text produced in the colonial New World), the subtle psychological and social comedies of Juan Ruiz de Alarcón (like Sor Juana, born in Mexico), or the multifaceted poetry of Matos, some of whose work recalls the irreverence and suggestiveness of Thomas Morton's *New English Canaan* (1637).[12] The difference, however, is that while Morton only hints at bawdiness, the vitriolic Matos became, on occasion, quite explicit, even pornographic. Matos was one of colonial Brazil's two major figures. The other was Antônio Vieira, the influential Jesuit priest whose elaborate, often controversial sermons deplored the treatment of the Native Americans and the Africans imported as slaves (see Vieira, app. C). Vieira invites comparison with Puritan preachers, from Cotton Mather to Jonathan Edwards, for reasons as much political as theological.

Another reason often given for the paucity of nondidactic literary texts in colonial New England is that Calvinism, the prevailing religious doctrine of the colonists, viewed art as irrelevant to God's greatness (if not an outright affront to it), an attitude that encouraged an aesthetic stringency, or simplicity (the famous Puritan plain style), in artistic expression. Poetry, especially, was held in fairly low esteem by the Puritans, who thought of it primarily as a branch of rhetoric, a mode of persuasion, rather than as an imaginative genre. This perspective helps explain the gulf that separates the work of Bradstreet, and even of Edwards and Taylor, from the intellectual richness, thematic diversity, and stylistic brilliance of Sor Juana, Vieira, and Matos. In fact, Latin American writers with their less restrictive poetic legacy, were considerably more productive than the Puritans in two particular forms, lyric poetry and epic poetry. Among the Puritans, with their suspicion of artistic expression, poetry was largely—though (as Taylor's work demonstrates) not exclusively—a matter of mnemonic verse, didactic rhymes, historical versifications, funeral elegies, and personal or spiritual reflections (Foerster, Grabo, Nye, Carlisle, and Falk 11–14). Although exhibiting a "rich variety in type and manner," colonial poets tended "to subordinate art and artist to utilitarian design and communal identity," with the result, sometimes, of "a curious tension" between "cultural theological restraint and personal emotion" (Scheick 84). In addition to being as English in its origins as Brazilian literature was not merely European but Iberian, early New England literature and culture "shared the experience—and myth—of the English Reformation, marking England as an elect nation: the Virgin Queen as the great deliverer of Protestant England from Spain and Bloody Mary; the providential miracles of the Armada and Guy Fawkes Day; and the apocalyptic events . . . of Civil War, Regicide, and rule by the Puritan Saints" (Lewalski 24). In contrast, then, to the political, intellectual, and artistic matrix that gave rise to the elaborate and inventive verse written in viceregal Mexico or Peru, or in Brazil, there was in New England a fundamentally different approach to the production and appreciation of what we think of as lyric poetry.

In any discussion of the distinctions between colonial poetry in Brazil and the United States, the question of purpose looms large. Perhaps reflecting, more than anything else, the aesthetic and religious contrasts between Puritan Protestantism and baroque Catholicism, the poetry of such diverse figures as Taylor, Bradstreet, Michael Wigglesworth, and Phillis Wheatley suggests that it was written and read for reasons quite distinct from those that inspired the poetry of Juan del Valle y Caviedes (from Peru), Sor Juana, and Matos. Whereas their traditions and circumstances encouraged the Latin Americans to write "under the aegis of the baroque, defined not only as an artistic style, but also as a cultural complex" (Coutinho 68), the Puritans created a socially conscious literature that embedded itself in, and spoke to, a host of theological, political, and governmental issues.

The case of epic poetry is revealing, since, particularly in Spanish America, it seems to be tied to the militaristic nature of the Spanish conquest. For all their other difficulties, the English settlers did not contend with well-organized societies like the Aztecs and the Incas or with the fierce Huron and Iroquois nations, as did the French. As a result, epic poetry devoted to warfare is largely absent in the colonial literature of the United States, where vision poems, mock epics, and burlesques were a much stronger tradition (McWilliams 160, 164).[13] The experience of the English colonists was defined more by the "conquest of the continent than by any other factor," and while the story of their creation of a country is essentially epic, "it had as its protagonists not heroes or demigods but plain average citizens" (Parkes 24). Brazil, however, differs yet again from Spanish America, in that, as Freyre (81) and others have shown, the early Portuguese (like the early English) did not encounter civilizations as advanced or as warlike as those of the Aztec, the Maya, and the Inca (see also González Echevarría, *Oxford Book* 10). Yet Brazil also produced a number of epic poems, such as Bento Teixeira's *Prosopopéia* (1601), José Basílio da Gama's *The Uruguay* (1769), and Santa Rita Durão's *Caramuru* (1781).[14] Although these epics are uneven in quality and none matches *The Araucaniad* in sheer narrative drama, they succeed, at least tentatively, in introducing several nativist elements and a sense of cultural identity. Such a development constitutes, as it does in the United States, a first step in the establishment of an authentic national literature.[15]

Among the other literary genres practiced in the New World's colonial phase—drama, sermon, and narrative—the first presents an interesting case. When the Puritans closed the English theater in 1642, they put a damper on the role drama would play in the development of literature in the English-speaking New World. And, indeed, drama did not emerge until after 1750, when the decline of Puritanism had begun. Published in 1765, Thomas Godfrey's *The Prince of Parthia* is perhaps most famous for being the first play written by someone born in the English colonies. Drama was not a widely accepted genre, in fact, until after the American Revolution, "and did not become a distinguished form of American literary art until the twentieth century" (Foerster, Grabo, Nye, Carlisle, and Falk 15). In contrast, the theater was important in the development of New France,[16] New Spain, and Brazil, where, from the beginning, it was seen as a useful tool in the conversion of the indigenous peoples and in the creation of a national identity (Wasserman, "Theater"). Realizing early on that the Native Americans were responsive to drama and to performance-based theological instruction (possibly because of Native America's strong oral tradition), Jesuits like Manuel da Nóbrega and José de Anchieta effectively used a variety of theatrical devices, including poetry, music, and song, to convert the Indians. The dramatic productions offered by Anchieta, in particular, "bear more resemblance to the spectacle than to the theater, and thereby betray an important link with the Middle Ages," as do Nóbrega's "scholastically oriented" *Diálogos sobre a conversão do gentio* (*Dialogues on the Conversion of the Natives*), written some eight years after its author's arrival in Brazil (Hulet 1: 5). Finally, and again in contrast to the dim view of the theater taken by the Puritans in England, the theatrical tradition of both Spain and Portugal (particularly Spain) was rich and varied, enabling the theater in Latin America to play a central role in the development of early literature and culture.

Occasionally a part of Spanish American and Brazilian theatrical performances, sermons were also a fundamental element in New England's colonial literature. For the Puritans, sermons were important because they consisted of "verbal arrows" that were capable of piercing even the most "sin-hardened heart." "In sermons," it is said, "Puritan writers worked always for a simplicity and directness of style so that hearers could understand and, they hoped, be moved" (*Harper American Literature* 1: 98–99). In Brazil, as in Spanish and French America, the sermon was also a feature of early literary development. Unlike the straightforward, unadorned style favored by the Puritans, however, Brazilian clerics, such as Vieira, Antônio de Sá, and Eusébio de Matos, cultivated baroque texts that touched, often critically, on virtually every aspect of colonial life, from politics and economics to race and religion. Vieira in particular was a master of baroque oratory and argumentation; his disputatious sermons, in which he might challenge God in open debate, were characterized by hyperbole, elaborate conceits and allusions, antitheses, irony, and repetitions (see app. C). If we examine the roles played by sermonizing in colonial American literature, including the importance that oratory and the oral tradition generally had for Native Americans, the differences between the sermons of Mather or Edwards and those of Vieira would reveal the larger aesthetic and intellectual issues (Gongorism, for example, versus the Puritan "plain style"; Jesuit Catholicism versus Puritanism; relations among the European colonizers, the Native Americans, and the African slaves) that shaped colonial letters in the Americas.

The study of colonial narrative, too, yields illuminating comparisons. Taking the form of official reports and documents (including ships' logs), letters, and histories, narrative was, logically enough, the first literary genre to be extensively practiced in the Americas. The earliest narratives we have, those dealing with the European discovery of the New World (such as Columbus's journal entry of 12 October 1492 or his exaggerated letter to the Spanish sovereigns; Samuel de Champlain's accounts of the first French landfall in the New World; John Smith's early report; and Pêro Vaz de Caminha's strikingly tolerant and matter-of-fact letter about the Portuguese arrival in Brazil),[17] reflect not only the psychology of their authors but also the social, political and economic conditions in their countries of origin (see app. C for the Caminha document). Although the novel was officially banned in colonial Spanish America, French and English romances circulated freely, if clandestinely, in the Americas, helping lay the conceptual and technical groundwork for the development of the New World novel itself (Fitz, "First Inter-American Novels").

One specific narrative form, however, developed early in the Americas. The captivity narrative, as it has become known in the literary history of the United States (see Drimmer; Sayre), has its counterparts throughout the New World. Annette Kolodny even argues that "the single narrative form indigenous to the New World is the victim's recounting of unwilling captivity" (qtd. in Sayre 4). Gordon Sayre maintains, however, that the genre's importance "is unique to the English literature of America" and that it "is not central to colonial New Spain, New France, or Portuguese Brazil, even though Native Americans certainly did take many colonials captive in those regions" (4). In Spanish America, for example, the prototype of this form—and probably the original North American captivity tale—is *The Narrative of Alvar Núñez Cabeza de Vaca* (1542).[18] This riveting work offers a fascinating alternative to the perhaps better-known captivity narratives of John Smith, John Tanner, Olaudah Equiano, and Mary Rowlandson.

Brazil, too, has its captivity narratives, the most representative of which is Durão's *Caramuru*. In its nationalistic ethos, this canonical text "quite closely parallels the North American story of John Smith and Pocahontas" (Haberly, "Colonial Brazilian Literature" 62). Its ten cantos of occasionally verbose (if, at times, distinctly nativist) octaves tell the story of the shipwrecked Portuguese explorer Diogo Álvares Correia (who, after firing his weapon, is given the Indian name Caramuru) and his relationship with the people of the Indian princess Paraguaçu, who later becomes his wife. Intended as a national epic, to portray the history of Brazil from colonial times to the expulsion of the last foreign invader, the poem surprisingly enough sees Correia and Paraguaçu brought to Europe by French forces and married in Paris. Patriotically thwarting French plans to conquer Brazil, Correia and his wife (now an ardent convert to Christianity) return to Brazil, which is poised to fulfill its destiny. Depicted in highly Europeanized and unrealistic terms, Paraguaçu, on the voyage home, is granted a vision of Brazil's future, in which her husband becomes the first governor of the state of Bahia and whites and Indians together produce a new people for the new land.

The same motif, the sexual congress of a European man and a Native American woman, appears in Mexico in the story of Cortés and his translator and concubine Doña Marina, later to be known, more infamously, as La Malinche. In Mexico, however, as Myra Jehlen observes:

La Malinche . . . signifies treachery and thus a continuing if hopeless conflict. In the United States, the self-abandoning Pocahontas stands for romance or the resolution of conflict in the absorption of one participant by the other. Pocahontas enables John Smith not only, like Cortés, to conquer the original inhabitants but to absorb them into an English America. (71–72)

Seen from this perspective, the story of Paraguaçu more closely parallels the Pocahontas legend than that of La Malinche. Even so, the Brazilian epic is more directly tied to the idea of racial blending and the creation of a new people than is the American story. From Paraguaçu to the character Iracema, and from Antônio Callado's *Quarup* to Ribeiro's *Maíra*, Brazilian literature has cultivated the issue of racial mixing and specifically women's role in it—a role that, as many texts show, encompasses such topics as power, female sexuality, and cultural identity. In John Smith's perhaps apocryphal account in his *True Relation of Virginia*, the idea of interracial marriage is only hinted at. Like

Paraguaçu, however, Pocahontas was eventually converted to Christianity, baptized as Rebecca, and married to the settler John Rolfe, with whom she traveled to London. Rooted in issues of race, sexuality, religion, cultural probity, identity politics, and progeny, the early inter-American captivity narratives stress the importance of the female characters. The point at which all these factors converge is often the female captive, a figure whose story is nearly always emblematic of the entire New World experience in all its complexity.

Arguing that women prisoners in the eastern United States were mostly not abused by their Indian captors, Frederick Drimmer cites the well-known case of Rowlandson as typical. Rowlandson, who had been "taken captive by the Wampanoag and the Narragansett in King Philip's War, in 1676," remarks on how respectfully she was treated. Of her experience she wrote:

> I have been in the midst of those roaring lions and savage bears that feared neither God nor man, nor the devil, by night and day, alone and in company, sleeping all sorts together, and yet not one of them ever offered the least abuse of unchastity to me in word or action. (qtd. in Drimmer 12)

With a rich diversity of forms and expressions, the New World captivity narrative is yet another genre that would benefit from comparative study.

The slow decline of Puritanism, interrupted only by the spasm of the Great Awakening (1730–45), had run its course by the mid-eighteenth century, when the thirteen colonies were beginning to rethink their identity and their relations with Britain. Once again it is important to keep track of both the historical and the aesthetic differences in play here. By the 1750s and the dawn of the "American Enlightenment" (Ferguson 345), colonial literature, only slightly more than one hundred years old, was struggling with issues of cultural authenticity and political self-determination (368–89). The result was a literature that grew "out of a commitment to the general relation and spread of ideas" to the international "republic of letters" and to "the promise of republicanism throughout the world" (380). Although the ideas of the Enlightenment were slowly making inroads into Brazil, its impact on literature came chiefly in the form of a resurgent and now empowering nativism, inspired in no small measure by the French physiocrats, who stressed the importance of scientific research. Emphasizing the value of the land and of agriculture over trade and commerce (long championed by the mercantilists), the physiocrats gave Brazilians a newfound sense of national pride and identity. In the last five decades of the eighteenth century, more and more foreign ships dropped anchor in Brazilian ports, which were open to international traffic. "In 1759," Burns reports, "both French and English squadrons visited Salvador," while between 1792 and 1805 nearly ninety vessels from the United States, including a number of Yankee sperm whalers, made stops (*History* [2nd ed.] 93). Perhaps not as resolutely as the United States, and without the benefit of an entrenched republicanism (though its seeds were being sown), Brazil sought to establish its identity as a culture and to enter the international arena, in politics and economics as well as in arts and science.

Brazil did not keep pace with the political progress of the United States—its first, failed attempt at independence occurred in 1789.[19] Nevertheless, Brazil produced a number of first-rate writers and texts. The colony could point to authors and intellectuals like Matos; the combative, patriotic Jesuit priest Vieira; the poet and historiographer Sebastião da Rocha Pita, whose boastful *History of Portuguese America, 1500–1724* (1730) represents the first systematic effort to write a sociopolitical history of Brazil); and Nuno Márques Pereira, the author of the popular though tendentious narrative *Peregrino da América* (1728). The text, viewed by David Haberly as "the response of the Iberian Counter-Reformation to John Bunyan's *Pilgrim's Progress,*" is sometimes cited as Brazil's first novel.[20] Energized by the importation of two major European cultural institutions—the academy (intellectual societies that, featuring literary, scientific, and often utilitarian approaches to letters and life, suggest parallels with early Puritan writing) and the Arcady, which in the tradition of European arcadianism advocated a return to the "peaceful joys of Nature" and to the forms, themes, and tropes of "Greek and Roman verse"—the most innovative literature of late-eighteenth-century Brazil can be found in the work of three men of color: Inácio da Silva Alvarenga, the author of *Glaura: Poemas eróticos*; José da Natividade Saldanha, "an icon of emotional alienation and heroic nationalism"; and Domingos Caldas Barbosa, "the most authentically Brazilian voice of the poets of the late eighteenth century" and a writer not afraid to confront openly his nonwhite status (Haberly, "Colonial Brazilian Literature" 61, 63, 67–68). Citing their contributions to the formation of both a national literature and a national culture receptive to intellectual issues, one critic in fact has argued that the Brazilian arcadians deserve recognition as the first organized group of serious, committed writers in the Americas (Merquior 365).

The eighteenth century, a period traditionally derided in Latin American literary history as imitative and lacking in creative energy (see Torres-Ríoseco), has been undergoing a critical reevaluation in recent years. As a result, the time span is now regarded, like the early 1700s in the American colonies, as a crucial period of political growth, cultural development, and social consolidation. Yet if, as many believe, Benjamin Franklin epitomizes the spirit of the Enlightenment in the United States, he has no direct counterpart in Canada or in Latin America, where, in Latin America at least, the changing literary climate finds its parallel in the reigning social, political, and economic decay of the time. When we think about the New World literatures of the eighteenth century and the traditions from which they come, we should keep in mind, as Arturo Torres-Ríoseco contends,

> that while the New England Pilgrims were still feeding their souls with Biblical inspiration in the frigid atmosphere of village meeting-houses, Mexico and Peru had splendid universities where scholars vied in fame with the most distinguished names of the old continent. (42)

In Brazil, however, where the educational system, largely the province of the Company of Jesus, had tended to lag behind, the expulsion of the Jesuits in 1759 had a highly negative impact on intellectual and artistic activity.[21] Nevertheless, literature—by this time a permanent feature of Brazilian culture—continued to move forward. In the late 1700s, for example, the poets of the school of Minas (named for a state, Minas Gerais) created their own Vergilian eclogues, "all the while studying Diderot and Jefferson as they surreptitiously circulate[d] the Declaration of Independence and set about preparing their ill-fated conspiracy" of 1789 (Putnam, *Marvelous Journey* 83).

In what would become the United States, the early 1700s were dominated by the thinking of such figures as Locke, Rousseau, Franklin, Montesquieu, Newton, and Voltaire. The Enlightenment should therefore be considered the first intellectual and ideological movement to unify the English-speaking colonies, which until this time had been split by geographic, regional, and political differences. (The most explosive debate was over slavery, an issue that would also divide Brazil but that would not lead to civil war.) Although, as we have seen, Puritanism had been the formative ideology of the New England colonies, its influence over the southern colonies had been minimal. By the mid-1700s, however, the progressive ideas of the Age of Reason had begun to nationalize colonial leaders from Massachusetts to Virginia. Based on an unshakable belief in progress, in the perfectibility of humankind and its institutions, in the power of reason and in the benevolence of nature, the Enlightenment emphasized the primacy of science over theology, reason over faith, and skepticism over dogma (Foerster, Norman, Grabo, Nye, Carlisle, and Falk 169). As reflected in its utilitarian literature, the ethos of the time was orderly, optimistic, and progressive—in contrast, as we have seen, to the torpor that had fallen over Spanish American and (less so) Brazilian letters of the same period. Yet if, during the Neoclassic Age, the literature of the United States was still primarily derivative—dependent, for its themes and forms, on British models—in Latin America, where belles let-tres had been gestating for more than 250 years, an as yet inchoate national-ism was percolating. The feeling arose, in Brazil and other countries, that a distinctive national literature was emerging. An early example is Teixeira's *Prosopopéia*, a poem rich in the topoi of the Renaissance and in which "Amer-ican nature and the American man appear for the first time" (Torres-Ríoseco 212), confirming the idea that Portugal's New World colony was taking shape as an independent cultural entity.

To sum up, then, we can say that the Age of Reason was, perhaps, more important to the development of literature and culture in the English colonies, where its defining principles were ardently embraced. In Brazil, with its Je-suit Counter Reformation heritage, the impact of the Enlightenment was at least initially not as strong. Nevertheless, as Hulet notes, Brazil experienced rapid changes during this period. They derived largely from its "burgeoning economic importance (based [now] on gold and diamond mining) in the Portuguese world, [from] the transfer of the capital from Bahia to Rio and the resultant abrupt break with Baroque Bahian tradition," and from the "culminating event: the arrival of the royal family in 1808." (Indeed, as wags like to point out, Brazilian independence owes much to Napoleon and his in-vasion of Portugal in 1807, because it forced the transfer of the Royal Crown to Brazil, thereby giving Brazil a dramatic new importance.) Hulet goes on to say that, in the spirit and energy of the Age of Reason, a concerted effort was undertaken

> to raise Brazil to the cultural level of the dynamic northern lands of Eu-rope and, simultaneously, to found a bona fide functional and cohesive national intellectual atmosphere, first in Minas Gerais, in the last quarter of the eighteenth century in Rio de Janeiro, and in the first quarter of the nineteenth in Pernambuco as well.

Hulet concludes by asserting that even "in the earliest years of this development the emphasis was on an awakening nationalism or sense of Brazilianism"—

represented, for instance, in the descriptive poetry of Manuel de Santa Maria Itaparica and in the heroic poetry of José Basílio da Gama and Durão (76, 78–79). Critics of what they see (perhaps unjustly) as the "extreme artificiality" of the poetry produced in the Brazilian academies in the late 1700s have contrasted the poets with, primarily, "the famous and virile . . . bandeirantes" who "explored the hinterlands . . . in an epic struggle against the Indian and Nature" and in quest of gold and precious stones (Torres-Ríoseco 217). We might note that this very adventure provided a crucial part of the plot for John Updike's fablelike novel, *Brazil* (1994), in which a number of national myths, cultural institutions, and historical events are imaginatively woven together.

Earlier in the eighteenth century, an event occurred that scholars of inter-American studies should be aware of. The English defeat of the French army at Quebec in 1759 was a twist of fate that changed the destiny of North America and significantly altered its complex relation with Europe and with the emerging nations of Central and South America. The culminating battle of the French and Indian War (known, in Europe, as the Seven Years' War), the French defeat on the Plains of Abraham, just outside Quebec City, ended France's claim to the New World and made England the preeminent military force in North America. Although the French, because of the vast territory they controlled, were potentially in a more favorable position than the English, England had several major advantages. There were more than a million British colonists in North America at the time, compared with 65,000 French settlers scattered in a thin line from the Saint Lawrence seaway, through the Great Lakes, and down the Mississippi River valley. The British colonies also received more military aid from England than the colonists of New France did from France. Finally, the English enjoyed the support of the powerful Iroquois nation (in 1609, Champlain—who a year before had founded the city of Quebec, the first permanent settlement in Canada—aided the Huron and the Algonquin in their war against the Iroquois). Thus, after the marquis de Montcalm was defeated by James Wolfe at the Battle of Quebec, the Treaty of Paris (1763) forced France to surrender its primary New World colony. A few years later, in 1775, when the Revolutionary War broke out, the French Canadians were asked to join the American rebellion against England. But the Québécois, viewing the conflict as one between England and its colonies, remained neutral. Both during and after the war, however, 40,000 English-speaking colonists, loyal to Great Britain (and known as United Empire Loyalists), fled to Canada, settling mainly in Quebec and Nova Scotia. By 1763, then, England found itself the undisputed master of North America. As its colonies moved toward independence, their resentment of the once-dominant English came to influence how Americans perceived Brazil and—beginning in the same year as the French Revolution—its struggle for independence.

After 1763, in fact, the colonists began to think of themselves as Americans rather than as British, as a nation with its own identity and its own future. As a result, the American Revolution (1776) was essentially fought by the colonists to protect and consolidate rights they believed they already possessed. In 1789, the year the presidential electors met to choose George Washington as the country's first leader (an event that transformed the United States from a loosely knit confederation into a federal republic), Brazil was experiencing the *Inconfidência Mineira,* its first, ill-fated experience with independence. Burns writes, of this aborted rebellion, that it came about "partly from a reaction to a threat of improved tax collection and partly as the imperfect comprehension of enlightened thought." Its very occurrence, however, proved that the winds of change set in motion by the Enlightenment had begun to effect changes in the interior of Brazil (*History* [3rd ed.] 108–09).

THE POSTCOLONIAL PERIOD

After its revolution the United States was no longer a colony within a European imperial system but an independent nation, militarily and politically weak but blessed with a number of advantages. "Lacking any deeply entrenched economic group," the United States, in the years immediately following the revolution, possessed "vast natural resources, a rapidly growing population of producers and consumers, relative political stability and unity, and the protection of a government friendly to business" (Foerster, Grabo, Nye, Carlisle, and Falk 176). Business, not political idealism, had become the defining characteristic of the United States. In contrast to the experience of the United States, Spanish America would fight a series of bloody and protracted wars for independence well into the nineteenth century and would suffer from entrenched problems of rival dictatorships, poverty, illiteracy, and poor systems of taxation and income distribution. Brazil, although it won independence bloodlessly in 1822, would be dogged by archaic social, political, and economic structures.

As in the freshly minted United States, it had become important in Brazil to avoid what Daniel Webster termed the "servile imitation" of the European masters; it was also necessary to study such writers as Milton, Shakespeare,

Addison, and Pope (Foerster, Grabo, Nye, Carlisle, and Falk 183). Later in the century, writers sought to identify and cultivate themes and issues—the New World landscape, religion, racial mixing, slavery, the Indian, the roles of women, the frontier, and the interior—that were unique to the Americas and that could help define what it meant to be American or Brazilian. João Capistrano de Abreu, the preeminent Brazilian historian of the period and often compared with Frederick Jackson Turner, began around the 1870s to warn his compatriots of the dangers inherent in overeager importation of European thought. It was unwise, he cautioned, to cast Brazil in the European mode, because the histories of the two regions were very different and because to do so prevented Brazilians from seeing what their nation really was—and what it really needed. Viewing Portugal's traditional dependence on England as a political and economic relationship that had had deleterious consequences for Portugal, Abreu urged Brazil to avoid a similar alliance with the United States. That country, he feared, might seek to keep Brazil in a state of dependency and to exploit it as a base for controlling all of Latin America (Stuart Schwartz's introduction to Abreu xxvi–xxvii). Eschewing the traditional concept of history as the recording of great deeds performed by great men, Abreu instead synthesized the diverse, long-neglected threads of Brazilian historiography to narrate Brazil's evolution as a nation and as a culture. In his work he concentrated on hitherto marginal figures—especially slaves, Indians, and women—to focus on the creation of the authentic Brazil, which he regarded as the interior, the backlands (ch. 9 is devoted to this topic) rather than the coastal areas, with their connections to Europe and the rest of the world.

The nineteenth century saw, in addition to nation building, the incorporation, in the formative literature of North, Central, and South America, of the themes that Abreu later identified as distinctive to the New World. William Hill Brown's melodramatic narrative *The Power of Sympathy* (1789) is generally regarded as the first novel written and published in the United States; it was followed by Charles Brockden Brown's *Wieland* (1798) and *Ormond* (1799). Indulging the sentimental taste then in fashion, these texts established the novel in the United States—although for a long time the genre was not taken seriously. In Brazil, where the circulation of novels had historically been a more surreptitious affair, fiction is sometimes said to have begun in 1752, with Teresa Margarida da Silva e Orta's *As aventuras de Diófanes* (*The Adventures of Diófanes*), a work heavily influenced by the social and economic liberalism of Fénelon's *Les aventures de Télémaque* (Versiani; R. W. Sousa). Another early novel is by Antônio Gonçalves Teixeira e Sousa, whose lachrymose *O filho do pescador* (*The Fisherman's Son*) appeared in 1843. Although the text is widely regarded as being of little merit, the author's personal story is interesting: of mixed-race background from the provinces, he was determined to become a successful man of letters in the imperial capital, Rio de Janeiro. If the novel of the United States began to take form in the postrevolutionary period (an era of intense if uneven literary activity), the novel in Brazil has its origins essentially in the time of the boy emperor Pedro II, who at age fourteen ascended the throne (1840). Brazil's novel thus began as a cultivated literary genre when the nation was struggling to complete its slow but peaceful journey toward both political and cultural independence.

During the same period, the United States started to play a significant role in Brazil's development as a nation and as a culture. By 1865, for example, the United States had become the leading importer of Brazilian coffee and a number of other products, including rubber and cocoa (Burns, *History* [3rd ed.] 262), a state of affairs that led to closer political and commercial ties between the hemispheric giants. Brazil, thanks largely to its having peacefully gained independence from Portugal in 1822, did not suffer the fragmentation that characterized Spanish America during the first half of the nineteenth century. Under Brazil's parliamentary system, one guided by Pedro II, political parties rotated their terms in office.[22] Although the reign of Pedro II "was still the old patriarchal, slaveholding one of colonial days," it was a stabilizing and intellectually progressive regime, led economically, politically, and socially by a prince "destined to be one of the wisest and most liberal-minded that any country ever had." Pedro was a cultural as well as a political leader who encouraged the arts and "the development of a truly national culture" (Putnam, *Marvelous Journey* 139). Nevertheless, Costa believes,

> an essential part of understanding the empire is to explain the relative stability of the monarchical system (1822–89). Part of the explanation lies in the fact that economic and social structures did not undergo fundamental change during the seven decades of the empire. The Brazilian economy continued to be based on the export of tropical products, and Brazilian elites could agree about fundamental issues. They also created an army and a national guard to put down resistance. But, more important, the elites were able to maintain a system of clientele and patronage efficient enough to disguise racial and class tensions. (xx)

By the mid-nineteenth century, Brazil did not enjoy the economic might, the cultural unity, and the political strength of the United States, but neither did it suffer the devastating cultural and political balkanization that plagued Spanish America. It is against this cultural background that the work most critics regard as Brazil's first true novel, Joaquim Manuel de Macedo's *A Moreninha* (*The Little Brunette*), was published (1844). It is a hugely popular sentimental romance that can be regarded as "a classic of middle-class literature in both origin and appeal" as well as a work that makes subtle social and political observations, including commentary on the emerging issue of women's rights (Burns, *History* [3rd ed.] 147).

But while Macedo may have cultivated the urban social milieu of the imperial capital in the creation of his novel, the indigenous people inspired Brazil's most significant novelist of the mid-nineteenth century, José de Alencar, a writer who has been widely compared with James Fenimore Cooper (Wasserman, "Re-inventing"; Edinger, Introduction). "In Brazil as in our own country," writes Putnam, "it is the Indian theme that represents the transition from the older, neoclassic to the newer, romantic literature" (*Marvelous Journey* 142). Yet if the Indian is fundamental to the literature of both the United States and Brazil, there are important contrasts that dramatize the racial and social attitudes brought to the New World by the English and by the Portuguese. For example, while both the Portuguese and the English settlers clashed with the Native Americans during the years of conquest and settlement, the Portuguese avoided the essentially genocidal strife that characterized relations with the Native Americans in the United States until the final decades of the nineteenth century (143). Earlier in the nineteenth century, when the star of Romanticism was shining brightly in both North and South America, Cooper and Alencar had naturalized Walter Scott's historical romance into a unique form—one that, in the idealized images of the Native American it produced (especially in Brazil), became a powerful force in the creation of a New World ethos (Wasserman, "Re-inventing").

Trapped much more than the prose writers in an imitative mode, poets in the United States, also seeking to nationalize their work, found it difficult to escape the influence of the English masters of the era. The difficulty of their task can be seen in the work of Joel Barlow, whose attempt at a national epic poem, *The Columbiad* (1807), adopts a distinctly inter-American perspective by invoking not only Columbus but the celebrated pre-Columbian Inca monarch Manco Capac. Although Barlow's self-conscious project was not entirely successful, it underscores how important the epic form was, throughout the Americas, to the establishment of a hemispheric consciousness (Fitz, *Rediscovering* 48–69).

By the second half of the eighteenth century, literature in Brazil and the United States, for the first time and with some exceptions, developed under similar intellectual and aesthetic influences, chiefly from England, Germany, and France. Because of the social, political, and cultural disparities between the two nations, differences in the matter of reception remained. In Brazil, for example, the period was marked not only by a considerable increase in literary activity but also by the appearance of several outstanding works of imaginative literature. This blossoming is particularly evident in the poetry of the arcadians, who absorbed the best features of European arcadianism and then produced something new, verse that pulsed with the energy and vitality of Brazil. Speaking of the poets associated with the ill-fated *Inconfidência Mineira,* Haberly finds that Tomás Antônio Gonzaga, Cláudio Manuel da Costa, and Inácio José de Alvarenga Peixoto were "as talented as any of their European contemporaries" ("Colonial Brazilian Literature" 64). By this time, Brazil possessed, at least in an incipient form, a literature, one that, as Putnam sees it, was "far more impressive," by the late 1780s, "than what the English colonies of North America could show for the same period." But it is also important to remember that

> if the northern continent did not have the poets that Latin America did by this time, it had the political thinkers: a Jefferson, a Paine, a Franklin, and it was the newly formed United States of America that was to be the teacher on the political plane, the leader and inspirer of the forces of hemisphere democracy. (*Marvelous Journey* 90)

Writing primarily about the literature of Spanish America, Torres-Ríoseco, as we have seen, criticizes the late-eighteenth-century period for being socially, politically, and intellectually stultifying and for producing a literature that was too often imitative, sterile, and "decadent" (41–43). Literary historians in the United States, in contrast, have generally summarized the decades from 1776 to 1836 as a vibrant era of incubation and transition that would move literature from the political writing following the revolution to the mature texts of Washington Irving, William Cullen Bryant, and Cooper. William J. Scheick, for example, argues that "as the eighteenth century lengthened, the Puritan religious literary heritage in verse evolved into an Augustan-influenced, aesthetically self-conscious, and politically motivated poetry concerned with the emergence of America as a new, independent nation" (97). Arriving at a similar conclusion is Kenneth Silverman:

The time from the first Puritans and Mather to the Revolutionary generation and Franklin thus not only covers the complex transition from Puritan piety, idealism, and provincialism to the more secular, utilitarian, and cosmopolitan values of the American Enlightenment. It also marks the establishment of two enduring visions of America that have often competed for authority. (112)

Bryant is particularly interesting in that he has a parallel in Antônio Gonçalves Dias, a giant of Brazilian Romanticism whose best work is characterized by his lush descriptions of the tropics and by his convincing if idealized Indianism. In considering an American counterpart for Gonçalves Dias, Putnam notes that while the two poets celebrate their natural landscapes, Bryant, in his "New England coldness and restraint," remains a neoclassicist, whereas Gonçalves Dias, recalling both Keats and Lamartine, "has the superabundant vitality, the big-bellied exuberance of the romantic school." Gonçalves Dias, moreover, "with his fierce Whitmanlike rejection of the Old World and his whole-souled acceptance of the New," and with "his burning patriotism and love of his native soil," comes "near to being *the* national poet, one who was enthusiastically acclaimed by the people even before he was by the elite" (*Marvelous Journey* 113, 111).

By the late 1820s, only a few years after Prince Pedro, a great admirer of Rousseau and the philosophes, declared Brazil's independence, the United States had in place the elements of an authentic national literature: ambitious and talented writers, suitable subjects, an increasing number of printing presses (Brazil did not see its first printing press until 1808), a flourishing newspaper industry, magazines, bookstores, schools (both public and private), and libraries (*Harper American Literature* 1: 515). The decade of the 1820s in fact was decisive for American literature, since it saw the publication of such achievements as Irving's *The Sketch Book* (1819–20), Bryant's *Poems* (1821), three of Cooper's *Leatherstocking Tales* (*The Pioneers*, 1823; *The Last of the Mohicans*, 1826; *The Prairie*, 1827), and Edgar Allan Poe's *"Tamerlane" and Other Poems*. The influence of Irving, Poe, and Cooper would be felt in Brazil. Poe, for example, "the first American writer to succeed in creating a total life in art as a foil to the conflicts and frustrations of the human predicament" and "the finest critical mind of his generation" (Spiller 52), has long been linked with the Brazilian arch-Romantic poet Álvares de Azevedo, whose life and work epitomize the *mal du siècle* that characterizes high Romanticism in Brazil. As Putnam notes, Poe directly influenced Azevedo and other Romantics, "for the author of 'The Raven' and the *Tales of the Grotesque and Arabesque* was well known to Brazilians of this period." Putnam goes on to say that while neither Poe nor Whitman was as popular as Longfellow (presumably because of the latter's Indianist verse, with *Hiawatha* widely read in Brazil), Poe "had a following among the select few" (*Marvelous Journey* 119). In addition, as Afrânio Peixoto has shown, both Baudelaire and Joaquim Maria Machado de Assis (his translation of "The Raven" was influential in Brazil; see Bellei) praised Poe (127). The recognition of Poe's genius by Machado (as the writer is known in Brazil) is significant because, besides demonstrating acumen early in his career, it indicates the importance of critical theory, as well as tradition and innovation, to the Brazilian writer's sense of imaginative literature.

In 1837, Emerson's landmark essay "The American Scholar" appeared. It was a declaration of literary independence that could be said to speak for all the nations of the Americas. The publication of Emerson's famous talk and, the year before, the convening of the Transcendentalist Club inaugurate what many scholars have referred to as the American Renaissance, a period of creative energy and imagination that lasted until 1865. Undoubtedly the most glorious period of this flowering of American letters occurred from 1850 to 1855, when some of the New World's greatest works of literature appeared: Hawthorne's *The Scarlet Letter* (1850) and *The House of the Seven Gables* (1851), Melville's *Moby-Dick* (1851), Thoreau's *Walden* (1854), and Whitman's *Leaves of Grass* (1855). *Leaves of Grass* had a far-reaching influence in both Brazil and Spanish America. Of the novels published in Brazil in the 1850s, two deserve special note, even if they do not rise to the artistic and intellectual level of *The Scarlet Letter*, *Moby-Dick*, and *Leaves of Grass*. The first is an engaging work by Manuel Antônio de Almeida, the realistic picaresque novel *As memórias de um sargento de milícias*, 1852–53 (*The Memoirs of a Militia Sargeant*). The other is Alencar's Indianist novel *O Guarani* (1857), which was integral to the development of both Indianism and Romanticism in Brazil.

A Brazilian writer who, in the most startling ways, merged Romanticism with what would later be known as modernist forms, structures, and techniques was Joaquim de Sousa Andrade ("Sousândrade"). Born in Maranhão in 1833, Sousa Andrade spent several years working as a journalist in New York City. An ardent republican, he eventually developed a highly distinctive style, one that in its nature and scope is surprisingly parallel to Whitman's. Like the author of *Leaves of Grass*, Sousa Andrade, first with *Guesa errante:*

poema americano (1866; *Guesa the Errant: An American Poem*) and later, more spectacularly, with *O Guesa* (c. 1888; *The Guesa*), develops an epic vision not merely of America but of the Americas, one that reaches back to its pre-Columbian past for its roots (the hero of the poem, Guesa, is a descendant of the Incan royal family and "destined from childhood for ritual immolation" [Sousa Andrade 98]) and that in waves of surrealistic imagery, daunting neologisms, and different voices connects this past to, among other things, the "inferno of Wall Street" and to an imagined dialogue between President Grant and Dom Pedro, the Brazilian emperor who was visiting the United States. Highly prized by the Brazilian concretists, and especially by Augusto and Haroldo de Campos (whose influential *Re-visão de Sousândrade* [*Re-Vision of Sousândrade*] appeared in 1964), Sousa Andrade and his early inter-American vision have, after being long ignored, now established themselves as part of late-nineteenth-century Brazil's most unusual literary contribution.

This period is also significant for both Brazil and the United States because of slavery, a cancer that had plagued both countries since their colonial days and that by the mid-nineteenth century threatened to tear them apart. While the abolitionist movement in the United States was the most urgent force for social and political reform during the 1850s, Brazil too sought to expunge this pernicious institution. In 1850, for example, it established the Queirós Law, which abolished the slave trade. With the passage of the Golden Law of 1888, one year before the nation established itself as a republic, Brazil thus became the last country in the Western Hemisphere to divest itself of the buying and selling of human beings (Cuba had done so in 1886). Burns suggests that slavery endured as long as it did in Brazil because it was "indissolubly linked with the colonial past" and was one element of the "trinity" that ruled the nation—the other two were the latifundium and monoculture (*History* [3rd ed.] 225). Caio Prado, Jr. (401–03), and Manoel de Oliveira Lima (51–52), among others, agree. As Burns explains, "slavery made the archaic agricultural system function since it contributed the most vital ingredient, labor, which turned the land into wealth." Therefore, "abolition signaled Brazil's emergence into the modern world" (Burns, *History* [3rd ed.] 225). Unlike the United States, no one in Brazil "dared to make an outright doctrinaire defense of slavery in the second half of the nineteenth century," although in both nations "the slaveowners' spokesmen insisted that the slaves' living conditions were superior to those of European laborers," Costa writes. "They also made a point of stressing that in Brazil slavery was milder than in other countries," that "masters were more benevolent," and that "relations between masters and slaves were paternal" (163). Because of agriculture's dependency on slave labor, however, the practice continued for a time, clandestinely, in the northeast, where it was most firmly entrenched. The social upheaval caused by emancipation was such that even a work like Graça Aranha's otherwise forward-looking novel *Canaan* (1902) featured an elderly former slave who reflects nostalgically on the security and paternalism of the plantation days, in contrast to what he sees as the despair and isolation of a modern world gone to pieces.

The connection between abolitionist poets in the United States, like John Greenleaf Whittier, and Castro Alves (see app. C) has been clearly established (see Braga). Another interesting link between the hemispheric giants is the Brazilian reception of *Uncle Tom's Cabin*, which was translated into Portuguese as early as 1853 and has something of a counterpart in Bernardo Guimarães's *A escrava Isaura*, 1875 (*The Slave Girl, Isaura*). Like a number of American abolitionist novels, "where the slave protagonists are often quadroons or octoroons," *The Slave Girl* "emphasizes the heroine's light skin"; apparently the writer assumed that "white middle-class readers would more readily empathize with a quasi-white figure" (Stam 77). Recognized as "Brazil's only important abolitionist novel," *The Slave Girl* may have been influenced by Harriet Beecher Stowe's famous work "and, perhaps, by Dion Boucicault's 1861 play, *The Octoroon*." As Haberly notes, though, "there is no evidence" that the Guimarães narrative "in any way changed the attitudes of the Brazilian slave-owners who bought and read" it (" Brazilian Novel" 146).

As important as the Enlightenment or neoclassicism was to the development of literature in Brazil and the United States, by the latter half of the eighteenth century the early signs of Romanticism were in evidence. In Brazil, for example, José Basílio da Gama's epic *O Uraguai* (*The Uruguay*) dramatically chronicles the 1756 revolt of the Jesuit-led Indians against the combined forces of Spain and Portugal).[23] The work gains much of its lyricism from vivid descriptions of the Brazilian landscape and from powerful characterizations of the people who inhabit it. One critic has suggested that "Basílio da Gama is one of the earliest forerunners of romanticism in Latin America" (Torres-Ríoseco 219). Haberly writes:

> Da Gama's *Uraguai* . . . mixes fact and fiction in its account of warfare between Spaniards and Portuguese on one side and some 30,000 Indians commanded by Jesuits on the other. Its five cantos of blank verse are very often pure propaganda—but nonetheless are wonderfully resonant, filled with sublime Portuguese heroes, noble Indian allies, and villainous and

lascivious Jesuits. The nobility of some of da Gama's Indian characters, in fact, makes him seem a liberal Romantic born before his time, a great precursor of nineteenth-century Brazilian Indianism. ("Colonial Brazilian Literature" 62)

In the view of Massaud Moisés, Brazilian Romanticism started as a distinct and viable literary movement in 1836, with the publication of Gonçalves de Magalhães's *Suspiros poéticos e saudades* (*Poetical Sighs and Longings*) and ends with Aluísio Azevedo's naturalistic novel *O mulato* (*The Mulatto*) in 1881 (the same year that a major novel of the Americas, Machado's *The Posthumous Memoirs of Brás Cubas*, appeared).

In the United States, too, an interest in describing the landscape and the Native Americans took hold, particularly after 1780, as the nation commenced its westward expansion. Because the Romantic movement came to the United States during an awakening of national consciousness, it assumed, as in Latin America, a sense of nationalistic fervor that it had not had in Europe. In this incipient Romanticism, epitomized by the link between Cooper and Alencar, the literary histories of Brazil and the United States begin to engage each other systematically.

Although early Brazilian Romanticism was dominated by poetry, especially Indianist poetry, the movement gave rise to the writer many critics regard as the real catalyst in mid-nineteenth-century Brazilian literature, the novelist José de Alencar. Pertinent to inter-American studies, as we have noted, is Alencar's complex relation with Cooper, who many believe influenced Alencar and his approach to the Indianist theme. In *Como e porque sou romancista* [*How and Why I Am a Novelist*], however, written in 1873, he denies having been influenced either by Cooper or by Chateaubriand, arguing instead for his own original handling of this deeply American topic. One critic contends that in a work like *Iracema*, North Americans will recognize how Alencar, like Cooper, uses a Native American heritage to create both a national mythos and a "common past" for an already highly diverse population. "In many respects," Naomi Lindstrom writes, "*Iracema* embodies the same general type of project underlying the Indian-theme novels of James Fenimore Cooper." Cooper, she writes, was "determined to craft a national literature" and "felt a similar attraction to the era in which Indians and settlers first came into contact" (xiii). We can nevertheless compare the treatment of the Indian—and the treatment of relations between Indians and whites—in works like *The Last of the Mohicans* and *O Guarani* (1857; *The Guarani*) or *Iracema* (1865).

The latter novel (the title is an anagram for *America*) takes up the issue of miscegenation, a defining theme in Brazilian literature. A major difference between Cooper and Alencar is that while Alencar is very much the Romantic (he provides an idealized version of the New World noble savage), "Cooper is a transitional figure, with remnants of neoclassicism and foreshadowings of realism mingling with a budding romanticism" (Putnam, *Marvelous Journey* 150). Natty Bumppo, the central character of Cooper's *Leatherstocking Tales*, moreover, is a peerless wilderness scout, a "homespun philosopher and deadshot" who functions as "the personification of the democrat's ideal of the democratic man" (Spiller 32). Because Alencar does not cultivate this type of mythical figure in his works, his vast output lacks the unifying cultural effect it might have had. Nevertheless, as Haberly points out, the impact of Alencar, "who completely transformed both the nature and the status of fiction in Brazil" in the mid-nineteenth century, "cannot be overestimated." Nationalizing the genre and making it respectable, Alencar "established its peculiar mix of detailed realistic description and romantic ideology, and he largely created its major sub-genres" ("Brazilian Novel" 142, 144), including the regionalist novel—which, with *O gaúcho* (1870; *The Gaucho*), he effectively inaugurated as a genre in itself. One critic concludes that

> while North American ideology promoted myths of separation, and the doomed nature of love between white and Indian (for example in the novels of James Fenimore Cooper), Brazilian ideology promoted myths of fusion through what Doris Sommer calls "foundational romances" of love between European and indigene. Whereas U.S. tradition venerates the Euro American founding fathers, the Brazilian includes an indigenous mother. . . . While Brazilian literature lauded cross-racial heterosexual romance—Indian men loving white women (*O Guarani*) or Indian women loving white men (*Iracema*)—as the generative matrix of a mestiço nation, American literature stressed male bonding between white frontiersmen and the native American male. (Stam 11)

For readers interested in characterization and the issues of gender relations and power, Alencar's significance as a New World author may stem from the series of novels he wrote under the heading *Female Profiles*: *Lucíola* (1862), *Diva* (1864), and, most important, *Senhora* (1875). This work, which, as Roberto Schwarz has shown, was crucial to the establishment of the novel in Brazil (41–77), took a remarkably progressive position on the social, economic, political, and sexual rights of women in nineteenth-century Brazil. Both stylistically and thematically, Alencar's works refined the art of narrative and fostered the development of a national literature—one conscious of the exigencies of literary practice and of the problems faced by Brazilians of various social classes (Hulet 1: 334).

As the nineteenth century wore on, it was regionalism that sparked the movement away from Romanticism and toward realism. In Brazil (e.g., in *O gaúcho*), regionalism had been for a long time a matter of rural life in the provinces. In the United States, in the hands of such practitioners as Bret Harte, Sarah Orne Jewett, and, most brilliant of all, Mark Twain, regionalism began in a similar fashion, as a function of small-town, back-country life. More quickly than in Brazil, it turned to depictions of life in the city, which was becoming a metaphor for the rapid industrialization transforming the United States from a rural to an urban society. Stephen Crane's *Maggie: A Girl of the Streets* (1893), an ironic and naturalistic portrait of a girl driven to prostitution and suicide by events seemingly beyond her control, is often cited as initiating the shift to realism. As we shall see, the work has a compelling Brazilian counterpoint in *The Slum*, novel, published three years before *Maggie*, by the naturalist Aluísio Azevedo (see app. C).

An intriguing and unexpected comparison of this period, however, deals with two of New World literature's most renowned novels, *Huckleberry Finn* (1885) and Machado's *As memórias póstumas de Brás Cubas* (1880–81; *The Posthumous Memoirs of Brás Cubas;* see app. C). From the perspective of literary history, we can see that both works altered the ways the American novel would be written and read. We will compare the two novels primarily on the basis of style and structure rather than theme (see Mac Adam, *Narratives*), although even here the two influential New World narratives have more in common than we might initially think.

While the pungent vernacular of the unschooled, abused, and homeless Huck Finn would probably never be confused with the sly self-consciousness of the privileged and sardonic Brás Cubas, the distinctive first-person voice of each text emerges as its most engaging feature. Yet while Twain's daring use of a uniquely American idiom (as opposed to the genteel, more "literary" language of his predecessors) ranks as a significant innovation, *Huckleberry Finn* remains a realistic narrative that also functions as an allegory. In Machado's work, in contrast, we have both a new language (one as demotic as Twain's if more polished and, in its own way, also subversive of literary norms) and a new sense of narrative structure, in which the reliability of the text itself and of the narrator's voice is called into question. Machado, moreover, is experimenting in this essentially antimimetic novel with an issue that preoccupied him until his death—the role of the reader in the reception of a text. Here he goes beyond Twain.

Although as early as *Huckleberry Finn* Twain is clearly aware of the potential inherent in the narrator-reader relationship, Machado fully exploits it. First with Brás Cubas, then with a host of other narrators, he openly challenges the reader's ability to know what is going on. After 1880, Machado's reader is forced into a new and more active role in the novelistic experience: in text after text the reader is systematically manipulated and even led astray by the narrative voice.

An additional point of comparison has to do with slavery. Both Twain and Machado have been taken to task for not condemning slavery overtly in their novels, but a careful reader might argue that both works do criticize the institution although not in obvious ways. Up to the point (introduced in chapter 16 and expounded on in chapter 31) where Huck decides that he would rather go to hell than turn Jim in—which, as a poor white southerner reared in the social and political mores of Christianity, he knows he is supposed to do—*Huckleberry Finn* is in structural terms a nearly flawless narrative, especially if it is read as an ironic morality tale on the entwined issues of race, religion, and conduct in nineteenth-century America. After this point, however, Twain seems to lose his sense of purpose, and the sharp moral focus of the early chapters becomes blurred, overwhelmed by a rapid succession of sociopolitically allusive episodes. Indeed, the reader feels that the enduring appeal of the novel, its essential dignity, stems ironically from Huck's rough-hewn and gradual realization that Jim, the runaway slave, is a human being, not chattel to be bought and sold. Machado, in his novel, which is more innovative both stylistically and structurally, also criticizes slavery—in a similarly indirect fashion—but he does so, through one of his minor characters, by showing how the institution endures because it appeals to that shameful aspect of human nature that seeks to humiliate and exploit others—an aspect that capitalism, the economic system of choice, finds innumerable ways to justify and reward (a point that Machado makes here and elsewhere).

For reasons yet to be thoroughly elucidated, the naturalistic novel, as a genre following hard on the heels of the regionalist novel, was cultivated in Spanish America, Brazil, and the United States. Although good comparative studies of the topic exist (Loos; Sedycias), additional investigation is needed into a more fundamental question: Why was the naturalistic novel so intensely and deliberately practiced in the Americas? Perhaps the answer has something to do with the view of the New World as a social experiment, as a kind of sociopolitical laboratory where laws, customs, and mores can be changed, where the mistakes of the past (and of Europe's more rigid social structures) can be corrected or ameliorated. In Brazil, where the naturalistic novel may have been perceived along these lines, its primary exponents "plunged headlong into sociological research, psycho-physiological phenomena, and auto-analysis" (Torres-Ríoseco 244). A penetrating social critic if an undisciplined stylist, Aluísio Azevedo, the prototypical Brazilian naturalist, was influenced by Émile Zola's *roman experimental,* so much so that even in the acclaimed *O mulato,* his literary artistry often gives way to sociologically inclined commentaries on slum life, racial blending, sexuality, poverty, and both religious and racial hypocrisy (see app. C). A later work, *O cortiço* (1890; *A Brazilian Tenement;* reissued in 2000 as *The Slum*), is more successful on purely literary grounds. Like the earlier work, it offers (by means of the psychological development of the characters in tenement in Rio de Janeiro) a compelling portrait of lower-class life, one that, as noted earlier, suggests Crane's *Maggie: A Girl of the Streets.* Azevedo envisioned *The Slum,* considered by many to be his masterpiece, as the first in a five-part series of novels that would do for Brazilian civilization what Balzac's *Comédie humaine* had done for French society. Although this vast project was never realized (frustrated with the lack of an appreciative readership, Azevedo gave up writing not long after his novel was published), *The Slum,* which deals incisively with race, greed, and sexuality—has been a steady seller in Brazil since the early 1900s. In comparing the naturalistic novel in Brazil and the United States, we can conclude that if its impact on the genre of fiction was modest, the form contributed significantly to the ways the two cultures have viewed the sea changes that took place and the many social, political, and economic problems that resulted from them. The economic and moral repercussions of slavery, for example, which are central to *The Slum,* can easily be seen as part of the historical framework of all the Americas. In inter-American studies today, therefore, Azevedo's novel can initiate a useful dialogue on a number of resonant issues, including the status of women.

Two other writers from this period who made major advances in the art of fiction are Henry James and Machado. Apparently unaware of the other's existence, each one altered the novel's course of development in the Americas.[24] Although there is a small but growing bibliography of works that compare these two landmark narrativists (see, e.g., Putnam, *Marvelous Journey;*

Brakel; Fitz, *Rediscovering*), more work needs to be done. Readers familiar with the work of both authors could argue, for instance, that—in terms of his ironic and metaphoric style, his imaginative approach to narrative structure, his experimentation with unreliable narrators, his manipulation of the reader, and his thematics—Machado can be regarded as more modern, or modernistic, than James, who for all the subtlety of his art seems more conventional. In any event, the year 1881 was decisive for both Machado and James. In that year *The Portrait of a Lady*, the first of James's mature novels, was published, and Machado came out with his turning-point novel, *The Posthumous Memoirs of Brás Cubas*. Although both authors cultivated the short story form (see Brakel), their meticulous and imaginative craftsmanship of the novel has come to define their place of honor in the Americas, where Machado should be regarded as at least "on the level of Melville, Hawthorne, and Poe" (González Echevarría, *Oxford Book* 95).

In theoretical terms, too, James and Machado have much in common. Both experimented with the relation of the author to the text; with tone, verisimilitude, and intertextuality; and, perhaps most important, with point of view, including unseen narrators, self-effacing narrators, and unreliable narrators. Moreover, both the Brazilian and the North American sought to expand the reader's role in the production of a text's meaning, to question the link between a text and the reality it purports to describe, to manipulate the role of time in a narrative, to expand the role of irony in plot development, to contemplate the nature of language and its connection to reality, to analyze the levels and ranges of emotional response a character might have, and to create modes of narrative structuring (the "scenic" would, for both writers, be central, but for different reasons).

In *The Posthumous Memoirs of Brás Cubas*, for example, the seemingly affable narrator, whose witty voice charms the reader from the outset, reveals his selfishness and nihilism only indirectly in the novel's final lines. In *Dom Casmurro* the reader is led, again by a very convincing narrator, to a conclusion that, on reflection, may be very different from the one that should be reached. As if sitting in a jury box (with the narrator playing the role of prosecuting attorney), readers are forced to evaluate the facts and reach their verdict about what really happened.

Above all, James and Machado moved the art of fiction from its traditional focus on the external world to an examination of the tangled inner world of motivation, desire, and response to external events. More will be said about James and Machado in chapter 3; let it suffice to say, for now, that between the years 1881 and 1906, Henry James, Mark Twain, and Machado were three of the most sophisticated and original narrativists in the Americas.

In Brazil, the early twentieth century was blessed with another singular work, *Os sertões* (1902; *Rebellion in the Backlands*), by Euclides da Cunha. A nonfiction book that, especially in its stirring second half, reads like a novel, *Rebellion in the Backlands* (see app. C) chronicles the story of a short-lived but violent uprising in Brazil's impoverished northeast. The rebellion, led by a religious fanatic, Antônio Conselheiro, who preached that the newly formed (1889) Brazilian republic was "the supreme heresy," a "mortal sin," and the embodiment of the anti-Christ (162), lasted only from December 1896 to October 1897. It quickly became, nevertheless, a conflagration that challenged the principles of the still-unstable republic and questioned the identity of Brazil itself. As the text unfolds, the latter issue has as much to do with race, and the supposed results of racial mixing, as with political ideology (see Amory). Cunha's views on race were influenced by the accepted doctrines of the time, which we know to be false but that were widely promulgated by Buckle, Ammon, Lapouge, and Gobineau (like Cunha and Romero, the largely "self-taught sociologist" Oliveira Vianna was much taken by these theories; see Burns, *History* [3rd ed.] 317).

We should bear in mind that these pseudoscientific theories were widely accepted in the United States, where racial mixing was much less common than in Brazil and where, until the closing decades of the twentieth century, it had been a virtually unthinkable option (see Fitz, "Blood"). "Indeed," as Robert Stam writes, "it is symptomatic that Pat Buchanan, during his 1996 campaign for the Republican presidential nomination, warned that demographic changes favoring people of color would turn the United States into 'the Brazil of North America'" (15).[25] The widespread fear of the "mongrelization of the races," however, had infected American culture at least since the time of *The Last of the Mohicans* and *Uncle Tom's Cabin*, both of which inveigh against the supposed dangers of racial mixing. Although the literature of the United States has never addressed the issue as openly and as consistently as Brazilian literature has, it is nevertheless a powerful if volatile point of contact—and contrast—between these two New World societies.

A few years later, in 1922, an event of such cultural importance occurred that it changed the ways Brazilians would think of themselves and their nation. As Charles Perrone has observed, "More so than in any other nation in the Americas, the avant-garde of Brazilian Modernism had a tremendous impact on cultural discourses" in a number of fields, from art to politics (*Seven Faces* xi). Anita Malfatti, one of the driving forces behind the Brazilian modernist movement, had been a student at the Art Students League in New York City just after the 1913 Armory Show[26] and had witnessed firsthand the reaction of the American public to the new art that was being exhibited. This experience undoubtedly influenced her sense of purpose back in Brazil. Both the Armory Show and Brazil's Modern Art Week allowed the European avant-garde to penetrate what was still a largely parochial New World milieu. While the Armory Show focused on painting, Brazilian *modernismo*, which has more in common with European modernism than with the earlier Spanish American movement of the same name, featured innovation and experimentation in all the arts, with the new poetry, exemplified by the publication in 1922 of Mário de Andrade's *Paulicéia desvairada* (*Hallucinated City*; see app. C), occupying the focal point.

Another significant difference is that while the Armory Show altered the direction of American art and aesthetics, modernism in Brazil provoked a profound identity crisis, a dramatic rethinking of what it meant to be Brazilian and of what Brazil could—and should—become in the remainder of the twentieth century. From this fecund intellectual, artistic, and cultural matrix arose Oswald de Andrade's historic anthropophagy movement (see Campos). It sought to merge surrealist imagery with what its advocates felt was Brazil's indigenous primitivism, in an attempt to ground national identity in the pre-Columbian past—a past that was to be linked to future developments worldwide (see Andrade). Brazil, in other words, would engage the twentieth century as a modern nation by evolving from its most ancient nativist traditions. (While nothing of this sort would occur in the United States, where autochthonous traditions have been less widely celebrated, the Mexican poet and intellectual Octavio Paz would, with works like *Piedra de sol* [1957; *Sun Stone*, 1963], attempt to achieve something similar, only a few decades later.) Seeking, ironically, both to internationalize and to nationalize Brazilian literature, the early *modernistas*, led by Mário de Andrade, Patrícia Galvão, and especially Oswald de Andrade, made use of such forms of the European avant-garde as free verse, cubism (see Morse), expressionism, and futurism, to cultivate what they felt were nationalistic themes, linguistic usages, myths, motifs, and characters. Particularly important were the myths and legends of the Amazonian jungle, which was widely viewed by the early Brazilian modernists as the source of all that was most authentic, if not necessarily primitive, about Brazilian culture. As Stam points out:

> The 1920s were the period of studies of "primitive" cultures (Frazer, Levy-Bruhl, Freud), of the African researches of the ethnologist Leo

Frobenius, and of the appropriations of African and Afro American cultures by the likes of Picasso, Brancusi, and Klee. Oswald de Andrade noted that those who were exotic for the Europeans, that is, the Indian and black, were a quotidian, unexotic reality for Brazilians. Whereas European artists like Paul Gauguin, Blaise Cendrars, and Georges Bataille looked for a primitive world as an antitype to decadent Europe, Brazilian artists were more knowledgeable about that world and more aware of the limitations of European primitivism. (71)

"Americanist concerns," as Vicky Unruh observes, "were more openly evident" (130) in a number of creative works, such as Mário de Andrade's nationalistically mythopoetic *rapsódia*, or *rhapsode, Macunaíma* (1928) (app. C; see Moisés 393); Oswald de Andrade's highly influential 1925 collection of poetry, *Pau Brasil* (*Brazil Wood*), and his two experimental novels, *As memórias sentimentais de João Miramar* (1924; *The Sentimental Memoirs of John Seaborne*) and *Serafim Ponte Grande* (1933; *Seraphim Grosse Pointe*) (see app. C for both); and Ronald de Carvalho's paean to the energy and vitality of the New World, *Toda a América* (1926; *All America*).

Most interesting, from both a Brazilian and an inter-American perspective, is Oswald de Andrade's "Anthropophagy Manifesto" (1928), which "stresses Europe's debt to the New World for its conception of natural man, as set forth in writings by Montaigne and Rousseau, and that proposes instead the 'bad savage,' an all-consuming cannibal, as a New World model of cultural critique and capacity for creative assimilation" (Unruh 130). Reversing the established roles of both influence and reception and ironically commemorating the gastronomic fate of the Portuguese bishop Sardinha (Sardine) at the hands of Brazilian Indians, Oswald's droll but revolutionary proposal argues that New World artists and intellectuals must devour the European heritage to create something original and authentically American. His parodic use of Freud's *Totem and Taboo* (1913), for example, allowed him to introduce the European-defined themes of taboo and primitivism into what he considered the unique condition of Brazilian literature. Indeed, by transforming Freud's concept of taboo into a Brazilian totem and by establishing for it a different frame of reference, Oswald made Freud seem to serve the purposes laid out in his manifesto. Although Oswald's concept of anthropophagy and its symbolism for the future of Brazilian literature was based, perhaps, on a misinterpretation of Nietzsche, his image of the Tupi cannibal devouring would-be European colonizers remains a potent and influential cultural icon. As Stam argues (building on the work of Oswald de Andrade, Augusto de Campos, Alfred Jarry, and Francis Picabia):

> Although the cannibalist metaphor was also circulated among European avant-gardists, cannibalism in Europe, as Augusto de Campos points out, never constituted a cultural movement, never defined an ideology, and never enjoyed the profound resonances within the culture that it did in Brazil. . . . Synthesizing insights from Montaigne, Nietzsche, Marx, and Freud, along with what [de Andrade] knew of native Brazilian societies, he portrayed indigenous culture as offering a more adequate social model than the European one. (70–71)[27]

While the United States, with writers like Sherwood Anderson, John Dos Passos, Gertrude Stein, and Ernest Hemingway leading the way, witnessed during the 1920s a revolution of its own in fiction writing, the Brazilian modernist revolution begun so provocatively in February 1922 was more widespread, having by 1928 manifested itself in all aspects of artistic and theoretical endeavor.

In considering the literature, and especially the poetry, of Brazil and the United States during the early years of the twentieth century, we should note that writers from both countries were visiting Europe, where they absorbed new forms of artistic expression. Just as Oswald de Andrade challenged the complacency of Brazilian poetry and thought, so too poets like T. S. Eliot, Ezra Pound, and E. E. Cummings responded enthusiastically to the innovative themes and techniques of the European avant-garde. Pound, like Oswald de Andrade, was particularly influenced by Italian futurism, a revolutionary kind of writing that sought to incorporate the realities of the technological age. Filippo Tommaso Marinetti's famous "Manifesto Tecnico," published in Milan in 1912, provided the Brazilian *modernistas* with "key images and themes—electric light, ventilators, aeroplanes, workers' rights, engines, factory chimneys, dynamos, and mechanics" (Pontiero 248). While, early on, the poets of modernism in both the United States and Brazil sang the praises of an increasingly technological society, only later in the century, when the deleterious effects of this transformation became apparent, would they question the desirability of unchecked material progress—indeed, of progress itself.

In the United States at this time, the rise of religious fundamentalism can be seen as a backlash against what modernism championed—new ideas (many from abroad), advances in science and technology, political liberalism, and intellectual freedom generally. Reacting to the dislocation and disillusionment that modernism seemed to represent, such cultural lightning rods as Aimee Semple McPherson and Billy Sunday sought to purify American life by promoting a literal interpretation of the Bible, by embracing the eugenics movement, and by supporting isolation from the rest of the world. The assault on civil liberties (one marked by rabid anti-Communism, the Sacco and Vanzetti trial, racial strife,[28] and the National Origins Act of 1924) led to the formation of the American Civil Liberties Union as well as to vigilante groups like the Ku Klux Klan that were bent on attacking "political, religious, and racial minorities" (*Harper American Literature* 2: 1100–01).[29] The racial tension in the United States resonated in Brazil when, as Jorge Amado makes clear in *Tent of Miracles*, black culture was openly and violently persecuted (see app. C). As early as 1926, however, Freyre, activating the arguments of his mentor Franz Boas, was developing his famous theory (formalized in *The Masters and the Slaves*) that "miscegenation . . . had made Brazil a more homogeneous nation" (Burns, *History* [3rd ed.] 330). Although, from the 1950s on, a number of Brazilian intellectuals disputed Freyre's argument, it would continue to have intellectual currency, if only as a fable of Brazil's long-standing desire to be a true racial democracy (Skidmore, "Essay" 362).

Deliberately utilizing the forms and techniques of the European avant-garde, many writers of the early twentieth century, in both Brazil and the United States, produced works that rejected nativist provincialism but also employed distinctly American linguistic forms, themes, images, and motifs, many mythically based.[30] In particular, the advent of modernism in poetry, a watershed event for both countries, was characterized by themes not traditionally thought of as literary and by a radical style, in which the popular idioms of the New World would take precedence and in which such elements as free verse, prosody, fragmentation, collage, irony, parody, and montage would dominate.

In narrative a similar revolution was taking shape. In the United States, after its sobering experience in World War I, there emerged what has been termed a literature of disenchantment, symbolized by the image of the lost generation and epitomized, perhaps, by Hemingway's damaged and disillusioned characters. Brazil, after initially seeking to remain neutral, became the only South American country to declare war on Germany, on 23 October 1917. At the same time, it limited its involvement in the war effort to "furnishing supplies to the Allies, sending some army officers to Europe and a medical mission to France, and assigning a naval mission of two cruisers and four destroyers to patrol the South Atlantic with the English squadron"

(Burns, *History* [3rd ed.] 305). In contrast to the ambivalent, alienated narrative that came out of the United States' participation in the war (and confronted the materialism, bigotry, and hypocrisy of postwar American society), Brazilian narrative, as we shall see in chapter 3, entered a period of radical experimentation. Stemming in part from the experiments by Machado (*The Posthumous Memoirs of Brás Cubas* [1880–81], *Quincas Borba* [1891], *Dom Casmurro* [1900]), it continued through the twentieth century. In comparing the impact of the war era on Brazil and on the United States, we should remember that while both countries experienced economic growth (Brazil's industrial production, for example, doubled during the war and, by 1923, had tripled) and an increase in international respect (Brazil participated in the Versailles peace negotiations), Brazil—perhaps because it lost no soldiers in the bloody struggle—entered the 1920s with greater confidence and optimism, its artists and intellectuals convinced that they would at last establish Brazil's cultural independence.

But the economic bubble of the Roaring Twenties burst in October 1929, with the stock market crash—an event that had immediate repercussions throughout the Americas and the world. The Great Depression, seeming to symbolize the distorted values of the United States, erupted with stunning magnitude and severity. In Brazil as well as in the United States, the 1930s became the decade of socially conscious literature. Although in both countries a modernist concern for stylistic and formalistic experimentation lived on, there was a growing awareness that literature had a social responsibility, a moral obligation to address the urgent problems of the time. Two important cultural developments of the period are the fugitive movement (centering on Vanderbilt University and the writers John Crowe Ransom, Allen Tate, Donald Davidson, and Robert Penn Warren) and the first regional congress (organized by Freyre) held in the city of Recife, in Brazil's northeast, a region long viewed as paralleling, in history and development, the American South. Both the fugitives and Freyre's northeastern regionalists were reacting against what they felt were the pernicious effects, on vulnerable agrarian societies (the American South and the Brazilian northeast), of rapid, unchecked industrialization. The Brazilian northeasterners and the fugitives feared the destruction of their traditional, rural cultures by urbanization, modernization, and capitalism. The Brazilians had the additional burden of freeing themselves—their language, their literary forms and modes, and the norms of their intellectual discourse—from a longstanding "tradition of colonial subordination to Europe or the United States" (Freyre, qtd. in Ellison 25), a tradition of dependence decried by such intellectuals as Sílvio Romero and João Capistrano de Abreu.

Many of the misgivings about Brazil's tendency to accept foreign influences can be found in the work of Roberto Schwarz, who in a number of influential studies has led present-day Brazilians to rethink the factors at play in their sense of national identity. As John Gledson expresses it in his introduction to *Misplaced Ideas*, Schwarz is stimulated by the

> *unrealities* of culture, by the comic or tragic adoption of a set of ideas, an artistic form, or a fashion, which does not fit the actual circumstances of the writer or his audience. Whether it be the dominant liberal ideology of the nineteenth century in a country whose economy was based on slavery, or the flower-power optimism of the sixties in Brazil, a country under military rule and rapidly stumbling into extremely savage repression . . . the revelation that circumstances are relative only encourages him to find the common ground which will explain them. (x)

As Schwarz himself puts it, "We Brazilians and other Latin Americans constantly experience the artificial, inauthentic and imitative nature of our cultural life" and all too easily demonstrate an uncritical "high regard" for "the newest doctrine from America or Europe" (1, 2). One result, he argues, is that "since the last [i.e., nineteenth] century educated Brazilians . . . have had the sense of living among ideas and institutions copied from abroad that do not reflect local reality." To Schwarz, Brazilians have "become incapable of *creating things of our own that spring from the depths of our life and history*" (9, 10), an unsettling conclusion that speaks to the heart of the question of national identity.

In Brazil, the politically committed novel of the northeast established itself as the defining genre of the 1930s, while in the United States, the socially conscious fiction of the 1930s voiced the public's sense of outrage and protest. Evoking memories of the American Dust Bowl experience, both Queiroz and Ramos wrote novels (resp., *O quinze* [1930; *The Year 1915*] and *Vidas secas* [1938; *Barren Lives*]) that deal with the traumatic effects of drought and displacement. Queiroz, with works like *As três Marias* (1939; see Queiroz, *The Three Marias*, app. C) would later distinguish herself as a powerful voice for women. In addition to this, Fred Ellison has described, in *Brazil's New Novel* (a still-standard consideration of José Lins do Rego, Jorge Amado, Graciliano Ramos, and Raquel de Queiroz) several cases of direct and indirect influence connecting writers in Brazil and the United States during this tumultuous period. Amado's 1934 proletarian novel, *Suor* (*Sweat*), for example, was likely influenced by Michael Gold's *Jews without Money* (Ellison 93). Mary L. Daniel, too, notes the numerous links between the fiction produced in the two countries:

> [P]arallels may be seen in the case of the United States of the same period, a territory as vast and with as many distinctive regions as Brazil, in which the most vigorous literary output came precisely from the southern region (e.g., William Faulkner, Tennessee Williams, Erskine Caldwell, John Steinbeck, etc.) with its decadent plantations, "dustbowl" tragedies, and generally adverse circumstances. (172)

Amado's work in the 1930s, for example, can be compared with that of Twain and Caldwell, both of whom he knew and admired. In addition, several of Steinbeck's novels, including *The Grapes of Wrath* (1939), have close parallels in the Amado narratives of the period (Fitz, "Vox Populi").

An interesting question is whether Faulkner had the kind of impact in Brazil that he had in Spanish America, where, as several studies have shown (e.g., Cohn), his novels have been highly influential. Borges's brilliant translation of Faulkner's *The Wild Palms* (in 1940) is evidence of the latter's effect on the development of the *nueva novela hispanoamericana*, the "new novel of Spanish America" (Monegal, *Borges* 373). Faulkner's work was certainly admired by Brazilian writers in the 1930s and 1940s (a vital period in Brazil's intellectual history; see Morse 193–95; Monteiro) and indeed is currently experiencing something of a renaissance, with a number of his works recently being retranslated by major publishers. One could argue, nevertheless, that Brazil's narrative tradition was, by the 1930s, more innovative than Spanish America's and that the Brazilian novelists of the time did not need Faulkner's invigorating influence as much as their Spanish American counterparts did (see Fitz, "Faulkner").

The outstanding Brazilian novelist of the 1930s was Graciliano Ramos, often regarded as the direct heir of Machado de Assis. Influenced in his formative years by such writers as the Portuguese realist Eça de Queiroz, Zola, Balzac, Gorky, and Dostoevsky, Ramos produced, in the 1930s, four novels, the last three of which are considered classics of Brazilian literature. These extraordinary works—*Caetés* (1933), *São Bernardo* (1934), *Angústia* (1936; *Anguish*), and *Barren Lives* (1938)—dramatically demonstrate their author's skill at psychological analysis and his penchant for acute social commentary, a facet of his work revealing a grim determinism (the last three are in app. C). In *São Bernardo*, for example, the protagonist, Paulo Honório, is the epitome of the relentless entrepreneur, a New World type who, brooding over his wife's suicide, discovers that his material success, power, and position have in fact crippled him as a human being. Paulo's self-centered struggle to dominate ends up, ironically, causing the destruction of the people around him. In many ways Paulo is the quintessentially American self-made man whose story has been told many times, although rarely with such power, in the literature of the United States. The novel is also a stylistic tour de force: its short, staccato sentences; sparing use of adjectives and adverbs; and sober, restrained, and essentialist vocabulary are reminiscent of Hemingway, but in a more resigned, even bitter mode. In stark contrast to *São Bernardo*, which takes place largely in the external world of action and event, is *Anguish*, which in an almost unbroken interior monologue unfolds in the repressed recesses of the protagonist's disintegrating mind and which led to the designation of Ramos as the Brazilian Dostoevsky. Claustrophobic in its effect on the reader, *Anguish* is actually a downward-spiraling confession, one splintered by frustrated sexuality; flashes of lucidity; unfathomable tangles of memory, desire, and violence; and failed attempts at objective self-analysis. Only in the novel's final pages, which Ellison finds reminiscent of the Molly Bloom soliloquy at the end of Joyce's *Ulysses* (127), does the reader realize the depth of the protagonist's madness. *Barren Lives*, Ramos's final novel, differs from its three predecessors in using the third person. The reason for the shift is obvious: the characters depicted— husband, wife, and their two children—are poor, illiterate backlanders struggling to survive in the drought-stricken northeast. The choice of third person does not produce a sense of detachment, however, since, as in Faulkner's *As I Lay Dying*, the viewpoint is always that of the character most involved, including in one memorable chapter the family dog. A striking feature of *Barren Lives* is Ramos's subtle equation of the status of the humans and the animals in the story. Primarily through deft similes and metaphors, Ramos makes clear that in the harsh and barren *sertão*, or backlands, human beings are no different from the other animals with whom they share hunger, powerlessness, and exploitation. The story of Fabiano, Vitória, and the two boys, finally, is as intrinsically connected to the interior of Brazil's troubled northeast as the plight of the Joad family is to the American Dust Bowl in *The Grapes of Wrath*. Both works, justly regarded as pinnacles of the 1930s New World novel, poignantly dramatize the human struggle for survival in a hostile social and physical environment and the hope for a more just future.

The 1930s and 1940s were in Brazil a period of accomplishment in poetry as well as fiction. After the revolutionary period of modernism in the early 1920s, a host of writers emerged who would carry Brazilian poetry to new heights. Among them are four giants: Manuel Bandeira, Carlos Drummond de Andrade, Cecília Meireles, and João Cabral de Melo Neto (see Tapscott, app. C).

A versatile and influential poet, Bandeira evolved from the fairly conventional symbolism and Parnassianism of *A cinza das horas* (*The Ash of the Hours*), published in 1917, to structurally freer and thematically more iconoclastic texts like *Libertinagem* (1930; *Libertinage*) and *Estrela da manhã* (1936; *Morning Star*). Perhaps his best-known and most representative contribution to modernism, *Libertinagem* features poems that demonstrate his lyricism, colloquial voice, biting irony, and unexpected flashes of tragic humor. In *Estrela da manhã*, Bandeira continues to experiment with forms of free verse and metrical innovation while delving, with a sense of social consciousness, into the rich cultural history of Brazil's blacks—a subject matter being explored by another major poet, Jorge de Lima. In his later years Bandeira composed some concretist poems; his work significantly helped the form gain critical recognition.

Widely regarded as Brazil's most important contemporary poet, Carlos Drummond de Andrade is also one of its most respected. Although occasionally given to what are sometimes perceived as anti-American sentiments (especially regarding the materialism and cultural arrogance often associated with the United States), Drummond, as he is known in Brazil, is becoming better known, and admired, in the English-speaking world, thanks to some excellent translations of his work. In discussing Drummond's enthusiastic reception as a poet, Thomas Colchie, for example, argues:

> It may seem strange to the North American reader to hear greatness and accessibility attributed to the same poet. Rarely have the two coincided in our poetry, at least since Whitman. In Latin America, two of the greatest modern poets—the Chilean Pablo Neruda and the Brazilian Carlos Drummond de Andrade—have also been tremendously popular. (Colchie and Strand ix)

Colchie goes on to say that "no modern poet—not even Neruda—has managed to construct so intimate a rapport with his reader as Carlos Drummond de Andrade" (ix).

A distinctive and influential voice of the 1922 modernist generation, Drummond was, by the time *Alguma poesia* (*Some Poetry*) was published (1930), celebrated for his simple language; detached, at times despairing commentaries on the world about him; and, perhaps most characteristic, the ironic, self-deprecating humor that permeates his best work. In *Brejo das almas* (1934; *Fen of Souls*), which appeared in the depths of the depression, Drummond adopted a more somber and introspective attitude that exudes, like the work of so many writers of the time, a keen awareness of Brazil's social problems. *Sentimento do mundo* (1940; *Sentiment of the World*), which recalls Neruda's best political poetry, reflects a sense of solidarity in the face of war.[31] Drummond's concern with social and political issues continues in *A rosa do povo* (1945; *The Rose of the People*) and *Poesia até agora* (1947; *Poetry until Now*), works that speak, clearly and directly, to the common people.

Cecília Meireles is revered in Brazil as one of its most technically proficient, lyrical, and melodious poets. *Vaga música* (1942; *Vague Music*) provides ample evidence, as does *Mar absoluto* (1945; *Absolute Sea*). The later work, which wrestles, sometimes in a mystical fashion, with timeless questions, is structured on sea and water imagery. A few years earlier, in 1940, Meireles had taught and lectured on Brazilian literature and culture at the University of Texas and traveled extensively afterward. Unlike her more militant modernist colleagues, Meireles never broke with her traditional poetic heritage, choosing instead to refine it by stressing musicality, observation, and symbolism.

Probably the most celebrated member of the Generation of 1945, João Cabral de Melo Neto is widely regarded as a difficult, or hermetic, poet, whose economical, sometimes surrealist images are not easily deciphered. The winner of the prestigious Neustadt International Prize for Literature in 1992, Melo Neto too has been well served by his translators; Elizabeth Bishop was one of the most successful re-creators of his poetry in English. Influenced early in his career by Pirandello and Apollinaire, Melo Neto quickly found, in a series of original works, his own highly distinctive voices, themes, and tones. In *Pedra do sono* (1942; *Stone of Sleep*), for example, he presents poetry as a form of dream or hallucination, sustained by engrossing images and the imaginative wordplay associated with slippage between signifiers and signifieds. Three years later, however, *O engenheiro* (1945; *The Engineer*) essentially rejected the free association of his earlier effort in favor of a more laconic poetry, not so much written, as a poet might, but constructed, as an engineer might, tightly and hermetically. In *O cão sem plumas* (1950; *The Featherless Dog*) the reader notes the social consciousness that marked Melo Neto's best work from then on. One of his most famous and most anthologized compositions, "Uma faca só lâmina" (1955; "A Knife All Blade"; see app. C), is a stark, compelling poem that influenced the concretist poets. The work is organized around "three basic images," a bullet, a clock, and a knife (Nist 182); each contributes to the sense of impending violence pervading the poem. Also appearing in 1955, "Morte e vida severina" ("The Death and Life of a Severino"), like its predecessor, depicts, in spare, minimalist language, the poverty and violence of Brazil's northeast.

As if balancing the importance of Brazil's northeast during this period, Érico Veríssimo, one of Brazil's most popular and cosmopolitan writers undertook to write between 1949 and 1962 a three-volume history of southern Brazil, the land of the *gaúcho* (cowboy) and of a history very different from that of the northeast. Epic in its scope and focusing on the region's social, political, and economic development from the mid-eighteenth century to the end of World War II, *O tempo e o vento* (*Time and the Wind*; see app. C) chronicles the interlocking stories of three families through several generations of growth. Reminiscent in many ways of James Michener, Veríssimo proved adept at merging what in the hands of a lesser writer could have been a narrowly regionalistic view of life and times in southern Brazil with a generous and expansive view of the human condition. In *Time and the Wind*, he integrated the Brazilian experience into the larger human experience and thereby helped establish a growing international following for Brazilian literature.

Dominated by the good-neighbor policy, relations between Latin America, whose raw materials were needed for the war effort, and the United States intensified during the 1940s. A number of American universities, including Vanderbilt, Texas, North Carolina, and Tulane, saw the potential of Brazil in particular and initiated programs in Portuguese and Brazilian studies. Although Brazilian literature was studied in the United States, it was mostly dwarfed by its Spanish language counterpart. We might note, incidentally, that while the literature of the United States had achieved international recognition by 1940, Latin American literature (in contrast to the literature of Spain) did not attain similar legitimacy until the 1960s. The importance of Brazil, however, was recognized early on, as attested by the publication in 1948 of Samuel Putnam's *Marvelous Journey*, a groundbreaking comparative study of Brazilian and American literature through the postwar period.

In Brazil, the 1940s were dominated by an intense regionalism, especially in the northern half of the country, while in the south a more urban, introspective, and cosmopolitan trend was developing. In both countries, hitherto marginalized groups made their presence felt as well. In the United States, for example, Richard Wright's *Native Son* (1940) and *Black Boy* (1945) were published; shortly afterward, Jorge de Lima brought out *Poemas negros* (1947). Lima, who had cultivated a black consciousness in the novel *Calunga* (1935), also wrote "Essa negra Fulô," 1928 ("That Black Woman Fulô"), a famous poem that facilitates a comparative study of the social, political, and sexual condition of women slaves in the United States and Brazil. Another significant event occurred in 1944, when Abdias do Nascimento, inspired by a performance of Eugene O'Neill's *The Emperor Jones*, founded the Teatro Experimental do Negro in Rio de Janeiro. Over the next two decades, Nascimento's politically committed group became a focal point for Brazil's artistic and intellectual community in its efforts to promote black culture in Brazil and to force Brazil to confront its racial problems. Women writers too sought to have their voices heard. In addition to Mary Beard's *Woman as a Force in History* (1946), which explored history as far back as the Middle Ages to establish the principles of the women's movement, the mid-century period saw the emergence in the United States of a number of outstanding women writers, including Katherine Anne Porter, Zora Neale Hurston, Eudora Welty, and Tillie Olsen.

In Brazil, the issues germane to the condition of women in Western society are compellingly laid out in Lygia Fagundes Telles's *Ciranda de pedra* (1955; *The Marble Dance*; see app. C) and especially Clarice Lispector's *Perto do coração selvagem* (1944; *Near to the Wild Heart*; see app. C). Destined to alter the development of modern narrative in Brazil, Lispector's novel won the respect of writers, critics, and readers around the world. The text (the title comes from Joyce's *A Portrait of the Artist as a Young Man*), with its poetic yet menacing depiction of a young Brazilian woman's mind, its celebration of female power and sexuality, and its subversive interrogation of androcentric culture, contrasts vividly with the masculine world of Jorge Luis Borges's better-known *Ficciones*, which epitomized the famous "new narrative" of Spanish America in the 1960s. Stylistically, structurally, and thematically, *Near to the Wild Heart* should be regarded as a landmark, as one of the most revolutionary novels of the mid-twentieth period, in either North or South America.

In the 1950s the connection between Brazilian and American literature intensified. Ezra Pound's *Cantos*, for example, and the poetry of E. E. Cummings and William Carlos Williams (along with that of Mallarmé, Joyce, and Apollinaire) were important in the development of concretist poetry, a form that combines the spatial and verbal aspects of language into a unified semiotic expression. The early Brazilian concretists, principally Décio Pignatari and the brothers Haroldo de Campos and Augusto de Campos (see app. C, "Two Concrete Poems"), had discovered a reference to the semantically elusive word *noigandres* while studying the *Cantos*. As a result, they were referred to as the Noigandres group during the formative years of Brazilian concretist poetry, from 1952 to 1956. Alluding both to the Provençal troubadour Arnaut Daniel (who employs it in one of his songs) and to Pound (who had extensively praised Daniel as an inventive poet-singer), *noigandres* was put to use by the São Paulo poets as "an emblem of free artistic experimentation," as the unofficial name of their group, and as the title of the poetry series they published (Perrone, *Seven Faces* 28). The theoreticians of concretism were captivated by Pound's "musical interests and his relational ideogrammic method of composition (in *The Cantos*), which, inspired by Fenollosa's studies of Chinese characters, counterposed and juxtaposed related elements drawn from different sources with visible effects" (29). In contrast to poets of the modernist rebellion of 1922—who had used imported forms in their attempt to create an authentic literature—practitioners of concrete poetry hoped to export their work and thereby demonstrate to a worldwide audience the validity and originality of Brazilian culture. According to Charles Perrone, "concrete poetry was more important in the reshaping of Brazilian lyric than it was in that of any other nation, and the central role of concretism in Brazilian literature—notwithstanding cited resistance and unresolved controversies—has no real parallel in other countries" (*Seven Faces* 59). Apropos of the success of this decisive if controversial movement, Caroline Bayard, writing from a Canadian perspective, has argued that the "historian of concrete poetry would look upon the Brazilian theoretical texts as the richest and most articulate contribution," while Claus Clüver maintains that "there is no real US-American equivalent to the Brazilian concrete ideogram" (qtd. in Perrone, *Seven Faces* 60, 61).

As for the narrative at mid-century, the most important event in Brazil is undoubtedly the appearance in 1956 of the mythopoetic and linguistic tour de force by Guimarães Rosa. Emir Rodríguez Monegal has called *Grande Sertão: Veredas* (*The Devil to Pay in the Backlands*; see app. C) "one of the most complex works of fiction ever produced in Latin America" (*Borzoi Anthology* 2: 678). Achieving a scope and technical mastery that recalls the best of Faulkner (see Valente), *The Devil to Pay in the Backlands*—perhaps because of its less than reliable English translation—has never had the kind of influence in North America that it deserves, particularly in the light of the warm reception the "new Latin American narrative" had in the United States in the 1960s. Summing up Rosa's importance in Brazil and Spanish America, Monegal, one of earliest critics with expertise in the literatures of the two traditions, asserts that Rosa was "generally recognized as the greatest Brazilian novelist since Machado de Assis." He goes on to say that "if Machado radically transformed nineteenth-century narrative, Guimarães succeeded in completely revolutionizing the style and diction of twentieth-century narrative." Indeed, at the time of his death in 1967, Rosa was "beyond dispute Latin America's greatest novelist" (Monegal, *Borzoi Anthology* 2: 677, 679). It was also during the mid-1950s that John Barth, struggling to complete his first novel, came across the recently published English translations of Machado's three best-known novels, *Epitaph of a Small Winner* (as it was titled in the original translation, by William Grossman; retranslated by Gregory Rabassa as *The Posthumous Memoirs of Brás Cubas*), *Philosopher or Dog?*, and *Dom Casmurro* (see app. C). Impressed by what he later called Machado's "postmodern" artistry and seeing in it the solutions to problems he was facing in his manuscript, Barth, in *The Floating Opera* (1956), thus owes a great deal to the three Brazilian texts (Fitz, "Influence" and "John Barth's Brazilian Connection"; Barbosa). In the realm of theater, Jorge Andrade's powerful drama *A Moratória* (1955) brings to mind the plays of Arthur Miller, whose influence Andrade has acknowledged. Finally, the 1950s saw the supplanting of Brazil's traditionally subjective and impressionistic criticism by Anglo-American New Criticism, introduced into Brazil by Afrânio Coutinho, who had spent the years 1942 to 1947 at Columbia University (Heyck).

Like the 1950s, the 1960s was an important time for Brazilian literature and its reception in the United States. The now-legendary Boom in Latin American literature was created, of course, primarily by such Spanish American masters as Pablo Neruda, Carlos Fuentes, Mario Vargas Llosa, Borges, and García Márquez. Less well known were the narrative achievements in Quebec, where another "new novel" emerged during the 1960s. Revolutionary in both form and content, the Québécois *nouveau roman* of the 1960s developed quickly as a form of social protest and, with its emphasis on "*joual*" rather than "proper" European French, as a voice for the liberation of the people and culture of Quebec. With writers like Gérard Bessette, Claire Martin, Marie-Claire Blais, Jacques Ferron, Jacques Godbout, Hubert Aquin, and Réjean Ducharme leading the way, the new novel of Quebec also began to experiment with the relations between the act of writing and the creation of an identity; with first-person metafictions; with nonlinear plot structures;

and with such issues as time, memory, politics, religion, and sexuality. It was comparable in many ways to the *nueva novela* of Spanish America and, in Brazil, to the distinctive *novo romance*, which was being cultivated by writers like Lispector, Maria Alice Barroso, Nélida Piñon, and Osman Lins. Overshadowed by the success of the Boom writers, the Brazilian authors of the 1960s and early 1970s were denied the kind of worldwide reception that allowed Spanish American literature to break out of its long isolation. A major event of the decade, therefore, was the publication in English, in 1967, of Lispector's *A maçã no escuro* (1961; *The Apple in the Dark*; see app. C)—a prototypical example of the lyrical novel (Fitz, "Lyrical Novel"), a form practiced by Hermann Hesse, André Gide, and Virginia Woolf. Other important Brazilian novels of the 1960s are Carlos Heitor Cony's *Pessach: A travessia* (1967), Autran Dourado's Faulkner-like *A barca dos homens* (1961) and *Ópera dos mortos* (1967),[32] and Piñon's *Fundador* (1969). For John Gledson, *Ópera dos mortos* (translated as *The Voices of the Dead*; see app. C) is "perhaps the best, though the most somber, novel of the decade" ("Brazilian Prose" 201). As Gledson observes, "of course the Boom reached Brazil as it did everywhere else in the world, and produced a sense of inadequacy, obscurely bound up with political frustration" (199). This sense of frustration with the political situation in Brazil was poignantly expressed in best sellers like *Quarup* (1967; see app. C) and *Bar Don Juan* (1972), both by Antônio Callado.

An additional—and lamentable—effect of the Spanish American Boom was that it may have delayed the foreign reception of Brazil's great master Machado de Assis. Although there is no proof that the reception of a work like *The Posthumous Memoirs of Brás Cubas* was delayed by the Boom, it has long puzzled Brazilianists that Machado, whose work was in so many ways the prototype of the new fiction emanating from Latin America, was so roundly ignored through the 1960s. In 1880–81, with the publication of this novel, Machado essentially did for Brazilian narrative what Borges would do for Spanish American fiction in the late 1930s and early 1940s—freed it from the constraints of rote realism. In the Americas, his formal recognition (beyond the range of Luso-Brazilianists, at least) would have to wait for a provocative 1990 essay in the *New Yorker* by Susan Sontag. Assessing Machado's importance as a writer, Sontag rather unceremoniously relegates Borges to silver-medal status in the history of Latin American narrative. Discussing Machado's essential "modernity" by comparing him (and his sly, digressive style) with a host of other international writers, Sontag declares that she is "astonished that a writer of such greatness does not yet occupy the place he deserves"; she suggests that he has been "marginalized" by "Eurocentric notions about world literature." She goes on to say:

> Even more remarkable than his absence from the stage of world literature is that he has been very little known and read in the rest of Latin America— as if it were still hard to digest the fact that the greatest author ever produced in Latin America wrote in the Portuguese, rather than the Spanish, language.

Remarking that Brazil has often been regarded by Spanish-speaking South America "with a good deal of condescension and often in racist terms," Sontag avers that Borges, whom she views as "the second greatest writer produced on that continent, seems never to have read Machado de Assis" ("Afterlives" 107). Although Machado is steadily achieving the acclaim he merited among scholars of Spanish American literature (see, e.g., González Echevarría and Enrique Pupo-Walker; Monegal, *Borzoi Anthology*), his name is not automatically mentioned in the same breath as Borges, Juan Rulfo, Julio Cortázar, Gabriel García Márquez, Carlos Fuentes, and Mario Vargas Llosa as Latin American fiction's innovators.

Although the modernist aesthetic of the 1920s and 1930s "had failed to revolutionize the [Brazilian] stage" (George 75), it produced one extraordinary play, Oswald de Andrade's notorious *O rei da vela* (*The Candle King*). Unfortunately, only in the late 1960s was it accorded the attention it had earned. Written in 1933 and published in 1937 but not staged until 1967, *The Candle King* is the theatrical version of Oswald's "Anthropophagy Manifesto." A character named Mr. Jones is a predatory and exploitive American capitalist who feeds off Brazil's financial woes. Beyond this exceptional work, as David George points out, the Brazilian stage has evolved to the point that provocative comparisons can now be made between the Brazilian theater and such playwrights as Jean Anouilh, Bertolt Brecht, Noël Coward, Alfred Jarry, Amiri Baraka, Clifford Odets, Eugene O'Neill, Luigi Pirandello, Jean-Paul Sartre, August Strindberg, and Tennessee Williams. The works of many of these authors, moreover, are staged in Brazil and interpreted in the context of pressures and conflicts that afflict Brazilian society (see, in app. C, Rodrigues, Suassuna, and Szoka). The violence inherent in racial, class, and gender conflict, for example, was the focus of Fernando Peixoto's late-1960s staging of *Poder negro* (*Black Power*), a Brazilianized version of Jones's *The Dutchman*; José Celso's direction of the Odets play *Awake and Sing* (translated as *A vida impressa em dólar*, or "life printed on a dollar," the subtitle of the original play) was "extremely well received" in Brazil, where the play's social concerns and its critique of the values driving American society were viewed as applying to Brazil as well (George 60–61).

The 1960s was also the era of *cinema novo*, or new cinema, a highly respected movement that established the Brazilian film industry as a vital and creative force. Featuring such international classics as *Vidas secas* (*Barren Lives*), by Nelson Pereira dos Santos, and *Terra em transe* (*Land in Anguish*) and *Deus e o diabo na terra do sol* (*Black God, White Devil*) by Glauber Rocha, *cinema novo* brought Brazil to the attention of the world. Finally, the 1960s was the decade of the bossa nova, Brazilian popular music disseminated in the United States, on the strength of such songs as "The Girl from Ipanema" and "One Note Samba," by jazz greats including Charlie Byrd, Stan Getz, and Vince Guaraldi. In the other direction, the music of Bob Dylan, John Cage, and Jimi Hendrix had a significant influence on Brazilian musicians and composers like Gilberto Gil and Caetano Veloso, the driving forces behind the powerful *tropicália* movement of the late 1960s, which sought to effect "a critical revision of Brazilian culture" through both musical and nonmusical means, nationally and internationally (Perrone, *Seven Faces* 102, 106–07). Elaborating on the sociopolitical importance of Brazil's "poetry of song" during this period, in which Brazil lived under a repressive military dictatorship, Perrone writes that, "given the early experience of noted singer-songwriter Bob Dylan, it is interesting to note, in comparatist perspective, how the phenomenon of the poetry of song in Brazil was, relative to the Anglo-American realm, so much more diversified and contextually important" (xiv). The 1960s are also memorable, finally, because—as a result of the increasing strategic significance of Brazil and Portuguese Africa to the United States—the United States Senate declared Portuguese to be a "critical language" for Americans to learn. As might be expected, the declaration spurred the study of Portuguese language and Brazilian culture at colleges and universities across the country.

Although suffering under the stifling effects of the dictatorship and its "economic miracle" (which in fact benefited the few at the expense of the many), Brazilian literature of the 1970s made remarkable advances, some of which expanded Brazil's intellectual and artistic presence in the hemisphere. In 1971, for example, the American publisher Alfred Knopf was still producing the translation (*The Devil to Pay in the Backlands*) of Rosa's epic masterpiece *Grande Sertão: Veredas*. As noted earlier, a flawed translation may have prevented this novel from attracting the attention in the United States that its Spanish American competitors were enjoying. The reception of Brazilian literature in Spanish America, however, took a major step forward with the English-language publication, in 1978, of Mario Vargas Llosa's *Pantaleón y las visitadoras* (*Captain Pantoja and the Special Services*) and, three years later, of the Peruvian master's *La guerra del fin del mundo* (1984; *The War of the End of the World*); both were deeply influenced by Cunha's extraordinary *Rebellion in the Backlands*.[33] A similar development was occurring in the poetry of Carlos Nejar, some of whose post-1973 work (e.g., *Casa dos Arreios*) evinces a distinctly Pan-American consciousness, in which a progressive sense of Latin American unity emerges as a creative force. In an earlier collection of poems, *Sélesis* (1960), Nejar generates parallels between the mythic hero of the Pampa—a vast region that includes parts of Argentina, Uruguay, and Paraguay as well as Brazil—and the American cowboy of the Old West. A function, no doubt, of life under the dictatorship, Brazil's so-called marginal poetry movement produced some subtly effective work during the 1970s. Although often associated with the outlook and tradition of Sylvia Plath, Ana Cristina César, for example, a key voice in women's literature in Brazil, also demonstrates a direct link to the poetry of Elizabeth Bishop. The American poet spent many years in Brazil and, in addition to her own work (much of which deals with the country, its beauty as well as its problems), translated a number of poets, including Drummond de Andrade, whose work she was the first to translate into English. César's well-known poem "Travelling" takes the key line of Bishop's "One Art" ("The art of losing isn't hard to master," which she renders into Portuguese as "Perder é mais fácil que se pensa") and builds her own poem around it.[34] In "Travelling," moreover, César creates an unidentified character named Elizabeth who plays a significant if mysterious role in the poem's development. Bishop also translated *The Diary of Helena Morley*, a work that, first published in the United States in 1957, may actually be better known than her poetry translations. Reflecting the English ancestry of her father, Helena Morley is the pseudonym for a Brazilian woman, Senhora Augusto Mario Caldeira Brant, whose charming story as a girl growing up in a small inland town (Diamantina, located in the state of Minas Gerais) during the final years of the nineteenth century comes vividly to life as *Minha vida de menina* (the text translated by Elizabeth Bishop). Greatly praised by the poet Manuel Bandeira and the novelist George Bernanos (who, when it first appeared in Brazil in 1942, was living in Brazil as an exile), the narrative impressed Bishop greatly. *As Duas meninas* (1997; *The Two*

Girls), a study of Morley's diary by Roberto Schwarz, shows that, in its social context and in the development of its protagonist, the diary can be compared with Machado's *Dom Casmurro* and its female character, Capitu. Praising *The Diary of Helena Morley* as one of the underappreciated achievements of Brazilian literature, Schwarz explains why the book had such a pronounced effect on Bishop, her outlook, her sense of Brazil, and her poetic production.

The 1970s should be remembered, overall, as the decade in which a new women's literature emerged in Brazil and became, in the years following Lispector's death (1977), a force for change—literarily, socially, and politically. With its gradual *abertura*, or "opening," Brazilian culture was, by the early 1980s, starting to throw off the shackles of the hated *ditadura*. As Darlene Sadlier puts it:

> The years following Lispector's death witnessed a budding of feminist literary scholarship in Brazil and a significant rise in the number of novels and stories written by women. By the mid-1980s, women writers were achieving a recognition that history had long denied them, and they became the topic of national and international conferences. . . . As a result of *abertura* and the rising feminist consciousness, the Brazilian publishing houses began producing anthologies that promoted the new "women's literature." (6)

Characterized by what the critic Fábio Lucas termed its "bankable eroticism," women's writing of the 1980s dealt openly with a variety of issues germane to women and sexual love. The candor was "a phenomenon new to Brazilian literature" (qtd. in Sadlier 8). A noteworthy outcome of the liberated women's writing is that the nation's fabled sensuality was revealed to be a construct of male desire—one, indeed, intended for male consumption. The situation began to change in 1982, when *Muito prazer: Contos eróticos femininos* (*Very Pleased to Meet You: Erotic Short Stories by Women*, ed. Márcia Denser) appeared, to great acclaim. Empowering Brazilian women with a radicalized sense of self and of sexuality, *Muito prazer*, as Denser and Sadlier note, was "intended to prove that women have something to say about sex— especially sex between women. The stories of lesbian love in the volume are among the first on this topic published by women in Brazil" (Sadlier 8). Other important works in the same vein, like Olga Savary's collection of erotic poetry, *Carne viva* (*Live Flesh*), soon followed. With the collapse of the dictatorship in 1985, Brazil's writers and intellectuals turned their attention to postmodernism and its applicability (or lack thereof) to Brazil and to Latin America generally. The debate reached something of a climax in the "Pós-tudo" affair, the dispute over cultural authenticity set off by the publication of a poem, "Pós-tudo" ("Post-Everything"), by Augusto de Campos in 1984 (see Perrone, *Seven Faces* 149–82).

The 1990s saw Brazil struggling with its financial woes and trying to assert itself as a major player in world affairs. Its writers, artists, musicians, and athletes continued to gain international respect and admiration, even after the debacle of its loss to France in the finals of the 1998 World Cup (a momentary lapse more than atoned for by Brazil's brilliant 2-0 victory over Germany in the 2002 Copa). The anthropologist and social critic Roberto DaMatta emerged as one of the new interpreters of Freyre's arguments about race and equity in Brazil. For DaMatta, as Thomas Skidmore summarizes his position,

> the essence of the Brazilian character [resides in] the structural relationships and accompanying values bequeathed by the highly hierarchical society of early Portugal and its slave-holding American colony. [DaMatta] analyzed the Freyre-type myth of his country's harmonious racial evolution . . . as the persistent rationale for what he frankly termed "our racism.". . . Like Darcy Ribeiro, DaMatta pointed to the colonial past as crucial in shaping Brazil's modern identity (361).

In another vein, DaMatta examines the role of Carnival in the social structures of Brazil and the United States:

> If we say that Carnival is a "rite of inversion," what happens when we have two Carnivals in societies that are clearly different in terms of institutions, history, and ideology? What exactly is inverted in each of the two Carnivals in these two different societies? If an "inversion" does really take place, how does each Carnival establish its dramatic field and its scenic levels? (117)

According to DaMatta, "the truly inclusive, open, and 'democratic' Carnival is in Brazil; the exclusive, discriminatory, and aristocratic-minded Carnival is in the United States" (128). In Brazil, where "the deepest social fear" is that of "being out of place," DaMatta observes, Carnival "temporarily suspends the precise hierarchical classification of things, persons, actions, categories, and groups in the social arena," whereas Carnival in the United States does not have this effect. Contrasting the New Orleans King of Carnival with the *malandro* or rogue figure who symbolizes Brazilian Carnival, DaMatta concludes that, if only temporarily, Brazilian Carnival transforms "the holistic hierarchy of everyday life into a fleeting moment dominated by magical individualistic equality," which constitutes the basis for the widespread, bittersweet view of Brazilian Carnival as the "great illusion" (130).

A wealth of talented women writers, including Leilah Assunção, Marina Colasanti, Helena Parente Cunha, Marilene Felinto, Hilda Hilst, Lya Luft, Nélida Piñon, Edla van Steen, and Lygia Fagundes Telles, have stimulated Brazilian literature into new areas of development. Piñon has been mentioned as a possible candidate for a Nobel Prize in literature. All the writers are gaining audiences through translation. Parente Cunha's superb novel *Woman between Mirrors* (1983), for example, enjoyed strong, steady sales in the United States, while Felinto's *The Women of Tijucopapo* (1982; trans. 1994) and Miriam Alves's *Finally . . . Us* (1995; trans. 1995) break new ground for black Brazilian women writers (for all three, see app. C).

In the cultural realm, Brazilian pop music found an appreciative audience in the United States in the 1990s. David Byrne, Arto Lindsay, and Beck, to cite three prominent names, are reinscribing the music of the *tropicália* movement into contemporary American popular music. A Beck song, "Tropicália" (a kind of anthem of the original movement), "borrows its weird noises and samba groove from a song by 'Os Mutantes' (the Mutants), an arty São Paulo psychedelic band of the late 60's," while Byrne has said that what drew him to *tropicália* music was both its musical sophistication and the political sophistication, its sense—echoing the spirit of Oswald de Andrade's "Anthropophagy Manifesto" of the late 1920s—that it was participating in the creation of "new forms of transcontinental bricolage that would inherently comment on Brazil's place in the world" (Marzorati 48–50).

At the dawn of the twenty-first century, then, Brazil, though frustrated by severe economic and political problems, can boast of a vital cultural scene that is making its presence felt around the world and of a flourishing national literature that is not only recognizing but also embracing its extraordinary diversity and creativity. Andrade's manifesto, for example, still commands attention as a radical, early-twentieth-century attempt to establish national identity and to define the country's relation with the international community. From the vantage point of the early twenty-first century, we can see that the central issue facing Brazilian literature continues to be the quest for authenticity. But can a nation so economically dependent and so marked by foreign influences hope to achieve an authentic national literature? Indeed, what does "authentic national literature" mean when international communication is instantaneous and when issues of influence, reception, and creativity are settled by computers? From the original cannibalists of 1928 to the *tropicalistas*, generations of Brazilian artists and intellectuals have sought to come to grips with these problems, to portray Brazil's traditional dependency in more honest and positive terms—terms that would allow it to participate, fully and equally, in the cultural exchanges that characterize the international scene. Yet because its cultural production continues to be adversely affected by its parlous economic status, Brazil is, in the early years of the twenty-first century, still more of a cultural receiver than sender, although, as contemporary Brazilian music and literature show, the situation is changing. Nevertheless, to understand and appreciate Brazil, we must explore the pernicious consequences of its longstanding dependency, of being continually hamstrung by "the vice of imitation" (Schwarz 11). As the world continues to learn about Brazil, the nation's unique contributions to world culture become more and more evident.

NOTES

1. For stylistic felicity and convenience, from time to time I use *American* in references to the literature of the United States.

2. By the early eighteenth century, France's North American position was potentially disastrous for England. Had the French moved to fortify, connect, and colonize their vast holdings, they almost certainly could have pushed the English into the sea. But they did not do so, with the result that England, not France, developed the militarily, economically, and politically stronger colony.

3. Although "a stated goal of colonization was the conversion of these heathen to heaven" (*Harper American Literature* 1: 104), there may be some question as to how hard the early English settlers—specifically the Pilgrims and Puritans—sought to accomplish this task, particularly compared with the French clerics (see *The Jesuit Relations* or the film *Black Robe*) or with the Spanish and Portuguese priests (Bartolomé de Las Casas, for example, or José de Anchieta, for some the founder of Brazilian literature). To judge from the historical record, the early English settlers were much less interested in converting the Indians they encountered than were the Spanish, French, and Portuguese.

4. For an interesting and provocative Brazilian perspective on race relations in Brazil and the United States during the late 1960s, see Jorge Amado's 1969 novel, *Tent of Miracles*. According to one of the characters, race relations in Brazil are better than in the United States precisely because of Brazil's long history of racial blending. For an in-depth look at the ways race and the designation of ethnic categories define residents of the United States, see Wright, "One Drop of Blood," which discusses multiracial people in the United States and the country's future as a racially mixed culture.

5. Skidmore believes that "five years of study in the US, mostly in the South with its Jim Crow laws and violent racism, deeply influenced Freyre, giving him a permanent point of reference in his future interpretations of Brazil." Skidmore also feels that the time Freyre spent as a graduate student at Columbia with Franz Boas, who "had become one of the first outspoken opponents of the scientific racism that still dominated academic thought in the North Atlantic world and Latin America," was decisive in his intellectual development (354).

6. Morison, for example, argues that England was overpopulated and needed a place to send its poor and unemployed; wanted markets for its textile (woolens) industry; needed the New World's precious metals; would be better off getting such commodities as olive oil, currants, and wine from its North American colonies than from Mediterranean countries; needed a short route to the Indies; had a "duty" "to propagate Protestant Christianity and prevent the Catholic Church from converting the entire native population of America" (48). See also Foerster, Grabo, Nye, Carlisle, and Falk (3–5).

7. The deep divisions between the two factions of Puritans, the Presbyterians (who controlled Parliament and whom Cromwell suspected of being sympathetic to Charles I) and the Independents (Cromwell's group), precipitated the war. Ironically, Cromwell, who had opposed absolutism, ended up ruling almost as absolutely as had the tyrannical Charles I. The Puritan penchant for absolute control is a major legacy to the Puritans struggling to build a society in the New World.

8. Although it may not have existed in written form, the political agreement that governed the Iroquois Confederation, which may have been formed around 1400, would antedate the Mayflower Compact.

9. The early French explorers and trappers, the *voyageurs* and *coureurs de bois*, are legendary for having achieved generally amicable relations with the Native Americans they encountered.

10. Burns reports that the first known shipment of African slaves arrived in Brazil in 1538 (*History* [3rd ed.] 495), while in New England the first African slaves were imported, on a Dutch vessel, in 1619.

11. Morison has written that "free popular education has been the most lasting contribution of early New England to the United States, and possibly the most beneficial" (70–71).

12. Scheick regards *New English Canaan* as "a mock elegy on an unsaintly camp follower" and notes that Morton's satirical poem "is hardly Puritan in sentiment." Observing that "Puritans were not bereft of a satirical impulse," he argues that they "did not particularly nurture satire" either, "whereas in the Southern colonies it publicly flourished, especially in late seventeenth- and early eighteenth-century newspapers. Southern colonial satire is more secular than the relatively scarce Northern variety. Southern colonial elegies, too, rarely allude to the Bible and, infrequently grim, they often are mocking or ironic in attitude" (86).

13. McWilliams writes that "the urgency of the republican mission, together with its long verse apologies, promptly obscured the possibility that the best-crafted poems of the era are mock epics and burlesques, rather than epics and panegyrics. . . . At a time when

Dwight, Barlow, Nathaniel Tucker, Richard Snowden, and others were worrying about the properly convincing way of elevating Revolutionary patriots to Homeric stature, [John] Trumbull showed that Toryism could be more memorably quelled by burlesquing the single combat and the epic simile" (164).

14. One of Basílio da Gama's Indian heroes has the same name, Cacambo, as the New World Indian in Voltaire's *Candide*. Some have suggested that Voltaire influenced da Gama, but both authors may have used the name of a real Indian. At any rate, as Garcia notes, the two characters have little in common save the name (37–38).

15. Another important writer from this period is Antônio José da Silva, often called the founding figure of Brazilian theater. Known as *o judeu*, or "the Jew," da Silva wrote comedies and operettas that reflected a distinctly national consciousness. Tragically, he was strangled and then burned at the stake by the Portuguese Inquisition in 1739.

16. The first known play written in French in North America was *Le Théâtre de Neptune*, a 243-line *reception* by Marc Lescarbot originally performed at Port Royal, November 1606. Although fanciful in its presentation, *Le Théâtre de Neptune* has a distinctively New World setting, four roles for "Indians," and a number of native expressions. Lescarbot, a Paris lawyer, was the first writer in French to envision the New World as a desirable escape from the corruption of the Old.

17. Although Caminha's letter was first composed on 1 May 1500, it was not published until 1817, a delay that precluded it from having the kind of impact on the European imagination that Columbus's 1492 letter had enjoyed.

18. Another captivity narrative is Carlos de Sigüenza y Góngora's *Los infortunios de Alonso Ramírez* (1690), in which a young Puerto Rican abandons his family to seek fame and fortune, only to be captured by English pirates. This first-person narrative marks an important step in the development of the Spanish American novel.

19. Brazil's initial bid for political independence actually involved, through Thomas Jefferson, the recently independent United States, the nation several Brazilian political leaders hoped would recognize their efforts.

20. The critic Artur Motta, for example, thinks so, although a somewhat stronger case can be made for Teresa Margarida da Silva e Orta's 1752 narrative, *As aventuras de Diófanes*.

21. The Jesuits would be expelled from Spanish America in 1767 and suppressed in New France from 1773 until 1842, when they were allowed to return, though in a much weaker capacity.

22. Pedro II had an official role in the opening of the Centennial Exhibition in Philadelphia, on 10 May 1876, and as a judge helped get Alexander Graham Bell's telephone reviewed at the exposition. Pedro II toured the United States for three months, and when he departed for Brazil, Whittier composed a poem in his honor.

23. For a cinematic version of this conflict, see *The Mission*.

24. James might have heard of Machado, whose important critical essay "O instinto da nacionalidade" ("The Instinct of Nationality") appeared in the journal *Nôvo Mundo* (*New World*), published in New York, on 24 March 1873. See Josué Montello, *Machado de Assis* (Lisboa: Verbo, 1972) 48.

25. Qtd. in Paulo Sotero, "Jirinovski do Patomac abala Nave Republicana," *O Estado de São Paulo* 25 February 1996: A18. Stam cites two other books, Peter Brimelow's *Alien Nation* and Michael Lind's *The Next American Nation*, as examples of worried authors who "speak in panicked terms of the 'danger' of the 'Brazilianization' of the United States" (366n25).

26. Organized by Arthur B. Davies and a group of artists committed to challenging the conservative nature of American art in the early 1900s, the Armory Show opened in New York in 1913 before traveling to Chicago and Boston. Influenced by European cubism and also by the postimpressionists, German expressionism, and fauvism, painters like Stuart Davis, Charles Demuth, and Charles Sheeler adapted the new techniques to their renditions of American life. See Milton W. Brown, *The Story of the Armory Show* (New York: Abbeville, 1988).

27. Stam writes, for example, that "the nihilism of Dada had little to do with what de Campos calls the 'generous ideological utopia' of Brazilian Anthropophagy. Radicalizing the Enlightenment valorization of indigenous Amerindian freedom, it highlighted aboriginal matriarchy and communalism as a utopian model. 'The Indian,' de Andrade wrote, 'had no police, no repression, no nervous disorders, no shame at being nude, no class struggle, no slavery'" (70–71).

28. One example is the race riot of 1921, in which whites in Tulsa, Oklahoma, went on a murderous rampage against the city's African Americans. See Tim Madigan's *The Burning: Massacre, Destruction, and the Tulsa Race Riot of 1921* (New York: Dunne–St. Martin's, 2001).

29. *The Harper American Literature* reports that "between 1920 and 1925, membership in the Klan rose from roughly five thousand to five million" (2: 1101).

30. In the modernist poetry of the United States, this mythic dimension most often came from anthropological and archaeological studies, like James Frazer's *The Golden Bough* (which Eliot made extensive use of in *The Waste Land*), which explored the myths underlying Western civilization. In Brazil the myths examined by the *modernistas* came from the Amazonian rain forest.

31. Colchie observes that while "Neruda is an intensely social poet: public, epic, even in matters as personal as love," "Carlos Drummond de Andrade is quieter, more lyrical and self-effacing, tenaciously private even while sharing Neruda's social concerns. Where they differ is in register" (ix).

32. The Faulkner novels that Dourado's work most recalls are *As I Lay Dying, The Sound and the Fury*, and *Absalom, Absalom!*

33. I owe this information to Efraín Kristal, of UCLA, who, in a conversation at Vanderbilt University in the fall of 1998, explained to me Vargas Llosa's use of *Rebellion in the Backlands* in *Captain Pantoja and the Special Services*. For a study of the influence of *Rebellion in the Backlands* on *The War of the End of the World*, see Wasserman, "Mario Vargas Llosa."

34. This line might also be translated as "Losing is easier than one thinks."

CHAPTER 3

Brazilian Narrative:
A Historical View

ORIGINS

As we saw in chapter 2, Brazilian literature lacks the kind of brilliant pre-Columbian past that characterizes much of Spanish America and its literature. The early Portuguese explorers did not encounter indigenous peoples whose civilizations were as sophisticated and complex as those of the Aztecs, the Maya, and the Inca. Although their flourishing oral traditions suggest that the Tupi-Guarani and the Tapuya (the two groups with whom the early-sixteenth-century Portuguese had the most contact)[1] possessed an imaginative literature, their impact on the development of colonial letters was minimal.[2] By the 1830s and the onset of Brazilian Romanticism, however, the Indianist tradition would become important to Brazil's identity as a nation and as a people. But in the formative years, the figures, genres, and themes of the Renaissance, then in full flower, represented the dominant culture. While it remained significant in Portugal, the Renaissance would give way, by the mid-sixteenth century, to the baroque, the movement that, as we have seen, exerted the greatest literary influence in colonial Brazil. Arguing that *ufanismo*, an exaltation of the natural beauty and fertility of the land and a celebration of Brazil as an earthly paradise, was the defining theme of early Brazilian literature, for example, Afrânio Coutinho believes that "it was under the aegis of the baroque, defined not only as an artistic style, but also as a cultural complex, that Brazilian literature was born" (68).

In Spanish America and the United States as well as Brazil, the earliest manifestations of literature appeared in two basic categories: the letters, logs, journals, official reports, and treatises written about the lands and peoples the Europeans encountered (many of these documents became the prototypes of *ufanista* writing) and the religious writings of such Jesuit clerics as José de Anchieta, Manuel da Nóbrega, and Fernão Cardim. Stemming especially from the first of these traditions—which culminated in Sebastião de Rocha Pita's *História da América portuguesa, 1500–1724* (1730)—a "nationalistic historiography" emerged, one that displayed a well-crafted "rhetoric of nationhood" (González Echevarría and Pupo-Walker 3: 3; see also Nunes, "Historiography"). In Brazil, as in Spanish America and, in a slightly different way, in what would become the United States, "proclamations of a national literature" found their sources in sometimes imaginatively written "political discourses" that sought a strengthened national identity and an end to colonial rule. In Brazil this enterprise was carried out by "political leaders, historians, literary scholars, and creative writers among others." Unlike the early literature of the United States, which maintained a fairly stable distinction between fiction and nonfiction, in Brazil

> romantic historians often blurred relationships between general and particular data, or between individuals and society. In many, such imaginative discourse is clearly linked to literary texts, such as the *Diálogo das grandezas do Brasil* (1618), by Ambrósio Fernandes Brandão. . . . Literature and history articulated an elaborate rhetoric of abundance and promise which was meant to feed national pride. (González Echevarría and Pupo-Walker 3–4)

While the blurring of fiction and nonfiction describes Brazilian historiography as late as the early nineteenth century (the Portuguese had even kept secret the existence of lands on the western side of the Atlantic), it also characterizes, as we will see in a moment, Spanish American letters at the outset—for example, in October 1492, Columbus began to assess his discoveries in the New World and to plan the presentation of his findings to the monarchs, whose continued backing he would need for future expeditions.[3]

In the light of this background, we can speak of Brazil's narrative tradition as beginning a few days after the arrival of the Portuguese on 22 April 1500 (at the height of the European Renaissance), when Pêro Vaz de Caminha, the official scribe for Pedro Álvares Cabral's fleet, wrote his famous "Carta de achamento," or letter of discovery. Generally considered the first example of Brazilian literature, Caminha's letter, an official report on what he and his companions observed, is interesting reading, especially when compared with Columbus's discovery document, written eight years earlier. Unlike the more-famous Columbus letter—which contains hyperbole and the rhetorical flourishes of chivalric romances, and of the epic poetry of the Renaissance—Caminha's tract is marked by a relative open-mindedness and objectivity; a self-consciousness about the Portuguese motives; and a clear, restrained, and unpretentious style. There is even a moment of comic relief, over the question of gold (a subject of deep concern to Columbus). Misinterpreting what he thinks the natives are saying, Caminha then realizes, with refreshing candor, that he has incorrectly decoded certain cultural signs. As he explains:

> [O]ne of [the Indians] noticed the Captain's collar and began to point with his hand to land and then to the collar, as if to say to us that there was gold on the land. . . . And he pointed to land and then to the beads and the Captain's collar, as if to give gold for the beads. Or rather we took this to be his meaning because we wished it to be so, while he really meant to say that he would take the beads and the collar together for himself. (qtd. in Monegal, *Borzoi Anthology* 1: 13)

Also notable is Caminha's tolerance of the Indians' dislike of European food and drink and of their nudity, which he seems to consider a sign of essential innocence: "They go naked without the slightest covering and pay no special attention to showing or not showing their shameful parts—and in this respect with as much innocence as they have in showing their faces" (12). David Haberly believes that "the subtext of Caminha's letter . . . is his conviction that he and his companions have somehow returned to Eden before the Fall—a fair and fertile garden whose inhabitants do not know shame." Focusing, apparently, on the potentially libidinous responses of the Portuguese men as they gazed at the naked Amerindian women, Haberly notes that Caminha's text implies that "within this garden even European sailors can regain the lost innocence of Adam, looking upon the *vergonhas* [in this context, "shameful parts"] of Indian girls" ("Colonial Brazilian Literature" 48). Caminha's candid, nonjudgmental, and detailed letter reveals as much about the attitudes and mores of the Portuguese (and Europeans generally) as it does about the indigenous people he met. Yet another important difference between Caminha's letter and Columbus's is that the Portuguese explorer's document was not published during his lifetime (it did not appear in print until 1817), whereas Columbus's had an immediate impact in Europe: it went through eight editions in Spanish and had a widely read Latin translation as well as an Italian verse paraphrase.

Finally, recent scholarship by Roland Greene has used the lens of imperialism to contrast the development of Spanish America and Brazil. The themes and figures of Petrarchism were "well disposed to counterpose or overlay different samples of the lived history of imperialism" in the colonial New World. Greene argues:

> [I]f Columbus is the first person of conquest, according to the representative anecdote of early modern imperialism, then Brazil is its quintessential object. Seldom discussed together, each one stands for a way of investigating the formation of the New World, through subjecthood or objectification respectively.

The spirit of objectification so pervades Brazilian culture, Greene contends, that it functions as a cultural marker connecting Brazil's colonial experience and such diverse twentieth-century phenomena as Carmen Miranda; the modernist journal *Klaxon*; the *Pau-Brasil, Antropofagia,* and *música popular brasileira* movements; and concretist poetry (9, 20–21, 131–33, 134).

We might instructively compare, as well, the discovery writings of John Smith with those from Spanish America and Brazil. A self-conscious promoter (like Columbus) and a battle-hardened adventurer, Smith could write objective, detailed descriptions and—as in Powhatan's alleged letter to him or his alleged salvation by Pocahontas—possibly apocryphal or at least misleading reports. In Powhatan's letter to Smith, the discourse ascribed to the leader of the Algonquin Confederacy may well be less what Powhatan actually said than what Smith, in an echo of Caminha's misinterpretation of the gold question, wanted him to say. It would be illuminating to undertake a comparative study of the English, French, Spanish, and Portuguese motivations behind their conquest of the New World and of the cultural implications of these motivations. Is it possible, for example, that the financially astute English settlers were as mercenary as the Portuguese, who have been called "notoriously commercial (rather than religious or cultural) in their imperialist attentions" (Greene 95)? If so, how do we explain the fact that the two cultures developed in such radically different fashions (a question that has long intrigued Brazilian intellectuals)? And how would the French and

Spanish fit into this scheme? What is clear—from the perspective of the conquerors, at least—is that in both North and South America the age of discovery and conquest quickly gave way to the calculated, self-serving policies of colonization.

THE EIGHTEENTH CENTURY

Beginning in the early 1700s, Brazilian writers faced two urgent problems, which would have to be resolved if Brazilian literature was to become a reality:

> how to find stylistic and thematic approaches to local reality, for despite the rebirth of faith in the land and its potential, it was clearly impossible to return to the essentially Medieval traditions of both the Jesuits and the *ufanistas*; and how to construct a literary society and achieve personal success in a colony still crippled by an inferior educational system, by limited intellectual opportunities, and by Portugal's refusal to allow printing presses to operate in Brazil. (Haberly, "Colonial Brazilian Literature" 60–61)

In Brazil, as elsewhere in the Americas, the eighteenth century was thus a period of transition from one cultural identity to another and a major step toward political independence. By this time, a feeling of nationality, of a national consciousness, had emerged, as well as a loosening of ties to the homeland. Portuguese settlers had mixed with the indigenous peoples, and their descendants felt a commitment to the land and to the civilization they were creating (see Coutinho 105). Part of the incipient nationalism was an awareness of prose as a literary genre (the epic and the lyric continued to be the most popular literary forms), although it should also be noted that fiction per se was not widely practiced, with the result that the novel, as a cultivated literary genre, was, "for all intents and purposes, nonexistent in the Brazil of that time" (Hulet 1: 78).

While narrative fiction as a distinct genre was rare in Brazil in the 1700s, the "representative example," according to Coutinho (98) and others, is Nuno Márques Pereira's prototypically baroque *Compêndio narrativo do peregrino da América* (*Narrative Compendium of the American Pilgrim*), which appeared in 1728.[4] Sometimes touted as Brazil's first novel, or its first novelistic narrative, the *American Pilgrim* is basically a fictionalized travelogue. Popular in both Portugal and Brazil during the colonial period (the book went through at least five editions), this moralistic, occasionally allegorical text recounts a journey from São Paulo, in the south, to Bahia, in the northeast. What is interesting now about the *American Pilgrim* is that the author, who evidently strove to inculcate virtue in the reader and to fulminate against what he took to be licentious behavior, found time to describe the natural beauty around him. Thus, in an early harbinger of Romanticism, he lauded the lush Brazilian landscape and the wildlife that inhabited it. The social sphere, too, warranted his attention: he condemned many of the artistic and recreational activities of the time, such as satirical and amatory poetry, comedies, certain dances, guitar playing, and "immoral" music. Loosely structured but blessed (its tendentious moralizing aside) with a clear and fluent style, the *American Pilgrim*, widely read in both Portugal and Brazil, retains its status as "the first imaginative prose work by a [Brazilian] native to be put into print" (José Veríssimo, qtd. in Putnam, *Marvelous Journey* 76).

A work with a greater claim to being Brazil's first novel or, at least, its most likely forerunner, is the sometimes ponderous and didactic *As aventuras de Diófanes* (the Adventures of Diófanes), by Teresa Margarida da Silva e Orta.[5] Although born in Brazil around 1712, Silva e Orta moved to Portugal when she was five and never returned to the land of her birth. She is nevertheless regarded by many critics as a Brazilian writer—indeed, as its first novelist. As noted in chapter 2, the work was influenced by Fénelon's *Les aventures de Télémaque*, although, according to Haberly, it is "modeled on Greek narrative" ("Colonial Brazilian Narrative" 61). Reflecting the liberal economic and political views of the French author, *As aventuras de Diófanes* (which was published in Lisbon in 1752 and enjoyed at least three subsequent editions) is notable for the sociopolitical ideas it advances, particularly those on the status of women. Like Fénelon, Silva e Orta (anticipating a basic tenet of Romanticism) believed that city life corrupts and that country life is restorative, that monarchs rule by divine right (but abuses of power must be checked), that society divides naturally into classes, and that the common people should be educated (Versiani 18). In contrast to Fénelon, however, Silva e Orta (who, for Versiani, may have been not only Brazil's but the New World's first novelist) opposed slavery, but she was less emphatic about the need for peace (18). While Silva e Orta was ambivalent about "the typically feminine conflict between the desire for freedom and the moral obligation of submission," she understood, as her female characters demonstrate, that "a woman's position in society was not equal to a man's" and that "a woman cannot live freely while she plays the feminine role" (Versiani 26, 25).

THE NINETEENTH CENTURY

The Beginnings of Fiction

Relatively tardy in its cultivation as a genre in Brazil, fiction came into its own in the 1830s; and although later in the century it emerged as the most powerful and inventive of Brazil's literary forms, initially it was neither very original nor very robust. After about 1850, however, the situation changed dramatically, for now "Brazilian fiction was unequaled in the rest of Latin America in terms of production and quality" (González Echevarría, *Oxford Book* 15). Yet even in its heyday, Brazilian literature, like culture, politics, and progress, remained a function of a tiny elite, perhaps two to three percent of the population. Because the remainder of Brazil's people—primarily poor, uneducated peasants, often the target of racial bigotry—were effectively isolated from the forward-looking aspects of their society, Brazil had difficulty developing, as a nation and as a culture, in the European mode. To be sure, some scholars have said that Brazilian literature evolved in ways "roughly parallel" to those of French literature, but Haberly, for one, finds this position basically untenable. Arguing that "the greatest Brazilian novelists of the period—José de Alencar, Joaquim Maria Machado de Assis, and Aluísio de Azevedo—do not fit neatly into any of the recognized European schools of fiction," he maintains that Brazilian fiction followed a unique line of development, one that was affected by European trends but, in fundamental ways, "followed its own path, with its own rules, and internal traditions and influences," in which "the needs and expectations of national leaders were at least as important as foreign models" ("Brazilian Novel" 137–38).

In the early decades of the nineteenth century, poetry still reigned supreme, as did the conventions and standards of the neoclassical Minas school; although prizing decorum and imitation, its adherents had still managed to produce first-rate verse. Another likely deterrent to the writing of fiction in the early 1800s was the fact that many French, English, and American novels were being translated into Portuguese and sold to the reading public, whose taste for fiction was thus slaked. That the novels of James Fenimore Cooper, for example, were available in Portuguese after 1837 (Daniel 128) complicated the already tangled thematic relation between his work and that of José de Alencar—who, as discussed in chapter 2, emerged later in the century as a central figure of the Indianist movement and of Brazilian letters generally. At the same time, the development of Brazilian fiction during this period was perhaps both helped and hindered by the popularity of the *fol-hetim*, or "serial," a hybrid form with a penchant for the sentimental and the sensationalistic and a tendency to blur the distinction between journalism (also in its infancy) and creative writing. At least one critic, David Salles, feels that the *folhetim* was geared to women readers (in Daniel 128).[6] Since its population base remained concentrated along the ample Atlantic coastline, Brazil "was much more receptive [to] and active in the commerce of ideas with the rest of the world" than Spanish America. González Echevarría acknowledges, though, that "Brazilian literature blossomed in the nineteenth century, with the publication of many *folhetins*, in which translations of the best European writers appeared." A major work that was first serialized was Manuel Antonio de Almeida's *As memórias de um sargento de milícias* (*Oxford Book* 15).

In summing up the evolution of Brazilian fiction in roughly the first half of the nineteenth century, we can identify three key events:

1. The sentimental novel was established. It was a genre that, in the hands of Joaquim Manuel de Macedo, its most skilled practitioner, tended toward the picaresque and featured the "contemporary Brazilian scene" in ways reminiscent of the comic theater of Martins Pena, who was instrumental in the creation of a national theater in Brazil (Daniel 133).

2. Nísea Floresta, a writer best known for her nonfiction treatise *Conselhos à minha filha* (1845; *Advice to My Daughter*) and for her "positivistic and abolitionist essay," published two didactic novels in Rio de Janeiro that dealt with the place of women in Brazilian society. Dionísia Gonçalves (Nísea Floresta was a pseudonym) had translated Mary Wollstonecraft's *A Vindication of the Rights of Woman* (first published in 1792) and arranged for its publication in 1832 (Daniel 135).

3. Almeida's *Memoirs of a Militia Sergeant* appeared in 1854–55, as a book. Although the reading public initially received it "with general apathy because of its break with popular romantic conventions," the work has become prized for its "earthiness" and "rollicking good humor," for "its documentary value as a mirror of urban life in Rio de Janeiro" during the Regency period, and for its "colorful gallery" of "Balzacian" social types (Daniel, "Brazilian Fiction," 135–36). Also reminiscent of Pena's social comedies, *Memoirs* offered an alternative to the popular but stifling tradition of the sentimental novel and, technically and thematically, paved the way for the work of Alencar and Machado.

The third text (after *Compêndio narrativo* and *As aventuras de Diófanes*) often advanced as Brazil's first novel is Antônio Gonçalves Teixeira e Sousa's *O filho do pescador* (*The Fisherman's Son*). Published in Rio de Janeiro in 1843, this treacly narrative is less moralistic and didactic than its rivals but, weighted down by its vapid characters and its tedious prose style, it never rises to the heights of an engaging novel. Yet for all Teixeira e Sousa's many weaknesses, his works bring the genre in Brazil almost to fruition, for, as Samuel Putnam puts it, the novel "was in the air, just as the epic had been at the beginning of the seventeenth century" (*Marvelous Journey* 139). Although a distinctly national literature really began with the poetry of such early Romantics as Antônio Gonçalves Dias—whose talent and mixed-race ancestry have led Massaud Moisés to regard him as the first authentically Brazilian poet in both sensibility and thematic concerns (122)—narrative from the 1850s on would steadily grow until becoming, by century's end, the genre in which the most original work was being done. We can conclude, then, that in the 1840s fiction assumed an enhanced respectability and that the publication of Macedo's *A moreninha* (1844; *The Little Brunette*) would herald the birth of the Brazilian novel proper.

In addition to the novel, another form of narrative was emerging in Brazil at this period. As befits its place in a mixed culture, the short story, according to K. David Jackson, developed from the tales and legends of the nation's indigenous and African heritages, from its folkloric traditions, and from its European heritage, although the third source is surely the most important one. Gaining recognition as a consciously practiced literary form in the nineteenth century, "the written Brazilian short story," one scholar feels, begins with the publication in 1841 of the short narrative "As duas órfãs" ("The Two Orphans"), by Joaquim Norberto de Sousa e Silva. Other critics believe that this honor should go to the "romantic tales of the grotesque and macabre by Álvarez de Azevedo," whose collection *Noite na taverna* (*Night in a Tavern*) employs "multiple narrators in the tradition of the *Decameron*" and, with Poe and Maupassant frequently mentioned as influences, "represents an artistic point of departure for the short story in Brazil." Regardless of the date of its formal origins, the modern Brazilian short story achieved excellence, for the first time, between 1882 and 1906, in "the formal perfection of Machado de Assis" (K. Jackson, "Short Story" 207–08). At the beginning of the twenty-first century, it has become one of Brazilian literature's strongest and most widely practiced genres.

A Look Northward

Before examining Macedo, the writer most critics now consider to be Brazil's first authentic novelist, we should consider the rise of the novel in the United States. In Brazil and the United States, the genre had long been regarded with skepticism and disfavor—if not outright condemnation—and for reasons not altogether dissimilar. In both countries, for example, the novel was considered an inferior, even pernicious form that, in contrast to a more ennobling genre like poetry, tended to exert a corrupting influence in society. Indeed, the novel was officially banned in colonial Latin America; in the 1700s in United States, where the novel met with more cultural resistance than in England, fiction was similarly discriminated against. "Although the novel encountered less public and ecclesiastical opposition after the [Revolutionary] war than earlier in the century, few men of substance believed it worthy of serious consideration as an art form." Others feared that there was little for the American novelist to write about—that America lacked suitably interesting or compelling subjects (Foerster, Grabo, Nye, Carlisle, and Falk 184–85). It was more prudent, many felt, to continue to imitate the themes and forms of established English writers, like Richardson, Sterne, and Scott, than to attempt a uniquely American novel, whatever that might be. Finally, post-Revolutionary America still had a deeply pragmatic approach to literature, a suspicion of any text that did not directly address the nature of the perceived world and did not seek to improve readers' lives.

Following their British models, American novels tended to fall into four categories (see Foerster, Grabo, Nye, Carlisle, and Falk 185): the novel of morality and sentiment; the Gothic novel (represented by Charles Brockden Brown, whom Foerster and his colleagues call "the most gifted novelist of the pre-Cooper years"); the satiric, or picaresque, novel; and the historical romance (a genre dominated by Scott, who was highly influential in nineteenth-century Brazil and in the United States). The work generally accorded the honor of being the first American novel, William Hill Brown's *The Power of Sympathy*, appeared in 1789; it was followed by Susanna Rowson's hugely popular *Charlotte Temple* (1790), which went into nearly two hundred editions. As we have seen, the sentimental and moralistic novel was widely practiced in Brazil and the United States, as was the historical romance, a genre that in both countries would play an important role in the cultivation of a national identity. The satirical novel, as we shall see, provides an especially interesting case: the greatest Latin American novelist and short story writer of the nineteenth century, Brazil's Machado, made imaginative use of Sterne's *Tristram Shandy* in creating a radically new kind of narrative, one that, built on irony and a metafictive self-consciousness, parodied its European forebears and satirized its Brazilian setting. What Machado, in *The Posthumous Memoirs of Brás Cubas*, does with Sterne is thus quite different from Sterne's legacy in the United States, where he is viewed chiefly as a progenitor of the sentimental or moralistic novel.

Joaquim Manuel de Macedo

The writer who, with *The Little Brunette* (1844), "launched the vogue of the novel in Brazil" was also "one of the prime movers of Brazilian letters throughout the Romantic period" (Hulet 1: 244). Instrumental in the development of the Brazilian theater and short story as well as poetry and the novel (he wrote about twenty novels), Macedo, a graduate of Rio's medical school, also established literary theory and criticism as viable activities in Brazil. Immensely important to the development of Brazilian literature for a number of reasons, he is most remembered today for *The Little Brunette*, a work that can boast of having gone through more editions than any other Brazilian novel. A prototype of the bourgeois sentimental novel, *The Little Brunette* offers an idealized, if "banal" and "touchingly naive," vision of middle-class society and its customs (Putnam, *Marvelous Journey* 137). Although Macedo, in the run of his career, depicted urban life as well as bourgeois manners, he shows his talent as a novelist in *The Little Brunette* in three crucial areas: he portrays some recognizably Brazilian social types (the little brunette herself, of course, but also the young swains who court her and the *moleque*, or rascally slave boy); he is adept at writing "fairly natural" and at times witty conversation among the characters; and, perhaps most surprising, he offers, against "the background of a patriarchal society," "a subtle appeal for a more equal education for women than was generally available at the time" (Daniel 134).[7] More engagingly written than Brown's wooden and overwrought *The Power of Sympathy* and featuring believable characterizations, lively dialogue, and a credible plot structure, *The Little Brunette*, for all its weaknesses, was instrumental in establishing the novel in Brazil.

Manuel Antônio de Almeida

A much more interesting—and successful—novel is Manuel Antônio de Almeida's *As memórias de um sargento de milícias* (*The Memoirs of a Militia Sergeant*), a lively, often humorous tale set in Rio early in the nineteenth century (app. C). Published serially (and anonymously) in the newspaper *Correio Mercantil* in 1852–53, it appeared in two volumes in 1854–55. Something of an anachronism, *The Memoirs of a Militia Sergeant* is a vividly realistic work written in the middle of Brazil's Romantic period. As Dorothy Loos has argued, its cool reception by the reading public may have been the result of this historical mismatch (25). Indeed, the "gentle social satire" that underscores the work was undoubtedly "antithetic to the sweet, sentimental life style extolling virtue, family and nation that was . . . recognized as the standard Romantic novelistic stance" (Hulet 1: 327). Arising from "two very different European prose traditions"—the "semi-picaresque, satirical English novels of the eighteenth century, like those of Fielding and Smollett, which Almeida . . . read in French translations" and "the early romantic *costumbrismo* of Spain and Portugal" (Haberly "Brazilian Novel" 140–41)—the Brazilian text (which finds its Spanish American equivalent in Fernández de Lizardi's *El periquillo sarniento* [1816; *The Itching Parrot*], generally regarded as Spanish America's first novel) presents an engaging panorama of *carioca* culture in the final years of Portuguese rule.[8] *Memoirs* describes in detail the customs and attitudes of the recently arrived Portuguese immigrants, the city's slums and shantytowns, its thriving black culture, its political intrigues and power structures, and the rural poor who come to the city in search of better lives. Indeed, in contrast to the two most important Brazilian novelists of the time, José de Alencar and Machado de Assis (who chronicled the lives of the middle and upper classes), Almeida deals, in his only novel, almost entirely with the lower classes. Beyond this, a striking feature of *The Memoirs of a Militia Sergeant* is its unexpected tone, the subtle vein of "near-Dickensian nostalgia" that it projects (Monegal, *Borzoi Anthology* 1: 293). For Putnam, in *Marvelous Journey*, Almeida is a "Balzacian realist" (149) who looks backward to a city that he had not personally experienced, a city that was rougher and freer than the Rio he knew and to which the Second Empire would affix an aura of respectability that he must have found meretricious (Monegal 294).

The primary source of the distinctive tone is the novel's "sarcastic, irreverent, and highly intrusive narrator," a sophisticated and knowledgeable observer whose unsentimental voice "is perhaps Almeida's most significant contribution to prose fiction in nineteenth-century Brazil" and whose knavish-cum-wily commentary on the action "controls his readers' reactions to the text, carefully explaining how they are to react to individual twists and turns in the plot and to the characters he describes and satirizes." As Haberly points out, echoes of this voice can be heard in Alencar's urban novels and in Machado's best work ("Brazilian Novel" 141). We could also argue that a keen awareness of and experimentations with the nature and function of the narrative voice constitute defining aspects of Brazilian fiction, from Macedo through Alencar, Aluíso Azevedo, and Machado and into the twentieth century, including such pivotal figures as Euclides da Cunha, Mário de Andrade, Oswald de Andrade, Patrícia Galvão, Graciliano Ramos, Clarice Lispector, Guimarães Rosa, Marilene Felinto, and Nélida Piñon. The long-standing concern with how a story gets told; with the relations among the narrator, the author, the text, and the reader; and with both language as a problem of epistemology and the theoretical underpinnings of realism as they apply to narrative fiction may help explain both why Brazilian fiction in the nineteenth century was able to improve so much in such a short amount of time and why it continues to be such a strong and vital genre.

José de Alencar

Although Almeida is a decisive figure in the development of the Brazilian novel scholars have long viewed José de Alencar as the creator both of a distinctly Brazilian novel and of a comprehensive and cohesive national literature. The author of nearly twenty novels, Alencar sought (as he discusses in the preface to his 1872 novel *Sonhos d'ouro* [*Golden Dreams*]) to tell the story of Brazil from its colonial beginnings to his own time. Given the extent and variety of his work, he essentially succeeded in doing so. Alencar was certainly aware of Cooper's works though he rejected, in *How and Why I Am a Novelist* (1873), the idea that the North American writer had influenced him, contending, in fact, that Cooper's best works were about the sea, not about Indians.

Throughout Latin America, in any event, Cooper was well known and respected as a writer of imagination and daring. Indeed, it has been argued that his *Leatherstocking* series

> was read most attentively and fruitfully not in Europe but in other parts of the Americas, where a collection of Spanish colonies and the single Portuguese one were pupating into nations and, like the United States, creating national literatures. They, too, looking for autochthonous subjects, found the opulent scenery and the original inhabitants sanctioned by the European discourse of the exotic and began to fashion from them a way of representing a non-European identity. Cooper showed that it could be done and was admired for it. (Wasserman, *Exotic Nations* 186).

Alencar's many novels, several of which can rightly be considered the "American offspring" of Montaigne, Rousseau, Chateaubriand, and Bernardin de Saint-Pierre (188), may be categorized into four groups: his early Indianist texts, his historical romances, his regionalist novels (regionalism was in both Brazil and the United States a significant force), and his urban novels (including what some scholars classify as his studies of women and their place in society).

Two novels exemplify his work in the Indianist vein: *O Guarani* (1857; *The Guarani*) and *Iracema* (1865). Recalling both Cooper and Chateaubriand, the texts depict the Brazilian Indian, male (in the earlier work) and female (in *Iracema*), as the epitome of the noble savage. Although the thought titillated him (as in *The Last of the Mohicans*), Cooper could not abide the idea of sex between a white woman and an Indian; Alencar, in contrast, makes this very theme the centerpiece of both works. Moreover, he takes up the issue of racial assimilation, so crucial to Brazilian culture generally, not merely from the perspective of race (as Cooper does, in his timorous way) but of gender and power as well (see Fitz, *Rediscovering* 83–92). Thus, in *The Guarani*, Peri, the quintessential noble savage, saves the beautiful Cecília, the daughter of the Portuguese-European colonizer, from drowning. In the novel's final, climactic scene, the two seem poised to consummate their "natural state" of "marriage."[9] Eight years later, however, in *Iracema* (app. C), Alencar reverses the conventional gender and power roles by having a beautiful Indian princess as the protagonist. The crucial difference in this work is that interracial sex is achieved; pregnant by Martim, the Portuguese soldier, Iracema bears a child, Moacir, whose mixed-race heritage represents the future of Brazil and its people. For Brazilians, *The Guarani* and *Iracema* (an anagram for America) are thus of mythic importance, for they portray a truly new world, in which the union of white and Indian implies, as Renata Wasserman believes, "not only a relaxation of [Europeanized] social constrainsts but also a weakening of all boundaries of being." In the idealized vision of an arch-Romantic, "the lines between masculine and feminine become blurred" and men have become feminized. "It is as if, with this blurring of differences, Alencar were toying with the creation of a true alternative to European culture, one that would fulfill the promise of renewal but would also demand a restatement of established distinctions between nature and culture, male and female" (*Exotic Nations* 210, 211). Referring to *Iracema*, "Alencar's masterpiece and the most popular of all his novels," Haberly believes that the author "goes even further in establishing the Brazilian creation-myth," for this seminal text's "intensely allegorical plot and rhapsodic language" set it "entirely apart from other nineteenth-century novels of Europe or America" ("Brazilian Novel" 143). From this perspective, the difference between Cooper, whose work upholds the attitudes of his race, gender, and class, and Alencar, whose texts are much less conventional, is clear. Although for both writers the Indian is pivotal, for Alencar the issue of the indigenous people is inseparable from the larger notion of miscegenation, a theme that speaks directly to what is, by Alencar's time, a defining if still inchoate feature of national identity. For Cooper, whose fear of racial mixing limited his vision, the Indian is a largely symbolic figure, essentially chaste, hypothetical, and circumscribed by the racial and sexual mores of the writer's time and place.

Perhaps the most successful of Alencar's urban novels is *Senhora* (1875; app. C). Along with the other novels in this group, it continues the examination of the situation of women in mid-nineteenth-century Brazil. The story of Aurélia, a beautiful, strong-willed young woman who, bucking social convention, determines to take control of her life, both sexually and financially, *Senhora* critiques the institution of marriage (particularly the dowry and the marriage of convenience) in the bourgeois culture of Brazil's Second Empire (1840–89). Deeply attracted to a man she feels has wronged her—by conducting himself in a way unworthy of her love—Aurélia, the *senhora* of the title, "chooses an unexpected revenge: to marry him but to keep total control of her bed and purse. A duel between husband and wife ensues, elegantly controlled but savage" (Monegal, *Borzoi Anthology* 1: 286). *Senhora*, then—like Gertrudis Gómez de Avellaneda's *Sab*, *The Blithedale Romance*, and *The Portrait of a Lady*—examines the legal, financial, and psychological ramifications of marriage as it affects women and their personal and public identities. Like Nathaniel Hawthorne's Zenobia, Aurélia is beautiful, intelligent, and socially well connected. Both Hawthorne and Alencar, moreover, arrange for an "irreconcilable dichotomy between reason and feelings to transform" their characters "into marbleized, statue-like forms." Even so, notes Catarina Edinger, "there is a cultural difference in the way the novels end: Alencar granted his heroine a happy ending whereas Hawthorne murdered his" (Introduction xiii; see also Edinger, "Hawthorne"). Reminiscent of Balzac (whom he greatly esteemed) and George Sand, as well as of Henry James and Hawthorne, Alencar, in *Senhora*, and *Lucíola*, examines urgent social problems (Haberly, "Brazilian Novel" 144).[10] In texts like *The Guarani* and *Iracema* he illuminates Brazil's slow, painful struggle to achieve a national identity.[11] In doing so, he paved the way for writers like Aluísio

Azevedo, Raul Pompéia, and Machado de Assis, who by the late 1800s would achieve world-class status.

Aluísio Azevedo

Hailed as the greatest of Brazil's naturalist writers, Azevedo gained notoriety in 1881 with the publication of *O mulato* (*The Mulatto*), an artistically un-even work that nevertheless offers a powerful expose of miscegenation, race relations, and class structure in nineteenth-century Brazil. By 1890, when *O cortiço* (*A Brazilian Tenement*) appeared, Azevedo had become a novelist of skill and insight (see app. C for both novels; *O cortiço* was later translated as *The Slum*). Notable for his psychologically and socially probing characteriza-tions, Azevedo—following the precepts of Émile Zola but breaking new ground as well—also became a determinist, who regarded the racial and sociopolitical environment of Brazil as one of his most important and influ-ential characters, one replete with its own mores, ideology, and conflicts. In addition to the cumulative emphasis reminiscent of Balzac and the Zolaesque portrayals of the ugly, the brutal, and the shocking (going further than Zola, Azevedo explored lesbianism, for example, as a function of both female desire and female empowerment), his work contains "idyllic moments, idealized descriptions, interventions of Nature, melodrama, plays of light and shadow," and "Poesque" moments of suspense, as well as "extraordinary insights into everyday life, social relations and class conflicts" (Hulet 2: 5).

Of his social significance, in fact, it can be argued that more than any other naturalist writer of his time—including Federico Gamboa of Mexico and Stephen Crane—Azevedo dissects "the complex process of adaptation and transformation of European literary ideology to the realities of the New World." As a result, "the naturalistic novel of Brazil addressed social questions unique to Brazilian society"—questions that were taboo to the Romantic and realist writers who preceded him (Sedycias 52–53). In the Americas, per-haps only Theodore Dreiser was as adroit in analyzing the social milieu of the time. Indeed, a comparative study of the two authors can shed light on their artistry and on the reasons why naturalism was such a productive movement in the New World generally and in Brazil and the United States in particular.

Raul Pompéia, Júlia Lopes de Almeida, and Adolfo Caminha

Although a number of narrativists of this period are worthy of attention, three stand out in the uniqueness of their work and in their significance, tech-nically, formally, and thematically, to the flowering of Brazilian fiction at the end of the nineteenth century: Raul Pompéia, Júlia Lopes de Almeida, and Adolfo Caminha. The narrative for which Pompéia is most famous, *O Ateneu* (1888; *The Atheneum*), is based on the author's student days at a boarding school in Rio de Janeiro. Taken, at the time of its publication, to be yet another example of naturalism, *O Ateneu* underwent something of a reconsideration. Concluding that its most salient features made it more of an impressionistic text, many critics emphasized the youthful narrator's tormented view of himself, his comrades, and his surroundings. These readers have focused on the setting's metaphoric overtones, and so for them the novel's final scenes, where the school burns down, suggest the improvements in Brazilian life that Pompéia believes the establishment of the Republic would bring.

For Haberly, the "best of the urban novelists who began publishing after about 1890" and the "only important female novelist between the eighteenth century and the publication of Raquel de Queiroz's *O quinze* [*The Year 1915*] in 1930," Júlia Lopes de Almeida can take credit for "a series of carefully drawn family chronicles" that, beginning with *A Família Medeiros* (1892; *The Medeiros Family*), "come closer than any other Brazilian texts to the standard model of European Realism" ("Brazilian Novel" 152). Widely regarded as "the first woman to achieve a national reputation as a major writer in Brazil" and praised by the literary historian José Veríssimo as a worthy successor to Machado de Assis (Sadlier 27), Lopes de Alemida has also been called "the Brazilian George Sand" (K. Jackson, "Short Story" 230).

Carefully written and maintaining the objectivity central to realism, the novels of the fin de siècle period depict a Brazilian social scene in the process of change. Interestingly enough, they do not focus, in any essential or ideological way, on the lives of Brazilian women of the period.

Probably the most unexpected novel of the period is Adolfo Caminha's fairly explicit story of homosexual love, *Bom-Crioulo* (1895; *The Black Man and the Cabin Boy*), a novel that still ranks as one of the most original achievements of the late-nineteenth- and early-twentieth-century period. Surprisingly similar to Alencar's *Iracema* in eschewing realism and, instead, reaching for the symbolic, mythic, and a sociopolitical significance of Brazilian society, *The Black Man and the Cabin Boy* nevertheless differs sharply from Alencar's forward-looking creation myth by offering a highly charged view of Brazil's metaphoric destruction. Because the love between Aleixo, the callow white boy, and Amaro, the black sailor (a runaway slave), can survive "only in the isolation of the ship," Caminha effectively "allegorizes Brazil—white Brazil—as pure and helpless, caught between the degradation of the nation's non-white population and the amoral decadence of European immigrants; like Aleixo, white Brazil will inevitably be destroyed in the process" (Haberly "Brazilian Novel" 151).

Joaquim Maria Machado de Assis

The story of Machado de Assis, Brazil's greatest writer, is bound up with the end of Romanticism and the reception of realism and naturalism, as well as with Machado's extraordinarily imaginative response to a variety of foreign influences (see app. C for a number of his works in translation). The many allusions that Machado makes to foreign artists, writers, and thinkers (including an allusion, in chapter 80 of *Dom Casmurro*, to Benjamin Franklin) internationalize his texts in ways that far exceed anything in the Americas up to his time. Long regarded as a Romantic (his pre-1880 work) who became an innovative, often iconoclastic realist (his post-1880 work [see Gledson, *Deceptive Realism*]), Machado transcended the literary conventions of his day to create a fundamentally antirealistic narrative—one that achieved for Brazil, with the appearance of *The Posthumous Memoirs of Brás Cubas* in 1880–81, the kind of stunning breakthrough achieved in Spanish America by Borges's *Ficciones* in the 1930s and by Faulkner in the United States. Although there is some justification for terming Machado a realist, such a definition undervalues his originality. It relegates him to being yet another New World imitator (albeit an innovative one) of yet another European artistic mode. A better, more productive approach, I believe, is to look more at his departures from the realistic tradition, a critical tactic that allows us to appreciate more fully his many technical innovations and strikingly different worldview.

Initially continuing the tradition of the urban novel as established by his predecessors Macedo, Alencar, and Manuel Antônio de Almeida, Machado would move, between 1878—and the publication of *Iaiá Garcia* (*Yaya Garcia*), the least romantic of his four early novels—and 1880, to a darker, more complex vision of society, a vision that would infuse his most brilliant novels and short stories. The result is that, as with Mark Twain and Faulkner, we are compelled to speak of Machado as an immensely complicated genius. Relying on parody, irony, and a diverse panorama of self-conscious, unreliable narrator-protagonists, his fictions give us glimpses of nineteenth-century Rio de Janeiro society. Often speculating on the nature of literary creation and reception (that is, on the act of reading), Machado's post-1880 texts thus seek to capture not the physical reality of his time and place but, again recalling Borges and Faulkner, the more complex notion of an aesthetic reality, one only tangentially connected to the physical world. "It is this perception of the fictive world as an independent reality," as Haberly observes, "which most sharply differentiates Machado from his predecessors and contemporaries," for he "understood that the novelist's task . . . was not to use fiction to describe reality, but to produce fictions within the context of a larger fiction" ("Brazilian Novel" 155–56). Flaunting their status as verbal artifices, his narratives function as their own realities. Machado's great contribution to New World narrative was to realize, perhaps more clearly even than James, that in successful fiction the symbols that give it form and meaning inevitably relate more to one another than to the physical reality that surrounds them. For Machado, the text itself (and, through it, the entwined processes of composition, narration, and reading) must emerge as the narrative's true subject, its true protagonist. Like Borges and Faulkner, Machado understood that a successful novel or short story is a self-contained semiotic system, an interrelated structure of text that, with the reader's participation, creates its own reality and its own significance. To the extent that extratextual meaning can be extrapolated from a text, it is the reader's act of interpretation, cued by a carefully integrated text, that does so. In terms of Western narrative, then, we can see that even early in his career Machado was experimenting not with the "disappearance" of the narrator, as Flaubert, James, and the adepts of the realist-naturalist schools were doing (Nunes 21), but with the new roles a narrator, text, and reader might play in relation to one another.

James and Machado are revered for moving the novel away from a reliance on social, cultural, and political events, on events occurring outside the individual, and toward the inner drama of consciousness, the struggle of the mind to comprehend and deal with its motivations and their consequences. Thus, both James and Machado examine the social and psychological complexity of moral issues and create characters who are capable of understanding the process by which consciousness affects human behavior. While James tended to weave together the highly subjective, private ruminations of an individual character with the objective, socially oriented ideologies and mores of a group, Machado after 1880 emphasized the role of language in the development of our consciousness, our outlook, and our discourse—in short, in the development of our identity and our sense of being (Fitz, "Metafiction"). This poststructural awareness of language not so much as a stylistic device (not even one purporting to show the ebb and flow of a refined consciousness, as in James's case) as the psycholinguistic force that—as Machado shows us in the novels *The Posthumous Memoirs of Brás Cubas, Quincas Borba,*

Dom Casmurro, *Esau and Jacob*, and *Counselor Ayres' Memorial* and in the short stories "Midnight Mass," "The Holiday," and "Final Request"—shapes our sense of who we are is perhaps what most distinguishes the post-1880 Machado from the post-1880 James.

At the same time, we should remember that *The Posthumous Memoirs of Brás Cubas* and *Dom Casmurro* (the plot of which offers a variation on Shakespeare's *Othello*), deal with one of the nineteenth century's—and the bourgeois novel's—defining themes, adultery.[12] Yet by emphasizing the craft of fiction itself rather than the story that seems at first glance to get told (a key issue in *Dom Casmurro*), both James and Machado changed the course of the novel, in Brazil and the United States. After James and Machado, fiction writing in the New World established itself as a valid literary project that helped determine the various forms narrative would take in the next century (see Fitz, *Rediscovering* 95–120).

Henry James is not the only American author with whom Machado can be compared. As suggested in chapter 2, Twain represents another link to the Brazilian writer. Unlike the connection between James and Machado, the one between Twain and Machado involves issues not so much of narrative technique as of theme, tone, and authorial attitude. The two writers are regarded, in their later works, as having become deeply disillusioned, even cynical. For Machado, the change is evident in his post-1880 work; for Twain, the shift is often dated from 1884, the year before the *Adventures of Huckleberry Finn* appeared (Spiller 119). In works as diverse as *A Connecticut Yankee in King Arthur's Court* (1889), *Pudd'nhead Wilson* (1894), and *The Mysterious Stranger* (published in 1916, six years after his death) and in such stories as "The Man That Corrupted Hadleyburg," Twain presents, beneath the comical veneer, a view of life that, as in Machado's later works, is highly skeptical of human nature and of our ability to resist violence, greed, and bigotry and is sorely distressed by our seemingly endless capacity for mendacity, hypocrisy, and self-delusion. Concerned more and more with cultural invasion and with the disturbing impact of the outsider's presence, Twain has been called "the first of Western writers to be aware of the nihilism latent in the crossing of cultural borders" (Fisher 641). This argument, particularly with regard to the question of nihilism, has been frequently raised in terms of Machado as well.

One of Machado's most accomplished stories from this period, "The Psychiatrist" (1881–82), benefits from a comparative reading with "The Man That Corrupted Hadleyburg."[13] Both texts explore what happens when a

fairly closed community must deal with a seductive and potentially transforming outside force.[14] In the case of Hadleyburg, which is not so much observed as exposed and distorted by its visitor (Fisher 641–42), the outside
force is the illusory promise of wealth and power. In Machado's provincial
town, Itaguai, which is "invaded" by the seductive but spurious claims of
science, the threat is the unquestioning and ultimately dehumanizing belief
in scientific rationalism as a panacea for society's ills. The basis of this late-
nineteenth-century disenchantment would seem to be, for both writers, their
reactions to the spate of deterministic pseudo-scientific theories (some racial
in nature) that were being promulgated in Europe and the Americas and gen-
erating a Darwinian vision of humans as devoid of free will and lost in what
Machado and Twain viewed as a mechanistic universe. Machado ridiculed
both positivism and its literary analog, naturalism, while Twain (especially in
What Is Man? and *The Mysterious Stranger*) was, as we have seen, appalled by
humanity's hypocrisy, avarice, and intolerance. The difference between the
despairing late Twain and the sardonic late Machado is, finally, one of degree.
The Brazilian writer avoided the debilitating nihilism and "paranoid pessimism that darkened Twain's final years" (Fisher 642). For Twain, the human
creature was little more than a function of self-interest, guilt, sham, violence,
and conformity. Machado, in *Esau and Jacob* (1904) and *Counselor Ayres'
Memorial* (1908), by contrast, was still laboring, with considerable skepticism, to portray the destructiveness of time, selfishness, and egoism, or self-
love (in this, he is close to Twain's critique of the cult of personal and cultural
self-interest), while continuing to explore the nature and potential of "the
narrative process itself" (M. Nunes 59).

A surprising comparison to come out of the authors' late period speaks
to the relation between "advanced" civilizations and those judged to be underdeveloped or backward. The "first of [Twain's] dark works" and "one of
the first parables of colonialization," *A Connecticut Yankee in King Arthur's
Court* can be read as "a slightly disguised version of his many contemporaries
who were carrying what they called the White Man's Burden of colonial education and integration into the modern world system." Machado's allegorical
1890 novel, *Quincas Borba*, which offers a subtle critique of the empire's social, political, and cultural policies and of its slavish devotion to the principles of Western thought, attempts something similar. The difference is that
in the Twain novel, the United States penetrates a "historically backward,
feudal society" in order to "modernize" it (the result of the modernization is

its destruction), whereas in the Machado novel, the United States, and the Western tradition generally, seeks to penetrate, control, and exploit a vulnerable and ill-prepared Brazil. Making a point that could easily be applied to Machado's text, Philip Fisher says that "Twain's book, like his great denunciations of the exploitation of the Congo in the early 1900s, was a thoughtful account of that most pressing of late nineteenth-century travel forms: the final mad scramble of the European powers to grab up and modernize whatever scraps were left of the underdeveloped world."

With *A Connecticut Yankee* and *Quincas Borba*, Twain and Machado have composed two parables of "cultural arrogance and its self-destructive naïveté" that can take their places, in the literature of the period, "alongside Conrad's *Heart of Darkness* with its idealist turned savage, Kurtz" (Fisher 643). Also, in contrast to Machado's unflinching commitment to the craft of the novel in his post-1880 works, Twain moved away from fiction after 1890, instead writing polemical pieces, satires, personal reminiscences, and autobiography. Finally, Machado and Twain lived during a time of great social change, to which Machado's *Quincas Borba* presents vivid reactions. While their responses as writers and intellectuals may in the end have been different, there can be no doubt as to the impact their art and their vision had on the development of narrative in the New World.

In summing up the importance of the nineteenth century to Brazil, Claude Hulet has written:

> The organization of Brazil as a nation took place during the last twenty years of the nineteenth century. It was a period of tremendous renovation, modification and reform. The Republic was formed, the slaves were freed, the laws were recodified, cities were modernized, the nation's frontiers were established, and the educational system was reorganized. Moreover, the writer, who had only gained a tentative acceptance in Romanticism, became a highly regarded intellectual force, even an integral part of society. (2: 3)

Similarly, John Gledson, in assessing the quality of nineteenth-century Brazilian literature, describes it as "without doubt the richest" in Latin America (Introduction, in Schwarz ix). As the 1800s drew to a close, Brazil, while still handicapped by a number of outmoded institutions and "misplaced ideas" and challenged by a persistent strain of intellectual and artistic authoritarianism (Reis), was poised, with Machado leading the way, to enter the international community of nations.

THE TWENTIETH CENTURY

In the early 1900s, Brazil and the United States were acutely aware of residing on the periphery of civilization. Both nations struggled to throw off their sense of cultural inferiority and to establish themselves as modern states. Moreover, in both Brazil and the United States, waves of immigrants and ideas from abroad would transform their societies, diversifying them in ways hitherto unimaginable. In this context we should keep in mind that before 1900 important European movements like Romanticism, realism, naturalism, and symbolism often took a decade or more to arrive in the New World. From about 1900 on, however, there would be no significant time lag between the emergence of cultural innovations in Europe and their appearance in North, Central, and South America. Thus the European avant-garde, in the first three decades of the twentieth century, found itself implanted almost immediately in the Western Hemisphere.

In the realm of social critique, for example, the "English theories of Positivism as propounded by Herbert Spencer gained adherents at the expense of the more orthodox theories of Comte," whose presence in Brazilian intellectual life had long held sway. For many Brazilians, as for many Americans, Spencer represented "the interrelationship of science, industry, and progress, a combination pointing to future glory through societal evolution." Spencer also made a number of observations, including racist statements, that "damned Brazil" (Burns, *History* [3rd ed.] 314, 166). It is in this context that Machado's 1891 novel *Quincas Borba* can be read as a withering critique of both positivism and Darwinian social theory; of the age's unshakable belief in progress; and of the impact racism, sexism, materialism, and the profit motive have on social organization.

Although Spencer's pronouncements on sociological, economic, and biological evolution were typically viewed in Brazil as elements of European positivism, in the United States they were more often interpreted as a justification for social Darwinism. Indeed, beginning in the late nineteenth century, a ruthless corporate capitalism had become the order of the day in the United States. Brazilians—exhibiting an intensified interest in the United States and in world affairs—"stood in awe of the rapid industrial progress of that northern republic, progress they very much hoped to imitate" (Burns, *History* [3rd ed.] 314), Machado's prescient warnings notwithstanding.

Rebellion in the Backlands and Canaan

While at the turn of the century Machado still reigned supreme as a narrativist, two important books by other writers appeared: Euclides da Cunha's work of nonfiction *Os sertões* (1902; *Rebellion in the Backlands*) and Graça Aranha's novel *Canaan* (also 1902; see app. C for both). The Cunha text continues to have a powerful impact on the nation. Aranha's work, a highly political if sometimes clumsily written treatise on Brazil as a dependent society, argues, through the polemics of the main characters, that the only authentic Brazilian is the product of racial mixing. It was this very proposition that, given the prevalent racial theories of such European thinkers as Henry Thomas Buckle, Joseph Arthur de Gobineau, Georges Vacher de Lapouge, and Gustave Le Bon, disturbed Brazilians. "What," Putnam asks, "was the use of striving for *brasilidade* (Brazilianism), when Brazil was so dubious an entity, and people, by the very fact of being a mixed race, were doomed to inferiority?" (*Marvelous Journey* 195). Examining Brazil's growing nationalism and the impact of the country's immigrants, Aranha is sharply critical of his homeland, bitterly denouncing its status as "a colonial regime disguised with the name of a free nation"—one that, feigning independence, is really at the mercy of foreigners (*Canaan* 196).[15] Regarded today primarily as an analytic *roman à thèse* rather than as a successful work of fiction, *Canaan*, its title ironically invoking the biblical image of Brazil as the promised land, nevertheless retains an important place in the development of contemporary Brazilian literature and thought.

Euclides da Cunha's epic masterpiece, *Rebellion in the Backlands*, is a work of more enduring significance that has gained worldwide acclaim. Although Cunha's extraordinary narrative is, on the most obvious level, an examination of the origins of the violent rebellion (in 1897) in Canudos, in northeastern Brazil, led by the religious mystic Antônio Conselheiro, it becomes an ambivalent, even skeptical rumination on the applicability of European thought to a quite different New World reality, largely inimical to the prevailing theories of the day. Cunha's work may have been influenced by Domingo Sarmiento's *Facundo* (1845) in setting up a similar contrast between civilization and barbarism (a dichotomy that also appeared in the discourse surrounding the antebellum United States and its own North-South schism).[16] In any event, *Rebellion in the Backlands* affords its author, schooled in the principles of Comte's positivism, an opportunity both to report on the events at Canudos and to interpret them. Reflecting positivist notions that were being promulgated, in Europe and the Americas, on the supposed degeneration of the races in the New World (a condition stemming, it was widely thought, from racial mixing), Cunha's text is deeply pessimistic about the future of Brazil's culture, which, by his time, was fundamentally the product of miscegenation. Yet Cunha's admiration for the courage and tenacity of the impoverished *sertanejos*, or backlanders, and their ability to adapt to their harsh environment pervades the book; indeed, he had difficulty accepting the pseudo-scientific argument that people of mixed race were destined to regress. At the same time, reflecting the theories of both Comte and Spencer, Cunha was a firm believer in the "great myth of unceasing progress so characteristic of the period . . . and was thus prepared to see the rebels simply as reactionaries" who could be redeemed by a proper education (Monegal, *Borzoi Anthology* 1: 323). As Cunha writes in one of the work's most famous passages:

> It was plain that the Canudos Campaign must have a higher objective than the stupid and inglorious one of merely wiping out a backlands settlement. There was a more serious enemy to be combatted, in a warfare of a slower and more worthy kind. This entire campaign would be a crime, a futile and barbarous one, if we were not to take advantage of the paths opened by the artillery, by following up our cannon with a constant, stubborn, and persistent campaign of education, with the object of drawing these rude and backward fellow-countrymen of ours into the current of our times and our own national life. (408)

Dramatizing the problem of the "two Brazils," the "backward," "barbaric" rural north and the "progressive," "wealthy" urban south, Cunha's text echoes a sentiment (in reverse) being expounded, early in the nineteenth century, about the growing rift between the northern and southern United States. As Porter says, "a tendency [in the United States] to look south and see a strange country is already apparent from the opening decades of the nineteenth century, but it is not until the 1830s that a critical boundary began to develop between an enterprising, vigorous, and civilized North, and a lazy, decadent, and barbaric South" ("Social Discourse" 354). A further parallel exists in the portrayal of the Confederate soldiers and Cunha's description of the captured rebels. Not even Nathaniel Hawthorne, for example, was immune to such attitudes. In an 1862 piece written by him for the *Atlantic Monthly*, he "viewed the imprisoned Southern soldiers he saw in Virginia as 'peasants, and of a very low order; a class of people with whom our Northern rural population has not a single trait in common.'" Hawthorne "had 'seen their like' in other parts of the world, but had not imagined such people 'to exist in this country.' In this instance, the South has become alien, a land of European peasantry" (qtd. in Porter, "Social Discourse" 354).

In a similar vein, Cunha would write of one of the captured *sertanejos*, "Here was a finished bandit, cast up by this backlands conflict, with a formidable legacy of errors resting upon his boyish shoulders. Nine years of life into which had been packed three centuries of barbarism" (408). In another echo of Hawthorne, Cunha declared, of the sense of alienation and estrangement that the victorious federal soldiers were feeling:

> Here was an absolute and radical break between the coastal cities and the clay huts of the interior. . . . They were in a strange country now, with other customs, other scenes, a different kind of people. Another language even, spoken with an original and picturesque drawl. They had, precisely, the feeling of going to war in another land. They felt that they were outside Brazil. (405)

As many critics have noted, however, for all his painstaking analysis and meticulous efforts to explain what happened at Canudos and, more important, why, Cunha failed to recognize the economic basis of the tragedy: the fact that the Brazilian northeast, which like the American South had long been crippled by a feudal sociopolitical structure that was ripe for revolt. This idea is given more play in Graciliano Ramos's *Vidas secas* (1938; *Barren Lives*) and in Mario Vargas Llosa's *La guerra del fin del mundo* (*The War of the End of the World*).

Although *Rebellion in the Backlands* is a unique book, written in a powerful, idiosyncratic style and rich in irony, startling metaphors, and dramatic structuring (part 2 reads more like a novel than like nonfiction), it has a counterpart in the literature of the United States: James Agee's *Let Us Now Praise Famous Men* (1941). Like Cunha, Agee seeks to explain the plight of a disadvantaged, rejected group, "to pry intimately," as he puts it with a self-consciousness that is at once highly political and disconcertingly moral:

> into the lives of an undefended and appallingly damaged group of human beings, an ignorant and helpless rural family, for the purpose of parading the nakedness, disadvantage and humiliation of these lives before another

group of human beings, in the name of science, of "honest journalism" . . . of humanity . . . [and] for money. (7)

While it is more autobiographical and lyrical than Cunha's work, Agee's text, which chronicles the lives of three Alabama tenant farmers caught in the throes of the Great Depression, is similar to the Brazilian's in its attention to detail; in its angry, indignant tone; and in its celebration of obscure, unsavory losers. Like Cunha's backlanders, they were forced to lead miserable lives, even as the rest of society, oblivious to their fate, was obsessed with its pious embrace of material progress. Both Cunha and Agee, then, focus not on the heroes of the dominant culture but on the survivors of its exploitation, its hypocrisy, and its greed—on the tenacity and resilience of a forgotten people.

It might be noted that although miscegenation is central to Cunha's text (as it is to *Canaan* and to Brazilian literature and culture generally), the issue is absent from Agee's work. *Let Us Now Praise Famous Men* casts the racial question as a rigidly enforced system of segregation, which Agee seems to understand as being ultimately destructive of the larger sociopolitical fabric. But in the early years of the twentieth century, the European-derived ideas about racially superior and inferior people were as widely disseminated in the United States as in Brazil. In both countries, many people found, in the theories of Spencer, a basis for sociopolitical organization that "not only glorified science and reason" but provided a scientific justification for controlling the "inferior" and racially mixed lower classes (Eakin 35). This attitude turns up, for example, in a canonical work of fiction, F. Scott Fitzgerald's *The Great Gatsby* (1925). Early in the novel, one of the main characters, Tom Buchanan, is lecturing his friends on a new book he has just read. He says, apocalyptically:

Civilization's going to pieces. . . . I've gotten to be a terrible pessimist about things. Have you read "The Rise of the Colored Empires" by this man Goddard? . . . Well, it's a fine book, and everybody ought to read it. The idea is if we don't look out the white race will be—will be utterly submerged. It's all scientific stuff; it's been proved. . . . This fellow has worked out the whole thing. It's up to us, who are dominant race, to watch out or these other races will have control of things. . . . This idea is that we're Nordics. I am, and you are, and you are, and—. . . And we've produced all the things that go to make civilization—oh, science and art, and all that. Do you see? (13–14)

But if Tom Buchanan's worldview calls for separation of the races and affirms the domination of the white race as natural law, in Brazil by the early twentieth century the situation is vastly different. In *Rebellion in the Backlands*, for example, Cunha, reflecting the flawed science he had been taught, declares what he believed to be the biological nature of the backlanders:

> An intermingling of races highly diverse is, in the majority of cases, prejudicial. According to the conclusions of the evolutionist, even when the influence of a superior race has reacted upon the offspring, the latter shows vivid traces of the inferior one. Miscegenation carried to an extreme means retrogression. . . . The laws of the evolution of species are inviolable ones. (85–86)

Appearing in a more optimistic light, miscegenation is also a major issue in Aranha's novel *Canaan*, published, like *Rebellion in the Backlands*, twenty-three years before *The Great Gatsby*. For Aranha—and calling attention to what Gilberto Freyre has termed Cunha's "racial pessimism" and "rigid biologic determinism" (Cunha, *Rebellion* 84n64)—the issue of mixing, racially and culturally, is the key to Brazil's future. He seeks to demonstrate, largely in the character Milkau (an idealistic German immigrant), that Brazil will eventually achieve its true identity and greatness through assimilation. The opposing view—that white Europeans and their ideas will dominate Brazil and subjugate its other peoples—is expressed by Lentz, another German immigrant, whose Nietzschean views on power, dominance, and racial matters parallel those of Tom Buchanan. During the 1920s *Canaan* "attracted wide attention in Europe and became well known to North Americans" (Putnam, *Marvelous Journey*, 205).

Lima Barreto

A novelist of the 1910s–1920s who may be considered more significant than Aranha, is Lima Barreto, a writer of mixed European and African ancestry. His output (four completed novels, a number of short stories and essays, and a journal) speaks, often angrily, for the downtrodden of Rio de Janeiro between 1890 and 1910. Like Macedo and Manuel Antônio de Almeida a novelist of the city, Barreto can usefully be compared with his contemporary Machado de Assis. Although they came from similar, disadvantaged backgrounds, Machado, seeking the path of the literary artist, would adopt a tone of cool irony, whereas Barreto, the militant social reformer, created texts that, while lacking in technical sophistication and occasionally fragmented, exude outrage at social injustice, with racial prejudice his fundamental theme. Indeed, while Machado offers little overt evidence of writing as a man of color, Barreto never allows his reader to forget the pernicious social, professional, and economic implications of this condition. Utilizing allegory, symbolism, and satire, Barreto vividly depicts Rio's lower classes, a segment of Brazilian society that other writers of the day chose not to deal with. His first novel, *Clara dos anjos,* which deals with the seduction and abandonment of a poor mulatto girl by a rich white man, was published posthumously (1923–24, in serial form); his second, *Vida e morte de M. J. Gonzaga de Sá* (*The Life and Death of M. J. Gonzaga de Sá*), appeared in 1919. The first of Barreto's novels published in his lifetime, *Recordações do escrivão Isaías Caminha* (*Memories of Isaías Caminha, Notary Public*), came out in 1909. Thought to have been influenced by Dostoevsky and to be partially autobiographical, this sometimes bitter work makes the hypocrisy and corruption of journalism its primary target. *Triste fim do Policarpo Quaresma* (*The Patriot;* see app. C), often judged to be Barreto's greatest accomplishment, appeared as a book in 1915. So did the last work published in his lifetime, the pungent political satire *Numa e a ninfa* (*Numa and the Nymph*). Heartened by the outcome of the Russian Revolution and perhaps convinced that widespread social justice was finally within reach, Barreto became a Socialist in the final years of his short life (he died at thirty-one, on the eve of Brazil's modernist revolt). Emir Rodríguez Monegal notes:

> In all his works, Barreto used satire very effectively to shatter the carefully preserved surface of Brazilian society, a surface that both Alencar and Machado . . . had already corroded with their irony. But Barreto went further than these predecessors, and opened the way for the successful social novelists of the 1930s and 1940s. (*Borzoi Anthology* 1: 434)

Literary Modernism

As we saw in chapter 2, the modernist revolt of the 1920s transformed the cultural landscape of both the United States and Brazil. One critic has argued in fact, that Brazil's Modern Art Week (in Feb. 1922) has no equal—"as a defining intellectual and artistic event"—in North American and Spanish American literary and cultural history (González Echevarría and Pupo-Walker 3: 7). Although the artistic and intellectual uprisings of the period manifested themselves in different ways, they had in common a desire to authenticate their societies, especially by establishing colloquial American English and colloquial Brazilian Portuguese as legitimate mediums for the creation of serious literature. In the 1920s, however, as the United States was becoming a world power, many of its writers—T. S. Eliot, Gertrude Stein, Fitzgerald, and Hemingway, for example—gained an international following and influenced the development of literary modernism throughout the Western world, including Brazil.

The ambivalence and disillusionment that mark much of post–World War I literature in the United States was exacerbated, many scholars feel, by racial discord, by xenophobia, and by the triumph of a rapacious form of capitalism. Greatly admired by the Brazilians of the time, this economic dynamism was aided and abetted in its development by pro-business government policies and rapid advances in technology. America's newfound affluence, and its enshrining of materialism and consumption as the true religions, became the envy of many peoples. Experience soon showed that the culture of commerce, tainted by racism and vitiated by greed, would contaminate societies to which it was exported. The acquisitive, exploitive practices of American corporations doing business with or in Latin America became a major source of hemispheric discord.

Deeply affected by his travels around the United States in the 1920s, Monteiro Lobato, a major Brazilian writer and intellectual, wrote *O choque das raças; ou, O presidente negro* (1926; *The Clash of the Races; or, The Black President*). The novel provided a Brazilian interpretation of some very American afflictions. An early example of Brazilian science fiction as well, *O choque das raças* deals with the pernicious social costs of political corruption, bigotry, and class and gender conflicts in a futuristic United States being torn asunder by violence, oppression, venality, and racial strife—traits that many feared the United States would export along with commercial products.[17] Lobato imagines a United States in which "the greater fertility and higher birth-rate of black Americans" leads to the election of an African American president. Whites take steps—"sterilizing Blacks via the use of radiation"—that suggest technology, and civilization, run amok (see Daniel 164). Although not optimistic about Brazil's potential for development and not particularly sympathetic to the modernist revolt, in *O choque das raças* Lobato showed that at least part of his vision for Brazil came from a clear understanding of the problems that the United States was facing and the ways in which Brazil, with all its handicaps, might avoid them.

Like the development of modernism in the United States, Brazilian

modernismo—which must be distinguished from the earlier and quite different Spanish American *modernismo*—was, culturally speaking, the most important event of the twentieth century (Fitz, *Rediscovering* 121–45). Driven
by both ideological and aesthetic pressures, it involved a self-consciously nationalistic adaptation of European avant-garde forms and techniques.[18] As in
the United States, modernism represented for Brazil a decisive step in its relationship with Europe and its own sense of cultural identity. "In general
terms," Mary L. Daniel observes, "the modernist movement in Brazil," which
began its ferment around 1915, "corresponds to the wider wave of van-
guardist reexamination of traditional values, styles, and methodologies accompanying the onset of the First World War throughout western Europe
and the Americas" (167). Inspired in the beginning by Italian futurism, *modernismo* evolved into a distinctly Brazilian, deeply nationalistic movement,
one that would revolutionize art and thought in Brazil and, as we shall see,
produce some of the nation's most seminal texts.

Oswald de Andrade and Mário de Andrade

Several prose writers are worthy of serious study, but two stand out: Oswald
de Andrade and Mário de Andrade. The more irreverent and experimental of
the two, Oswald de Andrade is studied today for two particular texts, *As
memórias sentimentais de João Miramar* (1924; *The Sentimental Memoirs of
John Seaborne*) and *Serafim Ponte Grande* (1933; *Seraphim Grosse Pointe*; see
app. C for both). The title of the first work obviously shows the writer's debt
to Machado's *The Posthumous Memoirs of Brás Cubas*. Oswald de Andrade
also demonstrates—particularly in his experiments with poetic prose and a
telegraphic, elliptical style (the influence of Marinetti and the futurists as well
as Blaise Cendrars, Jean Cocteau, and Mallarmé)—"the kind of prose that in
North American literature is associated with certain experiments by Gertrude
Stein, the early Hemingway" and "the early Dos Passos" (Monegal, *Borzoi
Anthology* 2: 498, 646). The sometimes scabrous punning, the ironic wordplay, and the fragmentation of the narrative into brief, epigrammatic chapters also suggest (in addition to Machado) the later, more iconoclastic work
of James Joyce, especially *Finnegans Wake*. The book helped liberate Brazilian fiction from the artificial restrictions of formal Portuguese aesthetics as
well as from a stuffy bourgeois morality. In the late 1920s, Andrade was for-
mulating his theory of anthropophagy, or cannibalism; his project culminated in the publication of his still-influential "Anthropophagy Manifesto"
(1928). It propounded the superiority of Tupi, a major indigenous language,

as well as of Brazil's native tradition, to the culture imported from Europe. With his famous line "Tupi or not Tupi, that is the question," Andrade was "reacting in a calculatedly outrageous manner against what he considered the repressive and censorious European tradition." Yet at the same time, Oswald was avidly devouring European thinkers like Sir James Frazer (as T. S. Eliot was), Lévy-Bruhl, and Freud, finding in them support for his belief that Brazil must consume and then reinvent European culture and that the country should cultivate its indigenous past—for him, its utopian state of nature (Monegal, *Borzoi Anthology* 2: 647).

Oswald was not the only Brazilian of the time to explore the Tupi language as the proper vehicle with which to express Brazil's national heritage. Barreto's *The Patriot* (1915) is a wry, ultimately sorrowful novel in which the humdrum existence of the protagonist, a low-level bureaucrat in the Ministry of War, is suddenly upset by a proposal he has written that calls for Tupi to be adopted as Brazil's official language. (It turns out that his superiors do not even know what Tupi is, much less its importance to Brazil's past.) A true patriot and, in the tradition of the boastful colonial *ufanistas*, an ardent advocate of Brazil's status as the most marvelous country in the world, Policarpo Quaresma is fired from his job (for writing official documents in Tupi, a language that ironically is judged to be an incomprehensible foreign tongue) and declared mentally ill. In addition, he fails as a farmer and in the end is exiled on the Island of Snakes. Even at the moment of death, when the reader might expect him to denounce the society that has treated him shabbily, after he had defended it faithfully for so many years, Policarpo still believes in Brazil, its past, its present, and its future.

De Andrade's other major work, *Serafim Ponte Grande*, appeared in the depths of Brazil's Great Depression, when Oswald, embracing Marxism, began to devote himself to writing avant-garde literature with a social conscience and strong political commitment. Although the two works are cut from the same aesthetically and culturally subversive cloth, they are substantially different; the later work is the more radical of the two. If, for example, the assault on conventional logic and semantic coherence in *The Sentimental Memoirs of John Seaborne* occurs internally, at the level of diction and syntax, in *Seraphim Grosse Pointe* it functions externally, manifesting itself primarily in the text's numerous and varied structural units, many of which emphasize the narrative's parodic and metafictional dimensions rather than the story of its protagonist. Overall, in fact, the structuring of *Seraphim Grosse Pointe* reflects the author's transference of the aesthetics of cubism and collage to the realm of narrative. "This second novel," writes Vicky Unruh, thus "greatly expands the Bakhtinian 'autocriticism of discourse' already present" in *The Sentimental Memoirs of John Seaborne* (115). That novel, in the comic way it re-creates the protagonist's life, can be thought of as a parody of the bildungsroman. And, as Mary Daniel notes, both texts

> are telegraphic, episodic works consisting of montages of travel narratives, sensorial and philosophical impressions, fragments of verse and letters, and parodic prefaces arranged in what might be called "cubist" style; both "antinovels" offer a carnivalization of a series of traditional literary forms in juxtaposition, including the initial copyright of the text. (168)

The other dominant figure of the time, Mário de Andrade, often described as the intellectual leader of Brazil's modernist revolution, is the author of several influential novels. *Amar, verbo intransitivo* (1927; *Fräulein*), which treats its unconventional theme "in a light-hearted yet Freudian manner," deals with a "German 'governess' whose main charge is to give young Brazilian men their sexual initiation" (Daniel 169). *Macunaíma* (1928; app. C) is a narrative that, injecting folklore into a vision of Brazil's sense of an authentically national literature, seeks to discover "the continuity between modernization and a primitive substratum" (Wasserman, *Exotic Nations* 222). Published to mixed reviews (possibly because readers were intimidated by its strange, synthetic language; its elusive, looping structure; its variegated mythmaking; its destabilizingly parodic aspects; its frank yet often playful eroticism; and its magical qualities), *Macunaíma* presents the story of its eponymous hero, a black Indian, whose ironic quest to regain a stolen tribal amulet leads him, in an early version of magic realism, through the many regions and communities of Brazil before returning him to the Brazilian jungle (see Stam 71; Daniel 170).[19] There, achieving a kind of apotheosis, he is transformed into the constellation Ursa Major. Conceived not as a traditional novel but as a *rhapsode* by its author (*Fräulen* was termed an *idílio* or "idyll"), *Macunaíma* consolidated Brazil's rich and varied mythological heritage—including myths introduced by European, especially Italian, immigrants—not into a coherent national myth, "literary language or character delineation but rather [into] the heterogeneous confluence of all the main ethnic, historical, and linguistic threads which had converged in the Brazilian national territory over the centuries since before the arrival of the first Europeans" (Daniel 170).[20] Recalling Joseph Campbell's *Hero with a Thousand Faces*, Macunaíma, like Mário's vision of Brazilian identity, is a work in progress, a character in a state of flux, a symbol perhaps of the dangers of rigidity and of the value of resourcefulness and imagination. He is the modern antihero, although transposed into the indigenous mode; the text (which, at the conclusion, the reader realizes is a story that a talkative parrot is relating to an unknown listener) develops through an "innovative, revolutionary language that Mário de Andrade invents for his work, respecting a popular native syntax and . . . transforming it into a new, flexible, expressive, recognizably Brazilian literary language recovered for writing." Moreover, as Renata Wasserman observes:

> In the trajectory from parrot to narrator to text, *Macunaíma* asserts cultural independence from the former colonial power. . . . Like Alencar, who began by forging a "Brazilian" language, Mário de Andrade finds in language the final and lasting affirmation of his work. In it man and parrot, culture and nature, join in the creation of the anarchic Macunaíma, who, if he does not solve the problems of exoticism, of domination, of economic and cultural dependency, finally becomes part of what is understood as Brazilianness by creating a different articulation of all these problems. He enters a national mythology in this now-basic text of Brazilian literature not only by redefining national identity in terms of disjuncture and incoherence but also by positing a different relation between the discourses of a powerful self and an other defined as dependent. (*Exotic Nations* 242–43)

Fiction from the 1920s to the 1950s

In the period between the wars, fiction became a brilliantly practiced genre. Fueled after 1920 by an energizing and liberating Freudianism and, in the 1930s by a reformist Marxism as well as by many writers' interest in the literary techniques of Joyce, Proust, and Kafka, narrative in Brazil and the United States reached new heights of sophistication and excellence. Afrânio Coutinho, for example, described the 1930s and early 1940s in his country as "a period of splendor . . . in which the fruits of the previous experimentalism" of Mário de Andrade, Oswald de Andrade, and others are gathered. Identifying the "golden age of modernist fiction between 1930 and 1945," Coutinho argues that, by this time, "Brazilian fiction has attained a well-defined physiognomy," replete "with its own, unmistakable, and peculiar structure" that "places it among the highest expressions of literature in the Americas" (245). Similarly, the years between 1920 and 1945 are commonly referred to as the "second renaissance" of American literature (the first was the generation of Emerson, Thoreau, Melville, and Hawthorne). In both countries a more developed awareness of narrative technique and theory emerged, as well as a steady movement away from realism and naturalism and toward such nonrealistic and nonmimetic elements as symbolism, myth, psychological time, fragmentation, montage, automatic writing, psychoanalysis, and stream-of-consciousness narration. While in the 1920s Americans and Brazilians traveled in Europe, studying in its salons and absorbing the intellectual ambience, the urgent social, economic, and political problems at home (and rising fascism abroad) drew these writers and artists, by the 1930s, back to the New World, where many would apply avant-garde techniques to characterize societies greatly in need of reform. In both Brazil and the United States, the tumultuous decade of the 1930s gave rise to some of the greatest works of fiction. In the hands of such masters as John Steinbeck, John Dos Passos (of Portuguese ancestry), Ernest Hemingway, Nathanael West, Thomas Wolfe, and William Faulkner in the United States and Patrícia Galvão (Pagu), Antônio de Alcântara Machado, Jorge Amado, Raquel de Queiroz, Graciliano Ramos, and José Lins do Rego in Brazil, the novel merged a keen social consciousness with innovative narrative forms. In addition, cross-fertilization between the hemispheric giants was evident. In Brazil, for example, Steinbeck's *The Grapes of Wrath* has long been thought comparable to Ramos's *Barren Lives*; both novels deal with downtrodden people forced off their land, by both natural and human-produced calamities, with no recourse but to flee across the country in search of decent lives. Steinbeck can be compared, as well, with Amado, as can Twain, Dickens, and Erskine Caldwell (three of Amado's favorite writers).[21]

But socially engaged fiction was not the only kind of high-quality narrative written in the 1930s and 1940s. Whereas northeasterners like Amado, Queiroz, Lins do Rego, and Ramos had a rural focus, the southern, urban orientation of Cyro dos Anjos, especially in his two best-known works, *O amanuense Belmiro* (1937) and *Abdias* (1945), recalls the technical sophistication, skepticism, and irony of Machado de Assis. *O amanuense Belmiro*, for example, features a protagonist who, unlike the characters in Amado, Queiroz, and Ramos, is an alienated bourgeois whose pseudoliterary life is dominated not by committed action but by escapist self-contemplation. The American novel *Look Homeward, Angel*, by Wolfe, in which the hero searches for a father figure in the violence and chaos of the modern world, presaged what is for many readers and critics contemporary Brazil's greatest novel, Guimarães Rosa's *Grande Sertão: Veredas* (1956; *The Devil to Pay in the Backlands*; see app. C).

Rosa, as noted in chapter 2, has often been compared with Faulkner (see Lowe; Valente). In August 1954, Faulkner spent a few days in São Paulo, visiting admirers there and commenting on the problem of race—a theme that figures prominently in his work and that is, of course, central to Brazilian literature. Although, as George Monteiro reports (104), *Sanctuary* and *Light in August* were at that time the two best-known Faulkner novels in Brazil, his work had been available in Portuguese there at least since 1945, when "A Rose for Emily" was translated (see McClendon).[22] In his article on *Absalom, Absalom!* and *The Devil to Pay in the Backlands*, Luiz Valente identifies Paulo Vizzioli as the "first scholar to undertake a comparison between William Faulkner and João Guimarães Rosa" and discusses the five points of contact that for Vizzioli justify a comparative study of these two great New World narrativists:

> The first is the manner in which Faulkner and Rosa transform the fertile tradition of literary regionalism by universalizing it into what Vizzioli calls "symbolic naturalism." The second is the prevalence of moral themes in their works, as the two writers deal with such questions as the nature of good and evil, the response to guilt and expiation, and the ways in which life is shaped both by individual choices and fate. The third is their preference for exceptional characters, whose actions test the limits of human suffering, endurance, and desire. The fourth is the challenge that the idiosyncratic style of both writers poses for the reader. The fifth is the similarity in their inventive narrative techniques, such as their use of stream-of-consciousness, their manipulation of point of view and their fragmentation of plot development. Vizzioli concludes by speculating on the possibility of a direct influence of Faulkner on Rosa. (149)

In addition to Rosa, Faulkner has been linked to a number of Brazilian writers, including Ramos, Lins do Rego, Machado, Adonias Filho (Merquior; Ellison), Maria Alice Barroso (Parker; Patai, *Myth*), and Autran Dourado (McClendon; Merquior; Patai, *Myth*; Gledson, "Brazilian Prose").

Yet for all that Faulkner was celebrated in Brazil, his influence was significantly different from his impact in Spanish America. There, as Deborah Cohn, following James Irby, has argued, "Faulkner's influence, in conjunction with that of other modern writers, represents a turning point in Spanish American literature" (15). This argument cannot be made for Brazilian narrative, for at least two reasons. First, Brazilian narrative simply did not need Faulkner's liberating example as badly as did Spanish American narrative—a genre that, until Borges, was overly dependent on European models and trends. In Brazil, the novel and short story had been radically altered by Machado de Assis as early as the 1880s and *The Posthumous Memoirs of Brás Cubas,* unquestionably the greatest Latin American novel of the nineteenth century and arguably the most innovative and engaging novel of the time in the hemisphere (see Gallagher). His work provided generations of Brazilian narrativists with the iconoclastic models they needed in order to undertake even more radical experimentations with theme, form, style, and structure. Unlike the dutifully realistic Spanish American novel of the late nineteenth and early twentieth centuries, the Brazilian novel, in the hands first of Machado and then of his artistic and intellectual heirs, rejected the limitations of realism and embarked on a new kind of narrative, a self-referential, semiotic system that called attention to itself as a verbal structure, or artifice (as Borges would later say), while not surrendering any of its sociopolitical significance. Building on Machado's groundbreaking efforts, then, the Brazilian novel of the 1920s and 1930s entered into a period of extraordinary inventiveness and creativity.

The second reason, closely related to the first, has to do with the unusual importance of Borges. In both theoretical and practical terms, the Argentine author revolutionized Spanish American fiction, facilitating in the process the later appearance of the "new novel," the narrative form that would be developed by such masters as Carlos Fuentes, Julio Cortázar, Mario Vargas Llosa, and Gabriel García Márquez (see Rabassa, "Nueva narrativa"). As a translator, theoretician, and creative writer, Borges had an impact on contemporary Spanish American fiction that has no parallel in Brazil. Two of his most important 1932 critical essays, "The Postulation of Reality" and "Narrative Art and Magic," in fact, outline what Borges would be trying to achieve in his *Ficciones* (see Monegal, *Borges,* 247–49) and, as such, stand in sharp contrast to Machado, whose most incisive theoretical pronouncements are integrated into the various discourses that are at play in his novels and short stories or, especially in his pre-1880 work, in the prefaces to them. In Brazil, although Faulkner was widely venerated, there was no Borges to translate Faulkner into Portuguese and thus facilitate his reception by a new generation of writers. As a consequence, it was the much earlier occurring Machado de Assis, and not Faulkner, who, by the second decade of the twentieth century, was already being looked to as the great emancipator of Brazilian fiction.

Fiction from the 1960s to the Present

When considering Brazilian fiction of the 1970s and 1980s, we cannot overestimate the significance of the dictatorship that began in April 1964 and stayed in power for twenty-one years. In spite of the brutal repression and censorship, however, several extraordinary novels appeared. Because of the unique circumstances of their creation, they gave new meaning to the term "politically aware." The authors who came of age under the *ditadura militar*, for example, found the writing of fiction itself to be a subversive act that could have serious, even fatal, consequences. Commenting on how the situation changed not only the nature of fiction that would be written but the way it would be read, Monegal has observed:

> Very different is the case of those writers who at the time of the army coup were still in their twenties. For them, writing in a society in which every thought, where even the least political subject (sex, for instance) became political because of the repression, was an experience which prevented them from handling the novel in purely literary terms, as a fictional artifact. They were (or became) committed novelists not because they wanted to change society but because writing novels was in their society at that time a committed activity, almost a subversive one. ("Writing" 19)

In choosing, often at great personal risk, to express themselves under these trying circumstances, the writers of the 1970s and 1980s had the dangerous, sometimes painful task of deconstructing long-held myths about Brazil, the foundations of its national identity, and its relations to other countries. According to Robert DiAntonio, "One can think of few other world literatures that exhibit such a passion for introspection and the refocusing of national ideals and myths." In fact, "by the mid-1980s the demythification of Brazilian history, cultural ideals, and myths had become acceptably mainstream" (ix–x). In the Brazilian novelists' obsession with historical and cultural self-analysis—a complex fusion of politics and aesthetic innovation—DiAntonio sees parallels with the efforts of German writers like Günter Grass, struggling to understand how and why their society gave rise to the Third Reich (183).[23] In addition to experimenting with style, structure, and thematic issues, the

writers of the dictatorship period demonstrated a deeply ironic and frequently skeptical vision of Brazil, one that

> underscored a common aim: to demythify the conception of a romanti-
> cized and stereotypical Brazil. Novelists dramatized the tension created
> between the national myths and the existing political and social reality.
> Even now [1989], after the "abertura," the practice continues unabated,
> for a nation passing out of a time of repression seeks to understand itself
> in both sociological and artistic terms. (DiAntonio 5)

In a sense, the writers of the 1970s and 1980s also felt obliged to challenge
Brazil's popular image of itself, to interrogate, often in unpleasant, disturbing, and parodic ways, Brazil itself, its history, its culture, and its traditions.

Epitomizing the process of unsparing self-appraisal is Silviano Santiago,
the author of several influential works of cultural criticism and fiction, one
of which, *Stella Manhattan* (1985), focuses on the tensions and interconnec-
tions that bind Brazil, the United States, and the rest of the Americas together.
Santiago formulated a widely accepted theory about modern Brazilian fiction. Since 1964 fiction in Brazil

> has become more aware of the problem of power, not only in the imme-
> diate political sense, but in such areas as the family, relations between the
> sexes in general, and even in language, and . . . what masquerades as a
> carnival of "alegria" ["happiness"; the word comes from a satirical song by
> Caetano Veloso] is in fact more self-aware, willing, and able, to take risks
> than anything that precedes it. (qtd. in Gledson, "Brazilian Prose" 203)

Santiago's theory thus encompasses the writers' struggles to deal, formally
and thematically, with life under the dictatorship and their more subtle innovations, largely thematic, that have characterized narrative since the 1980s.
Alienated by what they felt was the meretricious image the military regime
had promoted and exported, the writers of the post-1985 era saw an urgent
need to explore long-banned themes that, for these writers, defined Brazil as
it sought to heal its wounds and reestablish an authentic sense of self. Rising
to meet the challenge were a host of energetic, daring writers, including Antônio Callado, Ivan Ângelo, Sônia Coutinho, Darcy Ribeiro, Márcio Souza
(see app. C), Marina Colasanti, João Ubaldo Ribeiro, Lygia Fagundes Telles,
Moacyr Scliar, Lya Luft, Ignácio de Loyola Brandão, Lêdo Ivo, Murilo Ru-

bião, Edla van Steen (see app. C), Rubem Fonseca, Nélida Piñon, and Márcia Denser. Such formerly taboo themes as homosexuality, rape, exile, transgressive sexuality, drug use, violence, nihilism, and alienation could now be discussed (DiAntonio 5). In an explosion of long-repressed voices and themes, Brazilian literature began to recover from the devastating effects of dictatorship and from the false image it had promulgated worldwide.

Brazilian narrative, especially during this period, has an interesting parallel with its counterpart in the United States, where in what seemed to be "an increasingly fragmented, decentered world, contemporary fiction has been firm in its determination to celebrate the special authority of distinctly, 'minority' points of view," so much so that, in the United States as in Brazil, "contemporary writers may be said to have explored the moral authority of marginality" (*Harper American Literature* 2: 2577). The great difference, however, is that while the United States has witnessed a diminishing of the writer's role in society, it has also, as a culture, seen an intensification of "the narrowed focus, the increasing self-absorption, of American life," an obdurate devotion "not to the realization of some ideal conception of self but to the single-minded pursuit of one's own professional advancement—in the name of money, power, and status" (*Harper American Literature* 2: 2572–73). Such single-minded devotion to one's career was, even during the 1970s and early 1980s, virtually nonexistent in Brazilian literature. Although writers of both countries may be concerned with the nature and expression of power and with the inclusion of segments of their societies formerly judged to be marginal, in Brazil writers still have an important social function to perform and are not yet regarded as being irrelevant to larger sociopolitical issues. In the 1980s and 1990s, for example, artistic expression, one vital form of which is popular music, still possessed a strong political consciousness and function. Finally, in both Brazil and the United States, the final decades of the twentieth century saw a tremendous resurgence of short fiction. As we shall see, in fact, the postmodern short story is probably Brazil's most cultivated narrative form.

To appreciate the difference between Brazilian and American fiction in the 1970s, we can compare Joan Didion's novel *Play It As It Lays* (1970) and João Ubaldo Ribeiro's *Sargento Getúlio* (1971; *Sergeant Getúlio* [1978]). In the Didion work we meet an ambivalent character suffering from psychological trauma; in Ribeiro's novel we encounter a man whose identity—his moral vision and reason for existence—is based on keeping a promise. Crippled by painful personal experience and skepticism about what her culture truly values, Didion's protagonist, a young, out-of-work actress named

Maria Wyeth, whose dilemma poignantly captures the conflict at the heart of the postmodern American dream, finds it inconceivable that anyone could display passion for anything, including human relationships and political activism. For Getúlio, in contrast, nothing has meaning if he does not complete the violent mission he has accepted. A hired assassin, Getúlio lives by a code of brutality, yet he is also driven by a primitive ethical certainty, even in the face of betrayal and in the knowledge that if he keeps his word, he will be hunted down and killed. Conjuring up visions of an efficient backlands Achilles, he is a classical hero, inflexible in his integrity but caught up in the machinations and deceits of modern life and doomed by his refusal to compromise. Despite the violence of his world and of the violence he himself wreaks, Getúlio, who narrates the story in a voice that is shocking, sad, and funny, may earn the reader's respect if not sympathy. Rendered into a supple English by the author, *Sergeant Getúlio* ranks as one of the most unusual and powerful novels of the 1970s.

In the evolution of the post-1964 novel in Brazil, several other works stand out as well. Lygia Fagundes Telles's *As meninas* (1973; *The Girl in the Photograph* [1982]) depicts three young women whose separate but interconnected lives reflect the turmoil and tensions of the times (the years after the coup that ousted President Goulart, in 1964), including the torture of political prisoners (see app. C). The three women, each representing a segment of Brazilian society (the upper class, the drug culture, and the militant intellectual), live in Our Lady of Fátima boardinghouse, which in its repressive atmosphere serves as a metaphor for Brazil in the 1960s. A web of brooding, sometimes violent character studies woven together by internal monologues, *The Girl in the Photograph* portrays a Brazil reeling under the imposition of a dictatorship whose methods and effects the people can neither comprehend nor mitigate. In featuring three women as main characters, the novel provides a much-needed perspective on the dictatorship in its early days. Indeed, as the work of such outstanding writers as Telles, Piñon, and Lispector shows, women authors in the 1970s played an important role not only in voicing their opposition to the dictatorship but also in demanding improvements in social, educational, and health care services as well (see Schmink).

Another work published in 1973 is Lêdo Ivo's *Ninho de cobras* (*Snakes' Nest; or, A Tale Badly Told* [1981]; see app. C), a hybrid narrative that, recalling Faulkner, liberally mixes poetry (Ivo is an established poet), politics, reportage, allegory, and the mystery novel. Pointing out Ivo's keen interest in

Melville and Hawthorne, Jon Tolman notes the writer's "devotion to Dashiell Hammett and Raymond Chandler" as a possible explanation for the "mystery novel" element in *Snakes' Nest* (Tolman ii) as well as Ivo's use of allegory for political purposes. Utilizing an unreliable narrator and an acrid wit, the author examines the nature of good and evil and the problem of telling (or knowing) the truth in a repressive dictatorship, a structure that cannot tolerate honesty. As befits a political allegory, however, *Snakes' Nest* takes place not in urban Brazil in the 1970s but during World War II, in a corrupt and violent port city, Maceió, in the northeast. The parallels to the dictatorship are unmistakable, nonetheless.

Also manifesting aspects of political allegory is Ignácio de Loyola Brandão's *Zero* (app. C). Written in 1969, this extraordinary novel was not published in Brazil until 1975, a year after it came out in Italy. In 1976 it was banned by the Brazilian Ministry of Justice. The ban was lifted in 1979, following a national protest, and *Zero* became a best seller. Although the novel is set in the fictional Latíndia-America, its wealth of cultural detail suggests that the focus is Brazil. The name of its protagonist, José Gonçalves, refers to Brazil's "Joe Smith," its zero-like common man, and may remind American readers of Elmer Rice's Zero in *The Adding Machine*, as well as the human yo-yo in Thomas Pynchon's *V.* (Monegal, "Writing" 20). In the second half of the novel, as José is interrogated and tortured by the military police, his sufferings are compared with Christ's. What may be most striking for the non-Brazilian reader is that, however much it deals with death squads, torture, and ritual executions, the novel is driven not by despair but by hope, sustained, moreover, by a mordant and corrosive humor that both reflects and deflects the violent absurdity of our times. The revolutionary antihero of a revolutionary antinovel (which makes extensive use of collage; offers no logical or sequential action; features seemingly random juxtapositions, including pages divided into two sometimes conflicting, sometimes complementary columns of text; and has innumerable flashbacks and digressions), José Gonçalves seeks love and meaning in his life but finds instead a political regime, accountable to no one, controlling a society in which a barrage of media hype transforms the public into mindless consumers fixated on the "economic miracle" of the 1970s—any resemblance to the actual dictatorship is intentional.[24] The theme of marketplace propaganda may well resonate with Americans, whose culture has assumed a corporate mentality awash in wasteful, destructive commercialism. Indeed, in the novel's final two pages, three references to an unspecified "America" justify the reader's conclusion that, in its social and political relevance, *Zero* speaks to all the nations of the New World and to the very concept of America.

Also regarded as one of the decade's most representative novels is Ivan Ângelo's *A festa* (1976; *The Celebration* [1982]; see app. C). Moving backward and forward through time and using a variety of narrative types and tones, *The Celebration* shows that seemingly unrelated events are, like the fragmented text itself, fundamentally connected. The primary points of reference are the arrival in a Brazilian city of poor and hungry northeastern migrants and a birthday party thrown by decadent upper-middle-class professionals (the two events symbolize the wide gap between Brazil's rich and poor). *The Celebration* subtly skewers the pretentiousness, complacency, and self-centeredness of the bourgeoisie and, in so doing, enlists the reader's participation in imbuing the story with meaning and relevancy. The text that at the outset seems fragmented gradually reveals the close link between the two groups of characters. Ironically, the police use the unexpected confluence to justify their interrogation, degradation, and torture of both groups. Torture constitutes the novel's subtext, a metaphor for the abuse of power that Santiago refers to in his theory. In describing what he as a politically aware fiction writer seeks to accomplish in his work, Ângelo has said, "I hope to make the reader an accomplice not only in shaping the actual text, but in determining its significance, since my intention has been to provide wider participation in the terrible problems we face at the moment in Brazil."[25]

Published two years later, in 1978, and focusing on the plight of Brazil's indigenous peoples, Darcy Ribeiro's *Maíra* became something of an international sensation (see app. C). It challenges the popular belief, in Brazil and elsewhere, that there can be a successful compromise between the culturally rich but vulnerable Amazonian Indians and a Western capitalism driven by a consuming hunger for development. Questioning both the morality and the viability of the "economic miracle"—which was based on foreign investment in Brazil and was, as I noted, used abroad to justify the dictatorship—*Maíra* presents what some regard as a hopeless conflict, the struggle of a native people to survive in the face of the government's desire to attain first-world status. A good example of structural anthropology applied to the novel form, *Maíra* contrasts the traditional cultures of the Amazonian Indians with Christian mythology and ideology and with the frontier ethic of violence and exploitation that may inevitably destroy Indian life. Because of their nation's tragic confrontation with Indian culture, American readers should identify with the narrative in *Maíra*, an aesthetically complex work that reminds us that the price of one group's progress is often another group's extermination.

Santiago's *Stella Manhattan* broke ground for the Brazilian novel by intertwining sex, politics, and inter-American cultural relations in unexpected ways. The title character is the female alter ego of Eduardo da Costa e Silva, whom his father, embarrassed by his son's homosexuality and transvestism, sends to North America. With the help of his father's political crony Colonel Valdevinos Vianna, the young man gets a job in the Brazilian consulate in New York. Eduardo is approached by Vianna to help him bring out his female side, the sadomasochistic figure soon to be known in the gay community as the Black Widow. Through her connections to Brazil's military dictatorship, Stella is recruited by a group of Brazilian guerrillas living in exile in New York City. Set primarily in New York during the late 1960s, as the repression in Brazil was worsening, *Stella Manhattan* develops around four interlocking situations, all dealing with issues of power and dominance: the psychosexual tensions within the protagonist, Eduardo/Stella; the relationship between Eduardo/Stella and Vianna / Black Widow; the struggle between Eduardo/Stella and Vianna / Black Widow and the guerrillas seeking to bring down the military regime in Brazil; and the inter-American social and political connections that link Eduardo/Stella and Vianna / Black Widow to other ideologically charged groups, such as the Young Lords, anti-Castro factions, and the Black Panthers.

Although less militant than *Stella Manhattan*, another late 1980s novel, by Nélida Piñon, makes a political statement about Brazil. Subversively comic, Nélida's *A doce canção de Caetana* (1987; *Caetana's Sweet Song* [1992]) is a masterpiece of irony, allegory, and cultural criticism (see app. C; see also Santiago, "Hurried Midwives"). Set in Trindade, a small fictional city that recalls both Faulkner's Yoknapatawpha County and García Márquez's Macondo, *Caetana's Sweet Song* takes place in 1970, when the dictatorship was touting material progress as the panacea for Brazil's economic woes and Pelé was leading Brazil to an unprecedented third World Cup championship. Against this backdrop of outward success and illusory achievement, the citizens of Trindade, hopelessly (but humorously) ensnared in a variety of illusions and delusions, play out one well-intended but absurdist farce after another. Surviving on both its mythic past and on its citizens' unshakable faith in what they feel is its blessed future, Trindade serves, in this delightful yet biting novel, as a metonymy for the struggles of Brazil. The brilliance of the 1970 World Cup team (which many soccer enthusiasts regard as the greatest group of players ever assembled), for example, is ironically counterposed to a series of failures, miscalculations, and disasters, from the unhappy end of Caetana's operatic project to the injustices inflicted on Brazil and its people by the dictatorship.

Finally, we should mention Caio Fernando Abreu's *Onde andará Dulce Veiga?* (1990; *Whatever Happened to Dulce Veiga? A B-Novel*), which exemplifies the playful yet urgent nature of much Brazilian fiction in the 1990s (see app. C). *Whatever Happened to Dulce Veiga?* is both a detective novel and an ironic, postmodern, and very Brazilian reworking of the ancient quest narrative. Developing, on the most basic level, around a nameless, down-and-out journalist's search for a once-famous cabaret singer, *Whatever Happened to Dulce Veiga?* confronts a variety of larger issues: the problem of meaning, in life and in texts; the problem of national (and personal) identity in a culture historically open to foreign influences; and the need to maintain hope in a world in which the disparity between the rich and powerful and the poor and powerless grows ever larger. The United States as a cultural presence in Brazil is everywhere evident in the novel, which cites innumerable literary, cultural, and intellectual connections between the two nations and between Brazil and the rest of the world. In this sense, the conflicts that give the novel its tone of humor, distress, and malaise can be read as the logical result of the forces put into play by the tropicalistas and, before them, by Oswald de Andrade's "Anthropophagy Manifesto." Set in a nightmarish urban environment and peopled with characters who—because of their sexuality (the specter of AIDS haunts the narrative), their beliefs, or their occupation—represent the most marginalized of Brazil's citizens, Abreu's novel challenges the much-touted image of Brazil as an economic and racial paradise, presenting it instead as a kind of fantastic but failed utopia (not unlike the United States), yet one in which faith in a better future springs eternal.

The novel has not been the only narrative form to flourish in Brazil into the twenty-first century. Especially since the 1970s, short fiction has been experiencing a boom, in both quantity and quality. Indeed, the Brazilian short story is now on a par with work done anywhere in the world in this demanding form. Moreover, as one critic has said, "Brazil has contributed to world literature two undisputed masters" of this genre, Joaquim Maria Machado de Assis and João Guimarães Rosa. The name of Clarice Lispector, who, after 1960, helped transform the short story, might easily be added to the list (K. Jackson, "Short Story" 211, 223). Of the many present-day Brazilian short story writers, several names stand out: Rubem Fonseca, Lygia Fagundes Telles, Murilo Rubião, Samuel Rawet, Sônia Coutinho, José Veiga, Edla van Steen, Moacyr Scliar, Edilberto Coutinho, and Márcia Denser.

Although the applicability of magic realism to Brazilian literature remains a moot point (many scholars question whether it existed as a coherent movement, as it has in Spanish America), a number of writers have had the label attached to their work: Ariano Suassuna (esp. *A pedra do reino* [1971]), Veiga (*A máquina extraviada* [1968]; *"The Misplaced Machine" and Other Stories* [1970]), Aníbal Machado, Murilo Rubião (see app. C), Moacyr Scliar, Garcia de Paiva, Elias José, Lygia Fagundes Telles, and Eiko Suzuki. One of those who are skeptical about the term's aptness to Brazilian letters is K. David Jackson, who believes that "Magical Realism was little practiced in Brazil, forming instead a natural part of surrealist touches or poeticization applied to modernist narrative techniques" ("Short Story" 227). This explanation gains plausibility if we consider Machado de Assis's *The Posthumous Memoirs of Brás Cubas* to be an early forerunner of magic realism and if we include such later works as Mário de Andrade's *Macunaíma* and Érico Veríssimo's *Incidente em Antares* (1971; *Incident in Antares*). Mary Daniel has argued that the last work is reminiscent of the surrealistic qualities of García Márquez's *One Hundred Years of Solitude*, published only four years before, and that its principal town, Antares, "plays the same fictional role as Márquez's Macondo" (183). The question of magic realism aside, Brazilian narrative has, rather in the tradition of Kafka, extensively and systematically cultivated both grotesque humor and the absurd in dealing with the nation's topsy-turvy, often violent universe.

An important segment of Brazil's literature are a number of Jewish writers. Some—Clarice Lispector, for example, whose heritage is most evident in her final novel, *A hora da estrela* (1977; *The Hour of the Star* [1986]); Carlos Heitor Cony; Rawet; and Scliar—have become major fixtures in contemporary narrative. Currently claiming nearly 150,000 residents, whose ancestry is primarily Eastern European, the Jewish community has long had a presence in Brazil. The fiction of Scliar, like that of the American author Cynthia Ozick, deals in fairly obvious ways with traditional and mystical Jewish elements (see DiAntonio 113–14, 118); that of Lispector, also regarded as something of a mystic, is less overt. Although Scliar is widely regarded as the primary exemplar of contemporary Jewish Brazilian literature, Rawet, an immigrant to Brazil in 1936, is often said to be its pioneer. As the stories in *The Prophet* show, Rawet's best work illuminates an often overlooked aspect of Brazil's cultural complexity. Dealing with the immigrant experience, his moving tales and their poignantly drawn characters embrace such problems as alienation, displacement, and exile. Incorporating the work of such writers as Isaac Goldemberg (Peru), Mordecai Richler (Canada), Syria Poletti (Argentina), Lispector, Scliar, Cony, and Rawet, and including a number of American authors (among them, Philip Roth, Saul Bellow, Ozick, and Michael Gold), a comparative study of Jewish writing in the Americas would be a valuable project.

As in the United States and Europe, Brazilian postmodern fiction is strong; Roberto Drummond, Edilberto Coutinho, Caio Abreu, Márcio Souza, Silviano Santiago, and Chico Anísio are often mentioned as primary exponents.[26] Characterized by a pungent mixture of humor, satire, metaliterary play, parody, violence, intertextuality, the grotesque, and the absurd, contemporary fiction in Brazil also has a sharp political edge, which is "perhaps traceable to the years of military dictatorship" (K. Jackson, "Short Story" 229). One of Brazil's most widely read authors, Drummond is well-known for his funny but incisive pop style. Abreu, particularly in *Whatever Happened to Dulce Veiga?*, and Anísio develop a mordant and absurdist style that satirizes a variety of Brazilian and Western cultural institutions while also merging the traditional short story form with journalism, official discourse, propaganda, film, and television, especially the soap opera.

On the surface, at least, Brazilian and American fiction of the 1980s and 1990s differs, primarily because of Brazil's wrenching experience with the dictatorship, whose effects are slowly being extirpated. Although the United States' involvement in Vietnam had a profound impact on American society and although Watergate, the savings-and-loan scandal, and the Iran-contra affair challenged the national consciousness, the brutality of the military regime was devastating to Brazilians and to their images of themselves, their government, their sociopolitical institutions, and their country. It is this sense of betrayal and despair, along with the realization that their society would have to be not only rebuilt but rethought, that finds powerful expression in Brazilian fiction of the 1980s and 1990s. Brazilian writers were exorcizing the demons of their recent past while seeking to involve the nation in the international community more productively than before. While this penchant for self-examination characterizes American fiction as well, in Brazil it has had an unusual intensity. Roberto Drummond's wryly humorous *Sangue de Coca-Cola* (1985; *Coca-Cola Blood*), for example, parodies "the carnivalesque diversions created by the Médici government" while detailing "the grotesque and chaotic reality that lies just below the surface of a national myth" (DiAntonio 63). Something similar occurs in Edilberto Coutinho's *Maracanã, Adeus: Onze histórias de futebol* (1980; *Good-bye, Maracanã Stadium: Eleven Stories of Soccer*), a collection of short fiction that, employing sardonic wit and featuring typographical innovations (texts set in parallel columns), examines the country's passion for *futebol* in the context of its quest for a sense of national identity. Although cultural differences between them must be accounted for, DiAntonio is nevertheless correct in asserting that "Coutinho's stories, like Robert Coover's *The Universal Baseball Association, Inc.* (1968) and W. P. Kinsella's *The Iowa Baseball Confederacy* (1986), use a country's national pastime to explore larger issues—both national myths and societal and personal failings" (63). Noting the prevalence of narratives that subvert themselves and that feature multiple, conflicting narrators, Gledson feels that the tradition of "politeness and complicity," artfully exploited by Machado de Assis, has disappeared from Brazilian fiction, which, "with remarkable skill and variety, is exploring a country" and a culture dogged by fear and uncertainty and existing in what often seems a virtually permanent state of "tension and crisis" ("Brazilian Prose" 206).

In this fluid, uncertain, and sometimes dangerous cultural context, short story writers have shown a predilection for the themes of violence and alienation and for depicting the lives of formerly ignored groups, in particular the urban poor. In works like *Cemitério de elefantes* (1964), *O vampiro de Curitiba* (1965; *"The Vampire of Curitiba" and Other Stories*; see app. C), and *Abismo de rosas* (1976), Dalton Trevisan has created a stark and cruel, if funny, world that plumbs the lives of the exploited middle and lower classes in the cities (the works call to mind the spare milieus depicted by such minimalist writers in the United States as Robert Coover, Donald Barthelme, and Richard Brautigan).

The most celebrated of Brazil's urban story writers, however, must surely be Rubem Fonseca, the author of a number of works that are sorely in need of translation. Influenced by American detective fiction (see his *High Art* in app. C) and electronic gadgetry, Fonseca "depicts the crime, violence, degradation, and exploitation dominating the underworlds of Rio de Janeiro" in a way that demonstrates his "more complex literary, social, and Existential interests" (K. Jackson, "Short Story" 228). His controversial story "Feliz Ano Novo" ("Happy New Year"), from the collection of the same name published (and subsequently banned) in 1975, explores, in a dispassionate tone laden with irony, the nature of urban violence and depravity, sexual and otherwise. Another story, "Intestino grosso" ("Large Intestine"), stands as "one of the most important documents of contemporary Brazilian literature" (see app. C).[27] In discussing Fonseca's view of Brazil in "Large Intestine," Elizabeth Lowe has written:

> His first objection is to the "culture of development." Not only literature, but all of Brazilian culture, has been infected by the psychology of development. He uses a discussion on pornography, in ironic rebuttal to the censors who have accused him of being a pornographic writer, as a metaphor of the corruption of Brazilian thought and society.

Lowe goes on to observe that Fonseca's "final challenge is the concept of a 'pornography of death,' or the cannibalistic consumption of one generation by the next, both as an 'economy measure' to alleviate a severe shortage of protein, and as a type of purifying ritual" (110). This argument alludes, perhaps problematically, to Oswald de Andrade's anthropophagy movement and its significance for Brazil. Less sensational but no less significant may be Fonseca's declaration, in "Large Intestine," that writers—and art generally—must offset the dehumanizing effects of technocracy and function as opposition voices in society. Uninterested in posing as a populist, Fonseca is nevertheless regarded as "one of the most articulate spokesmen for the professional concerns and ideology of the modern Brazilian writer, to the extent that the title of his censored book, *Feliz Ano Novo* (*Happy New Year*), became a slogan of protest against intellectual repression during the Geisel regime" (Lowe 111).

As they did with the novel, women writers have transformed the modern Brazilian short story. The work of Nélida Piñon, for example, treats feminist themes in a personal and social context that makes them germane to the larger political realm. Often portraying metaphysical, allegorical, and symbolic characters and events that reflect her literary and philosophical cosmopolitanism, Piñon imbues her tales with a sense of human existence as an impenetrable struggle between our sense of what should be sacred and our all-too-regular experience of what is in fact profane. Her story "The Warmth of Things" (the title story in the collection *O calor das coisas* [1980]), for example, focuses on a mother's devotion to her son. In a grotesque, ironic rewriting of Kafka's "The Metamorphosis," the mother transforms the boy not into a giant insect but into an enormous meat turnover that may be a politicized Christian symbol. A sophisticated, erudite writer, with an earthy sense of humor and an abiding sense of history, Piñon shows affinities with such Spanish American writers as Alejo Carpentier and García Márquez (González Echevarría, *Oxford Book* 428).

Although, as mentioned in chapter 2, Márcia Denser served, in 1980, as a pioneer for women writers in Brazil with her anthology of erotic stories, *Muito prazer*, her 1982 collection *Diana caçadora* (*Diana the Huntress*) broke ground yet again in eschewing an overtly political message. Denser has said, "Com proselitismo não se faz literatura. Quem comer desse peixe vai vomitar" ("You can't make literature by proselytizing. Whoever eats of this fish is going to vomit"; qtd. in DiAntonio 184). Although sexual in nature, the 1982 stories—usually narrated, in tough, hard-boiled prose, by women—are the work of an author who disdains established notions of romantic love and refuses to moralize. Readers' individual responses to the text's treatment of such issues as desire, power, and the body represent acts of interpretation that reflect the changing concepts of female identity characterizing much Brazilian literature early in the twenty-first century. In the story "Tigresa" ("Tigress"), in which a young woman named Diana becomes (appropriately to her mythologically charged name) the sexual huntress instead of the hunted, Denser uses images of female sexuality to expose the hypocrisy and double standards of middle-class life in Brazil. According to DiAntonio, "Denser's post-modern poetics eschews the sociopolitical to focus upon relationships and personalities. She portrays the sexual battlegrounds of contemporary Brazilian life, the parties, bars, and motels." Commenting on what he sees as a parallel case in American literature, DiAntonio believes that the narratives in *Diana the Huntress* have "the texture and tone of Tama Janowitz's *Slaves of New York* (1986), especially the story 'O animal dos motéis' ("The Animal of the Motels")," and that Denser's writing "blends elements taken from popular culture like lyrics from Roberto Carlos and Caetano Veloso with allusions to the works of Hemingway and Cortázar" (183–84).

Sexuality is explored in various ways by Lispector (see Fitz, *Sexuality*), Lya Luft, Helena Parente Cunha, Hilda Hilst, Sônia Coutinho, Edla van Steen, Marina Colasanti, and Tânia Jamardo Faillace. Hilst, a prolific and, to some, hermetic writer who has been influenced by both existentialism and surrealism and has experimented with "point of view, typography, and syntax, making extensive use of a somewhat Joycean free-associative language," connects issues of sexuality to mortality (Sadlier 146). Luft, who is of German ancestry and grew up in Rio Grande do Sul, a German immigrant community, often writes of the "atmosphere of sexual fear and uncertainty surrounding her protagonists, whose dramas unfold in the claustrophobic space of the patriarchal home." In particular, she deals with the sundry obstacles and frustrations that confront lesbians as they seek individual identity in a culture not always receptive to female alterity. Sadlier observes:

> Luft's early works, *As parceiras* (1980; *The Partners*) and *A asa esquerda do anjo* (1981; *The Left Wing of the Angel*), are particularly effective in portraying the confusion of women brought up speaking German in the home and obeying the German community's strictly moral, patriarchal codes. Although these women are born in Brazil, they are taught early on to see "Brazilians" as "others"; the confusion that inevitably inflicts them is rooted in a hothouse atmosphere of nationalism and puritanism. (215)

In contrast to Luft's characters, Coutinho's tend to be middle-class women from Rio de Janeiro who find themselves trapped and frustrated, sexually and psychologically, in unsatisfactory relationships with men. In "Every Lana Turner Has Her Johnny Stompanato" (1985), Coutinho "writes a kind of deconstructive fiction, exploring the subtle, interchangeable relations among an authorial persona, a fictional character, a 'real' historical subject, and a consumer image of a Hollywood star" (Sadlier 228). The following passage exemplifies her style:

> Yes, there was the deeply tanned skin of the Beverly Hills swimming pools—or the beaches of the Zona Sul—the long, red fingernails, the platinum blond hair, and, on her beautiful face, traces of passing time. . . . On a misty Saturday afternoon, watching fraying clouds empty onto the tree-covered slopes of Corcovado, Melissa sees anew—I see anew—in a dizzying whirl of historic scenes, the similarities and differences between her and Lana Turner, beginning with the Anglo-Saxon Puritans' colonization of America and the arrival of exiled Portuguese with Moorish blood to Brazil. (trans. Sadlier 229)

Like Coutinho an author deeply conversant with Afro-Brazilian culture, Parente Cunha also pursues the theme of sexuality, especially as it relates to the country's racial past and present and to the changing expectations of middle-aged women in contemporary Brazil. Utilizing Brazil's African heritage as a mechanism for both psychological and sexual liberation, and in the tradition of Lispector (Fitz, *Sexuality*) allowing the act of masturbation to function subversively as a sign of female empowerment and self-realization,

Parente Cunha creates, in *Mulher no espelho* (1983; *Woman between Mirrors* [1989]), one of the most powerful and effective Brazilian novels of the 1980s (see app. C). Practicing a narrative technique that integrates several literary theories, such as structuralism, poststructuralism, feminism, and semiotics, into a fictional skein that comments on its own creation and its own authenticity, *Woman between Mirrors* dramatizes, from the perspective of a middle-class white woman, how changes in Brazilian culture reflect the more assertive roles women are assuming.

Yet another take on sexuality appears in works by Colasanti and by Faillace, both of whom deal, in quite different ways, with the troubled lives of young people in Brazil's middle and lower classes. Faillace in particular

> frequently writes about the difficulties children and adolescents encounter growing up in a world of drugs, crime, and sexual violence. Some of her most powerful and disturbing stories appear in *Vinde a mim os pequeninos* (1977; *Come unto Me the Little Ones*), whose protagonists include abandoned children, teenage mothers, and gang youths. (Sadlier 163).

A highly respected journalist, Colasanti, associated since 1975 with the women's journal *Nova*, has long written about women's issues in Brazil. Credited with creating the literary genre *mini-conto* ("mini–short story"), Colasanti is known for her tales of female eroticism. In "Menina de vermelho, a caminho da lua" ("Little Girl in Red, on Her Way to the Moon"), which originally appeared in Denser's *Muito prazer: Contos eróticos femininos* (1982), she offers "an unusual and unsettling depiction of preadolescent sexuality" (Sadlier 194; see 195–203 for translation of story). The story speaks poignantly about the cruel relations among sex, survival, and power that often characterize an environment beset by poverty, exploitation, and corruption.

In addition to those mentioned in the preceding pages, women writers and intellectuals such as Bella Jozef, Eliane Zagury, Lúcia Helena, Renata Pallotini, Edla van Steen, Rachel Jardim, Marilene Felinto, and Lygia Fagundes Telles are establishing themselves in the postdictatorship era as prime movers in yet another reformulation of contemporary Brazilian letters. Conscious of being historically and culturally distinct from their Spanish American and their North American counterparts and placing the issue of what it means to be a feminist and a woman in a perspective that links industrial nations and developing nations, Brazilian women writers are revolutionizing the ways Brazilians view themselves, their culture, and their relations with the world.

As we have seen, metaliterary play, the ironic grotesque, parody, and in-tertextuality are among the international trends characterizing the short story in Brazil today, though they are fully characteristic of the novel form as well. Often described as postmodern in its approach to form, tone, and style, the short story, according to K. David Jackson, features a number of specifically Brazilian features: synthesis of the Amerindian, African, and European tra-ditions; reinterpretation of Old World myths and indigenous legends; flour-ishing regionalism in themes, language, and characterization; extensive use of dialect and colloquial language; commitment to Brazilian Portuguese and its expressive possibilities; respect for local customs and key historical events; experimentation with discontinuous and poetic narrative structures; existen-tial and psychological portraits of the Brazilian character; and "the subtle analysis of the motivation, values, and relationships underlying a social world that seems deceptively familiar to the European or American reader, but that in fact embodies a decisive difference" ("Short Story" 231–32). That distinc-tiveness stems from the nation's colonial experience, its racial history, and its social, political, and economic structures. Inspired by such earlier writers as Machado de Assis, Guimarães Rosa, and Clarice Lispector and given new vi-tality by such contemporary practitioners as Piñon, Telles, Denser, Trevisan, Scliar, and Fonseca, the short story remains one of contemporary Brazil's strongest and most important literary genres.

NOTES

1. Current estimates of the number of Indians in Brazil when the Portuguese arrived in 1500 are 2.5 million.
2. If we include folklore in the definition of literature, then the Indian traditions had a significant effect on Brazilian culture. Tupi mythology, for example, lives on in the tales of Saci-perere, the one-legged Indian mischief maker, and in the figure of Iracema (the title of one of José de Alencar's most famous novels), "the captivating beauty with long green hair and a seductive voice who lures young warriors into the depths of the wa-ters" (Burns, *History* [3rd ed.] 17).
3. Because colonial authorities did not allow novels to circulate in the New World, non-fiction prose was the dominant genre. "Nonetheless," as Monegal notes, "fiction thinly disguised as fact, or fact generously contaminated by fiction, was the stuff of some of the most exciting chronicles, memoirs, and documents produced in Colonial times" (*Borzoi Anthology* 1: xv).
4. The full title is *Compêndio narrativo do peregrino da América, em que se tratam de vários discursos espirituais e morais, com muitas advertências e documentos contra os abusos que*

se acham introduzidos pela malícia diabólica no estado do Brasil. The didactic nature of the text is clear from the title's translation: *Narrative Compendium of the American Pilgrim, Consisting of Various Spiritual and Moral Discourses, with Many Warnings and Documents against the Abuses That, by Diabolic Malice, Have Been Introduced into the State of Brazil.*

5. In its first edition, its title was *Máximas de virtude e formosura* (*Maxims of Virtue and Comeliness*). In the three later editions, the title was changed to *As Aventuras de Dió-fanes*. No English translation of the work is known to exist.

6. Haberly reports, however, that as late as 1850, "at least 90% of Brazilian women were completely illiterate" ("Brazilian Novel" 139).

7. The text even features a reference to the British feminist Mary Wollstonecraft.

8. *Carioca* refers to anything relating to the residents of Rio de Janeiro.

9. Threatened by fast-rising waters, Peri tears a large palm tree from the ground and, using it as a raft, the two sail away.

10. *Lucíola* deals with prostitution, while *Senhora* takes up the subject of arranged marriages.

11. Alencar, for all his insight, did not recognize slavery—"which he strongly supported"—as Brazil's fundamental sociopolitical problem. For him the greedy pursuit of "uninherited wealth" was the "root of all evil" (Haberly, "Brazilian Novel" 144).

12. In his book *Adultery in the Novel: Studies in the Theory of Fiction* (New York: Oxford UP, 1979), Tony Tanner includes these two titles by Machado, along with such other nineteenth-century landmarks as *The Awakening, Madame Bovary, Anna Karenina, The Scarlet Letter,* and *The Age of Innocence.*

13. According to the Brazilian scholar Eugênio Gomes, the thematic structure of "The Psychiatrist" may have been inspired by Swift's *A Serious and Useful Scheme to Make an Hospital for Incurables*, but Machado goes further by virtually obliterating the "boundary between reason and madness" (qtd. by Grossman in Machado, *"The Psychiatrist" and Other Stories* ix [app. C]).

14. "The Psychiatrist" also bears comparison with Chekhov's "Ward Number Six" (1892) in that both stories, rife with irony, deal with a physician who ends up a patient in his own mental hospital.

15. The same problem, Brazil's dependency on foreign influences, was being examined by Machado, whose late novels *Quincas Borba* and *Esau and Jacob* depict the nation struggling to define itself in terms of such imported (and difficult-to-assimilate) concepts as modernity, liberalism, capitalism, and progress. Note that Aranha was well versed in the work of Nietzsche and the Scandanavian playwrights (Merquior 370).

16. Porter says the following: "The specific lines along which ideological opposition had formed are clear: civilization versus barbarism" ("Social Discourse" 354).

17. Despite the myriad ills that afflicted American society, Lobato was impressed by the strength and vitality of America's democratic institutions and, in a less idealistic vein, by the role the iron, steel, and petroleum industries had played in the country's economic development. On his return to Brazil in 1932, he campaigned vigorously for the development of these industries and for greater citizen involvement in government.

18. Born in the later years of the nineteenth century with the work of José Martí and Julián del Casal (in Cuba), Manuel Gutiérrez Nájera (in Mexico), and José Asunción Silva (in Colombia), but reaching its peak in 1888—with the publication of Rubén Darío's *Azul* (in Nicaragua), a collection of poems and short narratives—Spanish American *modernismo* was heavily influenced by the French movements Parnassianism and symbolism and the French poets Gautier, Leconte de Lisle, and Verlaine. Framing the issue in an inter-American context, we can point out that Spanish American *modernista* poetry exemplifies the arguments Edgar Allan Poe makes in "The Poetic Principle," although it is not known whether Poe's work exerted a direct influence. Escapist in nature, Spanish American *modernismo* dealt with little that was native to the Spanish-speaking nations of the New World. "It was exotic, in that it drew elements from distant sources. It was artificial—a mode of life and thought based on the imitation of alien ways, and the ignoring of realistic problems like poverty, illiteracy, and the oppression of Indian masses" (Torres-Ríoseco 88). In contrast, Brazilian *modernismo*, dating from 1922 but with its roots going back a decade, was deeply concerned with indigenous issues and the larger questions of thought, culture, and politics; these were often grafted onto artistic forms, techniques, and movements from the European avant-garde, such as free verse, cubism, and futurism. Far from escapist, this *modernismo* penetrated into all aspects of Brazilian society and culture and promoted a political and artistic agenda stressing an authentic national identity, a process the poet Menotti del Picchia described as the "Brazilianization of Brazil."

19. In one scene, Macunaíma becomes white after bathing in a pool of magical green water deep in the Amazonian jungle.

20. Brazil is formed by its European heritage, its Amerindian heritage, and its African heritage, in addition to the myths and traditions introduced by the immigrant nationalities (e.g., the Germans, Italians, and Japanese) who have enriched it.

21. Listing, in an interview with Selden Rodman, American writers that he knows and likes, Amado says that his "favorite is Mark Twain—as great as Dickens or Tolstoi—and among moderns, Hemingway, Sinclair Lewis, Upton Sinclair, Richard Wright, the young Steinbeck, and especially Erskine Caldwell" (122).

22. The Portuguese translation, by Oton M. Garcia (who also wrote an introduction), has the title "O segrêdo da Emília," and the story appeared in *Ribeu* 2.8 (1945): 116–28.

23. DiAntonio cites Osman Lins's masterpiece, *Avalovara* (1973), and the works of Nélida Piñon as exceptions to this comparison. *Avalovara*, which is structured around a palindromic Latin phrase, may be read in whatever sequence readers might prefer (see chap. 4). For those well versed in Spanish American fiction, this technique recalls Julio Cortázar's novel *Rayuela* (1963; *Hopscotch* [1966]).

24. The economic miracle lasted from 1968 to 1973 or 1974, when a worldwide petroleum shortage exposed the fragility of the miracle. Used to justify the repressive measures taken by the generals, the economic miracle boasted an average annual growth rate of about 11%, with inflation generally held in check at 20%. Benefiting from international prosperity, Brazil received almost unlimited foreign credit during these years, at

very low interest rates. Unfortunately, the Brazilian military accomplished its goals by keeping workers' salaries low, by suspending many civil liberties, and by setting up a dictatorship. Because wages failed to keep pace with prices, Brazil's working class lost much of its earning power. Although for many outside observers the miracle showed that Brazil could serve as a model for other Third World nations seeking to move up the economic ladder, it actually weakened Brazil's economy while exacerbating serious internal problems.

25. This quotation is from the paperback cover of *The Celebration*, trans. Thomas Colchie (New York: Bard Avon, 1982).

26. Although in *A Poetics of Postmodernism*, Hutcheon declares that postmodernism is "primarily European and American (North and South)" (4), and although she discusses several Spanish American writers and texts, her index does not show any Brazilian authors or have any reference for Brazil. The same is true for Brian McHale's *Postmodernist Fiction* (New York: Methuen, 1987) and Fredric Jameson's *Postmodernism; or, The Cultural Logic of Late Capitalism* (Durham: Duke UP, 1991). For a summary of postmodernism's relation to Brazil and its literature, see Perrone, *Seven Faces* 159–61; see also Santiago, "O narrador pós-moderno"; Caetano Lopes. Also recommended is Santiago's "Reading and Discursive Intensities." Studies focusing on how postmodernism relates to Latin America are in Beverley and Oviedo and in Yúdice, "Periphery" and "Capitalism."

27. Lowe, one of Fonseca's most perceptive critics, has translated this story; see *Review* 76 (1976): 69–75. Lowe includes a critical introduction.

CHAPTER 4

Brazilian Literature in English Translation

As the complex mechanism by which a work written in one language is reconstructed in another and can thus move beyond one linguistic community to reach readers in other cultures, times, and places, translation is vital to an all-too-often overlooked literature like Brazil's. Never a neutral or objective process, the work of the translator (who, as Rabassa has observed, must be the text's most careful and discerning reader) involves decisions that may be as political—that is, culturally sensitive—as they are aesthetic. More a creative writer than a linguist, the translator must make subtle interpretations that allow the work to be rendered in another language with a high level of stylistic fidelity to the original. Because Portuguese (the world's sixth most widely used language) is not frequently studied, even Brazil's greatest writers struggle to make themselves known outside the Portuguese-speaking world. Often lost, as we have seen, under the amorphous designation *Latin American*, Brazilian literature is a distinctive national literature, with its own themes, styles, cultural contexts, and periods of development. For those who do not read Portuguese or who do not read it well, translation is the only way Brazil can escape the isolation that has long prevented it from taking its rightful place among the dynamic literary nations of the Americas and of the world.

In the early years of the twenty-first century, we can say that Brazilian literature has been generally well served by its translation into English; we should note, though, that most of the translations occurred in the second half of the twentieth century. Nevertheless, the history of Brazilian literature in English probably began in the late 1880s, when two of its classics—Alencar's

Indianist, nationalistic idyll *Iracema* (originally translated by Isabel Burton), and Alfredo d'Escragnolle Taunay's *Inocência*—were published in London (see app. C for both works).[1]

Brazilian literature first made its appearance in the United States with Graça Aranha's controversial thesis novel *Canaan* (see app. C). In its "confused concept of race" (Wagley 261) and its focus on the thorny problem of Brazilian nationalism, including Brazil's cultural and economic relationship with the United States, *Canaan* generated a wide following during the racially charged 1920s (Putnam, *Marvelous Journey* 205).

This historically significant if aesthetically flawed novel gained an audience in the United States just as scholars there were starting to realize the many historical ties that, despite the disparities between the northern and southern nations, link the Americas. The eminent American historian Herbert E. Bolton, in fact, began offering his highly influential course History of the Americas, at the University of California, Berkeley, in 1919. Arguing that the Americas, North, Central, and South, had a common (if often unhappy) history—one that would provide the foundation for inter-American studies—Bolton's controversial thesis emphasized that Brazil, with its vast size, its historical parallels with the United States, and its wealth of natural resources, would become one of the New World's major nations. For this reason alone, Bolton thought, Americans should know much more about their hemispheric counterpart.

Two important works appeared in the 1920s: Isaac Goldberg's *Brazilian Tales* (1921) and his *Brazilian Literature* (1922) both enhanced the legitimacy of Brazilian letters by arguing that its development as an authentic national literature parallels the evolution of literature in the United States. The 1921 text—a small anthology of short stories by four Brazilian writers (one of whom, José de Medeiros e Albuquerque, Goldberg likens to both Maupassant and Poe)—marked the first time Brazil's prose master Machado de Assis was available in English in the United States.[2]

Driven in part by Bolton's innovative, comparative approach to American history and by the strategic imperative of inter-American relations in the pre–World War II years, interest in Brazil during the 1930s waxed and waned as Americans struggled to shed the isolationism and cultural arrogance that plagued relations between the United States and its hemispheric neighbors. Putnam, for example, reports (*Marvelous Journey* viii) that as of 1948 only twelve Brazilian novels had been translated into English (eight had appeared since 1943): Jorge Amado's *The Violent Land* (app. C), Aluísio Azevedo's *A*

Brazilian Tenement (listed in app. C under its more recent English title, *The Slum*), Graça Aranha's *Canaan*, Graciliano Ramos's *Anguish* (app. C), Paulo Setubal's *Domitila*, Taunay's *Inocência*, and Érico Veríssimo's *Crossroads* (app. C) and *The Rest Is Silence*. Two collections of short stories had also been published in the United States, Goldberg's *Brazilian Tales*, as noted, and, with Goldberg as the translator, *Brazilian Short Stories*, by Monteiro Lobato, a writer sometimes compared with Mark Twain. For a variety of reasons, then, by the third decade of the twentieth century Brazil had begun to make its presence felt in the United States.

During the cultural rapprochement that characterized the war years, American interest in Brazil picked up considerably. Samuel Putnam credits the war and the good-neighbor policies of the time with educating Americans about Brazilian literature and the many affinities it has with their own literature (*Marvelous Journey* vii–viii). Besides Sylvia Leão's *White Shore of Olinda* (written in English and published in 1943), two sociologically important and still-influential texts, both superbly translated by Putnam, were published in the 1940s: Euclides da Cunha's *Rebellion in the Backlands* (Putnam's version re-creates the drama, doubt, outrage, and bitter irony of the original; see app. C) and Gilberto Freyre's scholarly work *The Masters and the Slaves*.[3]

Exemplifying the Pan-Americanism of the times were several literary anthologies that situated Brazilian letters in the context of Spanish American literature and presented a more balanced picture of Latin America's two great literary traditions. Dudley Fitts's *Anthology of Contemporary Latin American Poetry* (New Directions, 1942), for example, contains translations of poems by such Brazilian luminaries as Manuel Bandeira, Carlos Drummond de Andrade, Jorge de Lima, and Murilo Mendes, while Angel Flores and Dudley Poore's *Fiesta in November: Stories from Latin America* (Houghton, 1942) offers "Sea of the Dead," an excerpt from one of Jorge Amado's most successful novels, *Mar Morto* (1936). This work, in another superb translation by Gregory Rabassa, is available in English as *The Sea of Death* (app. C).

Undoubtedly reflecting their publishers' fear of offending their readers, two of the novels on Putnam's list of works translated by 1948 were, in their English versions, severely bowdlerized: Amado's *The Violent Land*, translated by Putnam (Knopf, 1945), and Azevedo's *A Brazilian Tenement*, rendered into English by Harry W. Brown (McBride, 1926). Of the latter novel, João Sedycias notes, "When it was first translated from Portuguese into English . . . certain key passages in the original text dealing openly with sex were purposely left out" (58). Similarly, Amado's novel (its subject matter, the often bloody struggle over control of Bahia's lucrative cacao plantations, has been compared with events surrounding the California gold rush) was shorn in its English version of its many sexual scenes.

Finally, mention must be made of Veríssimo's *Brazilian Literature: An Outline* (Macmillan, 1945), written originally in English. This popular critical study generated interest in Brazilian literature and culture in the United States of this period. A respected intellectual and participant in both the Organization of American States and the Pan American Union, Veríssimo was a frequent visitor to the United States. His delightful travel journal *O gato preto em campo de neve* (1941; *The Black Cat in the Land of the Snow*) became a basic text for Portuguese study at a number of American colleges and universities.

After the war, Brazilian literature continued to make slow but steady progress in its penetration of the American consciousness. The most significant event during this period is the appearance in rapid sequence of three of Machado's greatest novels: *Epitaph of a Small Winner* (translation of *As Memórias póstumas de Brás Cubas*, by William L. Grossman, 1952; retranslated by Gregory Rabassa as *The Posthumous Memoirs of Brás Cubas*);[4] *Dom Casmurro* (trans. Helen Caldwell, 1953);[5] and *Philosopher or Dog?* (translation of *Quincas Borba* by Clotilde Wilson, 1954; retranslated by Rabassa in 1998).[6] The faithfulness of all three translations, which captured the spirit and the letter of Machado's metafictive irony as well as his structural innovations, enhanced Machado's reception in the United States. In that society in the 1950s, his acerbic iconoclasm could have been expected to catch the eye of a number of writers, including (as we saw in chapter 1) John Barth, who became an early admirer of Machado's work.

Although Barth was quick to see the brilliance of what he felt were Machado's "proto-post-modernist" techniques, few others were as enthusiastic.[7] In fact, as Daphne Patai has shown ("Machado in English"), many of the reviews of the three novels indicate that readers were not only misinformed about Machado's identity and intentions but mistaken or superficial in their critical comments. Some reviewers even disparaged *Dom Casmurro*, which Helen Caldwell has judged to be "perhaps the finest of all American novels of either continent" (1), for "irrelevant discourses" and a "thin" narrative line whose style becomes "annoying to the reader who expects a steady advance toward a climax" (Webster, qtd. in Patai, "Machado in English" 113). Another reviewer called it a tale that seems "slight and unsubstantial" (Herring, qtd. in Patai, "Machado in English" 114). Although several critics (beginning in 1953 with the American Waldo Frank) have praised *Dom Casmurro* for its artful ambiguity (particularly in the plot's ostensible conflict, whether or not the character Capitu was guilty of adultery), only Barth, a novelist given to anti-realistic tendencies, realized that Machado's achievement—the creation of a new kind of narrative and a new reader—put him very much ahead of his time. Nevertheless, Barth, because of his two famous essays "The Literature of Exhaustion" (1967) and "The Literature of Replenishment" (1980; for both, see app. C), neither of which mentions Machado, is more closely linked in the American mind to Julio Cortázar, Gabriel García Márquez, and Jorge Luis Borges than he is to the Brazilian master. Had Barth praised Machado in his two pieces, he would probably have made it easier for American readers to appreciate Machado's narratives. Not until late in the twentieth century, with the publication of the Noonday editions of his work—featuring introductions or afterwords by such influential figures as Elizabeth Hardwick and Susan Sontag—did the Brazilian writer receive the recognition he deserved in the United States.

Yet when we think about the breakthrough achieved, in the United States, by "Latin American" (typically taken to mean Spanish American) writers in the 1960s, the as-yet unanswered question is, Why was Machado de Assis—who as a novelist is widely regarded as superior to his Spanish American colleagues—all but ignored during the years of the Boom? Was the reason faulty marketing or promotion? Was some cultural disconnect taking place, one that perhaps overvalued the exotic Spanish American fiction of the time while undervaluing the decidedly unexotic work of Machado? Or was Machado simply misinterpreted by American critics, who may have been unprepared for the subtleties of this "unknown Latin American" author?

It might also be argued that Machado's meticulous dissection of the platitudes, posturings, and false assumptions on which empires are built and maintained went unheeded in the 1950s by American critics, a class of readers basking, along with many others, in the glow of a great victory at the end of a terrible world war and perhaps looking more for an affirmation than for a withering critique of empire. The American critical establishment of the time may simply not have been receptive to Machado's unique brand of disenchantment and skepticism, particularly as these touched on such issues as the legitimacy of power structures, the problems of cultural integrity and moral conduct in a capitalist society, and (most obvious in *Philosopher or Dog?*) the damage caused by political and economic relations (at the international level) based on exploitation and dependency. In short, the American literary intelligentsia of the 1950s may have found it more convenient to dismiss an idiosyncratic Latin American who had the temerity to challenge many of the fundamental arguments about social, political, and economic development that were rapidly being transformed into rigid dogma during the great ideological struggle between East and West that characterized the cold war era.

Troublesome to all who admire Machado's artistry, this issue (along with its nettlesome corollary: Why was Amado winning popularity and critical acclaim whereas Machado was not?) remains an enigma surrounding the reception of Brazilian literature in the United States during the 1950s and 1960s. One plausible answer is that, by any standard, Amado is a marvelous storyteller, a writer blessed by the ability to create memorable characters, to keep several plots spinning at once, and to hold the reader's interest every step of the way, while Machado's brilliance lies in his technical fireworks, in the depth of his intellectual and philosophical ruminations, in his wry sense of humor, and in his subtle manipulation of the reader. We'll examine Amado in more detail later in this chapter.

As Machado becomes more widely read in the United States, however, his readers should understand the nature of the translations of his works. This understanding is especially important for *Dom Casmurro*, which most scholars of Brazilian literature regard as his finest novel. As of 2002, at least three English translations of this masterwork were available, yet they are far from equal in quality and reliability. First is the venerable Caldwell version, originally published by Noonday Press in 1953 and still highly serviceable; second is the 1992 British translation by R. L. Scott-Buccleuch, published by Peter Owen; third is the most recent rendering, by John Gledson (Oxford UP, 1997), who is like Caldwell a noted Machado scholar (app. C). Without venturing into the complexities of comparative translation analysis, we can say that the Caldwell and the Gledson versions are reliable in connecting the reader not only to Machado's most obvious themes (e.g., adultery, jealousy, time, memory, and desire) but, more important, to his subtle, modernistic irony; his disillusionment; and his narrative self-consciousness. One notable difference between these two versions is that Gledson's contains notes that explain the significance of the many place-names, references, and allusions. Readers of Caldwell's rendering are given less guidance in the sociopolitical milieu of Machado's time, but they may gain more insight into the structural complexities and subtleties of the text itself, where, it may be argued, Machado's creative genius is most easily discerned.

Another, less apparent difference, relating to style (always the most difficult aspect of a writer's craft to translate), is that Gledson has made a conscious effort to "stick to Machado's own punctuation"; punctuation was of keen interest to Machado. The result is that "the run-on effect caused by the paucity of full-stops" (*Dom Casmurro*, translated by Gledson, xxiv, xxv), coupled with Machado's extensive use of the semicolon and the ellipsis (the latter, in addition to deepening the ambiguity, fosters readers' involvement in the construction of the text's meaning), allows the contemporary English-language reader to appreciate Machado's ironic, metafictive, and metaphoric mode of writing. Caldwell's version also preserves much of Machado's style, although it does not replicate quite so deliberately the way his sentences were written and read and therefore what their impact on the reader would be. Gledson's translation of *Dom Casmurro*, then, does not correct or improve Caldwell's version so much as it offers a more culturally based alternative to it, replete with a foreword (by the translator) and an afterword (by the Brazilian scholar João Adolfo Hansen) that situate Machado as a writer of a particular time and place and explain the intricacies of his artistry and outlook.

At the risk of nitpicking, however, we should examine in detail one particular difference between these two versions of *Dom Casmurro* that affects how the reader responds to a decisive passage. Chapter 55, "A Sonnet," deals with the writing of an unfinished poem, a poem that the self-conscious, perhaps duplicitous narrator-protagonist, Dom Casmurro, is able to interpret in a variety of ways (and in a metaphoric reenactment of the reader's response to the text). As he pens the memoirs that constitute the novel, Don Casmurro is an old man seeking to reconstruct his life, even though he is dubious about the medium of communication—language—about the filters of memory and intentionality, and about the act of narration itself. But Dom Casmurro has written only the sonnet's first line and its last, leaving the rest up to the reader (another demonstration of Machado's apparent interest in having the reader take a more active role in the creation of literature). Germane both to the sonnet and to the link between language and reality (the nature of the former may determine how we think about the latter), interpretation thus emerges as the central issue, even as the sonnet, with its missing middle, develops force as a symbol of the narrator's otiose life. The difference between the two versions has to do with the translation of the Portuguese word *sentido*, which can convey both "meaning" and "sense." Machado uses the word twice, in quick succession, but while Caldwell translates it as "meaning" both times, Gledson translates it first as "meaning" and then as "sense," breaking the repetition (and the register of ambiguity) that exists in the original. The Caldwell text reads as follows:

> Worn out with waiting, I decided to alter the meaning of the final verse by the simple transposition of two words, thus:
>
> Life is won, the battle still is lost!
>
> The meaning turns out to be exactly the opposite, but perhaps this in itself would coax inspiration. (112–13)

Gledson renders the lines differently:

> Tired of waiting, I thought of altering the meaning of the last line by turning it round, in the following manner:
>
> "The battle may be lost, but life is won!"
>
> The sense was exactly the opposite, but perhaps this might just bring the inspiration. (104–05)

When Gledson translates *sentido* first as "meaning" and then as "sense," he muddies the crucial point about meaning and the process of interpretation that Machado's original text makes, a semantic complexity that Caldwell's version, hewing more closely to the original syntax and diction, retains.

Finally, the reader of the two passages may have noted that the two versions differ in the sonnet's final line. In Machado's original text, the line begins with an allusion to life and ends with the Portuguese word for "battle": "Ganha-se a vida, perde-se a batalha!" In both its syntax and its caesura, Caldwell's translation is truer to the original than is Gledson's, which inverts the word order, and therefore destroys the rhythm of the original. In so doing, Gledson goes further than "a simples transposição de duas palavras" ("the simple transposition of two words"; Caldwell translation) called for in the original. Despite such problems, the Gledson version, with its notes and its attention to Machado's punctuation, has contributed to the positive reception of *Dom Casmurro* in the English-speaking world.

Lamentably, the third English translation will have the opposite effect and for that reason should be avoided by readers seeking to understand why this novel has been so widely praised. The translator of this "infamous" version, Scott-Buccleuch, "butchers the novel, omitting nine chapters and misnumbering the rest" (K. Jackson, "Madness" 15). The pivotal chapter 55, for example, which comes midway in the novel, links the two halves; furthermore, as we have observed, it develops the unfinished sonnet into a metaphor for the narrator's life, for the act of interpretation, and for the mystery of the human experience itself. Nevertheless, the chapter has been excised from Scott-Buccleuch's shorter, more streamlined and straightforward version. Indeed, as Patai declares, Scott-Buccleuch's unexplained decision to eliminate nine chapters is to alter the novel profoundly, to "enormously reduce the complexity and self-reflexivity of the original." Assessing the damage done to Machado's reputation, Patai says that "for those who believe the interest of the novel lies above all in Bento and Capitu's relationship, and who simply want to get on with the story, little damage will perhaps have been done. But to readers who want to know what Machado as a novelist is up to, the loss is inestimable." Seeking apparently to serve as an editor of the novel (which he seems to consider prolix and digressive), Scott-Buccleuch deletes "much of the metanarrative that is absolutely crucial to understanding Bento and his task in composing the story we ostensibly have before us"; these passages are sacrificed by the translator "in the interest (judging by the achieved effect) of advancing the plot" (Patai, "Machado in English" 97). Asserting what is termed the "moral right of the translator," Scott-Buccleuch gives us a *Dom Casmurro* that is less sophisticated than the original and that, in its abridgment, loses much of the novel's probing of the crucial aesthetic problem of verisimilitude and its interrogation of the concept of truth and of the reader's role in constructing it.[8]

A final question about Machado's availability in English concerns the many short fiction pieces he wrote. Like Henry James and Chekhov, Machado must be regarded as a master of the short story genre. (Paralleling his technical experimentations in the novel, his work on the short story form changed after 1881, becoming more sophisticated and psychologically insightful.) In addition, the Brazilian critic Augusto Meyer has compared "Machado's break in evolutionary continuity to that between Herman Melville's earlier works and *Moby-Dick*" (qtd. in Schmitt and Ishimatsu x). Although Machado wrote more than two hundred stories, fewer than fifty have so far appeared in English. Indeed, the first of his stories to be translated were apparently selected for a French collection published in 1910, two years after the author's death and one year after Anatole France feted Machado at the Sorbonne, in the Richelieu amphitheater, on 3 April 1909 (Goldberg 144). The tales that are in English, especially those written after 1881, number among his most respected. Aside from *Brazilian Tales*, mentioned earlier in this chapter, there are *"The Psychiatrist" and Other Stories* and *"The Devil's Church" and Other Stories* (see app. C for both works).

In tracking the evolution of Machado's presence in the mind of the American reader, we might note that a story from *"The Devil's Church"* collection, "Dona Paula," was selected by the editors for inclusion in the 1988 edition of the college anthology *Literature of the Western World*.[9] Sadly, however, Machado's entry lasted only one year; he was deleted from the following edition. His case might have been strengthened by a different story selection ("Midnight Mass," "The Psychiatrist," or "The Devil's Church") and by an introduction that situated him in the Western literary and intellectual tradition, pointed out the influences to which he responded, and elucidated his contributions to it. As the editors note, "Dona Paula" (1884), "with its close attention to its protagonist's stream of consciousness, its coolly ironic narrator, and its structural juxtapositions of times, characters, and value systems," represents the interiority and modernity of Machado's post-1880 narratives. Overall, however, as Jack Schmitt and Lorie Ishimatsu observe, "Machado's stories constitute an excellent satirical portrait of middle-class values and social structures in Brazil during the period of the Second Empire (1840–1890) and the first years of the Republic" (x) while also, especially after the late 1870s, achieving a universal appeal. In the later stories, Machado's experimentations with perspective and point of view; with irony, ambiguity, and unreliable narrators; with psychological conflict, hypocrisy, and alienation; and with time express the antirealism that animates his best work and demonstrate why it is Machado de Assis who created the first "new narrative" of the Americas.

The 1960s, then, are a kind of breakthrough period for Brazilian literature and culture in the United States. Besides Machado, several deserving writers, notably Carolina Maria de Jesus, Jorge Amado, and Guimarães Rosa, were translated and thus gained access to American readers. Appearing in 1962, de Jesus's scorching screed *Child of the Dark* offered an alternative to the generally sympathetic treatment that Brazil was experiencing in the United States. Ably translated by David St. Clair, *Child of the Dark* became a best seller in the United States, just as it had been in Brazil, where as *Quarto de despejo* it was published in 1960. Replete with powerful black-and-white photographs of its subjects and their environs and fueled by a sense of outrage, *Child of the Dark* presents a Brazil that had not been shown before and that was not a happy and prosperous place. Even more striking—given that the book appeared in the early years of the civil rights movement in the United States—is that the Brazil depicted here by its author, a poor black woman, did not have a smiling white face; it had a black face, and an angry one at that. Focusing on the impoverished inhabitants of a São Paulo slum in the late 1950s and written in the form of a diary, the work makes us see, smell, hear, and feel the pain—and cries of protest—of the *favelados*, who for lack of education and opportunity live in degradation and want. The author, whose literacy made her an atypical *favelada*, describes a part of Brazilian society vitiated by poverty, violence, racism, crime, vice, and, above all, hunger—the daily struggle for food is the book's signature theme. Written in the candid voice of a poorly educated woman who knew firsthand the desperate life she was portraying, *Child of the Dark* is, like *Rebellion in the Backlands* and *Let Us Now Praise Famous Men* before it, a scathing indictment of the abandonment of the poor and of a culture that would allow it to happen.

The enthusiastic reception of Amado in English is a fascinating if perplexing story, an example of the writer who is warmly received abroad while suffering controversy and criticism at home. Benefiting from the surging popularity of Brazilian music and film, and from the fact that *Gabriela, Clove and Cinnamon* provided an erotic, funny break from the racist, repressive, and conformist atmosphere of the 1950s in the United States, Amado's 1958 novel appeared to overwhelmingly positive reviews in 1962 (see app. C). Aside from its purely literary qualities, a significant part of the novel's appeal was the sensuality and exoticism that, for many Americans at the time, defined Brazil, a huge hemispheric neighbor about which they knew next to nothing but which held a certain fascination for them. The American reading public must have been titillated, for example, by Gabriela, a strong-willed protagonist who loved sex but found marriage confining, hypocritical, and inhibiting. Gabriela's creator and Brazil's most exported author, Amado is widely read, and his novels, most of them translated, have been highly successful in the global market. The problem, according to his critics, is that the books are often seen as pandering to the worst aspects of Brazilian (and Western) culture (violence against women, for example) and that, particularly after 1958 and *Gabriela,* they are less serious literature than facile marketing ploys.

Enormously popular with Brazil's growing but still limited domestic reading public yet excoriated by much of the country's intelligentsia, "Amado is virtually the only Brazilian writer to have had any international impact beyond academic circles" (Armstrong, *Third World* 134). This point may explain why Amado is the only Brazilian writer mentioned by the Chilean José Donoso in his widely read book on the history of the Spanish American Boom novels of the 1960s (*A Personal History of the Boom* [1977]). As late as 1987, the editors of *The Harper American Literature* cite only Amado from Brazil (along with Borges and García Márquez) in a reference to "South American" writers who have helped "internationalize" American literature and have become "as important to American literature as any writers from England or Europe" (2: 2578).[10] We could conclude that, in the minds of American readers, Amado's identification with Brazilian literature has become so pervasive that even many literary scholars (other than Brazilianists) know little about such widely translated and marketed writers as Machado, Clarice Lispector, Graciliano Ramos, and Nélida Piñon.

In any event, *Gabriela, Clove and Cinnamon*, a felicitous mixture of uninhibited sex, comic charm, and political intrigue and brimming with captivating characters (not the least is the "cinnamon-colored" Gabriela herself), became a best seller in the United States, ranking among the top twenty-five novels published there in 1962. In addition to the inherent goodness and insouciant sexuality of its racially mixed heroine (who for many readers epitomizes the beauty and vitality of the Brazilian people), *Gabriela, Clove and Cinnamon* exudes an enthusiasm for progress that reflects the economic and political policies of Brazil in the late 1950s. Earlier we observed that the novel served as a kind of antidote to the pessimism of the 1950s in the States. The critic Raymond Federman has a different explanation for the book's success in America. On the surface, at least, the 1950s had been "a period of social and economic optimism," in which "the key" issues were "the achievement of *success*" and the "*valorization* and *symbolization* of the American way of life" (1147). Because Amado's novel projects this image, the work may seem to valorize the economic and political climate of the United States—a feat that may have contributed to the warm reception *Gabriela, Clove and Cinnamon* enjoyed in the States.

Indeed, the novel's primary subtext may well be Brazil's need and ability to transform itself from a rural oligarchy, dominated by large landowners, into a modern nation-state, led by what Amado presents as a mutually beneficial union of commerce, the rule of law, and progressive social thought. As a social document, then, Gabriela's story highlights the "developmentalist enthusiasm" of "the Kubitschek presidency" (Gledson, "Brazilian Prose" 193). At the symbolic level, *Gabriela, Clove and Cinnamon* presents Brazil as a nation ready to shed its corrupt and violent ways and, embracing the progress, move forward, as the United States did a century earlier. From this perspective, Amado's post-1958 novels are, as Piers Armstrong argues, "uniquely compatible with international curiosity about Brazil." His many books respond to and satisfy "the appetite of international readers, which is shaped largely by perceptions of Brazil drawn from extraliterary sources" (*Third World* 134). Smoothly translated by James L. Taylor (who would soon become involved in an even more important translation project involving Brazilian narrative) and William L. Grossman (whose sensitivity as a translator was already evident in his rendering of Machado's *Epitaph of a Small Winner*) and catching the saucy tone of the original, *Gabriela, Clove and Cinnamon* presented a zestful and optimistic view of Brazil in the postwar era.

If Jorge Amado enjoyed commercial success in the United States of the early 1960s, another, even more celebrated Brazilian author, Guimarães Rosa, did not. Rosa, widely acknowledged to be postwar Brazil's most important narrativist, was very concerned about his reception by foreign audiences (Armstrong, "Translation" 68). Rosa wrote only one novel, *Grande sertão: Veredas* (1956), known in its flawed if serviceable translation as *The Devil to Pay in the Backlands*, which Alfred Knopf, perhaps capitalizing on Amado's success, brought out in 1963. Five years later, Knopf also published *"The Third Bank of the River" and Other Stories*, a collection of some of Rosa's best short fiction (both titles are in app. C). Skillfully translated by Barbara Shelby, who provides a short introduction, the stories present a Rosa who, as in the novel, mixes pathos with bathos in depicting a violent, mysterious world of bandits, fanatics, dreamers, and wanderers. Yet as the reader realizes in stories like "The Third Bank of the River"—which, for all its regional diction, meticulous description, and vivid characters, is carefully structured around a web of archetypal symbols—Rosa charges his tales with universal significance and imbues them with the ambiguities of the human experience. Brazilianists have long been puzzled that Amado, a writer of lesser vision and scope, has been so enthusiastically received in the United States while Rosa, an indisputable master of contemporary fiction, failed to catch on. Aggressive marketing by Amado's publishers, who recognized early on his appeal to the American reading public, is a major factor. Yet we should acknowledge that Amado has been more popular than Rosa in the United States simply because even in translation his novels, written in nonthreatening, accessible language, beguile readers with what many critics consider a false and misleading image of the sensuousness of Afro-Brazilian society. Rosa's language is both more complex and less entertaining. An aesthetically and intellectually chal-

lenging writer, Rosa constructs a fictional world that deals with the vicissi-
tudes of provincial life in the interior of Minas Gerais—a subject that lacks
the exoticism of Amado's colorful but often contrived Afro-Brazilian setting.

Rosa's work presented his translators, Harriet de Onís and James L. Taylor, with a number of unresolvable stylistic problems, chiefly in diction, register, tone, euphony, onomatopoeia, portmanteau words, syntax, and rhythmic
patterns. The original comes fully alive, in fact, only when read aloud, a quality that is lost in the translation and that underscores the original's link to the
sertão's rich oral tradition. For the reader who knows *The Devil to Pay in the
Backlands* in its daunting Portuguese (although distinctly Brazilian, it is laced
with neologisms, many from arcane or even speculative etymologies), the
translation simply cannot convey the verbal interplay or the deeply poetic nature of the original.

Ironically reminiscent of the medieval romance in structure (the chanson de geste), style, theme (the quest for the grail), and characterization
(Brazilian gunmen as knights-errant), *The Devil to Pay in the Backlands* also
suggests, especially for Americans, the Western, a form that is closely associated with certain fundamental features of United States cultural identity and
that is not especially receptive to foreign incursions. From this perspective,
Armstrong points out, the English version's "recasting of the protagonist, Riobaldo, from *jagunço* to cowboy or even hillbilly, rings as a betrayal of the
subtle aura of chivalrous *chanson*" ("Translation" 73) even as it threatens to
denationalize and enrich the Western as a narrative genre. American reviewers tended to construe Rosa's vast, reflective novel as a rather bizarre adventure story in the Western mode; their critical interpretation may have chilled
their response to the work even more than the abridged translation.[11] To an
American reader bred on the Western, *The Devil to Pay in the Backlands*—
particularly when shorn of the metaphysical richness of its mysterious, melodious, and evocative language—does seem like familiar territory. One must
wonder whether reviewers felt a certain reluctance to praise a sprawling text
that, coming from a culture so alien to them, presented itself not merely as a
sexually unorthodox Brazilian Western but as a profoundly philosophical
one as well.

Even so, the *jagunço* bands of the early twentieth century and the American outlaw gangs of the late nineteenth have enough in common that this
linkage, a common heritage of sorts, should have facilitated the reception of
The Devil to Pay in the Backlands in the United States. But it seems not to have.
Rosa's epic novel, never lacking in action, complex characters and relationships,

irony, humor, and high drama, uses the vast Brazilian *sertão*, or backlands, in a way that evokes the mythic West for Americans. Taking the form of an un-broken, self-conscious monologue by the protagonist, Riobaldo (a former gunman, now elderly and retired), who struggles to explain his life and its meaning to an unnamed listener, *The Devil to Pay in the Backlands*

> plays tantalizingly with the theme of homosexuality in a way that recalls some of Thomas Mann's masterly exercises. But Guimarães goes even further than the German master. At the very center of the novel he places an episode in which Riobaldo believes he has met the Devil himself. The primeval search for the father, diabolical temptation, frustrated eroti-cism—all these motifs are so intricately intertwined and interrelated as to make *Grande Sertão: Veredas* one of the most complex works of fiction ever produced in Latin America. (Monegal, *Borzoi Anthology* 2: 678)

Mincing no words, Monegal, a critic with a deep appreciation of Fuentes, Cortázar, Juan Rulfo, and García Márquez, concludes that Rosa, master of a form "in which he had no rivals," stands alone as modern Latin American lit-erature's most accomplished novelist (679).

While the English translation may not capture the original's stylistic in-ventiveness and semantic richness (Rosa himself apparently favored the Ger-man version [Armstrong, "Translation" 69]), it does convey some of its mythic and philosophical dimensions and re-create its dramatic intensity; the translation, in short, is exciting and easier to read than the original. The work remains, nevertheless, very much a novel of ideas, a genre that has never enjoyed great popularity in the United States, and for this reason too may have put off its initial reviewers. Concerned in particular with epistemologi-cal questions, the narrator's anxiously self-conscious monologue returns the reader time and again to the question of knowing (or, more specifically, of not knowing) and to the nature of life in a world that we cannot understand. As Kafka does, Rosa creates a world of signs that we cannot decipher and events that we can neither fathom nor control. *The Devil to Pay in the Backlands* gradually leads the reader (who can identify with the unnamed, erudite in-terlocutor) to confront the problem of interpreting the meaning of life, of making sense of what happens (or does not happen) to us. Ruminating on his mysterious past in order to discover his true identity and his proper place in the universe, the narrator, together with the reader, works to transform the novel into a quest for self-discovery, rooted in the chivalric romance but enriched by the myths, legends, and traditions of the High Plains–like *sertão*. The narrative, flowing toward the dramatic, surprising climax, becomes the story of a deeply human quest. Language emerges as the primary ontological force, a mode of existence in and of itself that, for author, characters, and reader, reflects and embodies the evanescent nature of life. Evocative of both Melville and Faulkner (and of the film *High Plains Drifter*), the text draws the reader into a struggle between good and evil, into an unsettling contemplation of the protean nature of reality, and into an attempt to decipher the present by means of the past.

Like Joyce's *Finnegans Wake* (1939), *Grande sertão: Veredas* is essentially an untranslatable text. Like Joyce, Rosa was a linguist who used many languages to create words and to give existing words new morphologies and, sometimes, new sound patterns and meaning. But the question remains: If a work cannot be fully translated, should we refuse to read an imperfect translation and thus miss out on the work, or, recognizing the limitations of the translation, should we get what we can from it? The question is pertinent to Rosa's novel, which should be required reading by anyone interested in the historical development of this genre in North and South America, even in a translation that lacks the poetry and mystery of the original.

Clarice Lispector, the third major force (along with Machado de Assis and Rosa) in twentieth-century Brazilian narrative, has also been extensively translated into English. Her fourth novel, *A maçã no escuro* (1961), was beautifully rendered into English as *The Apple in the Dark* by the renowned translator Gregory Rabassa (see app. C). It was published, again by Knopf, in 1967, only four years after *The Devil to Pay in the Backlands*. In his short but insightful foreword, Rabassa sums up Lispector's place in Brazilian literature and her importance to its narrative history. Interestingly, he observes that Lispector is more difficult to translate than Rosa because her texts are "less a matter of neologisms and re-creation than of certain radical departures in the use of syntactical structure, the rhythm of the phrase being created in defiance of the norms" (xii). Like Rosa's novel, *The Apple in the Dark* is both deeply philosophical and intensely conscious of the role language plays in the formation of our sense of identity and in our relationships with other people and the world about us. Unlike *The Devil to Pay in the Backlands*, however, it does not have an action-based plot, and this lack no doubt contributed to its poor sales and its failure to awaken American readers to the beauties of Brazilian narrative. Five years later, with the appearance of *Family Ties* (1972; *Laços de família* [1960]), Lispector appeared again in English translation (see app.

C). This time the rendering was done by the English scholar Giovanni Pontiero, who has translated other Lispector texts. Published by the University of Texas Press, a leading promoter of Latin American literature in the United States, *Family Ties* is still in print, a testament to the excellence of these stories and to the overall quality of these rather British-sounding translations.[12] For all its success, however, no other Lispector work was translated into English until 1986; then, in the next six years, no fewer than eight of her works were translated into English (Braga-Pinto 71). As with *The Devil to Pay in the Backlands,* Lispector's *The Apple in the Dark* did not benefit from the exploding popularity of Spanish American literature. In retrospect, the reason probably had less to do with a second-rate translation than with the differences between the narrative traditions of Spanish America and those of Brazil.

In the mid-1980s, however, Lispector, embraced by the French literary theorist Hélène Cixous as the epitome of *l'écriture féminine,* enjoyed an upsurge in recognition and international interest (see also chs. 2 and 3). As many scholars have pointed out, though, this embrace (some would say appropriation) of Lispector and her texts has not been without problems, particularly in the way Lispector is interpreted (see M. Peixoto 42–59 and Klobucka). Cixous's lauding of Lispector has reached such proportions that the Brazilian author may be gaining an identity among American audiences—especially those in English departments and women's studies programs—as the alter ego of Cixous, as "a French 'Clarice,' a character in a play of Cixous's own writings" (Braga-Pinto 12).[13] What César Braga-Pinto describes as the second period of Lispector's reception in the United States amounts to a transformation from an esoteric "Latin American" writer (whose texts evoke comparisons with Virginia Woolf, Djuna Barnes, and Jean Rhys) into an author whose work Cixous regards as the prototype of *l'écriture féminine,* a designation that has had both positive and negative effects on Lispector's reception in the United States.[14] Referring to Ronald Sousa's translation of *The Passion according to G. H.* (see app. C), a powerful if egregiously ignored novel of the 1960s, for example, Braga-Pinto writes:

> The translator's foreword to *The Passion* is a good mark of such a transformation. The translator no longer refers to concepts such as "existentialism" or "mysticism," but to questions related to "subjecthood" and "genre" (vii), language and the boundaries between literature and philosophy (viii), binary oppositions and "undecidability" (ix).

As César Braga-Pinto contends, this foreword not only reflects a new horizon of expectation but also contributes to the shaping of new interpretations according to it (71, 80–81).

Although, in the United States works such as *The Apple in the Dark*, *Family Ties*, *The Passion according to G. H.*, *Soulstorm* (a collection of late stories; see app. C), and *The Hour of the Star* (problematically translated by Pontiero; see Braga-Pinto 74; app. C) have established Lispector as a Brazilian narrativist of exceptional talent and imagination, the lyrical "fiction" *The Stream of Life* first embodied *écriture féminine* for Cixous and demonstrated the range of Lispector's poetic and philosophical approach to narrative.[15] Generally judged to be a successful rendering of Lispector and her famous style into English, *The Stream of Life* (translated by Elizabeth Lowe and Earl Fitz; app. C) was a conscious attempt to rewrite *Água viva* in late-twentieth-century American English and to replicate not only the content but, more important, Lispector's shifting tones, alternating registers, and deceptively simple diction.[16] Agreeing with Gregory Rabassa that the heart of Lispector's style is its surprising, even destabilizing syntax, the translators also kept Lispector's unusual (some would say idiosyncratic) punctuation. The task was not always achievable, because of the crucial difference between poetic ambiguity—one of the delights of Lispector's style—and mere confusion, the problem to be avoided in the translation. Finally, the translators sought to maintain the tone of the original. Encompassing a welter of emotional and intellectual states—including anger, humor, eroticism, frustration, despair, and hope—and flowing like water (one of the key metaphors), the work comes to life on a number of interconnecting levels. More poem than prose, *The Stream of Life* confirms Lispector's status as a distinctive writer of the Americas who humanizes the often abstruse concepts associated with poststructuralism (Fitz, *Sexuality*).

At least five other translations of Brazilian literature deserve special mention. One of modern Brazil's seminal texts, Mário de Andrade's *Macunaíma* was rendered into English by E. A. Goodland in 1984 (app. C). The novel is similar to Rosa's *The Devil to Pay in the Backlands* in that both texts, in Portuguese, make the peculiar language of their composition a major aesthetic concern. Goodland's version of *Macunaíma* successfully reconstructs the development of the novel's eponymous hero (more precisely, its antihero) and more or less captures the original's mythic dimensions. Where it falls short is in failing to re-create the aesthetic effect that makes the original a complex, influential text and that speaks, intertextually and parodically, to Alencar's myth making in *Iracema*. The text of the Portuguese version is itself an artificial language, "a deliberate and self-conscious geographic and linguistic amalgam, a composite of folkloric sources expressed in a collagelike language nobody actually speaks" (Unruh 126). As in *The Devil to Pay in the Backlands*, moreover, some particularly difficult phrases and sentences are omitted in the translation—a practice that tends to neutralize the language and, perhaps more troubling for the American reader, to disconnect it from its cultural moorings. The problem becomes most evident in the translator's struggles with the names of the flora and fauna of the Amazonian forest; since most of these plants and animals have no counterpart in the English-speaking world, attempts at translation end up being merely confusing. The result is an English rendering of the text that fails to achieve quite the same piquant sense of place and time that the original so effectively conveys.

Perhaps most problematic of all is Goodland's translation of the phrase that constitutes the novel's basic motif: "Ai! que preguiça! . . ." Functioning as the refrain of the "hero without any character" (as the novel's subtitle tells us), this key line, one of the most famous in present-day Brazilian literature, is translated as "Aw! What a fucking life!"[17] In the cultural context of the original, this rendition seems both too crude and too negative, while failing to express the essential, comedic lassitude, or sloth, of the hero whose story is meant ironically to embody that of Brazil.[18] Also missing in the translation is the original's ellipsis, a mark that lures the reader into a momentary contemplation of what has just been uttered. As a result of the deletion, the translation becomes more declarative, more assertive than the original and in the process loses much of the original's wryly parodic effect. At the same time, we must be grateful to the translator that such a pivotal—and daunting—work of modern Brazilian narrative exists in English at all. As with *The Devil to Pay in the Backlands*, it is better to know *Macunaíma* in an imperfect translation than not to experience the work at all.

Overcoming stylistic problems of a different sort is Catarina Feldmann Edinger's English version of Alencar's *Senhora* (1875; trans. 1994; app. C). This translation is notably successful in capturing the tones and nuances of dialogue that distinguish the Portuguese text. Convinced that a national literature could not emerge until a Brazilian vernacular was established, Alencar made use of a variety of speech forms and traditions, from the lowest to the highest, seeking to validate Brazilian Portuguese and its evolution away from the norms of continental Portuguese. Conscious of Brazil's indigenous past,

Alencar also wanted to incorporate the sounds and oral traditions of the Tupi language into his literary works, an effort that is most clearly evident in *Iracema,* which has benefited from a new English translation by Clifford Landers. In *Senhora,* the protagonist, because of a lucky financial situation, is able to speak from a variety of perspectives; each one has a distinctive tone, register, and diction. This stylistic feature makes Aurélia, the intelligent, strong-willed Senhora, compelling and believable, and Edinger brings the fluid, protean quality of her characterization across very well. As the reader comes to realize, Aurélia is not the haughty, disdainful, aggressive young woman she seems to be. The key to her social and psychological development is that she responds according to the situation she finds herself in; and her thoughts and conversations are re-created in the translation in such a way that the careful reader can readily follow the numerous shifts in tone that mark her ebb and flow as the novel's focal point.

Also highly successful in its English version is João Ubaldo Ribeiro's *Sergeant Getúlio* (app. C). It is a work that, as we have seen, ranks as a distinguished Brazilian novel of the 1970s. When it first appeared in Portuguese in 1971, critics hailed it for its extraordinary language, which, although clearly a literary invention, was felt to be an accurate, honest expression of the way many Brazilians think and speak. In this sense, *Sergeant Getúlio* adopts the genre of the language-conscious novel begun by Machado de Assis and continued by Mário de Andrade, Oswald de Andrade, Clarice Lispector, and Guimarães Rosa. Recalling both Mário de Andrade's *Macunaíma* and Rosa's *The Devil to Pay in the Backlands,* the language of Ribeiro's original text, simultaneously dialectical and invented, made the work difficult even for educated Brazilians to read with ease—so difficult, in fact, that the text's first English-language translator gave up in frustration, a turn of events that led the author himself to undertake the translation. The obvious question thus arises concerning *Sergeant Getúlio:* Is it a translation, or is it a rewriting, in English, of a Portuguese text? Either way, when one compares the two versions, it is obvious that the English rendering brilliantly re-creates the linguistic play and shock of the original, so that the American reader can be confident about experiencing its verbal pyrotechnics. In examining the two versions, we can see how Ribeiro handled some of the idioms and other linguistic peculiarities that separate the two languages—forms of address, cursing and profanity, the nomenclature of flora and fauna, puns, levels and types of humor, rhymes, rhythms, and euphonies. Although certain features of Brazilian Portuguese (the various ways to say *you,* the abundance of colorful obscenities) come across in the English version better than others, Ribeiro does a remarkable job in enabling the American reader to feel something like what a Brazilian reader feels when entering into the violent and corrupt yet often beautiful and funny world created in this novel.

In rather sharp contrast to the violent if heroic world of *Sergeant Getúlio* is Osman Lins's lyrical, erotic, and compelling novel *Avalovara*, which appeared in 1973 to great fanfare and then in a luminous English translation by Gregory Rabassa in 1980 (app. C). Constructed, mysteriously, around the letters of a Latin palindrome, SATOR AREPO TENET OPERA ROTAS,[19] and the infinite movement of a spiral linking the letters, *Avalovara* is an epic—a quest, simultaneously sacred, profane, and apocalyptic, to comprehend the nature and meaning of love. Focusing on the elusive relationship between a Brazilian Everyman, Abel, and three women, Roos, Cecília, and a character whose nominal identity is a mystical ideogram, *Avalovara* engages the reader, in a way that brings to mind both the Julio Cortázar of *Hopscotch* and the Thomas Pynchon of *V.*, in a cosmic struggle to understand the meaning of life, which the text presents as a function of space, time, and chance. In what is arguably his most masterful effort to date, Rabassa's marvelous translation, both supple and seductive in its English and faithful to the tones and registers of the original, gives the English-speaking world access to one of modern Brazil's greatest achievements.

Finally, a few words of praise must go to Helen Lane's sensitive and resourceful translation of Nélida Piñon's *The Republic of Dreams* (1989; the original appeared in 1984), the author's seventh novel but the first to appear in English (see app. C).[20] Weaving together two different worlds—the sensual, violent Brazil caught up in the chaotic process of its self-creation, and the interior realm of its inhabitants, the world of myth, vision, fantasy, and sexual impulse—Piñon's sprawling, mesmerizing text suggests that life is a republic of dreams, an unstable brew made up of illusion, delusion, and reality, always seasoned by desire. To an exceptional degree, Lane's translation captures the sinuousness of the Portuguese, as well as its dreamlike mystery and seductiveness, its questioning of the relation we wish to believe connects words to reality. At the same time, Lane's version is faithful to the original in that it can shift, often in a single line, from lyrical and philosophical speculation to graphic expressions of carnal activity. The destabilizing alternations of tone and register that mark the original are, with a few exceptions, recreated in an essentially seamless English translation, no small feat in a work of such complexity. Syntactically too Lane hews closely to the Portuguese, which is characterized by sentences that blur the differentiation between subjects and predicates, to accentuate semantically enriching ambiguities and uncertainties. This technique constitutes much of the original's appeal, and it is not lost in the English translation.

Overall, the view of Brazilian letters that we get by means of translation is that of a diverse literature that has long featured a strong, vital narrative tradition. The legacy dates to the colonial era, although it is most prominent from the time of Manuel Antônio de Almeida (whose novel *Memoirs of a Militia Sergeant* was recently translated; see app. C) and José de Alencar, in the mid-nineteenth century, to such important present-day figures as Nélida Piñon, Darcy Ribeiro, Antônio Callado, Rubem Fonseca, Autran Dourado, Moacyr Scliar, Helena Parente Cunha, Murilo Rubião, Edla van Steen, Ivan Angelo, Ignácio de Loyola Brandão, Marilene Felinto, João Ubaldo Ribeiro, Lygia Fagundes Telles, Silviano Santiago, and Lya Luft. Both the short story and the novel are actively cultivated in Brazil, and both seek to make readers "aware of language as a social phenomenon" while creating "narrations which subvert themselves (or each other, where more than one narrator is involved, as is frequent). Indeed language, in this sense, is usually an offensive weapon," one that demands tonal changes away from the temperate modes of Machado de Assis and toward voices that are more anguished, more candid. In the still-unstable postdictatorship era, Brazilian writers are in search of new tongues for a new nation, a nation still struggling to throw off the shackles of fear and oppression. With respect to literary production in this unstable sociopolitical scene, "it is not surprising if daring is often dogged by fear" and uncertainty (Gledson, "Brazilian Prose" 206).

At the turn of the twenty-first century, then, Brazilian fiction is alive and flourishing in translation, and most of its most interesting and engaging authors are available to the English-speaking audience. Although some pivotal authors (e.g., Lispector, Amado, Graciliano Ramos, Telles, and Machado) have been extensively translated, others, like Piñon, Fonseca, Luft, Santiago, João Ubaldo Ribeiro, and Parente Cunha, deserve to see more of their works brought out in English. Nevertheless, enough good translations of the major works exist that we can trace in English the development of a distinctly Brazilian narrative from its founding, with Alencar, in the 1850s and 1860s to its flowering, with Machado and the modernists, through such twentieth-century giants as Guimarães Rosa and Lispector, to present-day notables like Piñon, Lins, Abreu, and Luft.[21] Although many leading poets—including Mário de Andrade, Carlos Drummond de Andrade, Cecília Meireles, and

João Cabral de Melo Neto—and dramatists have been translated into English, Brazilian literature remains, at the dawn of the twenty-first century, a national literature distinguished in large measure by its rich, inventive prose narrative tradition.[22]

NOTES

1. Published in a single volume along with J. M. Pereira da Silva's *Manuel de Morais*, also translated by Burton, *Iracema* appeared in 1886, while *Inocência* came out in 1889. Although the title page of *Iracema* lists Isabel Burton as the translator, Frederick Garcia argues that Richard Burton did the translation (36). Henriqueta Chamberlain produced a more supple, up-to-date English version of the novel *Inocência* (1872), a work of transition between Romanticism and realism, in 1945.

2. The three stories by Machado are "The Attendant's Confession," "The Fortune-Teller," and "Life." The second volume, *Brazilian Literature* (published in the year of the modernist revolt), offered an outline history of writing and critical studies of some notable authors: Castro Alves, Machado, José Veríssimo, Olavo Bilac, Euclides da Cunha, Oliveira Lima, Graça Aranha, Coelho Neto, and Francisca Júlia.

3. *Rebellion in the Backlands* was published by the University of Chicago Press in 1944; *The Masters and the Slaves* was brought out by Knopf in 1946.

4. Grossman's English version was first published in 1951 in São Paulo as *The Posthumous Memoirs of Brás Cubas*. The text was released in New York the following year as *Epitaph of a Small Winner* (K. Jackson, "Madness" 15).

5. Although, as K. Jackson observes, "the first English version of *Dom Casmurro* was published in London in 1953" ("Madness" 15), copies were apparently circulating in the United States, where it was published in 1966: John Barth reports having read a copy at Pennsylvania State University, where he was teaching. The 1953 English version of *Dom Casmurro* carried an insightful introduction by the American critic Waldo Frank, who praised the text's striking ambiguity.

6. *Quincas Borba* was retranslated by Gregory Rabassa and published under its original title by the Oxford University Press in 1998. Often overshadowed by *The Posthumous Memoirs of Brás Cubas* and by *Dom Casmurro*, *Quincas Borba* is perhaps Machado's most poignant novel. The text functions as a critique of the concept of progress and of the novel as a genre; at the same time the work is a parodic allegory of Brazilian society during the Empire under Pedro II.

7. This is how Barth described Machado in a letter to me, 3 Apr. 1984.

8. A note on the copyright page says, "The moral right of the translator has been asserted" (4).

9. See *Neoclassicism through the Modern Period*, ed. Brian Wilkie and James Hurt, 2nd ed. (New York: Macmillan, 1988), vol. 2 of *Literature of the Western World*. I had written Hurt earlier, suggesting that he include some Brazilian authors, especially Machado, Clarice Lispector, and Guimarães Rosa.

10. A similar situation existed in the first edition of *Literature of the Western World*. The only Brazilian it included among "Latin American" writers who had "transformed Latin American literature . . . from a placid backwater of world literature into an important current in the main stream" was Jorge Amado (2: 2078 [New York: Macmillan, 1984]). Amado, and not Machado, Guimarães Rosa, or Lispector, is evaluated, along with Borges, García Márquez, Cortázar, and Vargas Llosa.

11. Ted Holmberg, writing in the *Providence Journal* (Apr. 1963), titled his review "Brazil's Wild West." Other reviews included Tom Schlesinger, "Brazilian Bandit Reminisces," *Virginia Pilot* 19 Mar. 1963; William L. Grossman, "Outlaw with a Problem," *New York Times* 21 Apr. 1963; Jack Conroy, "Outlaw and the Devil in Brazil's Backlands," *Chicago Sun Times* 19 May 1963.

12. Pontiero's other translations of Lispector's works (*The Hour of the Star* [1986], *Near to the Wild Heart* [1990], *The Foreign Legion* [1986], and *Discovering the World* [1992]; the original works were published, resp., in 1977, 1944, 1964, and 1984) have been subject to considerable criticism (see M. Peixoto 104n5; Braga-Pinto 73).

13. The University of Minnesota Press has published both *The Stream of Life* (*Água viva*) and *The Passion according to G. H.* (*A paixão segundo G. H.*) and *The Newly Born Woman*, one of Hélène Cixous's most famous works in the United States, as well as two books in which Cixous discusses Lispector's oeuvre: *Readings* and *Reading with Clarice Lispector*" (Braga-Pinto 80).

14. See Fitz, "Caracterização e a visão fenomenológica de Djuna Barnes e Clarice Lispector" ("Characterization and the Phenomenological Vision of Djuna Barnes and Clarice Lispector"), *Travessia* 14.14 (1987): 136–47.

15. Lispector herself termed this text a "fiction" as opposed to a "novel."

16. In a study of Lispector's English-language translations, Braga-Pinto says, "It is not surprising that the translation of *The Stream of Life* by Earl Fitz and Elizabeth Lowe is the most successful manifestation of Lispector's afterlife in English. Both translators have been dedicated readers of Lispector, and important agents in the promotion of her oeuvre in the United States" (92). See also *Clarice Lispector: A Bio-bibliography*, ed. Diane Marting (Westport: Greenwood, 1993): 7.

17. This subtitle, crucial to understanding the ironic nature of the hero, is omitted in the translation.

18. A more literal translation might be "Oh, what laziness!" or, less literally, "Oh, how lazy I feel!"

19. In English the sense of this palindrome is "The farmer carefully maintains his plow in the furrows" or "The plowman carefully sustains the world in its orbit" (see Rabassa, "Osman Lins" 31).

20. According to Piñon herself, in a talk given at Vanderbilt University, 18 Nov. 2000, an English translation of *Casa da paixão* (*House of Passion*) was done by Giovanni Pontiero (and read by Toni Morrison, then an editor at Random House) but the work was never published.

21. A list of key works that mark the evolution of Brazilian narrative and exist in English

translation might well include the following: (1) Romanticism: José de Alencar, *Iracema* and *Senhora*. (2) Realism and naturalism: Machado (who can also be read as a modernist antirealist), *The Posthumous Memoirs of Brás Cubas, Quincas Borba, Dom Casmurro, "The Psychiatrist" and Other Stories,* and *"The Devil's Church" and Other Stories*; Aluísio Azevedo, *The Mulatto* and *The Slum*; Euclides da Cunha, *Rebellion in the Backlands*. (3) Modernism: Mário de Andrade, *Macunaíma*; Oswald de Andrade, *The Sentimental Memoirs of John Seaborne* and *Seraphim Grosse Pointe*. (4) Later twentieth century: Clarice Lispector, *Near to the Wild Heart* (app. C), *The Stream of Life,* and *The Hour of the Star*; Guimarães Rosa, *"The Third Bank of the River" and Other Stories* and *The Devil to Pay in the Backlands*; Ignácio de Loyola Brandão, *Zero* (app. C); Lygia Fagundes Telles, *"Tigrela" and Other Stories* (app. C); Helena Parente Cunha, *Woman between Mirrors*; Nélida Piñon, *The Republic of Dreams*; Lya Luft, *The Island of the Dead* (app. C); Marilene Felinto, *The Women of Tijucopapo* (app. C); and Caio Fernando Abreu, *Whatever Happened to Dulce Veiga?* (app. C).

22. In *The Modern Stage in Latin America*, Oscar Fernández provides an excellent translation of Alfredo Dias Gomes's masterpiece *Payment as Pledged* (1960; *O pagador de promessas*). *Three Contemporary Brazilian Plays in Bilingual Edition*, edited and translated by Szoka and Bratcher, includes works by Plínio Marcos, Leilah Assunção, and Consuelo de Castro. Finally, *The Wedding Dress* (Rio de Janeiro: Funarte, 1998), translated by Joffre Rodrigues and Toby Coe (with a critical introduction translated by David George), contains five plays by the controversial Nelson Rodrigues. (For these translations, see app. C.)

CHAPTER 5

Conclusion: The Differences

In the preceding chapters, I have sought to compare Brazil's narrative tradition with that of the United States and at the same time to situate Brazilian literature in the larger context of world literature. To avoid the isolationism, prejudice, and parochialism that often plague literary study at the international level, I have emphasized why Americans in particular should know more about Brazil, its literature as well as its culture. More than five hundred years old, Brazilian literature, with its surprises and unexpected treasures, has produced some of the New World's most accomplished and imaginative works. When viewed objectively and appreciated as an organic whole, the poems, dramas, stories, and novels must be regarded as producing one of the most fertile and singular national literatures in the Americas. Indeed, it must be said that while the "Brazilian and Spanish American literary traditions are distinct," there is little doubt that "Brazil's is, with that of the United States, the richest national literature in the New World" (González Echevarría, *Oxford Book* xii).

As I have stressed throughout the book, Brazil and the United States have a great deal in common, especially their many cultural, political, and economic ties (which for the Brazilians can also be the source of bitterness and mistrust); their historical development; and their racial conflicts. As Randal Johnson and Robert Stam summarize this relationship, Brazil "is the New World country that most strikingly resembles the United States in both its historical formation and its ethnic composition" (17). Like the rest of North and South America, both countries began as European colonies, and from colonial days the experiences of the two nations show striking parallels.

Both engaged in wars of conquest that involved vast expanses of western territory and the near-extermination of Amerindian peoples; the cultural history of both is marked by a protracted struggle for emancipation from the mother country; both, with tragic consequences, cultivated slavery as an integral part of their economic development; both abolished the institution in the second half of the nineteenth century (Brazil in 1888, 23 years after the United States); finally, both would see waves of immigrants from all over the world pluralize, enrich, and diversify their societies (17).

Yet for all the similarities, crucial differences also exist between the evolution of Brazil and the United States that make studies of the sort undertaken here a risky and contentious affair.[1] More easily appreciated from the Brazilian perspective than from that of the United States, the essential problem is the relative imbalance, or inequality, with which we are forced to deal. In the year 2003, the United States found itself so hegemonically situated—culturally, politically, and economically—that any comparisons with the literatures or cultures of its hemispheric neighbors are fraught with both ideological and methodological stumbling blocks: questions of dominance and exploitation (what many view as cultural imperialism), of influence and reception, of evaluation, and of authenticity. Still, open-minded comparisons are what we must make if we are to attain a nuanced level of understanding and appreciation. We should recognize, in particular, that the chief difference between the Brazilian and the American experience is economic dependency, a factor that distorts not only the two nations' perception of each other but their ability to evaluate the other's cultural production as well. The United States is the richest and most powerful nation in human history, whereas Brazil, although wealthy in potential and in natural resources, struggles to feed, house, and educate its people, a high percentage of whom are under the age of twenty-one (Burns, *History* [3rd ed.] 485). Brazil's heavy reliance on the United States puts it and its culture at a disadvantage in any comparison with the United States. Looking at the historical record, we can see the heart of the problem: in the United States, "formal political independence led to real economic independence"; in Brazil, "formal independence from Portugal led only to British free-trade imperialism in the nineteenth century and to American domination in the twentieth" (Johnson and Stam 17). In 1968, only four years after the coup that put the military in power, the United States had established itself as the largest investor in Brazil, followed by France, Britain, Switzerland, and Germany. "The tragedy of Brazil," as Bradford Burns puts it, "has been its inability to achieve its enormous potential," with foreign interests profiting more from Brazil's riches than Brazilians have (Burns, *History* [2nd ed.] 527). In short, because of its ever-growing state of dependency (a situation exacerbated, ironically, under the military dictatorship, which encouraged foreign investment), Brazil has become a supplier of capital for the advanced industrial nations rather than a consumer of it.[2]

While Americans, accustomed to the economic and military dominance they have long enjoyed, tend not to consider how they and their culture appear to the rest of the world, Brazilians do, and the drastic imbalances they see between themselves and the United States have helped determine not only who is able to produce creative work but also how the artistic output is interpreted and appreciated. To understand Brazil and its culture, Americans must be aware of the volatile link between literature and politics that has existed there. In a country afflicted by illiteracy, hunger, poverty, and violence, literature—rarely the province of escapist aesthetes—has long been a weapon in the fight for social justice, and we should take this fact into consideration when comparing Brazilian letters with other national literatures. Given the continuing problem of illiteracy, for example, we ought not to be surprised at the significant role the electronic media play in the intellectual and political lives of the poor in Brazil. Even Brazilians who are unable to read and write can respond to popular music lyrics or to the messages conveyed in films and on radio and television. In a society where basic education is still not available to all, the writer—particularly the writer who participates in a widely disseminated television or radio interview—gains influence as a public intellectual in ways that most authors in the United States, where the idea of the public intellectual is largely discounted if not openly disparaged, could not.

The American reader seeking to understand Brazil and its literature must therefore seek to understand the turbulent and often iniquitous social, political, and economic context in which it is being written—and seen, listened to, and otherwise consumed. As Affonso Romano de Sant'Anna writes in his 1980 poem "What Kind of Country Is This?":

I live in the twentieth century. I'm off to the twenty-first,
Still the nineteenth's prisoner. (110)

Moreover, the American reader should become sensitive not only to the politics of translation and international publishing—which Brazilian authors are translated and published, and why?—but also to the impact of translated texts on the American consciousness of Brazil, on the image of Brazilian literature and culture these works produce, and on Brazil's consciousness of itself (Brazilians read, in Portuguese translation, a vast amount of foreign literature). There are, after all, major differences between such authors as Machado de Assis and Paulo Coelho or between Clarice Lispector and Jorge Amado, and discerning American readers, accustomed to making judgments based on their own traditions and values, must learn to recognize them.

The controversy surrounding Coelho offers a case in point. The author of six books "unabashedly" modeled on "inspirational works of the *Jonathan Livingston Seagull* genre," he is widely disparaged in Brazil (and elsewhere) as little more than a successful practitioner of New Age pablum. Nevertheless, Coelho's books, which have sold four million copies in Brazil and more than two million abroad (Patai, "Machado in English" 88–89), influence the way foreigners view the contemporary Brazilian narrative. If, worldwide, more people are reading *The Alchemist* (1993), one of Coelho's most successful novels, than are reading Machado, Rosa, Lispector, or Nélida Piñon, what is the impact on the perception of Brazilian narrative abroad? What impression is Coelho's work making on the world audience? For our purposes, we should remember that the American reader, aware of the problem of economic and cultural dependency, must not lavish praise on a text simply because it is Brazilian, the product of a disadvantaged nation; the work must be worthy, as serious literature, of our attention. Only then will we be on solid ground, critically speaking, and able to differentiate between works of greater or lesser artistic merit and cultural significance. To proceed in any other fashion is to risk casting aspersions on both the Brazilian text and the American reader.

Closely related to the role Brazilian literature has played in the nation's political development is the question of authenticity, an issue that has been percolating in Brazilian letters since the colonial era—when, as in the United States, writers struggled with the problem of cultural identity and the weight of the European literary tradition. Writers as diverse in outlook and style as Antônio Vieira, Gregório de Matos, and Sebastião da Rocha Pita sought early on to establish a uniquely Brazilian culture in the New World. The often acerbic work of Matos in particular has lived on in Brazil, exerting an influence even on contemporary writers. The modernists, especially Oswald de Andrade, saw Matos as the original revolutionary in the effort to attain the formal, thematic, and linguistic distinctiveness in literature that would help Brazil emancipate itself from the economic and cultural dependency that by the early twentieth century had enveloped it. Thus the quest for literary and cultural authenticity has dominated Brazilian literature much more than it did the literature of the United States, where by the mid-nineteenth century one could speak of an American literature. Although the Brazilian poet Gonçalves de Magalhães and the American poet Ralph Waldo Emerson published, at virtually the same time, intellectual declarations of independence, Brazil's struggle to realize such self-reliance would be a more difficult and drawn-out affair, lasting indeed up to the present day.[3] The question of authenticity, then, has burned longer and more intensely in Brazil than in the United States, and Americans must take this fact into consideration as they read Brazilian literature, particularly contemporary literature. As Burns puts it, "Like other nations of the vast and varied Third World, Brazil faces the challenge of economic and social development. Unlike most of those nations, Brazil possesses the potential for development. . . . In the case of Brazil, history not only illuminates the past; it also contains suggestions for the future" (Burns, *History* [3rd ed.] 491).

At the risk of oversimplification, we might say that the essential problem is one of interpretation, the perspective Americans take in reading a Brazilian novel or short story. Americans must be careful in judging a Brazilian text, song, or film. Long inundated by the sounds, images, and artifacts of American culture, Brazilians understand the United States much better than Americans understand Brazil, and this serious imbalance can lead Americans to be condescending and dismissive of Brazil; it can also sow the seeds of enmity and resentment among Brazilians. Some years ago, after a protracted discussion with a colleague in an English department over what I called the greatness of Machado de Assis, I was summarily dismissed with the following statement: "If this Machado de Assis is so good, why haven't I ever heard of him before?" Given the economics of the publishing industry and the relative obscurity with which Brazilian literature and culture have to contend, even a writer as brilliant as Machado has difficulty in gaining the international reputation he deserves. And while Machado, thanks to his availability in translation and to plaudits from V. S. Pritchett, Elizabeth Hardwick, Helen Caldwell, Susan Sontag, and John Barth, is acquiring a growing number of enthusiasts outside Brazil, other writers, notably Guimarães Rosa, remain underacknowledged in the international literary community.

As for the contributions Brazil makes to literature in the Americas and to world literature generally, five categories can be stressed: first, Brazilian writing's distinctive literature of discovery, conquest, and settlement; second, its strong, imaginative tradition of fiction, especially metafiction; third, the politically acute experimentalism of its modernist fiction; fourth, the diversity and vitality of its women's writing; and, fifth, its extensive and imaginative history of race-related writing.

In the first group, the literature of discovery, early writers like Pêro Vaz de Caminha; Manuel da Nóbrega; Ambrósio Fernandes Brandão; and, more prototypically, Sebastião da Rocha Pita assiduously cultivated an image of Brazil as the "earthly paradise" long imagined by medieval scholars. As is clear from the writing of Nóbrega, for example, God was thought to have created Brazil as a blessed land, a showcase of beauty, fertility, abundance, and human goodness.[4] The basis of the *ufanista* movement, this belief in the natural exuberance of Brazil's flora and fauna was to a degree mirrored in the literature of the early United States, where the accounts of Captain John Smith also contain Edenic references and pastoral overtones: "And then the Country of Massachusetts, which is the Paradise of all those parts" (*Harper American Literature* 1: 7). In contrast to the rhetorically fanciful *ufanista* vision of the New World as paradise, the more practical Smith, whose primary mission on reaching the wintry North American shores was to survive, saw his Edenic paradise as a sociopolitical utopia in which a natural abundance would have to be maintained by dint of hard work, perseverance, and discipline. Calling it New Canaan or New Jerusalem, the Puritans came to the New World convinced that it was their promised land, to be developed as they saw fit. In the beginning, the English settlers saw themselves forced, by circumstance and by Smith's military bearing, to apply such skills as fishing and hunting and to gather such items as fur, corn, and timber. While the English and the Portuguese settlers both saw the New World as a terrestrial paradise, their interpretations of it—and, perhaps more important, their sense of how their societies should relate to it—were quite different.

In regard to the second category, fiction and metafiction, we might note the extent to which self-conscious first-person narrators or protagonists populate Brazil's literary history.[5] Although metafiction—imaginative work that is openly concerned with the nature, processes, and assumptions of its own creation—characterizes numerous modern novels, Brazil is unique in that this mode of writing has long been a defining feature of its narrative tradition (Fitz, "Metafiction"). Indeed, self-consciousness not only about the New World experience but also about its writing marks the first document of Brazilian literature, Caminha's famous letter of discovery, a foundational document that lives on, often as parodic interpretation, in such contemporary novels as João Ubaldo Ribeiro's *Viva o povo brasileiro* (1984; *Long Live the Brazilian People!*) and José Roberto Torero and Marcus Aurelius Pimenta's *Terra Papagalli* (1997).[6] Self-consciousness appears in several other documents of the colonial period; while the attribute does not define them as literary texts, it suggests that a keen awareness of the process of writing and its relation to reality and to other texts has long been present in Brazilian literature. The tradition continues in the seminal work of José de Alencar, for many the founder of Brazilian letters, but not until Machado, in the second half of the nineteenth century, does it gain an undisputed master. Like Vladimir Nabokov, a metafictionist par excellence (see Gill) and an ironist as well, Machado broke ground in narrative theory and practice and in reader response. Beginning in 1880–81 with *The Posthumous Memoirs of Brás Cubas*, Machado, in a series of iconoclastic stories and novels, established himself as one of Western literature's innovators. So great is his presence in the history of Brazilian narrative that his legacy lives on through generations of writers. Thus we can speak of Machado's influence on such canonical narrativists as Oswald de Andrade (*The Sentimental Memoirs of John Seaborne* and *Seraphim Grosse Pointe*), Raquel de Queiroz, and Graciliano Ramos (*Anguish, São Bernardo*, and *Barren Lives*) in the 1930s, as well as on later innovators like Clarice Lispector (*The Stream of Life* and *The Hour of the Star*), Marilene Felinto (*The Women of Tijucopapo*), Helena Parente Cunha (*Woman between Mirrors*), and Caio Fernando Abreu (*Whatever Happened to Dulce Veiga?*). Probing, self-conscious narrative continues to flourish in Brazil as a creative force (in contrast to the often tedious, superficial postmodernism of many other literary cultures); it explores such politically charged problems as repression, violence, and cultural and economic dependency, especially in relation to issues of sex, gender, age, class, and race in a nation re-creating itself after the nightmare of a shattering dictatorship.

The innovative fiction of Brazil's modernist period represents the third area in which Brazil can make a contribution to inter-American and world literature. Texts like Mário de Andrade's *Macunaíma*, Oswald de Andrade's *The Sentimental Memoirs of John Seaborne* and *Seraphim Grosse Pointe*, and Patrícia Galvão's *Industrial Park* exemplify the characteristics of Western modernism while developing a distinctly Brazilian ethos, a skeptical view of the profound transformation that Brazilian culture, driven by the twin spurs of technology and industrialization, was undergoing in the 1920s, 1930s, and 1940s. Like Gertrude Stein and Ezra Pound in the United States, Oswald de Andrade in theory and in practice was the primary catalyst in Brazil's modernist movement, and, again like Stein's, his influence was widely felt (in the light of his importance to the *tropicalistas*, it is still being felt). Well versed in European modernism, Andrade, recalling Dos Passos as well, sought to renew the genres of poetry, fiction, and drama and to foster a social and political climate in the rapidly changing Brazil of the 1920s and 1930s that would be more receptive to the forms of experimental art that he—along with his modernist colleagues Anita Malfatti, Victor Brecheret, Mário de Andrade, and Galvão—was advocating. Integrating current ideas about music, painting, film, and literature, Galvão and the two Andrades, mixing the forms and techniques of the European avant-garde with political and economic issues and with the themes and myths of indigenous and African Brazil, revolutionized Brazilian narrative and expanded the cultural contexts of literary modernism, in Brazil and in the West generally.

A modernist who went even further in merging narrative and politics is Galvão, whose underappreciated 1933 "proletarian novel" *Industrial Park* joins a Marxist revolutionary fervor with both a militant feminism and a keen appreciation of cinematic techniques. "Recounting the failures of early industrialization through the stories of individual women and by daring to treat issues of abuse of workers, political confrontation, and sexual exploitation," *Industrial Park* depicts the city of São Paulo "in short, expressive, simple, and concise scenes" that bridge the gap between modernist experimentation and social realism. A rarity in the world of modernist fiction, *Industrial Park*, which paints an "authentic artistic and ideological portrait of its time," offers the reader "a woman's first-hand view of the rites of Latin American modernization" (Jackson and Jackson viii–ix). Galvão, who translated into Brazilian Portuguese such international masters as Joyce, Camus, Silone, Hemingway, and Faulkner, was imprisoned for four years and tortured as a political dissident under the Vargas dictatorship. *Industrial Park* (which she was forced to publish under a pseudonym, Mara Lobo) was so scathing a denunciation of the plight of urban female workers that the Brazilian Communist Party rejected it because of its "implicit anarchism" (K. Jackson, Afterword, *Industrial Park* 126). The novel circulated only among the intellectual elite, many of whom were actually parodied in the text. The rediscovery of Galvão late in the twentieth century expands our understanding of Brazilian modernist prose fiction and lends credence to the argument that the narratives produced in Brazil during this aesthetically and intellectually fecund period are the most innovative and politically engaged anywhere in the Americas.

The importance of Galvão to Brazil's modernist revolt underscores, as evidenced in the fourth category, the extent to which the Brazilian narrative has enjoyed the active participation of women writers. In Spanish America, male authors like Borges, Fuentes, Vargas Llosa, Rulfo, and García Márquez dominated the rise of the New Novel in the 1960s.[7] Since the 1950s in Brazil, however, the novel and the short story have been practiced by a number of outstanding women—and by male authors, like Osman Lins and Guimarães Rosa—who deal with issues of gender, sexuality, and power in nontraditional ways. In any discussion of women's writing in Brazil, Lispector must head the list. Debuting in 1944 with the novel *Near to the Wild Heart*, Lispector would change the course of Brazilian narrative by legitimizing the psychological, sexual, and political presence of women and by exposing the phallocentric social structures that distort the lives of both men and women in Brazilian culture. Lispector is not alone as a woman writer in Brazil, of course. Raquel de Queiroz, Maria Alice Barroso, Nélida Piñon, Lygia Fagundes Telles, Edla van Steen, Marina Colasanti, Márcia Denser, Lya Luft, and Sônia Coutinho are a few of the women who have energized and transformed contemporary Brazilian narrative.

The fifth category of Brazilian literature that might be brought to the table of inter-American or world literature deals with the explosive issue of race relations. Arguably "the only nation in the Americas to have achieved a synthesis akin to what used to be conceived of as a race," Brazil is a country whose culture truly is a "complex melting pot" (González Echevarría, *Oxford Book* 428). Much more than either Canada or the United States a racially mixed society, Brazil has long produced texts that interrogate the concept of race as well as the concept of mixed race—the latter topic, as we have seen, is a defining characteristic of Brazilian literature. Beginning in the colonial era with Gregório de Matos and running through the nineteenth century with writers like Alencar and Machado, the issue of Brazilian identity as a function of the melding of "three sad races" (as Haberly puts it) finds expression in a variety of later works as well: Machado's often-overlooked *Counselor Ayres' Memorial* (1908), Cassiano Ricardo's 1928 mythical modernist epic *Martim Cererê* (which celebrates Brazil, again portrayed as a Garden of Eden, as "the melting pot of the world, where the race and hope of the future" are being forged [see Hulet 3: 90]), Jorge Amado's *Tent of Miracles* (1969), Darcy Ribeiro's *Maíra* (1978), Marilene Felinto's *The Women of Tijucopapo* (1982), Helena Parente Cunha's *Woman between Mirrors* (1983), Nélida Piñon's *The Republic of Dreams* (1984), and the anthology *Finally . . . Us* (ed. Miriam Alves [1995]). *Tent of Miracles* lauds racial mixing and explicitly compares it with the racial situation in the United States in the late 1960s (one of the characters declares that North American racism is unacceptable to a Brazilian). Ribeiro's *Maíra* examines the Indians and their place in the modern Brazilian nation-state by asking whether cultural assimilation, viewed as another form of miscegenation, can ever work. Once again, as we see in the work of such Native American writers as N. Scott Momaday, Leslie Marmon Silko, and Sherman Alexie, the obvious parallels with the historical development of the United States and its literature cannot be ignored. Approaching these themes from a woman's perspective, Parente Cunha, Piñon, and the writers of *Finally . . . Us* take on the issues of patriarchy, Afro-Brazilian and inter-American culture, female identity, and female sexual expression as well as the economic, political, and sexual foundations of Brazilian civilization, including the role African slaves, indigenous peoples, women, and emigration have played in it.

Whether read as a national literature, as an American or New World literature, or as a world literature, Brazilian letters has much to offer the reader in search of a new cultural literacy. Western European in origin (although, given Portugal's status, it was also the product of an already marginalized European nation), it has been heavily influenced by non-Western (particularly African) forces as well as indigenous ones. We can read Brazilian literature therefore as a hybrid, one that since its inception in 1500, has been acutely aware of itself, of its difference from its European roots, and of its need to define itself. The issue of definition, as we have seen, has dominated Brazilian literature since the beginning of the twentieth century, from the modernists to the *tropicalistas*, and involves virtually all aspects of Brazilian life and culture. The new literacy with which we must learn to read Brazilian literature is, as Sarah Lawall envisions it, one "based on cultural expression," one that "must be understood not as the reproduction of a particular content but rather as the ability to *process* information . . . so as to take part in common discourse" (284), whether in the context of American or world literature. As it evolves in the twenty-first century, Brazilian literature will continue to be read in a variety of ways, but always as a complex, dynamic, and politically conscious force that appeals to traditionalists seeking new "great authors" to integrate into their reading lists as well as to advocates of cultural studies, Third World literatures, and literary theory.

American readers of Brazilian literature will be treated to an interesting double perspective: they will see the development of a national literature that, with certain key differences, should remind them of their own; and, more important in terms of cross-cultural literacy, they will discover what it means to read, write, and interpret literature in a nation riven with social problems and dependent, culturally and economically, on their own. In realizing this, American readers may come to see why Brazilians—despite their admiration for the United States—have become suspicious of and resentful about the virtual ownership of Brazil by American and European financial interests. At the same time, "in the sheer diversity" of its own once-marginalized voices, American literature has become more international in its sense of identity and development (see *Harper American Literature* 2: 2578). As the twenty-first century rolls on, the United States is steadily assuming a more inter-American outlook, in which Brazil will occupy a special place. American readers must nevertheless remember that they are reading Brazilian literature from a privileged position, one that does not always, or easily, facilitate understanding, of oneself or of the other. This tension vis-à-vis the United States marks much of Brazilian literature, especially since the early twentieth century, and the American or world reader must grasp what it means—for Brazilians, for Americans, and for the world audience generally—for the extraordinary strength and vitality of Brazilian letters to be fully appreciated.

NOTES

1. For Putnam, the key cultural difference between the United States and Brazil "has its roots in the Old World, in Protestant England and in the mellow Catholic civilization of Portugal with its large admixture of pagan elements—a Catholicism that in the new land was soon to be still further tempered by contact with native animism and an imported African fetishism. It is the two different ways of looking at life, the Latin and the Anglo-Saxon, developed over long centuries and given a religious embodiment, that present the basic contrast" (*Marvelous Journey* 7–8; see also Ribeiro 19–40).

2. Burns reports, for example, that between 1965 and 1975 (i.e., during the first eleven years of the dictatorship), the ten largest foreign companies in Brazil invested $98.8 million but remitted $774.5 million abroad. During this same decade the international agribusiness conglomerate Anderson Clayton "invested $1.6 million in Brazil while taking out $16.8 million in profits and dividends. *Business Week* advised its readers that the South American giant offered the highest level of profits in the world" (*History* [3rd ed.] 349).

3. Emerson's famous "American Scholar" address dates from 1837, while Gonçalves de Magalhães's "Ensaios sobre a história da literatura do Brasil" ("Essays on the History of Literature in Brazil") appears in *Niterói* 1 (1836): 132–59; his preface to *Suspiros poéticos e saudades* (*Poetical Sighs and Longings*) appears the same year.

4. Working on information about Brazil and its native peoples that was supplied to him by the French colonist Durand de Villegaignon, who from 1555 to 1559 spent time near Guanabara Bay, the present site of Rio de Janeiro, Montaigne wrote "Des Coches" and "Des Cannibales" and formulated his theory of the natural goodness of men, one based, we now know, on impressions of the Tupi.

5. Nelson Vieira, of Brown University, has long been interested in precisely this phenomenon.

6. For a more detailed examination of the relation between Caminha's *Carta* and Torero and Pimenta's *Terra Papagalli*, see the dissertation by Leila Lehnen, Vanderbilt University, 2002.

7. For an extended discussion of this issue, see Payne and Fitz.

Brazilian Music

Ever since the lilting rhythms of the bossa nova in the late 1950s and early 1960s, Brazilian music has been a major presence in the United States. Musicians of all stripes have embraced the myriad forms of Brazilian musical expression that have made their way into the American market. From jazz musicians like Stan Getz, Charlie Byrd, Vince Guaraldi, Herbie Mann, and George Duke to contemporary virtuosos like Diana Krall and Yo-Yo Ma, and from such diverse ensembles as the Pat Metheny Group, Manhattan Transfer, the High Llamas, the Beastie Boys[1] and David Byrne to postrock groups like Stereolab—and yet including such icons as Ella Fitzgerald, Joan Baez, Aretha Franklin, Frank Sinatra, and Sarah Vaughan[2]—artists have been integrating the sounds and modes of Brazilian music into their own compositions (see McGowan and Pessanha 175, 182–83). At the international level, the influence of Brazilian music has surpassed even that of soccer and unquestionably outstripped that of literature. Only the United States has had a greater impact on the development of international popular music than Brazil. The jazz flutist Herbie Mann, for example, believes that "there's an amazing magical, mystical quality to Brazilian music. Their music is paradise" (qtd. in McGowan and Pessanha 4). Although to many listeners in the United States it is simply part of the popular Carlos Santana and Ricky Martin–driven Latin sound, Brazilian music, felt by some to be "gentler" than its Spanish cousins, owes its essential difference, according to the celebrated musician Caetano Veloso, to the mellifluous sounds of its distinctive language: "Portuguese," avers Veloso, "is a much cooler, calmer, softer language than Spanish. . . . It's much more nuanced" (qtd. in Jones).

Music permeates all aspects of Brazilian society. For many Brazilians it has been a source of escape from the struggle against poverty. In the 1960s and 1970s, however, popular music took on a political dimension that has merged sound and sense into an effective form of protest and has given voice to individuals and groups long excluded from the political process (see Woodall). Immediately following the 1964 coup, popular music split into two factions—the cultural nationalists, who, seeking to defend what they felt was authentic Brazilian music, found their most ardent supporters among those associated with the MPB or *música popular brasileira* movement, and the Jovem Guarda, or "Young Guard," "a homegrown rock movement led by Roberto Carlos, who would later rival Julio Iglesias in the international market for *música romântica.*"

> The nationalist left regarded the Jovem Guarda as politically and culturally removed from Brazilian reality. The early MPB camp objected especially to the use of electric instruments in Brazilian music, just as orthodox folk-music fans jeered Bob Dylan for using an electric guitar at the Newport Folk Festival of 1965. The Jovem Guarda and international pop maintained a strong presence on urban airwaves, but the MPB approach dominated a series of popular-music festivals in São Paulo and Rio de Janeiro that marked the epoch of the late 1960s. (Perrone and Dunn 19)

It is no exaggeration to say that popular music in Brazil remains a political force to be reckoned with. Considering the role it plays in Brazilian society, Chris McGowan and Ricardo Pessanha argue, moreover, that it possesses three defining qualities:

> It has an intense lyricism tied to its Portuguese language heritage that often makes for beautiful, highly expressive melodies, enhanced by the fact that Portuguese is one of the most musical tongues on the earth and no small gift to the ballad singer. Second, a high level of poetry is present in the lyrics of much Brazilian popular music. And last, vibrant Afro-Brazilian rhythms energize most Brazilian songs, from samba to baião. (4)

Brazilian music first made its presence felt in Europe early in the twentieth century, when the maxixe, a lively, sometimes provocative dance-hall music, gained a large following. Created in Rio de Janeiro around 1880 by Afro-Brazilian musicians performing at parties in lower-class homes, *maxixe,* which McGowan and Pessanha regard as the first genuinely Brazilian dance form, "was a synthesis of lundu, polka, and Cuban habanera with additional voluptuous moves performed by the closely dancing couple. . . . Maxixe gave as erotic and scandalous an impression as lundu had one hundred years earlier and lambada would one hundred years later" (19).

As Charles Perrone observes, Brazilian popular music made inroads into the United States during the 1930s and 1940s with the film performances of Carmen Miranda, whose image and demeanor influenced Americans' perception, during this troubled period, of Brazil and its culture (*Masters* xix). Many of Miranda's films featured a new kind of music, simultaneously vivacious and sensuous, that was soon identified with Brazil itself. Exemplified in Ary Barroso's delightful song "Aquarela do Brasil" (recognized, in the United States and elsewhere, simply as "Brazil"), the new sound—which under Barroso's adroit hand provided the sound track for several Walt Disney films—became known the world over as samba.

By the 1950s the lines of influence began to run the other way. The samba, a nationalistic expression that had, largely through the Carmen Miranda films, struck a chord in the United States, was transformed in instrumentation and arrangements by North American ballroom orchestras and by the big-band sound generally (Perrone, *Masters* xix). With its American connection now established, the hybridized samba was practiced more and more by middle-class musicians in Rio de Janeiro and São Paulo who, led by João Gilberto, were bent on shaping the new sound (see Castro). With the appearance in 1959 of Gilberto's classic *Chega de saudade* (*No More Blues*), an album regarded by many as the "bible of bossa nova" (Perrone, *Masters* xx), the new sound became known as the bossa nova, the "new way." Although the bossa nova movement of the late 1950s "brought structural modifications to the samba, as well as innovations in performance style," it "did not replace the traditional samba." Instead, it offered "a new alternative for the middle- and upper-class listening public" (xx). In doing so, the bossa nova, embraced by influential American jazz musicians and pop stars, linked the Brazilian middle class with America's musical intelligentsia as well as with America's record-buying middle class. As Ruy Castro observes:

> [T]he bossa nova craze in the United States was longer and deeper than snapshot memories suggest. The new Brazilian sound had, after all, been making major incursions into the American pop scene for years before the Brits made theirs: the soundtrack from the popular 1959 Franco-Brazilian film *Black Orpheus*, for instance, gave American audiences an early taste of bossa nova's gliding groove, and Getz and Charlie Byrd's 1962 hit version of the bossa anthem "Desafinado" upped the dosage. In the wake of Getz's phenomenally successful collaborations, bossa nova records became an obligatory pit stop on the career path of every sixties pop singer from Elvis ("Bossa Nova Baby") to Edie Gorme ("Blame It on the Bossa Nova"). Jazz musicians got the message, too. Stan Kenton, Duke Ellington, Coleman Adderley, Dave Brubeck, Gerry Mulligan, Wes Montgomery, George Shearing, Oscar Peterson—all made bossa nova albums, many of them perhaps only too aware that the warmly inviting Brazilian import represented cerebral modern jazz's last chance at staying on the pop radar. (x)

Thus it was that, in the United States in the early and mid-1960s, a number of Brazilian musicians—notably João Gilberto, Antônio Carlos Jobim, Sérgio Mendes, and Astrud Gilberto (her captivating voice helped make "The Girl from Ipanema" a hit song in the United States)—became staples of the popular music scene. And the legendary album *Jazz Samba*, recorded in 1962 by the guitarist Charlie Byrd and the saxophonist Stan Getz, helped ignite the bossa nova craze. Merging easily with American "cool" jazz, bossa nova quickly won over American audiences and entered the permanent repertoire of a number of American musicians. Some of Jobim's tunes, in fact, such as "Triste" ("Sad"), and the still-infectious "Wave," became contemporary standards that influenced the directions American popular music would take. Like samba before it, bossa nova established itself as a staple on the international music scene, and its leading figure, Jobim, has gained a stature that rivals that of "George Gershwin, Duke Ellington, and other composers of Western popular music" (McGowan and Pessanha 6; see also Perrone, *Masters* xxv; Roberts 124).

The 1960s also saw the intensification of a cultural exchange between Brazilian and American musicians, composers, and singers that continues to this day. Especially in the areas of jazz and pop, the music produced by these collaborations has been nothing short of marvelous. In particular, guitarists and percussionists, including Airto Moreira and Flora Purim, have gained acceptance for a highly popular subgenre, jazz fusion, which—very much in the spirit of Brazilian music of this fecund period—blends North American jazz with other forms of popular music.

While the subtle Brazilian-inspired transformation of jazz was taking place, Brazilian music was itself changing, as the *MPB* movement merged music and musical forms, both in and outside Brazil, into yet another eclectic sound. In its integration of political awareness, "rhythm, melody, harmony, and lyrics," the work these performers created quickly became "one of the richest bodies of popular music ever to come from one country" (McGowan and Pessanha 6). At a 1967 festival, for instance, two young Bahian musicians, Caetano Veloso and Gilberto Gil, introduced the *som universal* ("universal sound"), in which Brazilian sounds and rhythms are played on electric instrumentation:

> Gil and Veloso were soon leading the insurgent movement of Tropicalism, which critiqued orthodox cultural nationalism and renovated Brazilian song by creatively engaging with vanguardist experimentation and international countercultures. . . . Taking cues from the radical iconoclast Oswald de Andrade and his proposal of *antropofagia*, or aesthetic anthropophagy, the Tropicalists aggressively devoured foreign information and styles, especially rock, but also tango, bolero, and mambo. (Perrone and Dunn 19–20)

As Veloso himself would later write of this experience, "The idea of 'cultural cannibalism' fit us, the Tropicalists, like a glove. We were 'eating' the Beatles and Jimi Hendrix" (qtd. in Perrone and Dunn 20).

Brazilian music continued to attract an international following during the 1970s, with MPB artists in particular gaining the attention of American audiences and performers. Wayne Shorter's 1975 album *Native Dancer*, which showcased the work of Milton Nascimento, was "particularly well-received," while "Brazilian percussionists made many contributions to jazz and fusion ensembles"; some of them even relocated permanently to the United States (Perrone and Dunn 20). "Brazilian music—its rhythms, instruments, harmonies, melodies, and textures—would have an enormous influence on American music from 1962 on." Percussionists like Airto Moreira, Dom Um Romão, Édison Machado, Milton Banana, Naná Vasconcelos,

Laudir de Oliveira, Guilherme Franco, and Paulinho da Costa—"all of whom recorded and toured with numerous jazz, rock, and pop artists in the United States"— led the way (McGowan and Pessanha 173). As the jazz flutist Herbie Mann would note, "In all fusion bands, the drummers slip into a jazz-Brazilian groove almost automatically," to the extent that, by the 1970s, "it became almost a matter of fact for every band to have a percussionist. But all the colors were Brazilian-influenced. Before that, the Latin drummers just played congas, timbales, and bongos" (qtd. in McGowan and Pessanha 173). In Europe, too, Brazilian instrumentalists and singers were becoming "an expected part of performance circuits" (Perrone and Dunn 21).

By the next decade, Brazilian popular music was firmly entrenched in North American culture, so much so that a "phenomenon dubbed Brazilian Wave occurred in all areas of the industry (recording, broadcasting, performance, publishing, media coverage)." Although reminiscent of bossa nova twenty years earlier, Brazilian Wave was much more diverse. "While bossa nova had operated with stylistic homogeneity, Brazilian Wave was defined by heterogeneity, the only overall common ground being national origin." A particularly energetic aspect of the wave's appeal was rock music. "Following the flirtations with Anglo-American rock'n'roll and subsequent variations in the 1960s and 1970s, there flourished a full-fledged movement in the 1980s." It touched virtually all elements of Brazilian culture and reached its zenith in the Rock in Rio Festival of 1985, "when Brazilian Rock (sometimes referred to as 'BRock') came of age" in a "seven-day megaconcert" that coincided with Brazil's return to "civilian governance after twenty-one years of military rule" (Perrone and Dunn 21, 23).

Four years after the end of the dictatorship, and probably in response to its repressive measure, the lambada, a sexy song-and-dance style that had its roots in Brazil's slave-owning past, became something of a dance craze in parts of the United States. Although the lambada, featured in at least one film released in the United States, was perhaps more of a commercial enterprise than an artistic one, it was also part of a liberating musical movement sweeping through Brazil's northeast during the 1980s and 1990s. In seeking to discover the essential appeal of Brazilian music, McGowan and Pessanha write that it has "a profound ability to move the soul. In its sounds and lyrics, it reflects the Brazilian people—their uninhibited joy or despair, their remarkable capacity to celebrate, and the all-important concept of *saudade* (a deep longing or yearning)" (6).

When rap music appeared in Brazil in the 1990s, São Paulo was its center. While several Brazilian rap groups have "appropriated the performance codes, sartorial accouterments, and hand signs of L.A.-style gangsta rap," the "leading rap formation, Racionais MC, recorded 'Periferia é periferia (em qualquer lugar)' ['Peripheries are Peripheries (Anywhere)'], which pointedly situates the poverty and violence of metropolitan São Paulo in global perspective." Some proponents of "nationalist positions in popular music" may object to Brazilian rap's overly enthusiastic embrace of New York and Los Angeles rap, but one can argue that Brazilian rap "is merely an updated version of *embolada*, a rapid-fire sung verse form from the rural northeast." Perrone and Dunn, though, make a distinction when it comes to Brazilian reggae, "because the model music is from a peripheral country":

> In Brazil, as elsewhere in the developing world, reggae first emerged as a contestatory music of black liberation before entering the mainstream. The foremost Rio-based group, Cidade Negra, began as a "protest" group and, after commercial success, recorded with Jamaican dance-hall star Shabba Ranks and with Gabriel o Pensador, a celebrated Brazilian rapper. The vocalist of that ensemble, Toni Garrido, was chosen to play the lead role in *Orfeu* (1990) [with the result that] the heterogeneity of musical practice in the present-day *favela* [slum] resounds on the film's sound track. (27–28)

The other outstanding feature of Brazilian popular music of the 1990s, besides its roots in social criticism, was the rapid expansion of the role played by gifted and innovative women. Dramatically increasing their presence in Brazil's music scene were vocalists like Marisa Monte, Daniela Mercury, Daúde, Vania Bastos, Cássia Eller, Leila Pinheiro, Monica Araújo, and Selma Reis. Zizi Possi produced outstanding albums like the 1994 *Valsa brasileira* (*Brazilian Waltz*). Song writing is another area in which Brazilian women have made great strides. Building on the work done earlier by Joyce Lee and Rita Lee (the latter formerly with Os Mutantes), "a whole generation of talented female singer-songwriters has arrived, including Rosa Passos, Zélia Duncan, Adriana Calcanhoto, Junia Lambert, Fernanda Abreu, and Marisa Monte. Daniela Mercury also writes some of her own songs" (McGowan and Pessanha 206).

At the turn of the century, Brazilian music is more pervasive in American (and world) culture than it ever was, even during the era of the bossa nova. Veloso made an eleven-city tour of the United States during the summer of 1999, for example, and a host of other Brazilian singers and musicians—including Milton Nascimento, Gal Costa, Gilberto Gil, Chico Buarque, and Chico Science (who, along with his band, Nação Zumbi, performed at New York City's Central Park SummerStage in 1995)—continue to win fans and gain plaudits from the critics across the land. In summing up the "profound influence" Brazilian rhythms, song writing, and percussion have had on American and global music, Herbie Mann has observed that it is now commonplace to have artists like "Djavan recording in Los Angeles, and Manhattan Transfer in Brazil, and they are all using people who have been listening to Herbie Hancock and Ivan Lins. That is, it all gets so crossed that each in turn re-influences the other" (qtd. in McGowan and Pessanha 183). Thus Brazilian music, in all its richness, variety, and political consciousness, has established itself as a force in the United States.[3] Brazilian culture has as well, as witnessed by the growth of immigrant communities in New York, New England, and Florida. In Rio de Janeiro's 1999 Carnival, the samba school Império Serrano even "paid homage to Brazilian emigrés with the theme 'Uma rua chamada Brasil' ['A Street Called Brazil'], referring to Forty-sixth Street, the commercial center of Little Brazil in New York City." These developments may suggest "a reduction in anxiety about U.S. cultural and economic influences in Brazil," as well as the emergence of transnational allegiances and identities among Brazilians living abroad.

> While there can be no question that the flow from abroad, especially the United States, is much greater to Brazil than vice versa, [it is also true that] Brazilian musical creativity may more than compensate for economic disadvantage. The constant influx of musical information from abroad has proved to be not only musically fruitful in so many ways but useful as well for reflections on cultural practice, social concerns, modernity, nationality, and globalization. (Perrone and Dunn 31)

Strengthened by the commitment to be an important part of Brazil's sociopolitical process, Brazilian music, as it creates for itself a global audience, remains "as playful, open, vibrant, imaginative, and self-renewing as ever" (McGowan and Pessanha 206).

Although making no pretense at completeness, the following list includes artists, groups, songs, and terms that are useful for American and world audiences to know. In preparing this list, I have relied heavily on the work of Charles Perrone. I recommend his writings, in addition to those of Christopher Dunn, Robert Stam, Chris McGowan, Ricardo Pessanha, and John Storm Roberts, to anyone seeking to explore modern Brazilian music, its leading practitioners, its impact in the United States, and its sociopolitical dimensions. I apologize to artists not on the list; the omission was not intentional.

Almeida, Laurindo: A Brazilian guitar master who often paired with the saxophonist Bud Shank in the 1950s, Almeida was one of the first Brazilian musicians to gain a following in the United States (Perrone, *Masters* 217). Almeida could re-create, in his inimitable style, many American and English pop hits. On his CD *Laurindo Almeida: Virtuoso Guitar* (Laser Light 15 296), for example, he gives beautiful renditions of such standards as "Yesterday," "Just the Way You Are," "Copacabana (at the Copa)," and "Tomorrow" (from the Broadway show *Annie*).

"Amor em paz" ("Once I Loved"). One of the many bossa nova hits by the hugely successful collaboration of Vinícius de Moraes (the lyrics) and Antônio Carlos Jobim (the haunting score).

Azymuth: Consisting of Ivan Conti, José Roberto Bertrami, and Alex Malheiros, this progressive jazz trio, which blends jazz, samba, and funk, has gained an international following. In England its single "Jazz Carnival" went gold in 1979; *Telecommunication* became a top-ten jazz album hit in 1982 (McGowan and Pessanha 180).

Bailes funk: Funk music, and funk dances (*bailes funk*), are popular in Brazil, attracting large, often boisterous crowds. "Contemporary Brazilian funk-oriented musicians include Ed Motta, Sandra de Sá, Cláudio Zoli, Luni, Skowa e Mafia, and Hanói Hanói. Fernanda Abreu . . . took the funk-dance music route with her much lauded 1995 album *Da Lata*" (McGowan and Pessanha 205).

Barroso, Ary: The author of "Aquarela do Brasil" (watercolor of Brazil), a samba tune better known internationally as, simply, "Brazil," Barroso in the 1940s was one of the most influential figures in the early exportation of Brazilian music. Walt Disney featured "Aquarela do Brasil" in his 1942 animated film *Saludos Amigos* (McGowan and Pessanha 30). Many of Barroso's songs were performed by Carmen Miranda in her movies. Still popular, "Aquarela do Brasil" also serves as the theme song for *Brazil*, Terry Gilliam's 1985 black comedy about life under a futuristic totalitarian regime.

Ben, Jorge: A very popular singer-musician of the 1960s and 1970s, Ben got his start in the competitions held in São Paulo and Rio de Janeiro. "The festivals were designed to promote popular music of a national orientation and were clearly dominated by the sounds of Bossa Nova and derivative forms, such as stylized regionalist compositions. The adolescent rock of the 'escapist' Youth Guard was shunned; one festival expressly prohibited the use of electric instruments," because it was perceived by some as yet another symbol of Yankee imperialism (Perrone, *Masters* xxix–xxx). Rod Stewart's song "Do Ya Think I'm Sexy?" appears to borrow so extensively from Ben's "Taj Mahal" that charges of plagiarism were brought against the Scottish singer. The case was eventually settled out of court (Rohter, "Tiger" 2–3).

Bethânia, Maria: The sister of Caetano Veloso and a star in her own right, Bethânia (the first to record, in 1965, one of Caetano's songs) produced a Brazilian version of Victor Herbert's "Sweet Mystery of Life" ("A rosa dos ventos"; Philips 6349 005) in 1971 (Perrone, *Masters* 48, 66, 121, 203). She was also a leading figure in the politically aware MPB movement from 1965 to 1985.

Blakey, Art: Blakey was one of the earliest American jazz musicians to recognize the genius of Brazil's Milton Nascimento. Even before establishing himself in his homeland, Nascimento, along with João Gilberto, had toured the United States with Blakey (Perrone, *Masters* 135).

Blanc, Aldir: Blanc was a premier, if controversial, songwriter of the 1970s. Often working with the guitarist João Bosco, he "is best known as an analyst of social customs and behavior." Blanc's songs, reflecting "daily life in modern urban Brazil," focus on the "anonymous inhabitants of inner city neighborhoods, working-class suburbs, or hillside slums, often vagabonds, hustlers, criminals, or victims of crime" (Perrone, *Masters* 166).

Bosco, João: The other half of the celebrated duo Bosco and Blanc, he is "a dexterous and imaginative guitarist who combines folk and popular rhythms, Bossa Nova (jazz) and traditional harmonies and classical technique in a distinctive style. His heavily syncopated attack on the guitar often imitates patterns of Brazilian percussion instruments" (Perrone, *Masters* 166).

bossa nova (new way or new manner): This famous music blossomed in Brazil in the late 1950s and during the 1960s in the United States, where, merging with jazz techniques, it was popularized by Stan Getz, Charlie Byrd, and Vince Guaraldi, among others. Reflecting middle-class values, bossa nova was criticized at home for being "a culturally estranged product that contributed to the alienation of the Brazilian public by turning away from the samba, the true tradition of the people, and encouraging adulation of North American values" (José Ramos Tinhorão, qtd. in Perrone, *Masters* xxv). Nevertheless, "Whatever controversies Bossa Nova may have provoked, it became enormously popular in a short time, at home and abroad, and left a lasting mark on popular music in Brazil" (xxvi).

Brown, Carlinhos: Brown is the stage name of Antônio Carlos Santos de Freitas, one of contemporary Brazil's most innovative bandleaders, songwriters, and percussionists. He took his name from the American soul music legend James Brown, whose music and dance moves he admired. Brown was "the founder and director of Timblada, a percussion-dominated ensemble that has enjoyed local and international success" and has aligned itself with "the expressive cultures of 'globalized black youth' without referencing the specific struggles of black communities in Brazil or abroad" (Perrone and Dunn 29).

Buarque, Chico: Perhaps the most widely respected figure in Brazilian popular music in the 1980s and 1990s and a songwriter-musician whose best work is both "popular" in its themes and "erudite" in its technical refinement and lyricism, Buarque "is best known as a social critic who voices popular sentiment in crafted musical molds, but his sensitive sentimental songs have been equally successful." As Perrone observes, "Buarque's output is marked by the intensification of social themes and diversification of formal approach" (*Masters* 1–2).

Byrne, David: The former lead singer of Talking Heads, Byrne has helped integrate Brazilian musicians and music into the world music scene. Released in 2001, the album *Look into the Eyeball*, for example, features several Brazilian styles, modes, and musicians; his successful label Luaka Bop cultivates Brazil as well.

"Cálice" ("Chalice"): One of Chico Buarque's most famous protest songs, along with "Construção" ("Construction"), "Cálice," coauthored by Gilberto Gil, uses religious allusions to portray the unjust silencing of an individual—and, by extension, of populace—by an unnamed political authority.[4] The Portuguese title, as Perrone points out, is a homophone of the imperative *cale-se,* ("Shut up!"), which "represents imposed silence, censorship, and victimization" (*Masters* 33–34). Although the song was not censored when it first appeared in a São Paulo newspaper, officials prevented Buarque and Gil from performing it in public, an act of repression that suggests the political potency of Brazilian popular music in the 1970s.[5] Indeed, Brazilian protest music, as Bradford Burns notes, "provided a most effective form of communication in a land where half the population was illiterate" (*History* [3rd ed.] 454).

"Canção da América" ("Song of America"): Written in collaboration with Fernando Brant and expressing a Pan-American sensibility, "Canção da América" is one of Milton Nascimento's best-known songs fostering friendship among the nations of the Americas.

Carvalho, Beth: Carvalho, a popular and successful samba singer during the 1970s, is a star of the MPB movement. Thanks to her treatment, samba, long regarded as a mainstay of the lower classes, became a unifying force with a strong "cross-class appeal" (Perrone, *Masters* xxxiii, 203–04).

Cazuza: Born in Rio de Janeiro in 1958, Cazuza (Agenor de Miranda Araújo Neto) is "one of the most incensed and incendiary songwriters and vocalists of his time in Brazil." In songs such as "O nosso amor e a gente inventa" ("We Invent Our Love") and "Brasil," Cazuza decries the injustices in his country (McGowan and Pessanha 195). The onetime leader of Barão Vermelho (Red Baron), "perhaps the only Brazilian rhythm-and-blues band to achieve widespread popularity," Cazuza died of AIDS in 1990, but not before one album, *Ideologia,* received prestigious awards and two others, *O tempo não pára* (*Time Doesn't Stop*) and *Burguesia* (*Bourgeoisie*) won "critical adulation and multi-platinum sales" (McGowan and Pessanha 195).

César, Chico: Combining his northeastern heritage with "influences from Tropicalismo and the Caribbean," César, a singer with a commanding stage presence, also "writes powerful, well-crafted songs. His beautifully poetic lyrics explore personal and profound themes with clever wordplay and verbal invention" (McGowan and Pessanha 152–53). His albums *Aos vivos* (1995) and *Cuscuz clã* (1996) have been widely acclaimed.

"Chuckberry Fields Forever": Reflecting his eclectic, international appreciation of music, Gilberto Gil's rocker "both pays homage to one of the black originators of rock and roll [Chuck Berry] and parodies the artsy Beatles song 'Strawberry Fields Forever.' In Gil's text, an irreverent profession of faith follows a chapter from the history of popular music in the Americas." Brazil must play a part, Gil believes, in recognizing the African roots of rock and roll in the New World (Perrone, *Masters* 121; Perrone also provides an English-language version of the lyrics).

"Construção" ("Construction"): Along with "Cálice," this work by Chico Buarque is one of the most significant protest songs. It "obliquely narrates the fatal fall of a bricklayer. . . . The concrete referent—construction work, a structure being built—is a homologue for the melody and the text, which are meticulously designed with measured dimensions and calculated structural balance" (Perrone, *Masters* 24). Semantically and melodically, the song is thus as much a "construction project" as the building it describes.[6]

Costa, Gal: A preeminent *tropicalista* vocalist as well as a collaborator of both Gilberto Gil and Caetano Veloso, Costa has been featured in concerts in New York and Los Angeles. Two of her songs (both written by Gil)—"Mini-mistério" ("Mini-Mystery"), "a know-thyself song that satirizes consumer mentality," and "Cultura e civilização" ("Culture and Civilization"), "which has been interpreted as an early expression of Afro-Bahian pride and as an affirmation of Brazilian counter-culture" (Perrone, *Masters* 107)—illustrate the political significance of Brazilian popular music.[7] "Culture and Civilization," David Brookshaw has written, "affirms its author's physical identity as an Afro-Brazilian ('my hair, beautiful as a lion's mane'). However, the yearning for the matrix is not expressed as a romantic Africa, but as Salvador, Gil's native city. Thus it combines a manifestation of both ethnic and regional identity" (qtd. in Perrone, *Masters* 221).

Djavan: A popular singer-musician in the 1980s, Djavan is also well known abroad, where many of his hit songs are covered by a variety of artists. Djavan tends to eschew protest songs, favoring instead love songs and "a sophisticated, rhythmically vibrant, pan-American style that is his alone" (McGowan and Pessanha 97–98).

Estrangeiro (*Stranger*): Released in 1989 and now available in CD (Elektra/Musician 9 60898-2), *Estrangeiro* remains one of Caetano Veloso's most influential albums.[8] Using, ironically, the motif of the other who comes to Brazil to understand (or possess) it, the album suggests at first the alienated Latin American artist in the metropolis but then subtly develops a distinctly Brazilian focus (Perrone, *Seven Faces*, 106). As Perrone describes this well-known song-poem, "The quasi-recitative opens with different impressions of a national symbol—Rio de Janeiro's Guanabara Bay"—and then names some of the many foreigners, including Paul Gauguin, Cole Porter, and Claude Lévi-Strauss, who came to Brazil to decipher its mysteries. "On a more metaphorical level," as Perrone notes, *Stranger* "refers to the vagaries of vision (blindness vs. insight) and perception itself. The song text plays out as a colorful dream sequence with apocalyptic strains that both questions touristic images of Rio and constructs a lyric self at odds with conventional interpretations of the city, the nation, and its guiding values" (106). Interestingly, at the song's conclusion, Veloso sings, in English, "Some may like a soft Brazilian singer / but I've given up all attempts at perfection," a line that recontextualizes and redirects a line written by Bob Dylan on the jacket of *Bringing It All Back Home* (Columbia CS 9128, 1967): "my songs're written with the kettledrum in mind / a touch of any anxious color. obvious. an' people perhaps like a soft brazilian singer . . . i have given up at making any attempt at perfection." Veloso anticipates negative "reactions to a particular vision and, in the context of Brazilian popular music in the U. S. market or of antirock sentiment in Brazil, [affirms] the individual course of the persona/composer, who follows aesthetic instinct rather than fashion or proscriptive values" (106–07).

"A Felicidade" ("Happiness"): Composed by the bossa nova song-writing team of Jobim (the beautiful music) and Moraes (the evocative lyrics), this song-poem—from the Academy Award–winning film *Black Orpheus* (1959)—about the ephemeral quality of happiness has become a standard of American popular music.

"Feminismo no estácio" ("Feminism in a Borough"): This composition by Bosco and Blanc deals with "women's liberation from the point of view of an inhabitant of one of Rio's older mixed lower-middle- and working-class neighborhoods." More specifically, the wry samba confronts the problem of "sexual equality in a context where traditional values still tend to prevail. Blanc hints at the class-bound limitations of feminism as it has been practiced in Third World Brazil—its restrictions to the minority, the educated middle class—and at the need to alter perspectives when considering the implications of feminist action for common people" (Perrone, *Masters* 187–88).[9]

Gabriel o Pensador (Gabriel the Thinker): A popular rapper, Gabriel, from Rio de Janeiro, is highly political. His controversial song "Tô feliz (matei o presidente)" ("I'm Happy [I Killed the President]") was banned in 1992. Directed at the soon-to-be-impeached president Fernando Collor de Mello, the song resulted in Gabriel's signing as an artist for Sony. Gabriel's songs attack bigotry, poverty, and domestic violence in Brazil (McGowan and Pessanha 205).

"A Garota de Ipanema" ("The Girl from Ipanema"): This famous bossa nova composition captivated audiences worldwide during the 1960s. Although, ironically enough, something of a flop in Brazil, "The Girl from Ipanema," as sung by Astrud Gilberto, won the Grammy Award for Record of the Year (1964). "It was the first song that universalized Brazilian music" (Page, qtd. in Buckley 2). The song was inspired by a teenager who would stroll past the Veloso Bar on her way to Ipanema beach in Rio. Regular patrons of the Veloso, the composer Antônio Carlos Jobim and the poet Vinícius de Moraes were mesmerized by her grace and beauty and wrote the song in her honor.

Gil, Gilberto: A major figure in Brazilian music, committed to freedom of expression and "engagé populism," Gil, along with Caetano Veloso, "is noted as one of the founders and leading interpreters of *tropicalismo* and as a leader who attacks convention and opens the way for diversification and experimentation in MPB" (Perrone, *Masters* 91). In the 1970s, Gil developed an Afro-American dimension to his music (see *Refavela*, Philips 6349 329; "Chuckberry Fields Forever"). Although some critics saw this influence as an aspect of cultural imperialism by the United States, Gil's music corresponded to the political and cultural movement Black Rio, which emerged in working-class sections of Rio de Janeiro. "Disenchanted," as Perrone says, "with the middle-class MPB of Rio's beach districts . . . black youth sought an outlet via musical forms that were associated with the rising tide of black consciousness in the United States, from the civil rights movement to black power and ethnic pride" (124).

Gilberto, Astrud: In 1963, Gilberto, then twenty-three and married to João Gilberto, was in a New York City recording studio when Stan Getz, the saxophonist who helped bring bossa nova to the attention of the American public, asked her to sing "A Garota de Ipanema" in English. "The Girl from Ipanema" became an international hit. Gilberto's career lasted through the 1980s.

Gilberto, João: The force behind the shift from samba music to the bossa nova beat (his legendary 1959 album *Chega de saudade* uses the term *bossa nova* for the first time), Gilberto is a central figure of the bossa nova in Brazil and the United States. In the 1960s, there was "a veritable explosion of Bossa Nova" music, although many North American interpretations, like those by Charlie Byrd, Vince Guaraldi, and Stan Getz, "tended to be of the instrumental variety" (Perrone, *Masters* xxv).[10] The popular album *João Gilberto: Live in Montreux* (Elektra Musician, 9 60760-4) features his distinctive voice and guitar playing. Outstanding songs (with English lyrics provided) include "Menino do Rio," "Retrato em branco e preto," "A Garota de Ipanema," "A felicidade," and "Adeus América." In 2000, along with Cactano Veloso, Gilberto won a Grammy for Best World Album, for *João: Voz e violão*.

indigenous music: Although not as great a force as African-based music, indigenous music has had an impact. As McGowan and Pessanha observe, "There is Indian influence in some Brazilian popular music, as seen in songs by musicians like Egberto Gismonti and Marlui Miranda, instruments like the *reco-reco* scraper, and traditions such as the *caboclinho* Carnaval groups. But generally one must journey to the remote homelands of the Yanomâmi, Bororo, Kayapó, and other indigenous groups to hear their music" (9–10).

"Insensatez" ("How Insensitive"): A product of the Jobim-Moraes songwriting team, this tune, often rerecorded, was a bossa nova hit of the early 1960s.

Jobim, Antônio Carlos: One of the first musicians to promote bossa nova, in the late 1950s and early 1960s, Jobim ranks as a master of Brazilian popular music and of its export around the world. His skills as a composer and his influence as a musician were largely responsible for the success of the bossa nova in the United States.

Kaoma: The creation of two French entrepreneurs; Jean Karakos and Olivier Lorsac, Kaoma was a "multinational group" (with a Brazilian lead singer, Loalwa Braz) that performed lambada songs in Europe, where it became a sensation in 1989. Its 1990 album, released as *World Beat* in the United States, "went gold and hit number 1 on the Billboard Latin music chart" (McGowan and Pessanha 155–56).

lambada: Originating in the northeastern state of Pará in the 1970s, the lambada dance was "a new hybrid, mixing elements of merengue, maxixe, samba, and forró dances. In it, couples press tightly together, the right thigh of each between the other's legs, and dip and swirl sensually to up-tempo, high energy rhythms" (McGowan and Pessanha 155). By the late 1980s, the lambada, regarded as the epitome of Brazilian sexiness, had become popular in Europe (especially in France, where a lambada compilation was issued by Carrère) and North America. In 1990 the film *Lambada: The Forbidden Dance* was released.

Lee, Rita: Originally part of the group Os Mutantes, Lee became a successful solo artist who was labeled, in the 1970s and 1980s, the first lady of Brazilian rock (McGowan and Pessanha 189). Packing her lyrics with "irony and irreverence," she "moved in the direction of an upbeat, light pop-rock sound flavored with various Brazilian rhythms and touches," although, as she shows in the 1987 song "Brazix muamba" (which protests the nation's many social problems and criticizes the nuclear power plants, Angra 1 and 2, outside Rio), she has not lost her political consciousness.

Lobão: Lobão (born João Luis Woerdenbag in 1957) has a sound that is "heavy, percussive, and energetic" and that mixes samba and rock, two genres not usually brought together. A collaborator with the American jazz keyboardist Ronnie Foster, on the 1989 album *Sob o sol de Parador* (*Under the Parador Sun*—an "ironic reference to the Paul Mazursky film *Moon over Parador* about a dictator in a fictional South American country called Parador"), Lobão has also written protest songs. In "Eleito" ("The

Elected"), for example, Lobão and co-writer Bernardo Vilhena, "castigate the ineffectual and unpopular Brazilian president José Sarney, who fought against free elections when the populace demanded them in 1984" (McGowan and Pessanha 194–95).

maxixe: A lively, often provocative music-and-dance form that was very popular in European dance halls before, during, and after World War I.

Mendes, Sérgio: An internationally popular musician of the 1960s (he had several gold albums in the United States during that period, including *Brazil '66* and *The Fool on the Hill*), Mendes "stepped out of his usual mold with *Primal Roots* (1972), which included folkloric styles in the mix, and the Grammy-winning *Brasileiro* (1992), which showcased rising Bahian songwriter Carlinhos Brown and fused MPB and Rio samba with axé music and funk" (McGowan and Pessanha 72).

Moraes, Vinícius de: Already renowned in the 1950s as a poet, diplomat, and public figure, Moraes went on to make a name for himself as a popular-music lyricist. The movie *Black Orpheus* (1959) was based on a verse play of his, *Orfeu da conceição*, and contained several of his (and Jobim's) songs, including "A felicidade" and "Manhã de carnaval" ("Carnaval Morning"), both of which became staples of the burgeoning bossa nova movement. Not only did Moraes establish and promote the new movement; he imparted status and dignity to the lyrics of Brazilian popular music (Perrone, *Masters* xxiii–xxiv), paving the way for the literary and sociopolitical dimension that, particularly in its MPB form, it would take.

Moreira, Airto: Moreira "spearheaded the Brazilian 'percussion invasion' of the late 1960s and 1970s that infused American jazz with new rhythms, percussive textures, and tone colors" and, with his wife, the singer Flora Purim, displaced Sérgio Mendes as the best-known Brazilian in the United States (McGowan and Pessanha 169). After moving to the United States, Moreira worked with such jazz artists as Miles Davis, Paul Winter, Wayne Shorter, Cannonball Adderley, Paul Desmond, George Duke, and Chick Corea, while with Paul Simon Moreira played the *cuíca*, a small drumlike instrument, on Simon's 1972 hit single "Me and Julio down by the Schoolyard" (McGowan and Pessanha 169–71).

música popular brasileira or MPB (Brazilian popular music): According to Charles Perrone, the initials MPB were "used to designate original composition rooted in or derived from Brazilian traditions, usually with acoustic instrumentation. In this sense, MPB was distinguished from international pop music and rock and roll in the early sixties' style of such groups as the Beatles, which used electric instrumentation" (*Masters* x). Growing from the bossa nova, MPB, as represented by Gilberto Gil, Caetano Veloso, Gal Costa, João Bosco, Aldir Blanc, Maria Bethânia, Chico Buarque,

Milton Nascimento, and others, can be socially conscious in its messages and appeals to the educated middle class and to less advantaged groups. MPB was a political force, particularly for young people, in the 1960s, 1970s, and 1980s.

Os Mutantes (the Mutants): Founded in 1966 and undergoing several transformations until breaking up in 1978, Os Mutantes has been called the first "artistically important rock band in Brazil" (McGowan and Pessanha 188). The group was initially associated with Gilberto Gil, later with Caetano Veloso. In 1968, at the International Song Festival in São Paulo, the members angered many people by wearing plastic clothes while accompanying Veloso in his famous protest anthem "É proibido proibir" ("To Prohibit Is Prohibited"). Widely regarded as outrageous and nonconformist, the group influenced the development of both Brazilian and international rock. In the United States they were admired by both Nirvana and the Posies, "both of which discovered the Mutantes' recordings in later years" (Perrone and Dunn 189).

Nascimento, Milton: A central figure of MPB and a highly successful singer-musician abroad, Nascimento, through many recordings and performances in the United States (which began as early as 1968), has established strong links to jazz musicians the world over. A distinctive vocalist, he has developed a "cult following" in the United States and has actively promoted "a cooperative Pan Americanism," a musical brotherhood and sisterhood of the Western Hemisphere (Perrone, *Masters*, 204, 203).

Pascoal, Hermeto: A colorful and creative figure, Pascoal is famous for making innovative music not only with traditional instruments but with found objects and environmental sounds. His 1984 composition "Tiruliruli," for example, takes a phrase from a soccer announcer's play-by-play and, repeating it again and again and adding harmonies, turns it into "a quirky but strangely affecting short piece." In 1970, Pascoal played piano on the Miles Davis LP "Live-Evil" (McGowan and Pessanha 167, 168).

Pereira, Nazaré: Well known in Europe, where she has established a following on the strength of her unique stylizations of *carimbó* (an Afro-Brazilian song-and-dance-form that is played on her 1988 album *Ritmos da Amazônia*) and other northeastern musical styles, Pereira is becoming popular in other parts of the world as well (McGowan and Pessanha 154).

Purim, Flora: Singing "with great passion in Portuguese and accented English, with a sensuous voice that was alternately smooth and husky," and making use of "an amazing array of vocal effects," including "squeaks, moans, cries, electronic distortions, free-form scatting, and precipitous glissandi," Purim became "the most successful jazz-fusion singer of the 1970s, both artistically and commercially." Along with her percussionist husband, Airto Moreira, Purim has worked with a number of jazz artists, including Herbie Hancock, Thelonious Monk, Stan Getz, Duke Pearson, Gil Evans, and Chick Corea (she sang and wrote songs for his band for two years). In 1974 she was named best female jazz vocalist by *Downbeat* magazine; in 1989 she teamed with her husband and Mickey Hart (drummer in the Grateful Dead) on the album *Dafos*; and two years later she vocalized to Hart's "world-music drumming-and-percussion fest *Planet Drum*" (McGowan and Pessanha 172, 173).

Ramalho, Elba: Born in the northeast in 1951, Ramalho was "a national-class handball player, a drummer in an all-girl rock band, and a sociology student before journeying to Rio as a singer for the northeastern group Quintero Violado. Besides being a fine vocalist, Ramalho is a stage and screen actress, appearing in plays such as *Lampião no Inferno* (directed by Azevedo) and in the Ruy Guerra film *Ópera do malandro*" (McGowan and Pessanha 150).

Regina, Elis: A beloved vocalist and a fixture of MPB, Elis Regina, who was born in Porto Alegre in 1945, had a number of hit records and worked with some of Brazil's most accomplished composers. Her version of Jobim's "Águas de Março" ("The Waters of March") is still a classic. Regina was also well known for her stage shows, which blended the musical dynamism of live concerts with the drama of traditional theater. She died of a cocaine overdose in 1982, at the height of her career.

"Samba de uma nota só" ("One Note Samba"): Another of Jobim's seminal compositions, "One Note Samba" is a kind of bossa nova manifesto that demonstrates the form's economy of linguistic expression and its careful integration of semantics and melody, of sound and sense. Along with "Desafinado," another still-popular classic, "One Note Samba" embodies "the ideal Bossa Nova aesthetic of subdued, subtle, and polished expression" (Perrone, *Masters* xxiii).[11]

Science, Chico: Chico Science and his band, Nação Zumbi (Zumbi Nation), were closely associated with the *movimento mangue*, "mangue beat," or (with a play on computer terminology) "mangue bit" ("mangrove movement," "mangrove beat," or "mangrove bit"), a musical form from the city of Recife, in the early 1990s. The movement is a fusion of "traditional forms with funk, rap, and heavy metal"; its iconography "features a marsh-dwelling crab with brains, emphasizing native subaltern intelligence, and a parabolic antenna stuck in the mud, which suggests a purposefully unresolved dialectic between the social reality of the mangrove shantytowns of metropolitan Recife and a deterritorialized, technologically informed sensibility" (Perrone and Dunn 29). Chico Science died in a car crash in 1997.

Sepultura: Exemplifying the internationalization that characterizes Brazilian music, the "Phoenix-based Sepultura, a heavy-metal band originally from Belo Horizonte," is regarded by some critics as "the protagonist of a cautionary tale about the extreme Americanization of Brazilian music." Even so, the group is "symptomatic of the complexity of urban Brazil, which sustains a wide variety of youth subcultures." Moreover, "Septultura is the most successful Brazilian group in the international music market since Sérgio Mendes and Brazil '66" (Perrone and Dunn 24, 25).

Simone: A popular vocalist, Simone is well know for her work on the sound track of the film *Dona Flor and Her Two Husbands* and for her 1978 album *Cigarra* (EMI Odeon 064 421089D). Politically committed, Simone gave in 1979 "a now legendary concert at which she performed Geraldo Vandré's most famous protest song, 'Caminhando.' This was a courageous act, since the government's Abertura (Opening) policy had only recently curtailed heavy censorship and the military was still solidly in charge of Brazil" (McGowan and Pessanha 99). A gifted athlete, Simone was a member of the national basketball team before becoming a professional singer. She recorded her first album, *Simone*, in 1973.

tropicália, tropicalismo: Tropicalismo is one of the most interesting and culturally important movements to emerge from Brazil since the 1970s. Finding its most successful expressions in film and music (including lyrics), *tropicalismo*—inspired by the anthropophagous theories of Oswald de Andrade ("cannibalizing from folk culture, pop culture and foreign culture" [Jones 67]) and by the experiments of the concretist poets (Caetano Veloso has transformed several *concretista* poems into musical scores)—helped revitalize Brazilian popular music and its sociopolitical context by appropriating and recasting a number of forms and influences, both national and international. In the late 1960s, *tropicalismo* initiated a debate about Brazilian society: How can a nation crippled by archaic, antidemocratic traditions and ruled by a military dictatorship assimilate the mostly alien trappings of Western modernity, its materialistic sense of progress and its dubious ideas about equality? Caetano Veloso and Gilberto Gil emerged as *tropicalismo's* most eloquent advocates. Several songs ("Tropicália," for example, and the album *Tropicália, ou panis et circensis*, which critiques Brazilian society allegorically) incurred the wrath of the dictatorship's censors; and in late 1968, when Veloso and Gil were placed under house arrest in Salvador, the *tropicalista* movement came to an end.[12]

Uakti: Taking its name from a mythological figure from the Amazon rain forest and making its own instruments, Uakti "was formed in the mid-1970s by Marco Antônio Guimarães, who had studied at the University of Bahia with the legendary composer Walter Smetak, a sort of Swiss-Brazilian Harry Partch who created new musical systems and instruments" (McGowan and Pessanha 181–82). Manhattan Transfer's Tim Hauser, who worked with the group in 1987 when Transfer was recording its album *Brasil*, has said of Uakti's music that it is "very spiritual" and "makes you feel like you're in a band two thousand years ago" (qtd. in McGowan and Pessanha 182). Uakti's innovative work can also be heard on Paul Simon's *The Rhythm of the Saints*.

Vandré, Geraldo: Another key figure in MPB, Vandré was the center of a controversy when in 1969 his song "Walking" was deemed "subversive" by the military authorities and banned.[13] Although Vandré, like Veloso and Gil (and in a sense Chico Buarque), was forced to flee Brazil, his work, sung in the streets in cities and in rural areas, became in the 1970s a rallying cry for opponents of the dictatorship. General Luís de França Oliveira, who was in charge of public security in Rio de Janeiro and who had called the song subversive, cautioned that "Walking" was "a musical cadence of the Mao Tse-tung type that can easily serve as the anthem for student street demonstrations" (qtd. in Burns, *History* [3rd ed.] 462).

Veloso, Caetano: One of Brazil's most respected musicians and cultural commentators, Veloso is an international celebrity whose eclectic music "veers from the Afro-Brazilian rhythms of his native province Bahia to the cool jazz collaborations of Miles Davis and Gil Evans" and from the Beatles and bossa nova to Arnold Schoenberg and George Clinton (Jones 67). On the album *Livro* (Nonesuch, 1999), Veloso still practices what he describes as "subversive Pan-Americanism," a term that recalls the late 1960s, when he was a prime mover in the tropicalismo movement. Along with João Gilberto, he won a Grammy in 2000 for *João: Voz e violão*, voted best world album. A translation of Veloso's autobiography, *Tropical Truth*, was published by Knopf in 2002.

Villa-Lobos, Heitor: A world-renowned modernist composer, Villa-Lobos, in works like the acclaimed *Bachianas brasileiras* (*Brazilian Bachs*), merged the European avant-garde with Brazilian themes, forms, and motifs. He allied himself in the 1930s with the National Socialist culture of the Vargas regime and wrote classical and popular music based on folk themes and utilizing indigenous instruments (Armstrong, *Third World* 204).

Xuxa: Born in 1963 in Rio Grande do Sul, Xuxa (Maria da Graça Meneghel) has created children's music, for her hugely successful TV Globo children's show, and released her own albums, which feature "catchy songs written by top pop songwriters" and are "slickly produced and heavily promoted by Globo." In the early 1990s, Xuxa was "the biggest-selling recording artist in Latin America"; in Brazil alone, her albums often sold more than two million copies (McGowan and Pessanha 204).

Zé, Tom: A socially conscious *tropicalista* from Bahia, Zé is well known for his song "Parque Industrial" ("Industrial Park"). Like Patrícia Galvão's 1933 novel of the same title, it satirizes the supposed benefits of an export economy and criticizes the sexual and racial stereotyping central to advertising and a consumer society. "Parque Industrial" also challenges the easy acceptance by many Brazilians of "pro-development ideology." The "Brazilianized pronunciation of the English refrain 'Made in Brazil' is," as Perrone sees it, "the scornful song's keynote" (*Masters* 61). Zé's later work, like *Fabrication Defect* (an album released in the United States in 1998), "stands out as a radical attempt within popular music to theorize the asymmetries of economic and cultural power in a global context" (Perrone and Dunn 20–21).

NOTES

1. The songs "I Don't Know" (from *Hello Nasty*) and "Twenty Questions" (*Sounds of Science*) were inspired by the bossa nova and by the music of Jorge Ben and Antônio Carlos Jobim (particularly his "Waters of March").
2. On *Sarah Vaughan: Brazilian Romance* (Chrome CBS, FMT 42519), for example, Vaughan, accompanied by Paulinho da Costa, George Duke, Hubert Laws, Tom Scott, and Ernie Watts, sings several songs by, and with, Milton Nascimento.
3. In Brazil, which suffers from widespread illiteracy, maldistribution of income, sexism, classism, and racism, popular music plays an important role in the country's political development and in its cultural discourse. The socially conscious and political lyrics of MPB, the popular music movement, stand in contrast to the often banal lyrics of popular music in the United States.
4. For English translations of some of the lyrics, see Perrone, *Masters* 33.
5. "Cálice" was eventually cleared by the censors, and by early 1979 it had become a top-ten hit.
6. Perrone (*Masters* 24–28, 34, 207) offers an excellent analysis of the song's musical and political qualities and provides an English version of its famous lyrics.
7. These songs were recorded by Costa on *Le Gal* ("Mini-mistério," Philips R 765 126; 1970) and on *Gal Costa* ("Civilização e cultura," Philips R 795 098L; 1969).
8. English versions of its songs are provided on the Elektra/Musician CD.
9. An English version of this song appears in Perrone, *Masters* 187–88.
10. See, e.g., *Brazilian Byrd* (The Best of Times, PCT 9137); *The Vince Guaraldi Trio: Impressions of Black Orpheus* (Fantasy OJCCD-437-2; F-8089); and *Stan Getz: The Best of Two Worlds*, which features Gilberto and his classics "Waters of March" (composed by Antônio Carlos Jobim) and "Picture in Black and White" (Columbia, CK 33703).
11. For an English version of this song, see Perrone, *Masters* xxii.
12. In 1969, both Veloso and Gil were forced to flee Brazil; they lived as exiles in London.
13. For an English version of some of the song's lyrics, see Burns, *History* [3rd ed.] 462.

Brazilian Film and Video

Like Brazilian music, although probably not as well known, Brazilian film has made its presence felt on the world scene. To appreciate its impact and its historical development, we should realize, as Randal Johnson and Robert Stam observe, that Brazilian cinema did not begin with the film that won first prize at Cannes in 1962, *O pagador de promessas* (*The Given Word*), or with *Black Orpheus* (1958; see also Veloso, "Orpheus"), actually a French film set in Brazil, or with *O cangaceiro* (1953), "the double prize-winner at Cannes and distributed in twenty-two countries," or even with the Carmen Miranda films. Brazilian film actually got its start "only six months after Lumière revealed his *cinématographe* in Paris in 1895," when Rio de Janeiro held the first screening of the "omnigraph," and in 1898, when the Italian Brazilian Affonso Segreto set up the country's first filmmaking equipment and production company (19). Although Brazilian film production grew during those early years, its influences, and the standards by which it would be judged, were foreign. As a result, Brazilians interested in the new art form would have difficulty nurturing an autonomous and authentic national film industry. Reflecting the economic dependency of the nation as a whole, the fledgling industry relied on foreign concepts, technologies, and financing, a situation that would plague it for years to come. In a larger sense, however, the problems Brazil's film pioneers faced were analogous to those of most Brazilian intellectuals of the period, whose legitimacy was defined by their ability to "import and absorb cultural goods from Europe" and the United States (Johnson, *Film Industry* 23).[1] Brazilian film is thus older than people might expect. In spite of periods of accelerated growth and activity, though, not until the 1960s and the *cinema novo* ("new cinema") did it achieve international celebrity.

Under the entrepreneurship of such figures as Paschoal Segreto (said to be the model for the character Laje da Silva in Lima Barreto's novel *Recordações do escrivão*

Isaías Caminha [*Memories of Isaías Caminha, Notary Public*]) and José Roberto Cunha Salles (a prominent member of Rio's illegal gambling industry, the *jogo do bicho* or "animal game"), Brazilian film entered a period of expansion—built on the concept of "entertainment centers"—that was financed, in part, by exhibitions of pornographic films. By about 1910, following significant increases in the supply of electricity to Rio de Janeiro, the cinema had become a popular diversion (Johnson, *Film Industry* 25–26). As improvements were made in both quality and quantity, the period came to be known as the golden age of Brazilian film.

In 1909, Giuseppe Labanca established the first Brazilian film studios, which produced successful versions of *Uncle Tom's Cabin* and *The Merry Widow*, while Cristóvão Guilherme Auler, another early leader in the industry, was responsible for *Paz e amor* (*Peace and Love*), a musical revue and political satire of the president, Nilo Peçanha, that ranks as "the most successful film of the first two decades of Brazilian cinema." The film industry benefited financially from the efforts of Francisco Serrador, a Spaniard who emigrated to Brazil in 1905 and within six years had gained control of the domestic market and secured outside investors, obviating the need for "the traditional family or partnership ventures that had characterized the industry to this point." After 1911, however, the production of feature films dropped drastically, largely because United States filmmakers were exporting their work to Europe, Latin America, and elsewhere. The domination of the Brazilian film industry continued into the 1920s, when "American films occupied over 80% of the Brazilian market." By the end of the decade, Brazil had become America's fourth largest market, trailing only Britain, Australia, and Argentina (Johnson, *Film Industry* 31, 36).

According to Johnson and Stam, the major filmmaker of the 1920s and 1930s was Humberto Mauro, who is credited as well by Glauber Rocha—one of the giants of *cinema novo*—with being "the most important precursor" of the movement (qtd. in *Brazilian Cinema* 24). In that period, however, Brazilian film was still in the grip of foreign influences, including the European avant-garde, which made its presence felt in a number of Brazilian films. One of these, Mário Peixoto's *Limite* (1930; *Limit*), was praised by Sergei Eisenstein as a "work of genius" that utilized "a technique of multiple narration" and "experimented with duration and montage as well as with subjective camera movement" (qtd. in Johnson and Stam 24).

With the advent of sound, the Brazilian film industry was energized; finally, practitioners believed, they could break free of foreign dominance. Ironically enough, an American, Wallace Downey, made Brazil's first commercially successful sound film, *Coisas nossas* (1931; *Our Things*). If sound movies did not liberate Brazilian film, as many had hoped they would, the 1930s witnessed the birth of an authentic, highly influential genre, the *chanchada* (see Shaw). "Partially modeled on American musicals (and particularly on the 'radio-broadcast' musicals) of the same period, but with roots as well in the Brazilian comic theater and in the 'sung films' about carnival, the *chanchada* typically features musical and dance numbers often woven around a backstage plot." Beginning in 1935 with Adhemar Gonzaga's *Alô, alô, Brasil* (*Hello, Hello, Brazil*) and featuring the talents of Carmen Miranda, this popular genre degenerated in the early 1970s (when some of the dictatorship's most brutal oppression took place) into puerile but lucrative sex comedies known as *pornochanchadas*. In its original form, however, the *chanchada* fostered, despite its idealized depiction of Brazilian society, "an authentic link between Brazilians and their cinema" (Johnson and Stam 26–27).

Women began to make serious inroads into the Brazilian industry during the 1930s and 1940s. Carmen Santos, for example, already known for her work as an actor and a producer, founded her own studio, Brasil Vita Filme, which she placed under the technical direction of Mauro. Another celebrated actor of the period, Gilda de Abreu, wrote and directed *O ébrio* (1946; *The Drunkard*), an immensely popular melodrama of which five hundred copies—a national record—were made (Johnson and Stam 27).

Another important development occurred in the late 1940s when a group, led by Matarazzo Sobrinho and with links to São Paulo's industrial bourgeoisie, sought to capitalize on the popularity of the *chanchada* but to undercut what they called the genre's vulgarity by founding a production company, Vera Cruz Films. Modeled on the Metro-Goldwyn-Mayer Studios, Vera Cruz (before it went bankrupt in 1954) "produced eighteen feature films, the most famous of which was Lima Barreto's *O Cangaceiro* (1953), . . . one of the few to have successfully reached a foreign public" (Johnson and Stam 27–28, 277). Although Vera Cruz significantly "improved the technical level of Brazilian cinema," the studio was "flawed in its very conception" by seeking "to create First World cinema in a Third World country." Powered by "elitist values," it ignored "the tastes, interests, and real situation of the Brazilian people" (28–29).

In a kind of cultural quid pro quo, Brazilian filmmakers utilized their ability to parody foreign films. Carlos Manga, for instance, produced successful spoofs of such Hollywood classics as *High Noon* and *Samson and Delilah*. Other films that were satirized included *King Kong* and *Jaws* (23).

Arising from the long-simmering desire for cultural and political renovation (one result was the election of the prodevelopment Juscelino Kubitschek as president in 1955), the *cinema novo* movement burst on the scene just as many Brazilians felt that the nation was finally emerging from chronic underdevelopment. Lasting from about 1960 to 1972, *cinema novo*, as Ismail Xavier sees it, stems from Rocha's famous 1965 manifesto (one that recalls Frantz Fanon's *The Wretched of the Earth*, published four years earlier). The Brazilian film industry, Rocha believed, should be "an aggressive art cinema with national and political concerns" that could assert "its cultural value and ideological strength through its constant search for an original film style able to turn the scarcity of means into a channel for aesthetic experimentation" (1). Although *cinema novo* would eventually be challenged in this task by *novo cinema novo* ("new, new cinema"), in its glory years in the 1960s it succeeded in authenticating and internationalizing the country's filmmaking. Yet beyond its importance to the development of film, the *cinema novo* movement, artistically and philosophically, expanded on issues that the writers of the *modernista* movement had dealt with in the 1920s. Comparing *Macunaíma*, Mário de Andrade's 1928 narrative *rhapsode*, with its 1969 film version, Johnson argues,

> Cinema Novo is, in fact, deeply rooted in the problematic faced by literary Modernism, which had attempted to democratize Brazilian art through a stance of cultural nationalism, rejecting a critical imitation of European models in favor of an interest in popular forms of expression and the culture of native Brazilian peoples. (Johnson and Stam 178–79)

With the landmark film *Macunaíma*, however, *cinema novo* moved into its final, "cannibal-tropicalist" phase, in music, theater, and the cinema, as it "emphasized the grotesque, bad taste, *kitsch*, and gaudy colors" and "played aggressively with certain myths, especially the notion of Brazil as a tropical paradise characterized by colorful exuberance and tutti-frutti hats à la Carmen Miranda" (38–39). Roberto Schwarz sees tropicalism as emerging "from the tension between the superficial 'modernization' of the Brazilian economy and its archaic, colonized, and imperialized core" (qtd. in Johnson and Stam 39).

Regardless of its failings, *cinema novo* constitutes a major achievement for Brazil. It made possible, in the 1970s, the participation of women and blacks as actors, writers, producers, and directors at a level never before seen in the nation, and it proved that Brazilian film could take on topics long regarded as taboo. Its role in bringing Brazilian film into the international arena was crucial to the establishment of Embrafilme, the state-supported enterprise. In 1974, when President Ernesto Geisel appointed filmmaker Roberto Farias as its director, Embrafilme began to play a decisive role in the evolution of Brazilian cinema—a role that, the filmmaker Carlos Diegues argues, was inherent in the goals of its political and aesthetic predecessor, the *cinema novo* movement (see Johnson and Stam 43, 45; see also Johnson, "Literature").

By the 1990s, television, which has more successfully negotiated the nation's economic crises of the 1980s, became a major competitor, especially the immensely popular *Telenovela* (see Rohter, "Brazil").[2] As Stam, Vieira, and Xavier observe, "Television has now largely taken over the role of adapting Brazilian literary classics. Jorge Amado, Graciliano Ramos, Érico Veríssimo, Guimarães Rosa, Machado de Assis, Lima Barreto, Rubem Fonseca, and Dias Gomes are among those whose work has passed through the electronic adaptation machine." Still, cinema is not neglecting its traditional connection with Brazilian (and world) narrative, for, as these critics also note:

> Among the literary adaptations now under way in the cinema are Paulo Thiago's version of Lima Barreto's *Triste Fim do Policarpo Quaresma* ("The Sad End of Policarpo Quaresma"), Walter Lima Jr.'s version of *Memórias de um Sargento de Milícias* [from the

novel by Manuel Antônio de Almeida], Bruno Barreto's version of Fernando Gabeira's *O Que É Isto, Companheiro* ("What's This, Comrade!"), Suzana Amaral's version of Rubem Fonseca's *Caso Morel* ("The Morel Case"), Guilherme de Almeida Prado's version of Júlio Cortázar's *A Hora Mágica* ("The Magic Hour"), Norma Benguel's version of [Alencar's] *O Guarani*, Carlos Diegues's version of Jorge Amado's *Tieta do Agreste* (with Sonia Braga in the title role), Leilany Fernandes Leite's version of Rachel de Queiroz's *Memorial de Maria Moura*, Bruno Barreto's version of *O Que É Isso, Companheiro* ("What Kind of Behavior Is This, Comrade?"), Hugo Carvana's version of Fernando Sabino's *O Homem Nu* ("The Naked Man"), and Emiliano Ribeiro's version of Lygia Fagundes Telles's *As Meninas* ("The Girls"). (Johnson and Stam 469)

In summing up the state of Brazilian film and of the contributions of the *cinema novo* movement, Johnson and Stam identify three chief characteristics: (1) the appeal of many films crosses class lines, since the intended audience is not just the intelligentsia; (2) filmmakers have the technical expertise to produce high-quality work; (3) content and style cover a broad spectrum, including science fiction, political commentary, fantasy, and historical re-creation (45–46).

Since the 1960s, Brazilian film has struggled with censorship and political repression, with inadequate funding (Embrafilme was abolished by President Fernando Collor de Mello in 1990 as part of his privatization drive) and related economic problems, and with the saturation of the domestic market by foreign films. Despite these challenges, the Brazilian film industry remains aesthetically and technically inventive, intellectually resourceful, and committed to growth and development, nationally and internationally. If (for the immediate future at least) Brazilian cinema seems unlikely to regain the strength it enjoyed in the 1950s, 1960s, and 1970s, neither is it likely to die out. Although it may, in the long run, "maintain a minimal autonomous existence as national feature film and coproduction, while also 'disappearing' into the larger universe of the audiovisual—into television, into video, into cable, the short film, music video, and into the work generated by video computer technologies" (Stam, Vieira, and Xavier 469), the Brazilian film industry's ability to recover and move forward should never be doubted (see Nagib).

What follows is a listing of films, terms, and artists that readers interested in this dynamic, influential aspect of Brazilian culture should become familiar with. For anyone wishing to pursue these issues in depth, the works of Randal Johnson, Ismail Xavier, and Robert Stam, which I rely on here, are recommended.

Andrade, Joaquim Pedro de: An original participant in the *cinema novo* movement, Andrade directed such major films as *Garrincha, alegria do povo* (1963), about one of Brazil's greatest soccer players and the significance of the game for Brazilians; *The Priest and the Girl* (1965); and, most important, *Macunaíma* (1969), his must-see version of the novel of the same name. *Macunaíma* was released less than a year after the promulgation of the extremely repressive Fifth Institutional Act. Johnson and Stam argue that the film is "an ideological radicalization of Mário de Andrade's original text and perhaps the most successful re-evaluation and re-elaboration of the Brazilian Modernist Movement. Its coded language of revolt represents an extremely aggressive attack on the continued exploitation of Brazil by the international capitalist system" (82). Joaquim Pedro de Andrade had planned to produce a film version of Gilberto Freyre's *The Masters and the Slaves,* but, because of his untimely death, the project was never realized. Had the film been made according to the plans Andrade had for it,

> it would have dramatically staged (and critically updated) Freyre's theories. . . . An examination of the script reveals that the film would have orchestrated a polyphonic encounter among Brazil's various source cultures, with their conflicts, alliances, and wars. Instead of presenting history as closed and uncontested, de Andrade planned to have the film envision Brazilian history through a polycultural grid, [one that would become a] vehicle for serious reflection on multicultural historiography. (Stam 13)

Benguell, Norma: Benguell directed the film version of *O Guarani,* the Alencar novel of 1857 that features a budding romance between a pristine "noble savage," Peri, and Cecília, the daughter of a Portuguese settler. As Stam notes, the Benguell film was released at about the same time that Disney's *Pocahontas* reached American movie theaters (12). Later, focusing on "the true story of the modernist 'muse,' Patrícia Galvão," the author of *Industrial Park,* Benguell brought out *Eternamente Pagu* ("Eternally Pagu") in 1987 (Stam, Vieira, and Xavier 457).

Black God, White Devil (*Deus e o diabo na terra do sol*): Directed by Glauber Rocha and redolent of both Euclides da Cunha's *Rebellion in the Backlands* and Guimarães Rosa's novel *The Devil to Pay in the Backlands,* this 1964 film "centers on the trajectory of the cowherd Manuel and his involvement with God (Sebastião) and the Devil (Corisco), and with messianic mysticism and the *cangaço* (social banditry)" (Johnson, *Cinema* 129).

Black Orpheus (*Orfeu negro*): This famous and beautiful film, which did so much to project in the international community an image of Brazilian society in the second half of the twentieth century, was the creation of the French director Marcel Camus and a Brazilian, mostly black cast. An Academy Award winner in 1959, *Black Orpheus* re-creates the ancient myth of Orpheus in the context of Brazilian Carnival. The film, decried by Vinícius de Moraes, the author of the successful play *Orfeu da conceição,* on which it was based, was a commercial flop in Brazil, where it was said to project a false impression of the country. Carlos Diegues's 1999 film *Orfeu* offers a powerful contrast to it (*see* Diegues).

Carolina, Ana: Emphasizing humor, sensuality, and "transgression," Carolina is one of Brazil's most exciting directors. (407). Her first feature film, *Mar de rosas* (1977; *Sea of Roses*), "anatomizes a grotesque family" living "in an atmosphere of surreal banality à la Ionesco. It is as if, as Paulo Perdigão puts it, 'Jules Feiffer's black humor and Samuel Beckett's dramaturgical absurdity were made to rendezvous on the Via Dutra [the highway that links Rio and São Paulo]'" (Stam, Vieira, and Xavier 407–08).

Central Station (*Central do Brasil*): Nominated for an Academy Award for Best Foreign Film in 1998, *Central Station* (directed by Walter Salles) portrays a retired schoolteacher in Rio de Janeiro who, barely able to scrape by, ends up aiding an orphaned boy in a quest across the rugged backlands for his father, who has deserted the boy and his mother. Recalling *Pixote* (which see) in its unsparing depiction of the poverty and violence that envelop Brazil's disadvantaged (especially its abandoned children), *Central Station* ultimately becomes a guarded paean to hope and compassion.

cinema novo: The advent of *cinema novo*, in the 1950s and 1960s, marks the beginning of the modern film in Brazil. Part of a surge of cultural transformation and nationalism that was sweeping Brazil and that also involved music, theater, and literature, *cinema novo*, as Johnson observes, evolved through three phases: (1) from 1960 to 1964, the year of the military coup; (2) from 1964 to 1968, the year of the Fifth Institutional Act, which set up martial law; (3) from 1968 to around 1972, a period marked by the suspension of habeas corpus, the intensification of censorship, and the institutionalization of torture. During this time, "It was difficult for filmmakers to express their opinions directly, and [as with Andrade's *Macunaíma*, 1969] allegory became the preferred mode of cinematic discourse" (*Cinema* 2–3). As the repression, violence, and censorship worsened, such leading *cinema novo* directors as Glauber Rocha, Rui Guerra, and Carlos Diegues fled Brazil for Europe. By 1973 the *cinema novo* movement was effectively over, and filmmakers began to cultivate more individualistic forms of artistic expression rather than set their work in one of the two sociopolitically charged locations—the arid, impoverished backlands and the *favelas* or slums of the urban poor—that tended to characterize *cinema novo films*. In 1998, New York's Museum of Modern Art sponsored a retrospective festival of *cinema novo* films.

City of God (*Cioade de Deus*): Directed by Katia Lund and Fernando Meirelles and based on a book by Paulo Lins, this disturbingly violent but visually stunning 2003 film depicts the evolution of 1960s street gangs in a Rio de Janeiro slum. Recalling Hector Babenco's *Pixote* as well as *The French Connection* and *Pulp Fiction*, *City of God* explores the impact of the international drug trade, poverty, and a culture where brutality is not only commonplace but accepted in the lives of a variety of young people, many of whom, the victims as well as the victimizers, are still children.

Diegues, Carlos: Like Joaquim Pedro de Andrade (which see), Diegues was a founder of *cinema novo*. In *The Big City* (1966), an early international success of the *cinema novo*, he dramatizes the plight of the urban poor, while in *Xica da Silva* (1976) he offers "a dynamic, colorful, noisy, playful celebration of a little-known historical figure," a female slave (Francisca "Xica" da Silva), whose rise to power becomes "a fictional re-creation of events that occurred in the state of Minas Gerais in eighteenth-century colonial Brazil" (Johnson and Stam 216, 217). *Bye Bye Brasil*, Diegues's eighth feature, was released in 1980 and featured at the New York Film Festival that year. A satiric comedy, *Bye Bye Brasil* questions the effects of Western-style progress on Brazil. Diegues's film *Orfeu* (1999), a popular reinterpretation of the play *Orfeu da conceição*, by Vinícius de Moraes, is a sober, often disturbing counterpoint to Marcel Camus's *Black Orpheus* (which see).

Disney, Walt: As part of Nelson Rockefeller's efforts during the 1940s to foster cooperation between the United States and Latin America, Disney was sent to Brazil to gather material for a series of Good Neighbor films. Among these, *Saludos Amigos!* (1941) and *The Three Caballeros* (1944) stand out as exemplary. *The Three Caballeros* appears occasionally on American television.

Dona Flor and Her Two Husbands: Directed by Bruno Barreto, *Dona Flor* (1976) has been immensely popular, in Brazil and around the world. The year it appeared, it was seen by ten million people in Brazil alone—surpassed in attendance only by *Jaws*, released in Brazil the same year (Stam, Vieira, and Xavier 389). Widely available on video, *Dona Flor and Her Two Husbands* is based on the novel by Brazil's most popular and widely translated author, Jorge Amado (see app. C). Featuring Sônia Braga and merging a wry comedic sensibility with a frank and earthy eroticism, this film has had, for better or worse, a significant impact on Americans' perception of Brazil and Brazilians. The work enjoyed "the most successful commercial run in the United States of any Brazilian film" and was "the most successful Brazilian film in history" (Johnson, *Cinema* 1, 88).

dos Santos, Nelson Pereira: A premier director and the guiding spirit of the *cinema novo* movement, dos Santos was developing the "aesthetic of hunger" (later made famous as a critical term by Glauber Rocha) as early as 1963. *Vidas secas*, a film dos Santos directed, with "its soberly critical realism, its sterling austerity, and its implicit optimism," "represents first phase Cinema Novo at its best" (Johnson and Stam 120). In describing his view of Brazilian cinema, dos Santos has written that "cinema must be seen as one more instrument of struggle, just as necessary as any other, in the sense of understanding and attempting to transform Brazilian society" (qtd. in Johnson, *Cinema* 162).

Duarte, Anselmo: Duarte is the director of *Pagador de promessas* (*The Given Word*), a poignant early *cinema novo* film that focuses on religious fanaticism in Brazil's impoverished northeast. The film is based on the 1960 Dias Gomes play (translated by Oscar Fernández as *Payment as Pledged*; see Woodyard). The film won the Best Film Award at the Cannes and San Francisco film festivals.

Exposure: This 1991 film, starring Peter Coyote and Amanda Pays, is the adaptation, by Walter Salles, Jr., of Rubem Fonseca's 1983 novel *A grande arte* (*High Art*, 1986; trans. Ellen Watson). The novel, set in modern Brazil and written in the mode of the detective thriller, recalls Raymond Chandler in its plot, tone, and character development. A "well-crafted genre film à la Hollywood" that "aims at an international audience," *Exposure* was recorded in English and "seems to look at Brazil through alien eyes" (Johnson and Stam 437).

Flesh (*A carne*): This Felipe Ricci film, adapted from the sometimes lurid naturalistic novel of 1925 by Júlio César Ribeiro, portrays a woman's sexual urges in a culture handicapped by, and not prepared to deal with, sexism and racism. A reviewer for the newspaper *Estado de São Paulo* described the film as "effectively conveying the nature of slavery"—a comment that is "an ambiguous recommendation given that the novel is in many ways antiblack" (Stam 60).

Four Days in September: Directed by Bruno Barreto, this Academy Award nominee for best foreign language film is based on events that took place in the repressive atmosphere of Brazil in the late 1960s. A small band of urban guerrillas kidnapped the American ambassador to Brazil, Charles Burke Elbrick, on 4 September 1969. When the ruling generals were forced to meet the guerrillas' demands—that an antigovernment manifesto be read over the radio and TV stations and printed in the papers and that the government free fifteen political prisoners and fly them to sanctuary in Mexico—the ambassador was freed, on 7 September. *Four Days in September* is widely available in video.

Gaijin: A Brazilian Odyssey: Directed by Tizuka Yamasaki, *Gaijin* recounts the difficulties the first Japanese immigrants to Brazil encountered. They were brought to Brazil to work on the coffee plantations of São Paulo and its neighboring states; their descendants would constitute one of the country's largest and most successful immigrant groups. Today the *Liberdade* ("Liberty") section of São Paulo contains more Japanese-speaking people than anywhere else except Japan.

The Grapes of Wrath: This American film is often compared with the film version of Graciliano Ramos's spare, laconic novel *Vidas secas* (1938; "Barren Lives"). Treating

similar subjects—drought and migration—the two works use "the trajectory of a
single family . . . to encapsulate the destiny of thousands of oppressed people."
Nevertheless, the social, political, and economic differences that distinguish the
United States from Brazil prevail: "The distance that separates John Ford's 1940
adaptation of Steinbeck's novel from Nelson Pereira dos Santos's adaptation of *Vidas
Secas* is the distance that separates Southern California from the *sertão* and Holly-
wood studio production in the forties from Third World filmmaking in the sixties"
(Johnson and Stam 120, 121).

Os Guaranis (*The Guaranis*): Adapted from the Alencar Indianist novel *O Guarani*
and directed by Antônio Leal, this 1908 film starred, as the Indian hero Peri, the
"popular Brazilian clown Benjamin de Oliveira," the "first black actor known to have
performed in a Brazilian fiction film" (Stam 60). The film no longer exists.

Guerra, Rui: Although born in Mozambique (also a Portuguese-speaking country),
Guerra was a defining figure of the *cinema novo* era. His masterpiece is widely judged
to be *The Guns* (1964). For the critic Roberto Schwarz, the work does not explain
human misery as much as it seeks to show how "misery and technological civilization confront each other" and how, in an impoverished society, the relationship between the oppressed and the oppressor is constantly changing (Johnson and Stam
130, 131–32).

The Guns (*Os fuzis*): Directed by Rui Guerra, this seminal 1964 *cinema novo* work
chronicles the entwined themes of hunger, repression, religious mysticism, and violence in Brazil. In so doing, it calls attention to the paradox of modern Brazil: How
can so much poverty and misery exist in a land so beautiful, so vibrant, and so rich
in natural resources?

The Hour of the Star (*A hora da estrela*): Directed by Suzana Amaral (a graduate of
New York University's film school), *The Hour of the Star* is the award-winning film
version of Clarice Lispector's 1977 novel. Focusing on an untrained refugee from
Brazil's impoverished, violence-ridden northeast, the work calls attention to the
chasm that exists between the nation's rich and poor. The film, which emphasizes the
protagonist's poverty and hopelessness, omits the anguished rumination on the sym-
biotic interaction among language, writing, and human existence that characterizes
the novel. Rather, it

> discards the reflexive structure of the Clarice Lispector source novella—by which a so-
> phisticated upper-class male narrator grapples with the problem of bringing to life a
> simple-hearted lower-class character—in favor of an unmediated third-person ap-

proach to its theme. . . . What the film achieves, finally, is an honest, often humorous lucidity within its self-defined limits. (Stam, Vieira, and Xavier 436, 437)

How Tasty Was My Little Frenchman (*Como era gostoso o meu francês*): One of the French Huguenots who in the mid-sixteenth century were settling the area around what is today Rio de Janeiro is captured by a tribe of Tupinamba and sentenced to death, although not before being made a member of the tribe, even being allowed to marry and to participate in tribal wars and work. An unsuccessful effort to escape is followed by the Frenchman's cannibalization. Exemplifying the captivity narratives of colonial inter-American literature and recalling Melville's *Typee*, the film's source was, as Richard Peña notes, "the diary of a German adventurer named Hans Staden, who, while in the service of the Dutch colonizers of Brazil, was similarly captured by some tribesmen, but escaped to tell the tale" (qtd. in Johnson and Stam 191). Made in 1971, *How Tasty Was My Little Frenchman*, with its motifs of anthropophagy and European–New World culture clash, also suggests Oswald de Andrade's famous "Anthropophagy Manifesto" of 1928.

Iracema: Based on José de Alencar's mythically charged romance of Brazil's founding as a racially mixed culture, the film, brought out by Jorge Bodansky and Orlando Senna in 1975, features a heroine quite different from Alencar's. Insisting, despite her appearance, that she is "white," Iracema struggles to find an identity in twentieth-century Brazil (which, of course, bears little relation to the setting of Alencar's Indianist idyll). Referencing the title of the novel only to "turn its idealism inside out," the filmmakers transform the novel's

> Pocahontas-like story of romance between the virginal Indian and the Portuguese nobleman [into] a brutal encounter on the Trans-Amazonian Highway between a cynical white trucker and an Indian adolescent forced into prostitution. In the novel, Iracema dies but her child with the Portuguese noble lives; in the film, however, there is neither child nor love. The characters do not generate the "seed" of the nation. (Stam 48, 287–88)

It's All True: Orson Welles's never-finished 1942 film evokes, from the Brazilian point of view, four interconnecting issues: "(1) Welles's nonracist approach to Brazilian culture; (2) the audacity of the project in cultural, aesthetic, cinematic, and racial terms; (3) Welles's relation to Afro-Brazilian culture and his working relationship with black Brazilians; and (4) the racial subtext to some of the opposition to *It's All True*" (Stam 109). Calling attention to the work of Rogério Sganzerla (whose 1985 "metacinema," *Nem tudo é verdade* [*It's Not All True*], combines "citations of *Citizen Kane* and *The Lady from Shanghai*" with a documentary style that "portrays Welles as the rebellious victim of the Hollywood studio system"), Stam, Vieira, and Xavier write that "Welles's utopian dream of real industrial and artistic collaboration between North and South America," as Sganzerla suggests, "violently challenged the neocolonial assumptions of the time and was therefore cut short" (Stam, Vieira, and Xavier 400; see also Page 8, 154, 422–23).

Land in Anguish (*Terra em transe*): This 1967 film by Glauber Rocha is, as Robert Stam argues, "an explosive study of art and politics in the Third World" (Johnson and Stam 149). It provides a satirical examination of the failures and contradictions of the Brazilian political left and of what Roberto Schwarz has labeled "the populist deformation of Marxism"—that is, "a Marxism that was strong on anti-imperialism but weak on class struggle" (Johnson and Stam 36).

Lesson of Love (*Lição de amor*): Based on the novel *Amar, verbo intransitivo* (1927; translated as *Fraulein*) by Mário de Andrade and directed by Eduardo Escorel, *Lesson of Love* "was among the most highly praised films released in Brazil in 1976." As Escorel puts it, the work is, "in the final analysis . . . a film about a repressive form of behavior, about a certain way of exercising repression," from the sexual to the political and from the family to the cultural (qtd. in Johnson and Stam 208). The self-reflective, "cinematographic" novel "consists of seventy-two rapidly changing scenes . . . as if each one were a filmic sequence. Many of the sequences themselves are partially composed of rapid successions of disparate and often unexpected images, as if each image were but one shot in a larger sequence." Yet, as Randal Johnson believes, the "principal link between this novel and film are Mário de Andrade's continued references to cinema" (Johnson and Stam 209–10).

Machado de Assis, Joaquim Maria: A writer who was well aware of the issues of race, gender, and class, Machado has had several major works adapted to film: "Paulo César Saraceni's *Capitu* (1968; based on *Dom Casmurro*), Nelson Pereira dos Santos's *Azyllo Muito Louco* (1970; based on 'O Alienista' ["The Psychiatrist"]), and Júlio Bressane's *Brás Cubas* (1985; based on *Memórias Póstumas de Brás Cubas*)" (Stam 33).

Macunaíma: Released as *Jungle Freaks* in the United States, this 1969 Joaquim Pedro de Andrade film is, according to Randal Johnson, "the culmination of the first three phases of Cinema Novo and the pacesetter for subsequent developments of Brazilian cinema" ("Cinema" 178). Exuberant and zany, and elevating "bad taste" to the level of aesthetic achievement, *Macunaíma* is "the first Cinema Novo film to be formally innovative, politically radical, *and* immensely popular with the Brazilian public" (Johnson, *Cinema* 25). The film adaptation of Mário de Andrade's influential modernist novel, *Macunaíma* is essential viewing for anyone interested in understanding contemporary Brazilian culture and politics. Although maintaining "the basic narrative structure of the novel," the film "introduces significant differences on other levels of the film's discourse"; it becomes "a critical reinterpretation and an ideological radicalization of Mário de Andrade's rhapsody cast in terms of the social, economic, and political realities of the late sixties" (Johnson, "Cinema" 178, 179–80).

Miranda, Carmen: A veteran of several Brazilian *chanchadas* and, later, the principal icon of a number of 1940s good-neighbor films, Miranda still sparks heated debate in Brazil, where many consider her "the passive instrument of North American imperialism, while others regard her as a kind of force of nature, somehow beyond good and evil. Beginning in the sixties," however, Sérgio Augusto observes, "she became the object of an international cult, when a fraternity of nostalgic camp-oriented cinephiles, almost invariably gay, rediscovered her films" (Johnson and Stam 359).

Omar, Arthur: A "prolific and inventive" figure in the production of short films that tend to be "full of fantasy, media consciousness, and intertextual allusion," Omar, in *The Inspector* (1989), reinterprets "the conventions of the police thriller by confronting the spectator with the corpses left by Rio's death squads" (Stam, Vieira, and Xavier 447, 448).

Pixote: Directed by Hector Babenco, this disturbing film portrays the lives of Brazil's abandoned street children, some three million in number. The winner of the New York Film Critics award in 1981 for best foreign film, *Pixote* confronts the violence, depravity, and exploitation that characterize modern Brazil. It also "forms part of an international genre—the street urchin film—that includes not only De Sica's *Shoeshine* (1946) but also Buñuel's *Los Olvidados* (1951) and Mira Nair's *Salaam Bombay* (1988)" (Stam, Vieira, and Xavier 412). In its subject matter the film also recalls Jorge Amado's 1937 novel *Capitães da areia* (*Sand Captains* or, for Ellison [98–100], *Beach Waifs*). While the film is brutally frank, however, the novel is marred by an excessive sentimentality.

The Plantation Owner's Daughter (*Sinhá moça*): A film from the Vera Cruz production company, codirected by Osvaldo Sampaio and "the Anglo Argentinean Tom Payne" and appearing in 1953, *The Plantation Owner's Daughter* is based on the novel by Maria Dezonne Pacheco Fernandes. Like *Gone with the Wind*, the Brazilian film "suggests a parallel between the heroine's personal struggle against what we now call patriarchy and the abolitionist struggle against slavery." It becomes, in its conclusion, "a kind of anti–*Birth of a Nation* . . . but this time in favor of a black cause," reminiscent of "the Chicana activism of the film *Salt of the Earth* (1954)." In 1986, *Sinhá moça* was adapted as a *telenovela*, or romantic TV serial, that "was fashioned after another black-related *telenovela—A escrava Isaura* [*The Slave Girl Isaura*; this title refers to Bernardo Guimarães's 1875 novel—whose formulaic conjunction of slavery, freedom, and romanticism it imitates" (Stam 138, 144–45, 149).

pornochanchadas: Deriving from the musical comedies and dance productions of the 1930s known as *chanchadas,* these financially successful films of the 1970s, filling the vacuum left by the demise of the *cinema novo* movement, have been described as "vapid erotic comedies" that, with the encouragement of the military dictatorship, "offer a cinematic portrait of the sexual alienation of the Brazilian petite-bourgeoisie" and "exalt the good bourgeois life of fast cars, wild parties, and luxurious surroundings, while offering the male voyeur titillating shots of breasts and buttocks" (Stam and Johnson 40). Representative titles include *A Bra for Daddy, Secretaries . . . Who Do Everything,* and *The Virgin and the Macho.*

Prates Correia, Carlos Alberto: Reconciling the "drive for auteurist expression with the constraints of the market," Prates Correia and his films are often linked to the state of Minas Gerais and to the work of such writers as Carlos Drummond de Andrade (*Cabaret mineiro; Cabaret in Minas*) and Guimarães Rosa. In *Noites de Sertão* (1984; "Sertão Nights"),

> we are symptomatically far from the oppressed northeastern *sertão* of *Vidas Secas* and *Black God, White Devil. . .* [Prates Correia] explores the Minas plantation universe and its figurations of desire, foregrounding the conflict between the patriarchal order and anarchic sexuality, in a filmic "translation" of the spirit of Guimarães Rosa. (Correia's most recent film is called *Minas Texas* [1986], in homage both to Wim Wenders' *Paris, Texas* (1984) and to [Correia's] own native region.) (Stam, Vieira, and Xavier 408–09)

Prison Memoirs (*Memórias do cárcere*): Directed by Nelson Pereira dos Santos, this 1984 film is based on *Memórias do cárcere* (1953), by Graciliano Ramos, who, charged with being a Communist, was imprisoned by Getúlio Vargas in the late 1930s. Focusing on Ramos's incarceration from March 1936 to January 1937,

> Dos Santos slightly tampers with the actual chronology of events in order to emphasize a downward spiral of degradation, so that Ramos begins as a relatively pampered political prisoner and ends as the abused victim of the aptly named "colônia," a virtual concentration camp on the Atlantic coast. . . . [The work] begins and ends with the Brazilian national anthem, at a time when patriotism was back in style in Brazil, precisely because of redemocratization. The anthem marks the film as a microcosmic statement, suggesting that Brazil has the aspect of a prison, yet one whose prisoners will soon be freed. (Stam, Vieira, and Xavier 426, 427–28)

Rocha, Glauber: For some the intellectual and artistic heart of the *cinema novo* move-ment, Rocha is remembered for three masterpieces of the genre: *Black God, White Devil* (1964), which deals, symbolically, with the drought- and poverty-stricken *sertão*, or northeastern backlands, and with the destitution, hunger, fanaticism, and violence that plague the region; *Land in Anguish* (1967), which, Robert Stam says, "points the way to a possible political cinema that avoids the twin dead ends of a con-descending populism on the one hand and an aridly theoretical reflexivity on the other" (Johnson and Stam 149); and *Antônio das mortes* (1968), a film that, also set in the troubled northeast, "amalgamates myth, mysticism, and reality into a filmic whole that is both epic and lyrical," as Terence Carlson explains (Johnson and Stam 169, 170), and that conjures up disparate images of the rebellion at Canudos, the tragic story so dramatically expressed in Euclides da Cunha's *Rebellion in the Backlands*.

São Bernardo: Leon Hirszman's cinematic version of the powerful Graciliano Ramos novel *São Bernardo* demonstrates the artistic link between the *cinema novo* move-ment and literary modernism in Brazil. It depicts a protagonist, the brutal Paulo Honório, whose rise to power parallels that of the rulers of the military dictatorship, who relied on violence, intimidation, bribery, and murder. Moreover, the film (re-leased in 1973)

> was made at a time when there was much talk in the international press of the Brazilian "economic miracle." The film exposes the miracle for what it was: a cruel deception. Paulo rises economically by a kind of miracle, but the miracle benefits only himself, just as the Brazilian economic miracle enriched an elite few at the expense of the oppressed majority.

The filmmakers argued, to the censors (who held the film up for seven months), that the work was "a scrupulously faithful rendition of a literary classic and a fitting trib-ute to Graciliano Ramos on the eightieth anniversary of his birth" (Johnson and Stam 205–207, 201).

Tent of Miracles (*Tenda dos milagres*): Based on the Jorge Amado novel, Nelson Pereira dos Santos's 1977 film "is one of a rare breed—a brilliant political film that succeeds in raising the consciousness of its audience and yet is thoroughly enjoyable to watch," according to Marsha Kinder. Regardless of the film's foundation in the Amado novel, its structure "is reminiscent of *Citizen Kane*," although the two heroes involved, one a powerful white man, the other an unlettered mulatto, differ greatly (Johnson and Stam 225, 226; see also Johnson, *Cinema* 207). A "film-within-a-film," *Tent of Mir-acles* is primarily concerned with "denouncing, albeit with a tremendous amount of humor, the racism so prevalent in Brazilian society," although it also "deals with

Brazilian cinema and its modes of production" (Johnson, *Cinema* 209–10). Arguing that "*Tent of Miracles* both supports and exposes the myth of racial democracy" in Brazil, Stam too finds that the film "critiques the myth by portraying a closet racist who unmasks himself when his daughter wants to marry one of 'them.' More important, the film suggests that the ideologically explicit and politically violent racism of the past has merely transmuted itself into the subtler mass-mediated racism of today" (305).

The Third Bank of the River (*A terceira margem do rio*): Adapted by Nelson Pereira dos Santos from the Guimarães Rosa story, this 1993 film is a French and Brazilian coproduction. Although dos Santos begins by developing the story that gives the film its title, he quickly moves to integrate four other Rosa stories into his discourse, and as "long as the film takes place in the interior of the country," it "remains close both to Rosa's mythic-rural literary universe and to the *sertão* of Dos Santos's own *Vidas Secas*" (Stam, Vieira, and Xavier 442).

Uncle Tom's Cabin: This American literary classic, widely known and influential in Brazil during the late nineteenth century (when Brazil too was struggling with the twin questions of slavery and emancipation), became a popular film (1909) in Brazil during its first *bela época* of filmmaking. This golden age dates from 1908, a year of significant activity in Brazil's nascent film industry, to 1911, when a flood of American and European films came to dominate the domestic market. (The *cinema novo* movement of the 1960s might be considered Brazilian film's second *bela época*.)

Vidas secas: Directed by Nelson Pereira dos Santos, the film version of Graciliano Ramos's superb novel of 1938 (translated as *Barren Lives*) reigns supreme, for many critics, as the masterpiece of *cinema novo*. "An area in which the film is imaginatively faithful to the novel concerns point of view. The Ramos novel is written from what might be called a subjectivized third-person point of view." While dos Santos retains "what we might call the democratic distribution of subjectivity," he also "creates subjective vision by camera movement" and "plays on diverse cinematic registers to transmit" the inner visions of the characters, one of the most striking of whom is a dog (Johnson, *Cinema* 177–78). "Rarely has a subject—in this case hunger, drought, and the exploitation of a peasant family—been so finely rendered by a style. Rarely have a thematic and an esthetic been quite so fully adequate to one another" (Johnson and Stam 120). The predilect theme of *cinema novo*—the depiction of rural poverty, hunger, dependency, injustice, and underdevelopment—is presented with an accuracy and poignancy that make *Vidas secas* an extraordinary account of survival in the harsh northeastern backlands.

White Passion (*Alva paixão*): Directed by Maria Emília de Azeredo and appearing in 1995, *White Passion* examines the troubled life of João da Cruz e Sousa, the most accomplished figure in Brazil's symbolist movement and a poet whose work is comparable to the French and German masters.

> As a prompter in the theater, Cruz e Sousa [who died in 1898, the same year that Brazilian cinema began] is the man who knows the lines but who cannot appear on stage. His poetry is appreciated, but his blackness is out of place in the literary milieu of Santa Catarina, one of the "whitest" regions of Brazil. The film ends with a flash-forward to the present with a shot of a young black boy sitting pen in hand in an impoverished schoolhouse. What is the fate, this ending implicitly asks, of the *contemporary* Cruz e Sousas? Can they avoid the kinds of tragedies that befell earlier black writers? (Stam 34)

Like the best of Brazil's popular music and literature, Brazilian cinema at its best has, as Robert Stam says, "demystified class society by laying bare the internal structure of its social relations" while examining, through "anti-illusionist strategies," "the process of [the] construction of the text itself" (Johnson and Stam 240). As we see from even a brief perusal of the highly selective lists in appendixes A and B, Brazilian music and film have developed both a high degree of sophistication and an acute sociopolitical awareness. The latter should remind us that all artistic expression functions in a historical context that we need to know in order to appreciate and understand the work. Representing vital traditions, Brazilian popular music and film are both flourishing (music perhaps more so than film), on the national as well as the international scene, and this success bodes well for Brazil's cultural, political, and economic globalization in the twenty-first century.

NOTES

1. In 1911, for example, a group of American business executives, along with their Brazilian counterparts, traveled to Rio de Janeiro to explore the "exploitability of the Brazilian market." In the next two decades, the fledgling Brazilian film industry "betrayed a wide range of foreign influences," including the European avant-garde (Johnson and Stam 22, 23–24).
2. As Stam, Vieira, and Xavier note, "Brazil's TV Globo is now the fourth largest private network in the world in audience and resources—while Brazilian cinema suffered the triple whammy of runaway inflation, urban crisis, and government neglect. And as the coup de grace, Brazilian television, unlike many of its European counterparts, has virtually boycotted national films. (In 1986, for example, out of 2,170 films screened on Rio's six television channels, only 35 were Brazilian)" (390).

Recommended Works of Brazilian Literature in English Translation

Abreu, Caio Fernando. *Whatever Happened to Dulce Veiga? A B-Novel.* Trans. Adria Frizzi. Austin: U of Texas P, 2000.

Alencar, José de. *Iracema.* Trans. Clifford E. Landers. New York: Oxford UP, 2000.

———. *Senhora: Profile of a Woman.* Trans. and introd. Catarina Feldmann Edinger. Austin: U of Texas P, 1994.

Almeida, Manuel Antônio de. *Memoirs of a Militia Sergeant.* Trans. Ronald W. Sousa. Oxford: Oxford UP, 1999.

Alves, Castro. *The Major Abolitionist Poems.* Ed. and trans. Amy A. Peterson. New York: Garland, 1990.

Alves, Miriam, comp. and ed. *Finally—Us: Contemporary Black Brazilian Women Writers.* Ed. and trans. Carolyn Richardson Durham. Boulder: Three Continents, 1995.

Amado, Jorge. *Dona Flor and Her Two Husbands.* Trans. Harriet de Onís. New York: Knopf, 1969.

———. *Gabriela, Clove and Cinnamon.* Trans. James L. Taylor and William L. Grossman. New York: Knopf, 1970.

———. *Jubiabá.* Trans. Margaret A. Neves. New York: Bard Avon, 1984.

———. *Sea of Death.* Trans. Gregory Rabassa. New York: Bard Avon, 1984.

———. *Tent of Miracles.* Trans. Barbara Shelby. New York: Knopf, 1971.

———. *The Two Deaths of Quincas Wateryell.* Trans. Barbara Shelby. New York: Knopf, 1965.

———. *The Violent Land.* Trans. Samuel Putnam. New York: Knopf, 1965.

Andrade, Carlos Drummond de. *Travelling in the Family: Selected Poems.* Ed. and trans. Thomas Colchie and Mark Strand. Additional trans. Elizabeth Bishop and Gregory Rabassa. New York: Random, 1986.

Andrade, Mário de. *Hallucinated City*. Trans. Jack E. Tomlins. Nashville: Vanderbilt UP, 1968.

———. *Macunaíma*. Trans. E. A. Goodland. New York: Random, 1984.

Andrade, Oswald de. *The Sentimental Memoirs of John Seaborne*. Trans. Albert Bork. *Texas Quarterly* 15.4 (1972): 112–60.

———. *Seraphim Grosse Pointe*. Trans. Kenneth D. Jackson and Albert Bork. Austin: New Latin Quarter, 1979.

Ângelo, Ivan. *The Celebration*. Trans. Thomas Colchie. New York: Bard Avon, 1982.

Aranha, Graça. *Canaan*. Trans. Mariano Joaquín Lorente. Boston: Four Seas, 1920.

Azevedo, Aluísio. *Mulatto*. Trans. Murray Graeme MacNicoll. Austin: U of Texas P, 1990.

———. *The Slum*. Trans. David H. Rosenthal. New York: Oxford UP, 2000.

Barreto, Lima. *The Patriot*. Trans. Robert Scott-Buccleuch. London: Collings, 1978.

Bishop, Elizabeth, and Emanuel Brasil, eds. and trans. *An Anthology of Twentieth-Century Brazilian Poetry*. Middletown: Wesleyan UP, 1972.

The Borzoi Anthology of Latin American Literature. Ed. Emir Rodríguez Monegal, assisted by Thomas Colchie. 2 vols. New York: Knopf, 1984.

Brandão, Ignácio de Loyola. *Zero*. Trans. Ellen Watson. New York: Avon, 1983.

Callado, Antônio. *Quarup*. Trans. Barbara Shelby. New York: Knopf, 1970.

Caminha, Pêro Vaz de. *Letter of Discovery*. Trans. Thomas Colchie. *Borzoi Anthology* 1: 11–13.

Campos, Haroldo de. "Two Concrete Poems." Trans. Mary Ellen Solt and Marco Guimarães. *Borzoi Anthology* 2: 776–77.

Cunha, Euclides da. *Rebellion in the Backlands*. Trans. Samuel Putnam. Chicago: U of Chicago P, 1967.

Dourado, Autran. *The Voices of the Dead*. Trans. John M. Parker. London: Owen, 1980.

Felinto, Marilene. *The Women of Tijucopapo*. Trans. Irene Matthews. Lincoln: U of Nebraska P, 1994.

Fonseca, Rubem. *High Art*. Trans. Ellen Watson. New York: Harper, 1983.

———. "Large Intestine." Trans. Elizabeth Lowe. *Review* 76 (Fall 1976): 69–75.

Galvão, Patrícia. *Industrial Park: A Proletarian Novel*. Trans. Elizabeth Jackson and K. David Jackson. Lincoln: U of Nebraska P, 1993.

Gomes, Alfredo Dias. *Payment as Pledged*. Trans. Oscar Fernández. *The Modern Stage in Latin America: Six Plays*. Ed. George Woodyard. New York: Dutton, 1971.

Ivo, Lêdo. *Snakes' Nest; or, A Tale Badly Told*. Trans. Jon M. Tolman. New York: New Directions, 1981.

Jesus, Carolina Maria de. *Child of the Dark*. Trans. David St. Clair. New York: NAL, 1962.

Lins, Osman. *Avalovara*. Trans. Gregory Rabassa. New York: Knopf, 1980.

Lins do Rego, José. *Plantation Boy.* Trans. Emmi Baum. New York: Knopf, 1966.

Lispector, Clarice. *The Apple in the Dark.* Trans. and fwd. Gregory Rabassa. New York: Knopf, 1967.

———. *Family Ties.* Trans. Giovanni Pontiero. Austin: U of Texas P, 1972.

———. *The Hour of the Star.* Trans. Giovanni Pontiero. New York: New Directions, 1986.

———. *Near to the Wild Heart.* Trans. Giovanni Pontiero. New York: New Directions, 1990.

———. *The Passion according to G. H.* Trans. Ronald W. Sousa. Minneapolis: U of Minnesota P, 1988.

———. *Soulstorm.* Trans. Alexis Levitin. Introd. Grace Paley. New York: New Directions, 1989.

———. *The Stream of Life.* Trans. Elizabeth Lowe and Earl Fitz. Minneapolis: U of Minnesota P, 1989.

Luft, Lya. *The Island of the Dead.* Trans. Carmen Chaves McClendon and Betty Jean Craige. Athens: U of Georgia P, 1986.

Machado de Assis, Joaquim Maria. *Counselor Ayres' Memorial.* Trans. Helen Caldwell. Berkeley: U of California P, 1972.

———. *"The Devil's Church" and Other Stories.* Trans. and introd. Jack Schmitt and Lorie Ishimatsu. Austin: U of Texas P, 1984.

———. *Dom Casmurro.* Trans. and introd. Helen Caldwell. Berkeley: U of California P, 1966.

———. *Dom Casmurro.* Trans. and fwd. John Gledson. Afterword by João Adolfo Hansen. New York: Oxford UP, 1997.

———. *Esau and Jacob.* Trans. Elizabeth Lowe. New York: Oxford UP, 2000.

———. *The Hand and the Glove.* Trans. Albert I. Bagby, Jr. Lexington: UP of Kentucky, 1970.

———. *Helena.* Trans. Helen Caldwell. Berkeley: U of California P, 1984.

———. *The Posthumous Memoirs of Brás Cubas.* Trans. Gregory Rabassa. New York: Oxford UP, 1997.

———. *"The Psychiatrist" and Other Stories.* Trans. William L. Grossman and Helen Caldwell. Berkeley: U of California P, 1963.

———. *Quincas Borba.* Trans. Gregory Rabassa. New York: Oxford UP, 1998.

———. *Yayá Garcia.* Trans. R. L. Scott-Buccleuch. London: Owen, 1976.

Matos, Gregôrio de. "The Satirical and Popular Muse" [a selection of poetry]. Trans. Thomas Colchie. *Borzoi Anthology* 1: 138–44.

Melo Neto, João Cabral de. *A Knife All Blade; or, The Usefulness of Fixed Ideas.* Trans. Kerry Shawn Keys. Camp Hill: Pine, 1980.

———. *Selected Poetry, 1937–1990.* Ed. and trans. Djelal Kadir. Additional trans. Elizabeth Bishop et al. Hanover: UP of New England, 1994.

Olinto, Antônio. *The Water House.* Trans. Dorothy Heapy. New York: Carroll, 1970.

Parente Cunha, Helena. *Woman between Mirrors.* Trans. Fred P. Ellison and Naomi Lindstrom. Austin: U of Texas P, 1989.

Piñon, Nélida. *Caetana's Sweet Song.* Trans. Helen Lane. New York: Knopf, 1992.

———. *The Republic of Dreams.* Trans. Helen Lane. New York: Knopf, 1989.

Queiroz, Raquel de. *The Three Marias.* Trans. Fred P. Ellison. Austin: U of Texas P, 1963.

Ramos, Graciliano. *Anguish.* Trans. L. C. Kaplan. New York: Knopf, 1946.

———. *Barren Lives.* Trans. Ralph Edward Dimmick. Austin: U of Texas P, 1965.

———. *São Bernardo.* Trans. R. L. Scott-Buccleuch. London: Owen, 1975.

Ribeiro, Darcy. *Maíra.* Trans. E. H. Goodland and Thomas Colchie. New York: Aventura, 1984.

Ribeiro, João Ubaldo. *Sergeant Getúlio.* Trans. Ribeiro. Boston: Houghton, 1978.

Rodrigues, Nelson. *The Wedding Dress* [includes additional plays: *All Nudity Shall Be Punished, Lady of the Drowned, Waltz #6,* and *The Deceased Woman*]. Trans. Joffre Rodrigues and Toby Coe. Rio de Janeiro: Ministério da Cultura–Funarte, 1998.

Rosa, Guimarães. *The Devil to Pay in the Backlands.* Trans. James L. Taylor and Harriet de Onís. New York: Knopf, 1971.

———. *Sagarana.* Trans. Harriet de Onís. New York: Knopf, 1966.

———. *"The Third Bank of the River" and Other Stories.* Trans. Barbara Shelby. New York: Knopf, 1968.

Rubião, Murilo. *"The Ex-Magician" and Other Stories.* Trans. Thomas Colchie. New York: Avon, 1979.

Sadlier, Darlene J., ed. and trans. *One Hundred Years after Tomorrow: Brazilian Women's Fiction in the Twentieth Century.* Bloomington: Indiana UP, 1992.

Souza, Márcio. *The Emperor of the Amazon.* Trans. Thomas Colchie. New York: Bard Avon, 1980.

———. *Mad Maria.* Trans. Thomas Colchie. New York: Bard Avon, 1985.

Suassuna, Ariano. *The Rogues' Trial.* Trans. Dillwyn F. Ratcliff. Berkeley: U of California P, 1963.

Szoka, Elzbieta, and Joe W. Bratcher III, eds. *Three Contemporary Brazilian Plays.* Trans. Szoka, Lydia Gouveia Marques, and Celina Pinto. Austin: Host, 1988.

Taunay, Alfredo d'Escragnolle. *Inocência.* Trans. Henriqueta Chamberlain. New York: Macmillan, 1945.

Tapscott, Stephen, ed. *Twentieth-Century Latin American Poetry: A Bilingual Anthology.* Austin: U of Texas P, 1996.

Telles, Lygia Fagundes. *The Girl in the Photograph.* Trans. Margaret A. Neves. New York. Bard Avon, 1982.

———. *The Marble Dance.* Trans. Margaret A. Neves. New York: Bard Avon, 1986.

————. *"Tigrela" and Other Stories*. Trans. Margaret A. Neves. New York: Bard Avon, 1986.

Trevisan, Dalton. *"The Vampire of Curitiba" and Other Stories*. Trans. Gregory Rabassa. New York: Knopf, 1972.

van Steen, Edla. *Village of the Ghost Bells*. Trans. David George. Austin: U of Texas P, 1991.

Veríssimo, Érico. *Crossroads*. Trans. L. C. Kaplan. New York: Macmillan, 1943.

————. *His Excellency, the Ambassador*. Trans. L. L. Barrett and Marie McDavid Barrett. New York: Macmillan, 1967.

————. *Time and the Wind*. Trans. L. L. Barrett. New York: Macmillan, 1951.

Vieira, Antônio. "How to Save Both Souls and Bodies." Trans. Thomas Colchie. *Borzoi Anthology* 1: 130–38.

————. Section of "Sermon for the Good Success of the Arms of Portugal against Those of Holland." Trans. unknown. Haberly, "Colonial" 59.

————. Untitled portion of sermon on the injustice of slavery. Trans. unknown. Qtd. in Burns, *History* [2nd ed.] 53.

APPENDIX D

A Brazilian Chronology

History and Politics

1494: With the Treaty of Tordesillas, Pope Alexander VI separates the Portuguese and Spanish zones of influence in the New World.

1500: The first European contact occurs when the Portuguese explorer Pedro Álvares Cabral and his crew arrive in the land that would become known as Brazil.

1538: The first known shipment of African slaves arrives in Brazil.

1555: The French vice admiral, Durand de Villegaignon, establishes a colony, France Antartique, in the

Literature and Culture

1500: Pêro Vaz de Caminha, Cabral's official scribe, writes his "Letter of Discovery," the founding document of written Brazilian literature.

1549: The first Jesuits arrive and, with their various educational activities, begin to form the foundations for a national literature and culture. Early Jesuits like Manuel da Nóbrega and José de Anchieta seek to interact with and respect indigenous cultures (but not cannibalism and polygamy). Anchieta uses theatrical performances in Tupi to help convert the Indians to Catholicism.

History and Politics	*Literature and Culture*
area around Guanabara Bay and present-day Rio de Janeiro.	
1565: Rio de Janeiro is founded by a Portuguese noble and soldier, Mem de Sá.	
1567: The French are expelled by the Portuguese.	
	1601: What many now consider the baroque era of Brazilian literature begins with the publication of Bento Teixeira's short epic poem *Prosopopéia.*[1]
1612–15: The French invade northern Brazil; they are forced out by the Portuguese.	
1624–25: The Dutch capture Salvador and then (in 1630) Recife and begin to occupy Brazil's northeast.	
	1640: The influential Jesuit priest and master of baroque oratory Father Antônio Vieira preaches his famous sermon on the success of Portuguese arms against the Dutch invaders.
1654: The Treaty of Taborda forces the Dutch to withdraw from Brazil.	
	1681: Gregório de Matos returns to Brazil from Portugal definitively and begins to compose colonial Brazil's most original and multifaceted poetry.
1695: Gold is discovered in the south central state of Minas Gerais.	
1697: Brazilian troops destroy Palmares, the largest and most powerful of the runaway slave citadels.	
	1724: The first of Brazil's highly influential eighteenth-century academies, the Academy of the Forgotten Ones, is organized in Salvador.

History and Politics

1727: Coffee begins to be cultivated in Brazil.

1759: Marquês de Pombal, the powerful prime minister of Portugal from 1750 to 1777, expels the Jesuits from Brazil.

1763: The national capital is moved from Salvador da Bahia, in the northeast, to Rio de Janeiro, in the southeast.

1786–87: Thomas Jefferson holds several meetings with José Joaquim de Maia concerning Brazil's gathering independence movement and how the United States might react to it.

1789: Brazil's first attempt at independence, the Inconfidência Mineira, fails.

1808: Fleeing Napoleon, the Portuguese royal family, the Braganzas, takes up residence in Brazil.

1815: Brazil is elevated by the Portuguese crown to the status of a kingdom.

1821: The Portuguese monarch, João VI, returns to Lisbon.

1822: Prince Pedro proclaims Brazil's

Literature and Culture

1730: Sebastião da Rocha Pita's *History of Portuguese America* is published in Lisbon.

1768: With the appearance of Cláudio Manuel da Costa's *Poetic Works*, Brazil's baroque period comes to an end. Arcadianism begins; Tomás Antônio Gonzaga becomes its most able practitioner.

1769: José Basílio da Gama brings out his epic poem *The Uruguay*.

1781: José de Santa Rita Durão sees his epic poem *Caramuru* published.

1808: Brazil gets its first printing press.

History and Politics

independence and is declared emperor.

1823: Brazil becomes the only Latin American nation to approve the Monroe Doctrine.

1824: The United States recognizes Brazil.

1831: Pedro I abdicates; a regency government is installed.

1840: Pedro II assumes the throne.

1850: The slave trade is eliminated by means of the Queiróz Law.

Literature and Culture

1833: Martins Pena writes *The Country Justice of the Peace,* Brazil's first comedy of manners. He helps found a national theater.

1836: The publication of Gonçalves de Magalhães's *Poetical Sighs and Longings* heralds the beginning of Romanticism in Brazil.

1844: Joaquim Manuel de Macedo sees his romantic fiction *The Little Brunette* appear.

1852–53: Manuel Antônio de Almeida's picaresque novel *The Memoirs of a Militia Sergeant* makes its debut.

1857: José de Alencar publishes *The Guarani.* Gonçalves Dias brings out another lyrical and indigenous work, *The Timbiras* (Timbiras is the name of an Indian tribe).

1865: Alencar's *Iracema,* one of Brazil's defining texts, appears.

1875: *Senhora,* one of Alencar's important later novels, is published.

1870s–80s: Positivism, an intellectual movement established by the French thinker Auguste Comte that stressed empirical analysis as

History and Politics

Literature and Culture

the basis for knowledge, becomes influential in Brazil.

1881: With the appearance of Aluísio Azevedo's *The Mulatto* the period of realism-naturalism begins in Brazilian literature. Machado de Assis's *The Posthumous Memoirs of Brás Cubas* appears.

1883: Castro Alves's *The Slaves* is published.

1888: The Golden Law abolishes slavery in Brazil.

1889: The Republic is established.

1890: Azevedo's naturalistic novel *The Tenement* is published.

1891: A new constitution, patterned after that of the United States, is written.

1891: Machado de Assis's *Quincas Borba* is published.

1893: Symbolism begins in Brazil with the publication of two works by João da Cruz e Sousa: *Missal* (prose poems) and *Broquéis* (verse).

1895: Adolfo Caminha publishes *The Black Man and the Cabin Boy.*

1897: The Canudos Insurrection breaks out.

1899: Machado's *Dom Casmurro* appears.

1902: Euclides da Cunha publishes *Rebellion in the Backlands*, while Graça Aranha publishes *Canaan*. These works mark the end of symbolism in Brazil and the beginning of the modernist period. An unsettled time of experimentation and innovation ensues as Brazil begins to look outward.

1906: Rio de Janeiro hosts the Third Pan-American Conference.

1907: Taking part in its first worldwide conference, Brazil is active in the Second Hague Peace Conference.

History and Politics	*Literature and Culture*
	1908: Machado de Assis dies. His final novel, *Counselor Ayres's Memorial,* also appears.
1910: Cândido Rondon, an army officer, becomes the first director of Brazil's Indian Protection Service.	
	1912: Oswald de Andrade returns from Europe and begins to promote in Brazil Marinetti's futurism and Paul Fort's new poetry.
	1914: Anita Malfatti, who has been studying at the Berlin School of Art and whose paintings show the influence of German expressionism, has her first exhibition in Brazil. Three years later, her work will introduce Brazilians to cubism.
1915: Nearly one million immigrants (esp. Italians and Germans) enter Brazil.	
1917: Brazil declares war on Germany and joins the Allied powers.	
	1920: Brazil's first modern university is established. Oswald de Andrade defends the creations of Victor Brecheret, an avant-garde Brazilian sculptor.
	1922: Modern Art Week, 11–17 February, begins in São Paulo. Mário de Andrade's *Hallucinated City* appears.
	1924: *The Sentimental Memoirs of João Miramar,* by Oswald de Andrade, is published.
	1925: Andrade publishes *Brazil-Wood.*
	1928: Andrade promulgates his "Cannibalist Manifesto;" Mário de Andrade publishes *Macunaíma*; Jorge de Lima publishes "That Black Girl Fulô."

History and Politics

1929: The beginning of the Great Depression devastates Brazil's economy.

1930s: Government-supported industrialization is initiated.

1932: Brazilian women gain the vote.

1937: Getúlio Vargas establishes the dictatorial Estado Novo or New State.

1938: Popularly known as Lampião, Virgolino Ferreira da Silva, the leader of the northeast's last great bandit gang, is killed by the authorities. As proof of his death, his severed head is displayed in several towns in the region.

1942: Brazil declares war on Germany and Italy and participates in World War II.

Literature and Culture

1930: Carlos Drummond de Andrade publishes his "Seven-Sided Poem."

1932: José Lins do Rêgo publishes *Plantation Boy* (which includes three of his novels: *Menino do Engenho*, *Doidinho*, and *Bangue*).

1933: Gilberto Freyre publishes his *The Masters and the Slaves*; establishes the importance of miscegenation in Brazil's history, and lauds Brazil's African heritage. Oswald de Andrade's revolutionary narrative *Seraphim Grosse Pointe* appears.

1935: Jorge Amado publishes *Jubiabá*, his depression-era novel of black life and politics in Salvador.

1936: Graciliano Ramos publishes *Anguish*.

1937: Oswald de Andrade completes his modernist and "cannibalistic" play *The Candle King*. It is not staged until 1967.

1938: *Barren Lives*, by Graciliano Ramos, appears.

1939: Rachel de Queiroz publishes *The Three Marias*.

1943: Jorge Amado publishes *The Violent Land*.

1944: Clarice Lispector publishes her celebrated first novel, *Near to the*

History and Politics	*Literature and Culture*
	Wild Heart. Abdias do Nascimento founds the Teatro Experimental do Negro and begins to emphasize the question of race relations in Brazil and to expand it into the political arena.
1945: The military deposes Vargas.	
	1946: *Sagarana,* a landmark collection of stories by Guimarães Rosa, appears.
1950: Vargas is reelected president.	
	1952: Concrete poetry establishes itself in Brazil through the Noigandres Group of São Paulo (Augusto and Haroldo de Campos and Décio Pignatari).
1954: Vargas commits suicide after being deposed by the military once again.	
	1956: Rosa brings out *The Devil to Pay in the Backlands.*
	1958: A paean to Brazilian optimism and exuberance, *Gabriela, Clove and Cinnamon,* one of Amado's most influential novels, appears; it becomes a best seller in the United States in the early 1960s. Brazil wins its first World Cup.
	1959: The film *Black Orpheus* appears to international acclaim. A new form of Brazilian music, the bossa nova, begins to gain in popularity.
1960: Brasília, a planned city in the interior of the country, becomes the new federal capital.	1960: *Cinema novo* begins to cohere as a social, political, and aesthetic movement. Lispector publishes *Family Ties,* a collection of highly influential stories.
	1962: *The Given Word* wins first prize at the Cannes film festival. The bossa nova becomes hugely popular worldwide.

History and Politics

1964: A military coup, aided by the United States, deposes President João Goulart; a new dictatorship begins.

1968: Heavy government censorship is imposed; violation means arrest, torture, even death.
1968–74: The years of Brazil's celebrated "economic miracle."

1969: Charles Burke Elbrick, the American ambassador to Brazil, is kidnapped by urban guerillas; he is later freed.

1974: General Ernesto Geisel is named president; the economy begins to falter, and the military dictatorship begins to lose its support.

Literature and Culture

1962–63: The *engagé* anthology of poetry *Street Guitar* is published.
1964: Ruy Guerra's politically charged film *The Guns* premiers.

1966: Chico Buarque's hit song "The Band" combines great popular appeal with incisive political commentary.
1968: José J. Veiga publishes *"The Misplaced Machine" and Other Stories.*

1968–69: Tropicalism (involving Caetano Veloso, Gilberto Gil, and Tom Zé, among others) enjoys its apogee. In a period of political repression, Brazilian popular music resonates with artistic complexity, intellectual seriousness, and political acumen.

1971: João Ubaldo Ribeiro publishes *Sergeant Getúlio.*
1973: Lispector publishes *The Stream of Life.* Osman Lins publishes *Avalovara.*

1975: *Zero*, Ignácio de Loyola Brandão's prize-winning novel of the dictatorship, is published in Brazil. It is banned by the Ministry of Justice in 1976.

History and Politics	*Literature and Culture*
	1976: Ivan Angelo's politically charged novel *The Celebration* is published.
	1977: Lispector's *The Hour of the Star* is published.
1978: Pressure mounts for a return to a democratically run government.	
	1982: Márcia Denser edits *Very Pleased to Meet You: Erotic Short Stories by Women*, establishing erotic writing by women as a viable genre in Brazil. Marilene Felinto's *The Women of Tijucopapo* also appears.
	1983: Helena Parente Cunha publishes *Woman between Mirrors*.
	1984: Nélida Piñon publishes *The Republic of Dreams*. Lya Luft publishes *The Island of the Dead*. João Ubaldo Ribeiro publishes *Long Live the Brazilian People*.
1985: With the election of Tancredo Neves, civilian rule is reestablished in Brazil.	1985: Brazil's TV Globo becomes the world's fourth largest television network.
	1987: Piñon's *Caetana's Sweet Song* makes its appearance. *Vera*, a film by Sérgio Toledo, debuts.
1990s: Brazil's women's movement becomes "the largest, most radical, most diverse, and most effective of women's movements in Latin America" (Skidmore, *Brazil* 207).	1990: Caio Fernando Abreu publishes *Whatever Happened to Dulce Veiga? A B-Novel*. Rubem Fonseca publishes *August*; it deals with the final days of Getúlio Vargas in 1954.
1992: President Fernando Collor de Mello is impeached.	
	1993: Nelson Pereira dos Santos adapts several stories by Guimarães Rosa to film with *The Third Bank of the River*.
	1995: With the return of governmental support, the Brazilian film industry begins to expand its activities once again.

History and Politics

Literature and Culture

1999: Following the release of his acclaimed album *Fabrication Defect*,
Tom Zé begins his first United
States tour. Enthusiastically promoted by such prominent musicians as Beck, John McEntire, and
David Byrne, Brazilian pop music
develops an international following
in the late 1990s.

2002: Luiz Inácio Lula da Silva, a populist, is elected president.

2002: Brazil becomes the first nation to
win the World Cup five times.

NOTES

The entries under "History and Politics" are based on the third edition of Burns's *A History of Brazil* (495–500).

1. See Moisés 35. All subsequent divisions of Brazil's literary history follow Moisés as well.

Critical Works Cited: An Annotated Bibliography

Abreu, João Capistrano de. *Chapters of Brazil's Colonial History: 1500–1800.* Trans. Arthur Brakel. Oxford: Oxford UP, 1997.

Written by the most influential Brazilian historian of the nineteenth and early twentieth centuries, this book, originally published in 1907, captures Abreu's significant contributions to Brazilian historiography: the attention Abreu paid to "marginal" figures; the importance he placed on transportation systems, schools, and economic structures; his concerns over the tendency of Brazilians to ape European and North American ideas; and his belief that the true, or authentic, Brazil was to be found not in the coastal areas but in the interior, the backlands (the *sertão*). The introduction is provided by Stuart Schwartz.

Agee, James, and Walker Evans. *Let Us Now Praise Famous Men.* Walden ed. New York: Ballantine, 1972.

As a social document, this famous text bears comparison with Euclides da Cunha's *Rebellion in the Backlands* (see Fitz, "Faulkner").

Aldridge, A. Owen. *Early American Literature: A Comparatist Approach.* Princeton: Princeton UP, 1982.

Aldridge, along with Stanley T. Williams, was one of the first scholars of American literature to take a North-South approach to the topic and to read the literature of the United States in the context of "Latin America," a term that, for Aldridge, covers only Spanish America (Brazilian literature is not mentioned). Still, many of Aldridge's comments are relevant to Brazil (one might, for example, apply his judgments about the poetry of Anne Bradstreet and Sor Juana Inés de la Cruz to the work of Gregório de Matos).

Amory, Frederic. "Euclides da Cunha and Brazilian Positivism." *Luso-Brazilian Review* 36.1 (1999): 87–94.

Amory argues that da Cunha, an enthusiast of Comte's positivism as a young man, later rejected the French school in favor of "English evolutionism or social Darwinism." Amory writes that "English evolutionism, not French Positivism, is writ large over the masterpiece of Euclides' maturity, *Os Sertões* [*Rebellion in the Backlands*] (1897–1900)" (91). If this new view of da Cunha's positivistic inclinations is accurate, then Brazil may have been more accepting of social Darwinism than previously thought.

Andrade, Oswald de. "Manifesto of Pau-Brasil Poetry." Trans. Stella M. de Sá Rego. *Latin American Literary Review* 14.27 (1986): 184–87.

A major document of early modernist poetry in Brazil, this declaration of independence for Brazilian poetry (and Brazilian culture in general) calls for "the counter-weight of native originality to neutralize academic conformity" (187).

Armstrong, Piers. "Guimarães Rosa in Translation: Scrittore, editore, traduttore, traditore." *Luso-Brazilian Review* 38.1 (2001): 63–87.

Armstrong discusses Rosa's keen interest in seeing his work translated and disseminated worldwide, as well as his active participation in contractual and editorial processes. Rosa, for example, commented critically on several translations that were being done and, in some cases, resolved particular problems in the final versions. But, as Armstrong makes clear, Rosa's confidence in his target-language fluency may have exceeded his literary capabilities in these languages, as can be seen in his correspondence with his original English-language translator, Harriet de Onís. The result is that Rosa may have "overestimated his own strengths and underestimated the difference between knowledge of foreign languages and the instincts of a native speaker" (71–72).

———. *Third World Literary Fortunes: Brazilian Culture and Its International Reception.* Lewisburg: Bucknell UP, 1999.

Striking a comparative perspective (emphasizing Brazil in relation to Spanish America and the United States), Armstrong examines such modern and modernist Brazilian writers as João Guimarães Rosa, Machado de Assis, Mário de Andrade, Carlos Drummond de Andrade, and Jorge Amado and evaluates their receptions abroad. Armstrong also discusses the importance of *Tropicalismo* and its leading practitioners, as well as the differences between Carnival in Rio de Janeiro and in New Orleans ("each is an inversion of prevailing social laws and mentalities, but in opposite ways"; 186).

Augusto, Sérgio. "Hollywood Looks at Brazil: From Carmen Miranda to *Moonraker.*" *Brazilian Cinema.* Ed. Randal Johnson and Robert Stam. East Brunswick: Assoc. UP, 1982. 352–67.

Augusto argues that beginning around 1933, the "key year in the long history of the cultural and economic invasion of Latin America by the United States" (357) and the year that Franklin Delano Roosevelt's good-neighbor policy was inaugurated, Rio de Janeiro gained a mystique as "the ideal site of enraptured romance" (355). Augusto provides a brief overview of how the Hollywood film industry has simplified, distorted, or elided the complexities of Brazil.

Barbosa, Maria José. "Life as an Opera: *Dom Casmurro* and *The Floating Opera.*" *Comparative Literature Studies* 29.3 (1992): 223–37.

Focusing on the motif of opera in Machado de Assis's *Dom Casmurro* and John Barth's *The Floating Opera* and on the relation between these two texts (*Dom Casmurro* influenced Barth's conception of his novel), Barbosa examines the ambiguity in the two works.

Barth, John. "The Literature of Exhaustion." *Atlantic* Aug. 1967. 29–34.

In this famous essay, Barth praises the influence of Borges on contemporary fiction writing. He does not mention Brazilian authors, although he was well acquainted with the work of Machado de Assis.

———. "The Literature of Replenishment." *Atlantic* Jan. 1980. 65–71.

In this follow-up to his 1967 piece, Barth discusses the invigorating work of García Márquez and Cortázar, in the context of postmodernism. Again, Barth does not mention Machado de Assis, whom he has referred to as the "proto-postmodernist" (Fitz, *Machado* 45).

Bellei, Sérgio Luiz Prado. "'The Raven,' by Machado de Assis." *Luso-Brazilian Review* 25.2 (1988): 1–23.

Arguing that "'appropriation,' not 'translation,' is what best explains 'O corvo'" (the Brazilian title of Poe's poem), Bellei discusses the "peculiar kind of anxiety of influence" that Brazilian writers experience and the way Machado's interpretation of Poe and "The Raven" relates to "the construction of nationality in literature" (12).

Bercovitch, Sacvan, gen. ed. *The Cambridge History of American Literature.* 8 vols. Cambridge: Cambridge UP, 1994.

Although it focuses on the United States, this study speaks, "inclusively" and "exclusively" (and often comparatively), to "all the other countries of the Americas, north and south" (1: 3). The work thus provides a pluralistic approach to the concept of American and, indeed, to inter-American literary study generally.

———, ed. *The Puritan Imagination: Essays in Revaluation.* Cambridge: Cambridge UP, 1974.

Bercovitch's introduction gives a good account of the reassessment of Puritan literature that was undertaken in the 1970s. As a result, we can see clearly the religious, historical, and aesthetic parallels between Puritan writing and the literature of colonial Brazil.

———. "The Puritan Vision of the New World." Elliott, *Columbia Literary History* 33–44.

In this short, insightful essay, Bercovitch lays out the basic premises of Puritan thought and reveals its application both to literary endeavor and to political organization.

Beverley, John, and José Oviedo, ed. *The Postmodern Debate in Latin America.* Spec. issue of *Boundary 2* 20.3 (1993).

In their introduction, which, although focusing on Spanish America, does refer to Brazil, Beverly and Oviedo observe that "in Brazil . . . *modernismo* and *posmodernismo* already correspond to the English meanings" (2).

Bolton, Herbert E. "The Epic of Greater America." *American Historical Review* 38 (1933): 448–74.

Arguing that the Americas share not an identical history but a common historical experience, Bolton calls for a new approach to what we think of as American history, one that integrates the New World experiences of Native America, Spain, Portugal, France, and England. This approach supplements, or counterbalances, "the purely nationalistic presentation to which we are accustomed" by offering up a "broader treatment of American history" (448). Bolton's argument thus affords us an intellectual justification for the development of inter-American literature as a field.

Braga, Thomas. "Castro Alves and the New England Abolitionists." *Hispania* 67.4 (1984): 585–93.

In this interesting article, Braga, pointing out patterns of influence and reception, discusses the connections between Brazil's great abolitionist poet Castro Alves and the New England abolitionists.

Braga-Pinto, César A. "An Other of One's Own: Clarice Lispector, Hélène Cixous, and American Audiences." MA thesis. San Francisco State U, 1993.

The author discusses Lispector's reception in the United States and her influence on Cixous. He considers, first, the status of Lispector as a canonical Brazilian writer. He then examines her writings in English translation, the nature (or quality) of the translations themselves, and the responses of American readers to her work. Finally, the author looks at French translations of Lispector's work and at her relation to French feminist theory, especially the elusive concept of *l'écriture féminine.*

Brakel, Arthur. "Ambiguity and Enigma in Art: The Case of Henry James and Machado de Assis." *Comparative Literature Studies* 19.4 (1982): 442–49.

Arguing that James's and Machado's best works are characterized by "their gaps, ambiguity, and open-ended nature," Brakel shows that the "unsolvable nature" of these works, "coupled with an illusion of solubility, is a large part of their survival value as literary touchstones." Both James and Machado saw their art as "a means of superseding the difficulties inherent in a totally empirical approach to life" (442, 443).

Buckley, Stephen. "Then, Now and Forever: 'The Girl from Ipanema.'" *Foreign Jour-*

nal, Washington Post Foreign Service, 18 Oct. 1999: A13. <http://www.
washingtonpost.com/wp-srv/WPlate/1999-10/18/0871-101899-idx.html>.

This short piece reflects on the life of the original "Girl from Ipanema" and the
impact she and the famous song have had on Brazilians and non-Brazilians alike.

Burns, E. Bradford. *A History of Brazil.* New York: Columbia UP, 1970.

Burns organizes this excellent history as follows: ch. 1, "In the Beginning"
("The Land," "The Indian," "The European," "Discovery and Confrontation,"
and "The Establishment of the Colony"); ch. 2, "The Colonial Experience";
ch. 3, "The Proclamation and Consolidation of Independence"; ch. 4, "The
Transformation"; ch. 5, "The New Brazil"; ch. 6, "Restructuring Society"; and
ch. 7, "Reform, Radicalization, and Reaction." Burns includes a useful appendix
that contains excerpts from some of the military dictatorship's Institutional Acts.

———. *A History of Brazil,* 2nd ed. New York: Columbia UP, 1980.

In what was long regarded as the standard English-language history of Brazil,
Burns examines culture and civilization from the nation's origins through the
1970s. He documents Brazil's long-standing relationship with the United
States and, by giving ample space to Brazilian literature, film, and music, integrates Brazil's cultural history into his narrative. His chronology of events is
highly useful, as is the section "Additional Readings."

———. *A History of Brazil,* 3rd ed. New York: Columbia UP, 1993.

———. *Latin America: A Concise Interpretive History,* 2nd ed. Englewood Cliffs:
Prentice, 1977.

This work is a fine study of the historical and cultural relations between the
United States and Brazil because it compares and contrasts Brazil's development as a nation with that of the countries of Spanish America. Thus readers
learn a good deal about Brazilian-American ties at the same time they discover
what makes Brazil unique in Latin America.

Caetano Lopes, Francisco. "A respeito da questão da pós-modernidade no Brasil."
Homenagem a Alexandrino Severino: Essays on the Portuguese-Speaking World.
Ed. Margo Milleret and Marshall Eakin. Austin: Host, 1993. 229–48.

Linking the question of postcolonialism to the cultural debate over the impact
and meaning of postmodernism, Lopes explores the possibility that much
contemporary Brazilian fiction is developing along postmodern lines. The author argues that postmodernism is as political and cultural as it is artistic and
intellectual.

Caldwell, Helen. *The Brazilian* Othello *of Machado de Assis: A Study of* Dom Casmurro. Berkeley: U of California P, 1960.

This famous study established the critical context for much Machado de Assis
scholarship. Caldwell provides a close reading of the novel *Dom Casmurro,*
which relies, openly and not so openly, on the characters and structure of
Shakespeare's play.

Campos, Haroldo de. "The Rule of Anthropophagy: Europe under the Sign of De-
voration." Trans. Maria Tai Wolff. *Latin American Literary Review* 14.27
(1986): 42–60.

Written by an esteemed Brazilian author and critic, this essay is divided into
several sections: "Avant-Garde and/or Underdevelopment," "Modal Nationalism vs. Ontological Nationalism," "The Baroque: The Non-infancy," "The
Baroque and the Rule of Anthropophagy," "Concrete Poetry: An 'Other' Constellation," and "The Alexandrian Barbarians: Planetary Redevoration." Discussing the contentious attitude of the Brazilian avant-garde toward European
and North American forms and influences, de Campos argues that "in Brazil,
with Oswald de Andrade's 'Antropofagia' ('Anthropophagy'), in the 1920s
(taken up again, in the 1950s, as a cosmic philosophical-existential vision, in
the thesis 'A Crise da Filosofia Messiânica' ('The Crisis of Messianic Philos-
ophy'), we get a strong sense of the need to consider the national element in a
dialogical and dialectic relationship with the universal" (43–44).

Carneiro, David da Silva. "The Story of Jefferson and Maia." *Brazil* 20.1 (1946): 8–9.

Carneiro describes the meeting between Maia, the young Brazilian revolutionary, and Jefferson, the sympathetic but cautious American diplomat.

Castro, Ruy. *Bossa Nova: The Story of the Brazilian Music That Seduced the World.*
Trans. Lysa Salsbury. New York: A Cappella, 2001.

Castro's entertaining account of the rise of bossa nova in Brazil during the
1950s defines the new music, shows how it related to Brazil's cultural milieu,
and explores how Brazilian culture was being exported abroad. Castro also examines the crucial role played by the genius and personality of João Gilberto.
Issues of influence and reception are extensively discussed.

Chamberlain, Bobby J. "Through Eagle Eyes: U.S. Brazilianists and Their Relationship to Brazilian Literature." *Hispania* 74.3 (1991): 604–09.

Chamberlain, a respected American Brazilianist, examines the pitfalls that may
occur when a "first-world" scholar seeks to study "third-world cultures." Arguing that if we allow "the norms of the dominant U.S. society" to serve as the
models for judging the efforts of other cultures, we will likely regard the literature and culture of Brazil "with some disapproval, as something exotic but ultimately flawed." He proposes an alternative approach that, if appropriately
applied, should eliminate Americans' biased reading of Brazil and its culture
(604, 605).

Chevigny, Bell Gale, and Gari Laguardia, eds. *Reinventing the Americas: Comparative
Studies of Literature of the United States and Spanish America.* Cambridge:
Cambridge UP, 1986.

This collection does not deal specifically with Brazil, but its excellent introduction and some of its essays touch on subjects germane to the Brazilian experience and its relationship to the United States.

Clemons, Walter. "A Gravestone of Memories." *Newsweek* 28 Sept. 1987: 74–75.
In reviewing Toni Morrison's *Beloved*, Clemons quotes Morrison, who had
traveled to Brazil to do research for the novel: "In Brazil . . . they've kept [referring
to records and slave narratives] *everything*. I got a lot of help down there" (75).

Cohn, Deborah N. *History and Memory in the Two Souths: Recent Southern and Span-
ish American Fiction*. Nashville: Vanderbilt UP, 1999.
Although Cohn's valuable book does not deal specifically with Brazil, its criti-
cal methodology and theoretical framework invite the reader to integrate the
Brazilian experience into its findings and conclusions. Parallels between the
American South, for example, and Brazil's Northeast have long been made (see
Putnam, *Marvelous Journey*; Freyre; Ellison). And while Faulkner's influence in
Brazil was not as crucial as it was in Spanish America, the Mississippian was
known and admired, early on, in Brazil (see Monteiro).

Colchie, Thomas, and Mark Strand, eds. and trans. Additional trans. Elizabeth
Bishop and Gregory Rabassa. *Travelling in the Family: Selected Poems by
Carlos Drummond de Andrade*. New York: Random, 1986.
This enlightening anthology of Drummond's poetry includes, in addition to
an informative introduction, excerpts from all his major publications, from
Some Poetry (1930) to *Passion Measured* (1980). The excellent translations
nearly always catch the elusive tones of Drummond's verse.

Costa, Emilia Viotti da. *The Brazilian Empire: Myths and Histories*. Rev. ed. Chapel
Hill: U of North Carolina P, 2000.
In this expanded version of the 1985 text, a new chapter deals with the situation of Brazilian women in the nineteenth century. In general, however, the orientation of this study is still on developing "a clear understanding of the
Brazilian elites from the beginning of the nineteenth century to the fall of the
empire in 1889" (xv).

Coutinho, Afrânio. *An Introduction to Literature in Brazil*. Trans. Gregory Rabassa.
New York: Columbia UP, 1969.
This useful introduction to Brazilian literature, as Rabassa notes in his preface,
organizes itself "according to stylistic movements rather than historical or ideological ones" (viii). Thus the work features such divisions as "From Baroque to
Rococo," "The Romantic Movement," "Realism, Naturalism, Parnassianism,"
and "Symbolism, Impressionism, Modernism." Coutinho does not minimize
the influences of history, theories, and social movements, but the book focuses
on the texts themselves (there are no plot summaries). An issue that informs the
study is the need to elucidate what is authentic in Brazil's literary culture.

Cunha, Euclides da. *Rebellion in the Backlands*. Trans. Samuel Putnam. Chicago: U
of Chicago P, 1967.
The dramatic study of a violent and bloody ten-month rebellion waged, from
December 1896 to October 1897 by a band of impoverished northeastern

peasants against the military might of the newly formed Brazilian republic, this classic of Brazilian literature, which, in terms of its being a searing portrait of the abandonment and abuse of the weak and poor by the strong and wealthy, recalls Agee and Walker's *Let Us Now Praise Famous Men*, is required reading for anyone who truly wishes to understand twentieth century Brazilian literature, music, and film.

DaMatta, Roberto. *Carnivals, Rogues, and Heroes: An Interpretation of the Brazilian Dilemma*. Trans. John Drury. Notre Dame: U of Notre Dame P, 1991.

The author, an anthropologist, focuses on "the perennial anti-democratic (and anti-egalitarian) Brazilian elitism that is characterized by an arrogant style of dealing with social and political differences. From this perspective, this text is a political denunciation of a set of social practices that nobody takes seriously in Brazil but that I am convinced are at the heart of the Brazilian power structure" (xi). In an intriguing chapter of ("Carnival in Rio and Mardi Gras in New Orleans: A Contrastive Study"), DaMatta examines similarities and differences between the two festivals.

Daniel, Mary L. "Brazilian Fiction from 1800 to 1855." González Echevarría and Pupo-Walker 3: 127–56.

———. "Brazilian Fiction from 1900 to 1945." González Echevarría and Pupo-Walker 3: 157–87.

These essays offer excellent coverage and concise commentaries. The second covers the major narrativists of the first half of the twentieth century.

DiAntonio, Robert E. *Brazilian Fiction: Aspects and Evolution of the Contemporary Narrative*. Fayetteville: U of Arkansas P, 1989.

Focusing on their aesthetic and political dimensions, DiAntonio offers interpretations of major works by some of the country's most important writers: Ivan Ângelo, Clarice Lispector, João Ubaldo Ribeiro, Darcy Ribeiro, Márcio Sousa, Moacyr Scliar, Ignácio de Loyola Brandão, and Murilo Rubião.

Dixon, Paul B. *Retired Dreams:* Dom Casmurro, *Myth and Modernity*. West Lafayette: Purdue UP, 1989.

Challenging the notion that Machado de Assis should be considered a realist, Dixon argues that, after 1880, Machado became more concerned with epistemology and ontology than with the description of life. He apparently began to see the inherent ambiguity of life, our inability to know with complete certainty what happens or what it means.

Donoso, José. *The Boom in Spanish American Literature: A Personal History*. Trans. Gregory Kolovakos. New York: Columbia UP, 1977.

Drimmer, Frederick, ed. *Captured by the Indians: Fifteen Firsthand Accounts, 1750–1870*. New York: Dover, 1961.

While Drimmer does not refer to Spanish American or Brazilian literature in his discussion of captivity narratives, his comments on this form in the early lit-

erature of the United States facilitate comparisons with similar works in colonial Latin America.

Eakin, Marshall C. *Brazil: The Once and Future Country*. New York: St. Martin's,
1997.

An excellent history that does not minimize cultural and intellectual factors,
this concise work provides a clear vision of modern Brazil, as a nation and as a
highly diverse culture. By explaining the points of contact that have long existed between Brazil and the United States, Eakin encourages further comparative thinking about the two hemispheric giants.

Edinger, Catarina Feldmann. "Hawthorne and Alencar Romancing the Marble."
Brasil/Brazil 4.3 (1990): 69–84.

In this engaging article, Edinger compares Aurélia, the protagonist of Alencar's
Senhora, with Zenobia, of Hawthorne's *The Blithedale Romance*. While both
Alencar and Hawthorne endow their characters with grace, beauty, and social
position, they create in them an unresolvable conflict, between reason and
emotion, that causes them to become, psychologically, like marble statues. As
Edinger observes, though, Hawthorne feels compelled to have Zenobia die,
but Alencar allows Aurélia to resolve her dilemma.

———. Introduction. *Senhora*. By José de Alencar. Trans. Edinger. Austin: U of
Texas P, 1994. ix–xviii.

Edinger gives an overview of the salient aspects of Alencar's *Senhora* (1875), an
early milestone in the development of the Brazilian novel. In *Senhora*, one of
Alencar's several "feminine portraits," the writer examines the place of women
in mid-nineteenth-century Brazil. "A romantic influenced by Balzac's realism,"
Alencar "developed a Brazilian consciousness" by "following French revolutionary models" (xi).

———. "Machismo and Androgyny in Mid-Nineteenth-Century Brazilian and
American Novels." *Comparative Literature Studies* 27.2 (1990): 124–39.

Edinger examines how mid-nineteenth-century novelists (Cooper, Hawthorne,
and Alencar) create female characters and how these women function in their
societies, in relation to men and to the power structure. Discussing the
machismo often associated with Latin American literature, Edinger writes,
"Not only do the feminine protagonists of these Brazilian novels [by Alencar]
come across as self-reliant and assertive, but the relationship between men and
women developed in the plots reveals purposes and sensibilities quite different
from the ones portrayed by Cooper, Hawthorne, or Melville." Moreover, "con-
trary to the usual point of view, it seems that, much more than the Latin males
who wrote or appeared in Brazilian literature in the mid-1800s, it is the Natty
Bumppos, the Ahabs, and even the Chillingsworths and Dimmesdales of
American literature who deserve the negative label of 'macho men.'" Finally,

seeking to clarify "a basic difference between the literatures of Brazil and the United States in the middle of the nineteenth century," Edinger writes that "the Brazilian literature of the time does not present as clear a division between popular and 'serious' literature as does the American" (124–25).

Elliott, Emory, gen. ed. *Columbia Literary History of the United States.* New York: Columbia UP, 1988.

Although this study focuses on the literature of the United States, it occasionally refers to such Spanish American figures as the Mexican philosopher Edmundo O'Gorman (who argued that America had to be "invented" immediately after its "discovery" [16]), Columbus, Cortés, Borges, and Álvar Núñez Cabeza de Vaca. Brazil is not mentioned, although the cultural context for its inclusion in a future edition is created.

———. "Poetry" (from the section "New England Puritan Literature"). Bercovitch, *Cambridge History* 1: 226–54.

Citing Anne Bradstreet, Michael Wigglesworth, and Edward Taylor as the most productive Puritan poets, Elliott discusses the forms that New England Puritan poetry took as well as its essential characteristics.

Ellison, Fred P. *Brazil's New Novel: Four Northeastern Masters: José Lins do Rego, Jorge Amado, Graciliano Ramos and Rachel de Queiroz.* Berkeley: U of California P, 1954.

Not to be confused with the French *nouveau roman* of the 1950s, Brazil's "new novel" is the socially aware fiction of the second-generation modernist movement. Appearing during the 1930s, these works, as Ellison shows, changed the novel's course of development in Brazil. Of particular interest are Ramos, one of the masters of Brazilian narrative, and Amado, the internationally acclaimed author who is bitterly challenged in Brazil for allegedly romanticizing poverty and for exploiting stereotypes of blacks and women. Ellison's study, which appeared before Amado became a controversial figure, analyzes the works of the early, more *engagé* (if less technically sophisticated) writer. Ellison's book is a must-read on the modern Brazilian novel, particularly that of the 1930s.

Federman, Raymond. "Self-Reflexive Fiction." Elliott, *Columbia Literary History* 1142–57.

Self-reflexive fiction has been a staple of Brazilian narrative since Machado de Assis, and although Federman examines writing in the United States in the 1960s and 1970s, his comments reveal many points of comparison between Brazilian and United States fiction in the postwar period (the nature of "new narrative" in the Americas, for example). Federman's discussion of the relevance of Sterne's *Tristram Shandy* to United States fiction in the 1960s might facilitate a comparison between that link and the influence of Sterne's novel on Machado and his post-1880 work.

Ferguson, Robert A. "The American Enlightenment, 1750–1820" and "What Is Enlightenment? Some American Answers." Bercovitch, *Cambridge History* 1:
345–46 and 368–89.

Ferguson's comments, while restricted to the United States, highlight the similarities and differences, in the literatures they produced in the late eighteenth
and early nineteenth centuries, between that country and Brazil.

Fisher, Philip. "Mark Twain." Elliott, *Columbia Literary History* 627–44.

Although Fisher's commentary on Twain makes no mention of Brazilian literature, it provides insight into Twain's art that apply to Brazilian literature of the
same period, especially to the work of Machado de Assis, with whom Twain can
be productively compared.

Fitz, Earl E. *Clarice Lispector*. Boston: Hall, 1985.

Covering all aspects of her output, this study emphasizes Lispector's importance as a Brazilian writer and her place in world literature; at the same time, it
explicates the unique stylistic and thematic qualities of her writing. It also provides a solid bibliography (up to 1985) of critical studies of her work.

———. "Clarice Lispector and the Lyrical Novel: A Re-examination of *A maçã no
escuro*." *Luso-Brazilian Review* 14.2 (1977): 153–60.

The article examines Lispector's mid-career novel from the perspective of Ralph
Freedman's definition of the lyrical novel and finds it prototypical of the genre.

———. "Faulkner, Agee, and Brazil: The American South in Latin America's Other
Tradition." *Look Away*. Ed. Deborah Cohn and Jon Smith. Durham: Duke
UP, forthcoming.

The argument made in the first part of the essay is that, because of the liberating influence of Machado de Assis (and his legacy of innovation and experimentation), Brazilian narrative in the 1930s and 1940s did not need Faulkner's
transforming presence as much as Spanish American fiction did. In the second
part, Fitz compares and contrasts Agee's *Let Us Now Praise Famous Men* and da
Cunha's *Rebellion in the Backlands*.

———. "The First Inter-American Novels: Some Choices and Some Comments."
Comparative Literature Studies 22.2 (1985): 361–76.

The essay considers the texts—from English and French Canada, the United
States, Spanish America, and Brazil—that are most often cited as the "first
novel" of their New World culture. The study establishes a basis for comparing
the rise of the New World novel and for evaluating its emergence vis-à-vis the
European (and American) traditions that were affecting its development.

———. "From Blood to Culture: Miscegenation as Metaphor for the Americas."
Mixing Race, Mixing Culture: Inter-American Literary Discourses. Ed. Monika
Kaup and Debra J. Rosenthal. Austin: U of Texas P, 2002. 243–72.

In addition to arguing that miscegenation typifies the New World experience,
and that racial blending has moved out of the realm of the biological and into

the cultural, the author notes the prohibitions on and prejudices against inter-racial unions that still exist in the United States.

―――. "The Influence of Machado de Assis on John Barth's *The Floating Opera*." *Comparatist* 10 (1986): 56–66.

The author explicates the ways in which Machado's three most famous novels (which Barth, struggling to complete his first novel, read in English transla-tion)—*Epitaph of a Small Winner, Philosopher or Dog?*, and *Dom Casmurro*—influenced the final version of *The Floating Opera*. The theme of nihilism, as it applies to Barth's work, is examined in the light of its relevance to the work of Machado. Fitz, aware of Machado's influence, also looks at Barth's main char-acters and their relationships with each other.

―――. *Inter-American Literature and Criticism: An Electronic Annotated Bibliogra-phy*. Iowa City: U of Iowa, 1998.

Accessed free of charge through the U of Iowa P Web site (www.uiowa.edu/~uipress/interamerican), this work has two parts: part 1 lists works of literature that involve more than one New World literary culture, including the Native American; part 2 focuses on critical works (books, book chapters, reviews, and articles) dealing with inter-American issues or demonstrating an inter-American frame of reference. Several Brazil–United States studies, on a variety of subjects, are listed, as are sources comparing Brazilian literature with other hemispheric and world literatures.

―――. "John Barth's Brazilian Connection." *New World* 2.1–2 (1987): 123–38.

Fitz offers an extensive discussion of the influence Machado de Assis and his three major novels had on Barth as he was completing his first novel, *The Float-ing Opera*. Issues of style, structure, and theme are explored, as are the areas of influence exerted by each Machado novel.

―――. *Machado de Assis*. Boston: Hall, 1989.

This introductory text discusses all of Machado's work, his famous novels and short stories as well as his lesser-known plays, poetry, and nonfiction. It evalu-ates Machado in the context of world literature. The author considers Machado essentially a modernist, who sought to escape from the confines of realism and to invent a "new narrative," replete with a "new reader" and a new way of think-ing about fiction and its relation to language and reality.

―――. "Metafiction in Latin American Narrative: The Case for Brazil; or, If Brás Cubas Were Here Today, What Would He Say about Spanish American Fiction?" *Mester* 26 (1997): 43–69.

Focusing on novels by Machado, the author argues that the Brazilian narrative tradition is "significantly different, in its development, from its better-known Spanish American cousin" and that "this difference is largely an issue of a partic-ular kind of self-consciousness, the kind that contemplates not only the process by which a text comes into being but its relationship to reality and to truth" (43).

————. *Rediscovering the New World: Inter-American Literature in a Comparative Context.* Iowa City: U of Iowa P, 1991.

This book demonstrates some possibilities for scholars engaged in inter-American literature, a fast-growing field that compares and contrasts the literary development of North, Central, and South America. Integral to this enterprise is the presence of Brazilian literature, by itself and in relation to the other literatures of the American, or New World, experience. Chapter 5, for example, discusses Henry James and Machado de Assis.

————. *Sexuality and Being in the Poststructuralist Universe of Clarice Lispector: The Différance of Desire.* Austin: U of Texas P, 2001.

Arguing that Lispector's narratives epitomize poststructural thought and that sexuality functions, in her best work, as the most humanizing marker of poststructuralism, the author examines Lispector's work in the light of such thinkers as Derrida, Lacan, and Kristeva.

————. "The Theory and Practice of Inter-American Literature: A Historical Overview." *Beyond the Ideal: Pan-Americanism in Inter-American Affairs.* Ed. David Sheinin. Westport: Praeger, 2000. 153–65.

This work, which summarizes the development of inter-American study in the twentieth century, proposes solutions to the methodological problems it faces and speculates on its future as a discipline.

————. "The Vox Populi of John Steinbeck and Jorge Amado." *Jorge Amado: New Critical Essays.* Ed. Keith Brower, Earl E. Fitz, and Enrique Martínez-Vidal. New York: Routledge, 2001. 111–23.

This essay, in a collection that discusses the work of Amado, concentrates on the development of the American and the Brazilian writers in the 1930s and 1940s. It compares and contrasts them as politically conscious novelists who achieve their greatest successes by chronicling, and giving voice to, common people struggling to survive.

Fitzgerald, F. Scott. *The Great Gatsby.* New York: Scribner, 1953.

In addition to questioning the materialism and greed that define the American dream, Fitzgerald's novel illustrates the extent to which theories of racial superiority had infected the United States, as they had Brazil.

Foerster, Norman, Norman S. Grabo, Russel B. Nye, E. Fred Carlisle, and Robert Falk, eds. *American Poetry and Prose,* 5th ed. Boston: Houghton, 1970.

This work, offering a historical and a critical survey of the development of American literature, features a comparative perspective that both facilitates the study of American literature in its diversity and promotes an examination of the literary histories of America's hemispheric neighbors.

Freyre, Gilberto. *The Masters and the Slaves: A Study in the Development of Brazilian Civilization.* Trans. Samuel Putnam. New York: Knopf, 1971.

Although Freyre's arguments have recently been attacked by a number of Brazilian intellectuals, his work should still be required reading for anyone seeking to understand the complex social, political, and economic institutions that make up Brazilian culture and civilization. The importance of miscegenation, for example, is central to Freyre's theories, as are his comparisons between Brazil's development and that of the United States and Europe.

Fukuyama, Francis. "The Great Disruption: Human Nature and the Reconstitution of Social Order." *Atlantic Monthly* May 1999: 55–80.

In discussing the "shared cultural values" that liberal democracies have long depended on, Fukuyama sets up a contrast between the cultural and political histories of the United States and Latin America (58–59). Arguing that "the disruption of social order by the progress of technology is not a new phenomenon," Fukuyama concludes that "our only hope [for a restructuring, or "renorming," of society and its values] is the very powerful innate human capacity for reconstituting the social order. On the success of this process of reconstruction depends the upward direction of the arrow of History" (56, 80).

Furtado, Celso. *Accumulation and Development: The Logic of Industrial Civilization.* Trans. Suzette Macedo. New York: St. Martin's, 1983.

The author asserts that "industrial civilization is the outcome of the convergence of two processes of cultural creativity: the bourgeois and the scientific revolutions" (1). The book explains how Brazil fits into this convergence and, indirectly, how its economic development compares with that of the United States.

Gallagher, D. P. *Modern Latin American Literature.* Oxford: Oxford UP, 1973.

While Gallagher uses the term *Latin American* to refer almost exclusively to Spanish American authors, he mentions a few Brazilians, including Machado de Assis (1, 5), Antônio Callado (4), and Guimarães Rosa (87–88). Indeed, his belief that Machado alone among nineteenth-century Latin American novelists is not derivative and immature is significant, as is his contention that Machado's novels were "like their counterparts in the twentieth century" imbued with a "farsic sense of 'waste'" (5).

Garcia, Frederick C. H. "Richard Francis Burton and Basílio da Gama: The Translator and the Poet." *Luso-Brazilian Review* 13 1 (1975): 34–57.

Garcia discusses the reasons behind Burton's interest in da Gama's epic—*O Uruguai*, as is clear from its famous notes, is antipathetic toward the Jesuits—and offers an insightful critique of Burton's translation (a first draft of *The Uruguay* was probably completed by April 1867, during Burton's sojourn in Brazil).

George, David. *The Modern Brazilian Stage.* Austin: U of Texas P, 1992.

Adopting a "performance-centered" approach and focusing on the companies that staged them as well as on the productions themselves, George examines the plays that have signaled the development of Brazilian theater since the 1940s. Although the methodology is not comparative, the text clarifies the importance of foreign authors and texts to the evolution of Brazilian theater.

Gill, Anne. "*Dom Casmurro* and *Lolita*: Machado among the Metafictionists." *Luso-Brazilian Review* 24.1 (1987): 17–26.

Gill examines the narrative self-consciousness and irony employed by Machado and Nabokov in these two memorable novels. She finds Machado to be "far more subtle" in his effect on readers' reception of the story and participation in the construction of the text's meaning.

Gledson, John. "Brazilian Prose from 1940 to 1980." González Echevarría and Pupo-Walker 3: 189–206.

Surveying Brazilian fiction in the postwar era, Gledson discusses three dominant elements: the 1964 military coup and the ensuing repression and censorship; the influence (in both the novel and the short story) of Guimarães Rosa—in particular, of *The Devil to Pay in the Backlands* and the "equally experimental" series of long stories, *Corpo do baile* [*Ballet Corps*] (both in 1956); and the growth of a serious reading public. Gledson asserts that "real, constructive change" in modern Brazilian literature "seems to have concentrated in two decades, the 1950s and the period from about 1975 (when censorship began to be lifted) to around 1985." The heyday of Brazilian literature contrasts with that of Spanish America, "where the 1960s were so crucial," a condition Gledson attributes to "political events and their tragic repercussions" (191).

———. *The Deceptive Realism of Machado de Assis: A Dissenting Interpretation of* Dom Casmurro. Liverpool: Liverpool Monographs in Hispanic Studies, 1984.

Taking exception to the view of the post-1881 Machado as an antimimetic modernist, Gledson argues that the Brazilian narrativist is essentially a realist, whose numerous technical innovations mask a coherent and critical vision of Brazilian society.

Goldberg, Isaac. *Brazilian Literature*. New York: Knopf, 1922.

In what is likely the first book-length study of Brazilian literature to appear in the United States, Goldberg seeks to educate other Americans about the literature and culture of Brazil. Published in the centenary of Brazil's independence, *Brazilian Literature* relates Brazilian writers and themes to the North American experience, a strategy that is a precursor to Putnam's more systematic comparison in *Marvelous Journey* (1948). After outlining the development of Brazilian literature, Goldberg devotes the remaining text to "representative" Brazilian writers: Castro Alves, Machado de Assis, José Veríssimo, Olavo Bilac, Euclides da Cunha, Oliveira Lima, Graça Aranha, Coelho Neto, Francisca Júlia, and Monteiro Lobato.

González Echevarría, Roberto. "Latin American and Comparative Literatures." *Poetics of the Americas: Race, Founding, and Textuality.* Ed. Bainard Cowan and Jefferson Humphries. Baton Rouge: Louisiana State UP, 1997. 47–62.

Latin American literature can, the author believes, create "a new, redefined comparative literature" that should enable the discipline to break away from a culturally arrogant Eurocentrism that, in his opinion, has stunted the growth of comparative studies (48, 47).

———, ed. *The Oxford Book of Latin American Short Stories,* New York: Oxford UP, 1999.

The editor, a renowned critic of Latin American literature, offers in his preface a concise summary of the development of the short story in Spanish America and Brazil (where it enjoys its status as a narrative form of great range, adaptability, and creativity).

González Echevarría, Roberto, and Enrique Pupo-Walker, eds. *The Cambridge History of Latin American Literature.* Brazilian Literature and Bibliographies. 3 vols. Cambridge: Cambridge UP, 1996.

Volume 1, although it focuses on Spanish American literature from its indigenous past through the nineteenth century, provides a basis from which to undertake solid comparative studies between Brazilian and Spanish American literature and their respective formations (an example is Antonio Benítez-Rojo's study of the nineteenth-century Spanish American novel in which he mentions Machado de Assis as a Latin American novelist of the period who, unlike his peers, possessed a profound understanding of the novel genre and how it might be further developed [434]). The essays in volume 2 deal with Brazilian literature from its inception to the present. The contributors point out, if not develop in depth, the many connections, differences, and parallels between Brazilian literature and other literatures of the world. Of Brazil's cultural identity, the editors write that "there is no doubt that Brazilian literature is a national literature as original and self-contained as French, Italian, or Spanish literature; its ties to a broader Latin American literature, however, are strong, if fluid and ever-changing over time" (3: xiii). All genres are covered (historiography, novel, short story, poetry, drama, popular literature, literary criticism, and the essay), and the final essay offers an interesting comparative study of Brazilian and Spanish American literature. Throughout, the varied relations between Brazilian literature and both European and North American literature are discussed.

Graham, Richard, ed. *Machado de Assis: Reflections on a Brazilian Master Writer.* Austin: U of Texas P, 1999.

This slim volume, consisting of essays by experienced scholars, is an excellent introduction to the controversy regarding Machado de Assis: How should he

be read—as a realist? as an antirealist or even a (post)modernist? or in some
other fashion? Machado's reception in English is also examined, as are some
existing English translations.

Greenblatt, Stephen. "Racial Memory and Literary History." *PMLA* 116 (2001):
48–63.

Greenblatt, concerned with the globalization of literature, proposes a new kind
of literary history. It rejects outmoded notions of literature as a force for national unity and calls for more of what he terms the boundary-effacing "cultural *métissage*" that characterizes our time (59).

Greene, Roland. *Unrequited Conquests: Love and Empire in the Colonial Americas.*
Chicago: U of Chicago P, 1999.

In his chapter on Brazil, "For the Love of Pau-Brazil: Objectification in Colonial Brazil," Greene argues that "Vaz de Caminha's direct and unique voice"
"bequeathed us the history of a colonial enterprise that is seen as corporate and
impersonal." He also asserts that "if Columbus is the first person of conquest,
then Brazil, which was discovered on 22 April 1500 during an expedition to India led by Cabral, is its quintessential object" (80).

Haberly, David T. "The Brazilian Novel from 1850 to 1900." González Echevarría
and Pupo-Walker 3: 137–56.

This readable essay examines the origins of the Brazilian novel and its development up to 1900 and the time of Machado.

———. "Colonial Brazilian Literature." González Echevarría and Pupo-Walker 3:
47–68.

Stressing the numerous foreign influences that were affecting its development,
Haberly discusses the evolution of colonial letters in Brazil, up to the late eighteenth century.

———. *Three Sad Races: Racial Identity and National Consciousness in Brazilian Literature.* Cambridge: Cambridge UP, 1983.

Featuring fine essays on Alencar and Machado de Assis, among others, this useful work examines the role of race in the formation of a national consciousness
in Brazilian literature. *Three Sad Races* is essential reading for anyone interested
in the application, to the literature of the United States, of Haberly's approach.

The Harper American Literature. Ed. Donald McQuade, Robert Atwan, Martha
Banta, Justin Kaplan, David Minter, Cecilia Tichi, and Helen Vendler.
Vols. 1 and 2. New York: Harper, 1987.

By including selections from such non-English authors as Christopher Columbus, Giovanni da Verrazzano, Alvar Núñez Cabeza de Vaca, and Samuel de
Champlain and by featuring examples of Native American literature and commentary, this anthology reflects the diversity of American literature. *The
Harper American Literature* thus facilitates inter-American literary study. More-

over, it provides a historical framework within which to situate the development of Brazilian literature and culture.

Heyck, Denis. "Coutinho, the 'Nova Crítica' and Portugal." *Hispania* 64.4 (1981): 564–69.

This article charts the conversion of Afrânio Coutinho from an admirer to a critic of Portuguese literature and its influence on Brazilian letters. It also discusses Coutinho's discovery of the principles of the New Criticism and how they might be applied to Brazilian literature.

Hoffman, George. "Anatomy of the Mass: Montaigne's 'Cannibals.'" *PMLA* 117 (2002): 207–21.

Framing his argument in the reception of the Mass by Native American people and in the context of the religious polemic between Protestantism and Catholicism, Hoffman examines how, near the end of "Cannibals," Montaigne "finally discloses his direct contact with three Brazilian natives in order that the reader may hear them share their views on Renaissance France" and how, with a comment on their dress (or lack thereof), he "seems to anticipate the sarcasm of Swift in returning to a European perspective only to parody its parochial views on natives' nudity" (207).

Hulet, Claude L. *Brazilian Literature.* 3 vols. Washington: Georgetown UP, 1974.

This work provides useful critical introductions to the periods of literary development and to their impact on the intellectual and artistic evolution of Brazilian letters, as well as to each author considered. The selections themselves, however, and the bibliographies are in Portuguese.

Hutcheon, Linda. *A Poetics of Postmodernism: History, Theory, Fiction.* New York: Routledge, 1988.

Offering both an analysis of and a critical commentary on postmodernism, Hutcheon discusses, in addition to representative North American and European writers, such Spanish American authors as Jorge Luis Borges, Gabriel García Márquez, Julio Cortázar, and Carlos Fuentes.

Jackson, Elizabeth, and K. David Jackson. Translators' Preface. *Industrial Park: A Proletarian Novel.* By Patrícia Galvão (Pagu). Lincoln: U of Nebraska P, 1993. vii–xi.

In this informative preface, the Jacksons outline the author's importance in modern Brazilian literature, especially in Brazil's politically charged modernist revolution of the 1920s and 1930s. They also discuss the main themes and stylistic traits of this unusual novel.

Jackson, K. David. "The Brazilian Short Story." González Echevarría and Pupo-Walker 3: 207–32.

In this concise, perceptive discussion of the genre, Jackson traces the history of the short story in Brazil, from its origins to its late-twentieth-century practitioners. He notes its distinctive periods of development, its illustrious authors, and the foreign and domestic influences that have shaped it.

―――. "Madness in a Tropical Manner." *New York Times Book Review* 22 Feb. 1998: 14–15.

In reviewing new translations of two of Machado's greatest novels, *The Posthumous Memoirs of Brás Cubas* (trans. Gregory Rabassa) and *Dom Casmurro* (trans. John Gledson), Jackson makes cogent observations about Machado's history in English translation, other translations of Machado's work—including the "infamous 1992 British translation, 'Dom Casmurro, Lord Taciturn,'" (15)—his style, and his celebrated stories, most of which have never appeared in English translation.

Jackson, K. David, and Yvette E. Miller. "Introduction: The International Context of Brazilian Literature." *Brazilian Literature.* Spec. issue of *Latin American Literary Review* 14.27 (1986): 7–8.

This issue, according to its editors, "seeks to place Brazilian literature in the international context of comparative literature, both in the sense of comparing Brazilian writers with those of other literatures and also through considering their participation in the broad thematic and stylistic currents of modern literature." Among the aspects of Brazilian culture discussed is anthropophagy. It has served "as a paradigm for the craft of literary composition in Brazil," in which "the rich fabric of ethnography, music, folklore, history, and language, to mention a few examples, has been exploited to create a synthetic focus for a national literature." The editors contend, as well, that "Brazilian writing is unique in the Americas for its background in Portuguese, African, and Asian contacts and for the individual and experimental translation of these traditions into works marked by imagination and vitality" (7).

Jackson, Richard. "Remembering the 'Disremembered': Modern Black Writers and Slavery in Latin America." *Callaloo* 13.1 (1990): 131–44.

In this study Jackson notes that "the search for the intimate history of the black slave is especially evident in . . . the Brazil-oriented literature of Gayl Jones, the black American author who is a specialist on Brazilian slavery, and in Toni Morrison's new novel, *Beloved*, which the 1987 Pulitzer Prize winner researched, in part, in Brazil." Although Morrison does not write about Brazilian slavery, "the Brazilian documents she used helped give her the perspective necessary to get inside the slave's mind" and to understand better "the difficulty of living black slaves faced everywhere" (132–33, 140).

Jay, Gregory. "The End of 'American' Literature: Toward a Multicultural Practice." *College English* 53 (1991): 264–81.

Examining only the literature of the United States, Jay calls for a revision of what has long been thought of as American literature and of American studies. "Our goal," he writes, should be "to construct a multicultural and dialogical paradigm for the study of writing in the United States," a paradigm that pays more attention to its Hispanic, Native American, and Chicano components. Jay is also concerned that a "Comparative American Literature" initiative might simply "end up repeating the history of colonial imperialism" (264, 268). Despite his use of the term *Latin America*, Jay discusses only Spanish American texts and authors; Brazil is not mentioned.

Jay, Paul. "Beyond Discipline? Globalization and the Future of English." *PMLA* 116 (2001): 32–47.

Although he does not discuss inter-American literature per se, Jay notes—in the context of changes sweeping English departments—the value of a less narrowly nationalistic approach to the concept of America and to American literature.

———. "The Myth of 'America' and the Politics of Location: Modernity, Border Studies, and the Literature of the Americas." *Arizona Quarterly* 54 (1998): 165–92.

Using the issue of border studies as his prime mover, Jay advocates a "reshaping" of American literature and of American studies. He is also concerned about the size and scope of the inter-American project and wonders how scholars might deal effectively with the tangle of "*historical* relations" that bind the Americas together (171, 172). The author uses the term *Latin America* to refer only to Spanish America; no mention is made of Brazil.

Jehlen, Myra. "Three Writers of Early America." Bercovitch, *Cambridge History* 1: 59–83.

Although she discusses the literature of the early United States partly in terms of Spanish American counterparts (e.g., the stories of Pocahontas and La Malinche), Jehlen draws no parallels with texts from early Brazilian literature.

Jesus, Carolina Maria de. *Child of the Dark: The Diary of Carolina Maria de Jesus.* Trans. David St. Clair. New York: Dutton, 1962.

One of the first Brazilian books to have a significant impact in the United States in the early 1960s, when a surge of interest in Brazil began to be felt, *Child of the Dark* (an intriguing read in conjunction with the film *Black Orpheus*) chronicles the struggle for survival of a poor black woman living in a *favela*, or slum.

Johnson, Randal. "Cinema Novo and Cannibalism: *Macunaíma*." Johnson and Stam 178–90.

Johnson offers a perceptive, meticulous comparison of Mário de Andrade's famous 1928 narrative (which he called not a novel but a *rhapsode*) and Joaquim Pedro de Andrade's equally famous 1969 film version, "released in the United States with the inane title, 'Jungle Freaks'" (178).

———. *Cinema Novo x 5: Masters of Contemporary Brazilian Film.* Austin: U of Texas P, 1984.

This study focuses less on *cinema novo* itself (which Johnson terms "the most important phenomenon in the history of Brazilian cinema" [xi]) than on five influential directors: Joaquim Pedro de Andrade, Carlos Diegues, Ruy Guerra, Glauber Rocha, and Nelson Pereira dos Santos.

———. *The Film Industry in Brazil: Culture and the State.* Pittsburgh: U of Pittsburgh P, 1987.

Providing an excellent historical summary of Brazilian cinema, from the late nineteenth century to the mid-1980s, Johnson discusses the complex relation between the Brazilian state and its cultural production.

———. "Literature, Film and Politics in Brazil: Reflections on the Generation of 1968." *Tropical Paths: Essays on Modern Brazilian Literature.* Ed. Johnson. New York: Garland, 1993. 183–98.

Focusing on Renato Tapajós's novel *Em câmara lenta* (1977) and Márcio Souza's *Operação silêncio* (1979), Johnson discusses the many films and narratives of the "mid-to-late 1970s"—the period of the *abertura*, or "opening," when redemocratization began—that depict the political events of the time. "Both works," writes Johnson, "are testimonies of the failure to 'realizar a transformação' ["realize the transformation"] through armed struggle against a repressive, authoritarian regime" (197).

———. "Tupy or Not Tupy: Cannibalism and Nationalism in Contemporary Brazilian Literature and Culture." *On Modern Latin American Fiction.* Ed. John King. New York: Hill and Wang, 1987.

According to Johnson, "in Oswald de Andrade, cannibalism becomes the underlying force of all social relationships. It is a new paradigm that expresses, in allegorical terms, the revolt of the colonized against the colonizer," and its goal is to ingest and consume the colonizing forces and create something new and unique while not being subsumed in the process. In Johnson's view, "the favoured weapons in this metaphorical deglutition" are "corrosive humour, irreverence, parody, and sarcasm" (50–51).

Johnson, Randal, and Robert Stam, eds. *Brazilian Cinema.* East Brunswick: Assoc. UP, 1982.

The standard text in its field, *Brazilian Cinema* has four parts: "The Shape of Brazilian Film History," "The Theory of Brazilian Cinema: The Filmmakers Speak," "Cinema Novo and Beyond: The Films," and "Special Topics and Polemics." Although part 1 offers a concise discussion of the history of Brazilian cinema, the book as a whole concentrates on the *cinema novo* of the 1960s. Part 4 contains an essay on Brazilian women filmmakers (Elice Munerato and Maria Helena Darcy de Oliveira) and one on Hollywood's view of Brazil.

Jones, Malcolm. "Troubadour with a Twist." *Newsweek* 12 July 1999: 67.

Jones discusses Caetano Veloso's music (including his history as a *Tropicalista*) and the artists whom contemporary Brazilian music has influenced. Veloso explains the popularity of Brazilian music by contrasting the "cooler," "softer," and "more nuanced" sounds of Brazilian Portuguese with the harsher sounds of Spanish.

Kinder, Marsha. "*Tent of Miracles.*" *Brazilian Cinema.* Ed. Randal Johnson and Robert Stam. Enlarged ed. New York: Columbia UP, 1995. 225–33.

Arguing that this celebrated film focuses primarily on "racial issues" and issues of "sexual politics" (225), Kinder also finds that though initially portrayed in conventional terms, as "objects of satire and ridicule," the female characters "turn out to be more progressive than those of the men around them in the same class or condition" (230).

Klobucka, Anna. "Hélène Cixous and the Hour of Clarice Lispector." *SubStance: A Review of Theory and Literary Criticism* 23.1 (1994): 41–62.

Undertaking a rigorous examination of Cixous's response to Lispector, of the influence the Brazilian writer has had on Cixous's work, and of Cixous's promotion of Lispector worldwide, Klobucka concludes that Cixous reads Lispector in ways that obscure some of the most transgressive aspects of the Brazilian's work.

Landers, Clifford E. "Translating and Transnationalizing Brazilian Literature and Culture." *Brasil/Brazil* 23.13 (2000): 55–67.

Landers, a translator of Brazilian fiction, laments the near-invisibility of Brazilian literature in the United States and then offers some explanations about why this situation has come about.

Landsman, Ned. *From Colonials to Provincials: American Thought and Culture, 1680–1760.* New York: Twayne, 1997.

Although Landsman focuses on the early development of the United States, he makes some observations that are useful to comparisons between colonial America and colonial Brazil—especially as the latter is differentiated from that cultural block known, in the United States, as "Latin America."

Lawall, Sarah, ed. *Reading World Literature: Theory, History, Practice.* Austin: U of Texas P, 1994.

Although the critical introductions and the essays in this book do not mention Brazil, they provide a useful theoretical context for integrating Brazilian literature into world literature. Lawall argues that a badly needed consciousness of world literature should help the cultures of the world undertake exchanges of information and viewpoints as a way to deal with disparities.

Lewalski, Barbara Keifer. "English Literature at the American Moment." Elliott, *Columbia Literary History* 24–32.

Lewalski's short, informative essay explains how the themes, forms, and concerns of early-seventeenth-century English literature shaped colonial literature in the United States in ways analogous to the mechanisms by which Iberian literature and politics influenced Brazilian letters of the period.

Lindstrom, Naomi. Foreword. *Iracema.* By José de Alencar. Trans. Clifford E. Landers. New York: Oxford UP, 2000. xi–xxiv.

In addition to offering a perceptive look at the novel's distinguishing features and a summary of its chapters, Lindstrom discusses the work in the context of both Brazilian and Spanish American literature of the period.

Loos, Dorothy. *The Naturalistic Novel of Brazil.* New York: Hispanic Inst., 1963.

Focusing on its most representative practitioners, this work is an excellent study of the naturalistic novel in Brazil. Loos also discusses the influence of Zola and the importance, to Brazilian culture and literature, of this genre.

Lowe, Elizabeth. *The City in Brazilian Literature.* Rutherford: Fairleigh Dickinson UP, Assoc. UP, 1982.

In this detailed, informative book, Lowe examines the impact of urbanization on Brazilian literature. Discussing the rural–urban dichotomy that has long framed the debate over national identity and cultural authenticity, Lowe also casts light on the dominant question of Brazilian history and culture: Should the country seek its identity through internationalization, or should it cultivate what is indigenous? The comparative approach used here is appealing, since it helps identify the connections Brazilian literature has with literatures of the rest of the world.

Mac Adam, Alfred J. *Modern Latin American Narratives: The Dreams of Reason.* Chicago: U of Chicago P, 1977.

In the sections on Machado, Mac Adam, focusing on genre, style, and content, argues that Machado's most famous extended narratives should be read not as novels but as satires.

———. *Textual Confrontations: Comparative Readings in Latin American Literature.* Chicago: U of Chicago P, 1987.

Although most of the discussions are on Spanish American literature, Mac Adam's perceptive comments about the Brazil writer Machado demonstrate the uniqueness of Machado's narratives and his importance to the evolution of the Latin American narrative.

Mann, Charles C. "1491." *Atlantic Monthly* Mar. 2002: 41–53.

Surveying new theories about the number of indigenous peoples living in the Americas before the arrival of Columbus and comparing recent theories by anthropologists, archaeologists, ecologists, historians, geographers, and others, Mann discusses the possibility that there were many more people in the Western Hemisphere than previously thought and that some of them (as in the Amazon region) were highly successful at "imposing their will on the landscape"—so much so, Mann says, that "in 1492 Columbus set foot in a hemisphere thoroughly dominated by humankind" (41).

Marx, Anthony W. *Making Race and Nation: A Comparison of the United States, South Africa, and Brazil.* Cambridge: Cambridge UP, 1998.

In analyzing the role of race in the United States and Brazil, Marx observes that while racial inequality has been more obvious in the former, it has been more hidden in the latter, because Brazilian racism is surreptitious. Marx notes that in the United States, gains in racial equality have come largely through sustained challenges in the courts, whereas Brazil has not turned to the legal system as much. The author also discusses the long-standing myth of Brazil as a racial paradise.

Marzorati, Gerald. "Tropicália, Agora!" *New York Times Magazine* 25 Apr. 1999: 48–51.

This article discusses how and why "Brazilian pop music suddenly finds itself the focus of America's late-1990s vanguard." It examines the influence that *tropicalista* music has had on such musicians and groups as David Byrne, Beck (Beck Hansen), Stereolab, Tortoise, and the High Llamas. Beck, Marzorati notes, even has a song called "Tropicalia" on an album that "borrows its weird noises and samba groove from a song by Os Mutantes (the Mutants), an arty São Paulo psychedelic band of the late 60's." Marzorati mentions "the ambivalence" the original *tropicalistas* felt "concerning Brazil's more and more Americanized, consumer-oriented culture" and the care they had to take with lyrics "about the constraints of living under a military dictatorship" (48).

McClendon, Carmen Chaves. "A Rose for Rosalina: From Yoknapatawpha to *Ópera dos mortos*." *Comparative Literature Studies* 19.4 (1982): 450–58.

Focusing on Faulkner's "A Rose for Emily" and Autran Dourado's novel *Ópera dos mortos* (1967), McClendon examines the numerous parallels between these two texts and suggests that "Dourado's 'bird' may have found its 'skeleton' in Yoknapatawpha County" (451).

McGowan, Chris, and Ricardo Pessanha. *The Brazilian Sound: Samba, Bossa Nova, and the Popular Music of Brazil.* Rev. ed. Philadelphia: Temple UP, 1998.

Offering a cogent historical summary of Brazilian music, from its multicultural origins to the present, this informative book, which includes photographs of musicians and translations of their works, shows why Brazilian music is as rich, varied, and vibrant as it is and why it is popular the world over.

McWilliams, John. "Poetry in the Early Republic." Elliott, *Columbia Literary History* 156–67.

McWilliams notes that, traditionally, few have found much that is "indigenously American" or "evocative rather than didactic" in the poetry of the revolutionary era. He casts light on a period of United States literature that provides a useful comparison with Brazilian colonial literature, which was developing a strong sense of nationalism.

Merquior, J. G. "The Brazilian and the Spanish American Literary Traditions: A Contrastive View." González Echevarría and Pupo-Walker 3: 363–82.

Beginning with the colonial era and working up to the present, this essay examines the many differences between Spanish American and Brazilian literature.

Miller, J. Hillis. Contribution. *Special Millennium Issue. PMLA* 115 (2000): 2062. Citing the need for curricular reform in language and literature, Miller mentions what he calls the "literature of the Americas" as an example of the "new regional, transnational, multicultural, multiethnic" program that will be needed in order to keep the humanities alive and relevant.

Moisés, Massaud. *A literatura brasileira atrevés dos textos.* 21st ed., rev. and augmented. São Paulo: Cultrix, 1999.

This venerable literary history is an excellent comparative context for studying the development of Brazilian literature. Its discussions of the defining literary periods are especially useful, as are Moisés's commentaries on the principal authors and texts.

Monegal, Emir Rodríguez. *Jorge Luis Borges: A Literary Biography.* New York: Dutton, 1978.

This comprehensive work, which stresses the often intimate connections between Borges's personal life and his writing, casts light on the genesis of some of Borges's most famous texts. Monegal, an authority on Brazilian and Spanish American literature, does not mention Brazilian writers, but the discussions of Faulkner's impact on Borges in the 1930s (and on Borges's subsequent rejection of realism in favor of "fantastic literature") indicate that Borges's shift occurred some fifty-five years after Machado de Assis's and the publication of *The Posthumous Memoirs of Brás Cubas* (1880–81).

———. "Writing Fiction under the Censor's Eye." *World Literature Today* 53.1 (1979): 19–22.

In this revealing article, Monegal shows how difficult it was for Brazilian writers under the dictatorship and how they learned to cope. Monegal discusses several works of this troubled period that, for a variety of reasons, stand out in the history of Brazilian narrative.

Monegal, Emir Rodríguez, assisted by Thomas Colchie, eds. *The Borzoi Anthology of Latin American Literature.* 2 vols. New York: Knopf, 1984.

This collection, the first to present Brazilian and Spanish American literature as an integrated, and authentic, Latin American cultural production, offers short but insightful introductions that contrast Brazilian literature with that of Spanish America and that point out the relation of both to European and North American works. The pieces that introduce each Brazilian author are especially useful.

Monteiro, George. "Faulkner in Brazil." *Southern Literary Journal* 13.1 (1983): 96–104.

This essay discusses Faulkner's six-day visit to Brazil in August 1954. A participant in the International Writers' Congress in São Paulo, Faulkner, whose visit was sponsored by the American State Department, was asked about the issue of race, in his novels and in the Americas generally. His response, surely of interest to Brazilians, was that, for him, "there are no races that are inferior or superior" and that "one of the preeminent problems on this continent is the problem of race" (99).

Moog, Vianna. *Bandeirantes and Pioneers.* Trans. L. l. Barrett. New York: Braziller, 1964.

Appearing in English translation in 1964, this influential work, written by a prominent Brazilian sociologist, ranks as one of the earliest efforts to compare the economic and political development of the United States and Brazil. Moog argues that the basic difference stems from North America's pioneers and Brazil's early settlers, the *bandeirantes,* who explored the interior of the country in search of gold, precious jewels, and slaves. Moog points out that while the pioneers believed in egalitarianism, social organization, and the communal good, the *bandeirantes* by and large did not. As Adolph A. Berle notes in his introduction, "The United States and Brazil are the two largest geo-political components of the Western hemisphere. What each thinks of the other may well determine the course of New World history. It is thus important that Americans should understand Brazil, and that Brazilians understand the United States. Brazilians know this" (9–10).

Morison, Samuel Eliot. *The Oxford History of the American People.* New York: Oxford UP, 1965.

In the preface, Morison declares that his "main ambition" in writing this work was "to re-create . . . American ways of living in bygone years" and to analyze how "basic American principles were established" (vii). To fulfill his goal, the author looks to other American nations and regions, such as the Indians, the Caribbean, Canada, and Latin America (including Brazil). The effect of this approach is to broaden the concept of "Americanness" to include an inter-American perspective, as Morison's volume does.

Morse, Richard. "Triangulating Two Cubists: William Carlos Williams and Oswald de Andrade." *Latin American Literary Review* 14. 27 (1986): 175–83.

Demonstrating how the American and the Brazilian authors utilize cubist techniques in their poetry, Morse argues that "Williams and Oswald were more radical than their fellow Modernists in stripping language of discursive, ready-made elements. . . . Yet," he says, "Both felt obliged to define, or *render,* the American scene and to abjure the cerebral imperatives of Modernism that led to *blague*" and both "began with the medium itself, language" (176).

Mulford, Carla, ed. *Teaching the Literatures of Early America.* New York: MLA, 1999.

Although not dealing with Brazil, this useful volume explains why the concept of "American" literature is expanding to include not only the literatures of the United States but also those of Canada and Spanish America.

Nagib, Lúcia, ed. *The New Brazilian Cinema.* London: Tauris, 2003.

Bringing together studies by film scholars and critics from Brazil, the United States, and the UK, this volume focuses on what it describes as the "remarkable renaissance of Brazilian Cinema, both feature length fictional films and documentary films" since 1994 (xv).

Nist, John. *The Modernist Movement in Brazil: A Literary Study.* Austin: U of Texas P, 1967.

In this respected study, Nist reviews the development of Brazilian modernism and then devotes chapters to its primary practitioners. He includes a useful bibliography.

Nunes, Benedito. "The Literary Historiography of Brazil." González Echevarría and Pupo-Walker 3: 11–46.

Arguing that "the ambiguous relationship between the Americas and Europe . . . disposed the countries of the Americas to the writing of their own history," Nunes explores how Brazilian identity, culturally and politically, is a function of Portuguese colonial society, the peculiarities of Brazilian Romanticism, and the development of a "national historiography" (11).

Nunes, Maria Luisa. *The Craft of an Absolute Winner: Characterization and Narratology in the Novels of Machado de Assis.* Westport: Greenwood, 1983.

This is a highly informative study of Machado de Assis, his early, "romantic" novels as well as his post-1880 efforts. These latter works are those for which he is most famous.

Oliveira Lima, Manoel de. *The Evolution of Brazil Compared with That of Spanish and Anglo-Saxon America.* Westport: Greenwood, 1975.

The 1914 edition was one of the earliest attempts to study the development of Brazil in relation to Spanish America and the United States. Although brief (it consists of twelve lectures delivered at Stanford University in 1912) and somewhat dated, this study highlights such fundamental issues as religion, political self-determination and independence, slavery, race relations, and miscegenation.

Page, Joseph A. *The Brazilians.* New York: Addison-Wesley, 1995.

An excellent overview of Brazil and its inhabitants, this readable book is divided into five sections: "Who Are the Brazilians?", "The Pyramid of Power in Brazil," "The Curse of Violence in Brazil," "Spiritual Brazil," and "In Search of What Makes Brazilians Brazilians."

Parker, John M. "Maria Alice Barroso." *A Dictionary of Contemporary Brazilian Authors.* Comp. David William Foster and Roberto Reis. Tempe: Center for Latin American Studies, Arizona State U, 1981. 14–15.

In discussing Faulkner's influence on Barroso, Parker writes that the novel *Um simples afeto recíproco* (1963) exemplifies "the long, clause-ridden Faulknerian sentences of the narrative and the multiple vision achieved through the statements supplied to the questioning narrator by a series of witnesses" (15).

Parkes, Henry Bamford. *The American Experience: An Interpretation of the History and Civilization of the American People.* New York: Vintage, 1961.

Emphasizing economic and cultural history, Parkes includes sections on Brazil, Canada, and Latin America. The section "Literature in America" is recommended as a starting point for comparisons with Brazilian literature.

Patai, Daphne. "Machado in English." *Machado de Assis: Reflections on a Brazilian Master Writer.* Ed. Richard Graham. Austin: U of Texas P, 1999. 85–116.

This informative essay examines Machado's reception in the English-speaking world and comments on the available translations of his key novels. Patai also discusses briefly the Brazilian publishing phenomenon Paulo Coelho (ranked, in 2002, as the world's second most widely published author, after John Grisham).

———. *Myth and Ideology in Contemporary Brazilian Fiction.* Rutherford: Fairleigh Dickinson UP, 1983.

In the chapters on Maria Alice Barroso and Autran Dourado, Patai notes similarities that link some of Faulkner's works (*The Sound and the Fury, As I Lay Dying,* and *Absalom, Absalom!*) with texts by the two Brazilian writers.

Payne, Johnny. *Conquest of the New Word: Experimental Fiction and Translation in the Americas.* Austin: U of Texas P, 1993.

Examining the impact of "Latin American" (read Spanish American) fiction in the United States in the 1960s, Payne argues that the American reception of the Boom writers distorted the historical basis of their works, so that it was understood as magical realism alone. Suggesting (along with other critics) that North American fiction was at something of a low point in its development, Payne believes that the Boom writing invigorated and inspired American narrative. He discusses the importance of translation in the dissemination of Latin American literature in the United States at the time.

Payne, Judith A., and Earl E. Fitz. *Ambiguity and Gender in the New Novel of Brazil and Spanish America: A Comparative Assessment.* Iowa City: U of Iowa P, 1993.

This work provides a comparative focus on the "New Novel" in Brazil and Spanish America in the 1960s. While Brazil embraces ambiguity and more open discussions of gender, Spanish America, tied to the patterns and restrictions of machismo, does not. According to the authors, the less-well-known Brazilian "New Novel" began earlier than the Spanish American form (indeed, with the publication of Machado's *The Posthumous Memoirs of Brás Cubas* in 1880) and reached its zenith with such writers as Clarice Lispector, Osman Lins, and Guimarães Rosa.

Peixoto, Afrânio. "American Social and Literary Influences in Brazil." *Books Abroad* 9.1 (1935): 3–5; *Books Abroad* 9.2 (1935): 127–29.

The Brazilian scholar summarizes the importance of the American Revolution for Brazilian artists and intellectuals of the late eighteenth century and briefly discusses the influences of such writers as Franklin, Cooper, Poe, Stowe, Longfellow, Twain, and Emerson on Brazilian literature. He also touches on the relatively more hospitable reception of the United States in Brazil than in Spanish America, which he finds "more mistrustful" (5).

Peixoto, Marta. *Passionate Fictions: Gender, Narrative, and Violence in Clarice Lispector.* Minneapolis: U of Minnesota P, 1994.

This concise study ranks as one of the best on the narratives of Clarice Lispector. Peixoto argues convincingly that Hélène Cixous has misinterpreted Lispector, portraying her as more passive and benign that she is. Peixoto writes, for example, that "the nurturing gentleness Cixous finds so repeatedly and exclusively in Lispector's texts and uses as her own method of reading, like a disguised straitjacket, ties Lispector to a limited interpretation" that reflects more of Cixous's interests as a writer and critic than it does of Lispector's texts (48).

Pereira, Luiz Bresser. *Development and Crisis in Brazil, 1930–1983.* Trans. Marcia Van Dyke. Boulder: Westview, 1984.

Incorporating economic and political commentary, Pereira explains how Brazil, "with the fifth largest land mass and the eighth largest population," has become one of the ten largest economies in the world and has developed "even while remaining on the periphery of the core economies," as Thomas C. Bruneau notes in his foreword (xiii). The author focuses on Brazil's transformation, between 1930 and 1983, from "an agrarian, mercantile economy into a capitalist, industrial society" (1).

Perrone, Charles A. *Masters of Contemporary Brazilian Song: MPB 1965–1985.* Austin: U of Texas P, 1989.

This rewarding book is a critical study of the MPB (*música popular brasileira*) movement of the 1960s and 1970s. Offering commentary on the sociopolitical significance of MPB as well as discussing its aesthetic qualities, the book—which focuses on six of the movement's leading composers and artists: Chico Buarque, Caetano Veloso, Gilberto Gil, Milton Nascimento, and the team of João Bosco and Aldir Blanc—demonstrates clearly why this vibrant movement had such an impact on Brazilian culture and its relationship with the rest of the world.

———. *Seven Faces: Brazilian Poetry since Modernism.* Durham: Duke UP, 1996.

Perrone discusses not only the poetry itself but popular-music lyrics as well, especially as they relate to the *Tropicalista* movement and to the nation's sociopolitical problems. There is an excellent chapter on concretist poetry, its importance to poetry, semiotics, and literary theory worldwide. Finally, Perrone notes the many points of contact between Brazilian poetry and such American and European figures as Poe, Bob Dylan, Pound, Cummings, John Cage, Joyce, Mallarmé, Rimbaud, Rilke, and Valéry.

Perrone, Charles A., and Christopher Dunn. *Brazilian Popular Music and Globalization.* Gainesville: UP of Florida, 2001.

Beginning with a 1959 song, "Chiclete com Banana," the authors examine the development of Brazilian popular music into a worldwide phenomenon, one that, by 2001, had influenced musicians and singers in virtually every country. Issues of influence and reception, and of the internationalization of Brazilian music and culture generally, are clearly discussed.

Pontiero, Giovanni. "Brazilian Poetry from Modernism to the 1990s." González Echevarría and Pupo-Walker 3: 247–67.

After a concise discussion of the influence of cubism and expressionism on Brazilian modernists early in the twentieth century, Pontiero charts the evolution of *modernismo*, to elucidate its principles and to identify its most representative writers. He then outlines the development of Brazilian poetry to the end of the twentieth century.

Porter, Carolyn. "Social Discourse and Nonfictional Prose." Elliott, *Columbia Literary History* 345–63.

In discussing the literature of the United States between Jefferson's presidency and the beginning of the Civil War, Porter touches on themes—including slavery, regional conflict, and the explosive intersection of politics and art—that resonate with Brazilian culture of the same period.

———. "What We Know That We Don't Know: Remapping American Literary Studies." *American Literary History* 3 (1994): 467–526.

Porter, focusing on "American" literature and "American" studies at the end of the twentieth century, advocates a revision of the courses we teach and the texts we use. As an indication of the need for such revision, she mentions García Márquez's comments on how Faulkner had influenced him. In a discussion of José David Saldívar's *The Dialectics of Our America*, Porter calls for a Pan-American literary history, one that would include Latin America (521). In using the term *Latin America*, however, Porter refers only to Spanish American texts, authors, and issues; no mention is made of Brazil or its literature.

Prado, Caio, Jr. *The Colonial Background of Modern Brazil.* Trans. Suzette Macedo. Berkeley: U of California P, 1967.

Although somewhat dated, this volume remains a basic text for those seeking to understand Brazil's development. Prado maintains that many of Brazil's present-day problems stem from social, political, and economic structures of the colonial period, which, the author believes, are only now being replaced by up-to-date systems.

Putnam, Samuel. "Jefferson and the Young Brazilians in France." *Science and Society* 10.2 (1946): 185–92.

Putnam explores in some detail the circumstances surrounding the April 1787 meeting between Jefferson, the minister plenipotentiary to France, and a group of Brazilians led by the young patriot José Joaquim da Maia. Careful not to commit the still weak United States to something it could not do (supporting a revolutionary movement in another New World country), Jefferson may have given the inexperienced Maia the erroneous impression that he was not interested in Brazil's cause.

————. *Marvelous Journey: A Survey of Four Centuries of Brazilian Writing.* New York: Knopf, 1948.

The first comprehensive comparative study of Brazilian and American literature, Putnam's book begins with the colonial era and ends at the mid-1940s. The work is especially good in examining the sociopolitical factors that shaped the two societies in their formative periods and in drawing parallels and contrasts between the writers of the "Romantic Liberation" (99–162). Putnam explains that the European influences on Brazil differed from the English influences on the United States. Putnam is one of the first commentators to discuss links between Henry James and Machado de Assis.

Rabassa, Gregory. "A Comparative Look at the Literatures of Spanish America and Brazil: The Dangers of Deception." *Ibero-American Letters in a Comparative Perspective.* Ed. W. T. Zyla and W. M. Aycock. Lubbock: Texas Tech UP, 1978: 119–32.

The author discusses the key differences between Spanish American and Brazilian literature and warns readers not to assume that what they think they know about one culture applies to the other.

————. "La nueva narrativa en el Brasil." *Nueva narrativa hispanoamericana* 2.1 (1972): 145–48.

Arguing that "el mayor novelista de todas las Américas es brasilero" (145; "the greatest novelist of all the Americas is a Brazilian"), Rabassa cites Machado as a forerunner of Latin America's famous "New Narrative" of the 1960s. Rabassa then discusses such later narrativists as Euclides da Cunha, Graciliano Ramos, Guimarães Rosa, Dalton Trevisan, Clarice Lispector, and Nélida Piñon.

————. "Osman Lins and *Avalovara*: The Shape and Shaping of the Novel." *World Literature Today* 53.1 (1979): 30–35.

The novel's translator, Rabassa, discusses the thematic and structural characteristics of *Avalovara* and, in the process, compares it to Julio Cortázar's *Hopscotch*. Instead of the circle, which as Rabassa notes has long served the novel well, Lins employs the spiral as the primary narrative base of his work (32).

Reis, Roberto. *The Pearl Necklace: Toward an Archaeology of Brazilian Transition Discourse.* Trans. Aparecida Godoy Johnson. Gainesville: UP of Florida, 1992.

In examining some canonical texts of Brazilian literature from 1850 to 1950— the "transition period" in which Brazil was transformed from a rural society to an urban one—Reis asserts that most of the literature produced during this time, including the so-called leftist literature of the 1930s, leaves basically unchallenged the elitist ruling structures. Thus the undercurrent of authoritarianism in Brazilian culture, Reis observes, is rarely questioned by the country's writers (Machado and Érico Veríssimo are the two exceptions for Reis).

Ribeiro, Darcy. *The Brazilian People: The Formation and Meaning of Brazil*. Trans. Gregory Rabassa. Gainesville: UP of Florida, 2000.

Written by one of Brazil's foremost intellectuals, this book proposes, according to Elizabeth Lowe, who provides the book's foreword, "a 'theory of Brazilian culture' that summarizes the author's thirty years of research, fieldwork, and contemplation on the contributions of the Indians, Afro-Brazilians, and many mixed-race variations to the distinct character of Brazilian nationality and culture." Ribeiro meditates on "the paradox of Brazil, a country of immense potential hindered by racial and class prejudice," she says (viii, xii).

Roberts, John Storm. *Latin Jazz: The First of the Fusions, 1880s to Today*. New York: Schirmer, 1999.

Roberts devotes considerable space to Brazil, its musical heritage, the many musicians Brazil has exported to the United States, and especially the impact they have had on the development of jazz. Of the marriage between American jazz and Brazilian bossa nova, Roberts writes, "It is ironic that one of the last mass-popular movements in jazz to date also should have been one of the very few 1960s phenomena whose roots in the 1950s were tenuous, and that it should at one and the same time have intrigued musicians by its rhythmic and harmonic subtlety, and the general public by its extreme accessibility" (115).

Rodman, Selden. *South America of the Poets*. New York: Hawthorn, 1970.

A kind of literary travelogue through Latin America, this book offers, in chapter 5 ("Brazil in Five Cantos"), interesting, brief commentaries on such modern Brazilian writers as Vinícius de Moraes, Euclides da Cunha, and Jorge Amado. Several comparisons are made between the cultural development of Brazil and that of the United States. For example, after summarizing Vianna Moog's *Bandeirantes and Pioneers* (1943), Rodman identifies the book's thesis: the differences between the two countries emerged from their experiences during colonial periods. Whereas the Brazilian *bandeirantes* ("flag-bearers") who conquered the hinterlands "had no public spirit or will for political self-determination," leaving in their wake "a land fit only for exploitation, a world where the only principle was the principle of authority," the North American pioneers believed in the value of work, were "devoted to the virtues of frugality and punctuality," and "had the capacity to organize for communal benefit" (93).

Rohter, Larry. "Brazil Builds Bigger and Better Telenovelas." *New York Times* 27 Aug. 2000, Television and Radio sec.: 21–23.

Observing the commercial success (in Brazil and, in translation, in a dozen countries in Spanish America) of the serial *Xica da Silva*, Rohter discusses the *telenovela*, a popular entertainment often described as the equivalent of the soap opera.

Rohter notes several points of comparison: (1) while some soap operas have been running for four decades, the telenovela has a beginning and end, usually after about 180 episodes; (2) while most soap operas are consigned to daytime programming, *telenovelas* enjoy prime-time airings five or six evenings a week; (3) most Hollywood stars regard soap operas as beneath their dignity, but even the biggest stars are recruited for the *telenovelas*; (4) the *telenovela*, unlike its counterpart, tends to take on controversial themes, including "agrarian reform, racism, abortion, environmental degradation, homosexuality, and corruption," as well as the more traditional themes of love, jealousy, and betrayal; and (5) the *telenovela* is more explicit in its handling of nudity and sexual matters (21).

———. "Tiger in a Lifeboat, Panther in a Lifeboat: A Furor over a Novel." *New York Times* 6 Nov. 2002: late ed. final, sec. E: 1 +. 14 Oct. 2003 <nytimes.com/ 2002/11/06/books/06NOVE.html>.

Although focusing on the controversy surrounding the many similarities between Moacyr Scliar's novella *Max and the Cats* and Yann Martel's *Life of Pi*, the article also mentions two similar cases (Daphne du Maurier's *Rebecca* and its relation to Carolina Nabuco's *The Successor* and the debt Rod Stewart's "Do Ya Think I'm Sexy?" is thought to owe to Jorge Ben's "Taj Mahal") where Brazilian writers and artists felt that their creative efforts were improperly copied or borrowed by others.

Sadlier, Darlene J., ed. *One Hundred Years after Tomorrow: Brazilian Women's Fiction in the Twentieth Century*. Bloomington: Indiana UP, 1992.

Featuring an excellent critical introduction examining the development of women's writing in Brazil, this anthology—which contains selections, many never before translated, from Brazil's best women writers—sheds light on the Brazilian narrative. Moreover, it presents comparative studies on Brazilian women's writing and women's writing in other parts of the world, particularly the United States.

Sant'Anna, Affonso Romano de. "What Kind of Country Is This?" Trans. Fred P. Ellison. *Latin American Literary Review* 14.27 (1986): 106–16.

This famous poem captures the essence of the pain, frustration, and anger that Brazilians, looking at the rest of the world, feel about the underdevelopment and foreign exploitation that plague their country.

Santiago, Silviano. "The Hurried Midwives of Time: Brazilian Fiction in the 1980s." *Tropical Paths: Essays on Modern Brazilian Literature*. Ed. Randal Johnson. New York: Garland, 1993. 223–29.

Santiago, a leading critic, observes that, during the 1980s, Brazilian writers, in an effort "to modernize the field of comprehension of the contemporary work of art, decided to take up again the modernist tendency to thematize the art of criticism in the literary work itself, making it self-reflexive"—a tactic that harks

back to Machado de Assis. Santiago asks, "How does one justify the divorce between literary production in the 1980s and contemporary criticism?" (227–28).

———. "O narrador pós-moderno." *Revista do Brasil* 2.5 (1968): 4–13.

Focusing on the short stories of Edilberto Coutinho, Santiago explores the implications of postmodernism for contemporary Brazilian literature and culture.

———. "Reading and Discursive Intensities: On the Situation of Postmodern Reception in Brazil." *Boundary 2* 20.3 (1993): 194–202.

Discussing Brazil's "greatest modern critic," Antônio Candido, Santiago argues
that in a "culturally 'underdeveloped' country such as Brazil, the problem represented by the spectacle/simulacrum distinction becomes particularly acute."
He observes that this problem "already has a history," directly related, as Candido outlined it, to the integral relation between underdevelopment and literature (195–96).

Sayre, Gordon M., ed. *American Captivity Narratives: Selected Narratives with Introduction.* New Riverside Editions. Gen. ed. Paul Lauter. New York:
Houghton, 2000.

Arguing that the captivity narrative is of special importance to the literature of
the United States, Sayre includes selections from French Canada and Spanish
America as well as from the English colonies. His book is intended to spur a
"broad, comparative conception of the American captivity genre" (4).

Scheick, William J. "The Poetry of Colonial America." Elliott, *Columbia Literary
History* 83–97.

According to Scheick, the poetry of the colonial United States was far more creative and complex than has traditionally been thought. Indeed, his discussion
of Edward Taylor's poetry suggests a connection, based on the aesthetics of the
baroque, between his work and that of Mexico's Sor Juana Inés de la Cruz or
Brazil's Gregório de Matos.

Schmink, Marianne. "Women in Brazilian *Abertura* Politics." *Signs* 7.1 (1981):
115–34.

Schmink examines the roles played by the women who were active in Brazil's
feminist movement and who, during the *abertura*—"opening": João Baptista
de Oliveira Figueiredo's decision in March 1979 to initiate a return to democratic government in Brazil—lobbied for social and political reform.

Schmitt, Jack, and Lorie Ishimatsu. Introduction. *"The Devil's Church" and Other
Stories.* Trans. Schmitt and Ishimatsu. Austin: U of Texas P, 1977.

This insightful essay summarizes Machado's career as a short story writer, discusses his outstanding characteristics, and places him in an international context.

Schwarz, Roberto. *Misplaced Ideas: Essays on Brazilian Culture.* Trans., ed., and introd. John Gledson. London: Verso, 1992.

Schwarz analyzes the evolution of Brazil's literature by comparing and contrasting it with Brazil's development as a nation-state and with its self-conscious intellectual formation. His basic argument, which he develops in provocative essays on such pivotal writers as José de Alencar, Machado de Assis, and Oswald de Andrade, is that liberal Western ideas have been "inappropriately copied in Brazil," where they have been "misplaced," and that since the nineteenth century, "educated Brazilians . . . have had the sense of living among ideas and institutions copied from abroad that do not reflect local reality" (8–9).

Sedycias, João. *The Naturalistic Novel of the New World: A Comparative Study of Stephen Crane, Aluísio Azevedo, and Federico Gamboa.* Lanham: UP of America, 1993.

Examining representative works by three New World authors—Crane, *Maggie,* from the United States; Azevedo, *O cortiço (A Brazilian Tenement),* from Brazil; and Gamboa, *Santa,* from Mexico—Sedycias compares and contrasts the phenomenon of the naturalistic novel.

Sena, Jorge de. "Machado de Assis and His *Carioca* Quintet." *Latin American Literary Review* 14. 27 (1986): 7–18.

In the context of the "contemporaneous free novel form," de Sena believes, Machado's final five novels represent "*a single experimental novel*—a 'Carioca' quintet." De Sena discusses the assessment of a writer like Machado, whose brilliance is obscured by the "inability" of the "great cultures . . . to see or accept anything outside of themselves" (9).

Shaw, Lisa. "The Brazilian *Chanchada* of the 1950s and Notions of Popular Identity." *Luso-Brazilian Review* 38.1 (2001): 17–30.

Focusing on the productions of the successful Atlântida studio, Shaw examines the role the song-and-dance films played in the creation of a popular identity in the 1950s, "a decade in which Hollywood's hegemony and the capitalist ethos were more prevalent than ever in Brazil" (17).

Silverman, Kenneth. "From Cotton Mather to Benjamin Franklin." Elliott, *Columbia Literary History* 101–12.

In discussing the writers, each emblematic of his period, and the emergence of the "Two American Dreams"—a hardheaded practicality and a vision of an ideal society—Silverman sets up an analytic framework for making comparisons between American and Brazilian culture (111).

Skidmore, Thomas E. *Brazil: Five Centuries of Change.* New York: Oxford UP, 1999.

After a short but convincing introduction, "Why Read about Brazil?," Skidmore takes the reader through a concise history of Brazil and the forces that have shaped it. Particularly engrossing are the sections on such urgent issues as the widening gap between the rich and poor in Brazil, education, health care, policies affecting women, and race relations.

———. "The Essay: Architects of Brazilian National Identity." González Echevarría and Pupo-Walker 3: 345–62.

Skidmore surveys the evolution of the Brazilian essay, observing in particular its interest in Brazilian identity, especially as the issue sheds lights on Brazil's relation to other cultures.

Sontag, Susan. "Afterlives: The Case of Machado de Assis." *New Yorker* 7 May 1990: 102–08.

Sontag describes her discovery of Machado as one of Western literature's modern masters. Calling *Epitaph of a Small Winner* "thrillingly original" and "radically skeptical," Sontag considers it "one of the most entertaininingly unprovincial books ever written"—a work that more sophisticated societies will find it difficult "to condescend" to (108). This provocative essay appeared, almost verbatim, as the foreward to Noonday's edition of *Epitaph of a Small Winner* (see next entry).

———. Foreword. *Epitaph of a Small Winner.* By Joaquim Maria Machado de Assis. Trans. William L. Grossman. New York: Noonday P, 1990. xi–xx.

Comparing Machado with such writers as Sterne, Natsume Soseki, Robert Walser, Italo Svevo, Robert Hrabal, and Beckett, Sontag—impressed by his iconoclasm and modernity—declares herself "retroactively influenced" by him (xix). "Machado is even less well known to Spanish-language readers than to those who read him in English," she concludes, because *Epitaph of a Small Winner* was translated into Spanish in the 1960s, about a decade after he had appeared in English (xix).

Sousa, Ronald W. "The Divided Discourse of *As aventuras de Diófanes* and Its Socio-Historical Implications." *Ideology and Literature* (1984): 75–88.

Sousa notes that *As aventuras* (1752), by Teresa Margarida da Silva e Orta, often cited as Brazil's first novel, was "a conscious imitation" of Fénelon's *Les aventures de Télémaque* and that, like its progenitor, it is steeped in political analysis (75).

Sousa Andrade [Sousândrade], Joaquim de. "The Inferno of Wall Street." Trans. Robert E. Brown, with the assistance of Augusto de Campos. *Latin American Literary Review* 14 (1986): 92–98.

This early modernist poem poignantly expresses the troubled relationship that, from the perspective of Brazil, existed between it and the United States in the early twentieth century.

Spiller, Robert E. *The Cycle of American Literature: An Essay in Historical Criticism.* New York: Free, 1967.

Spiller argues that American literature (like all literature) "has a relationship to social and intellectual history, not as documentation, but as symbolic illumination" (x). Spiller's historically based method facilitates a comparative study of American and Brazilian literature. His insightful discussion of American colonial literature, for example, can assist the reader in contrasting it with its Brazilian counterpart.

Stam, Robert. *Tropical Multiculturalism: A Comparative History of Race in Brazilian Cinema and Culture.* Durham: Duke UP, 1997.

As he describes how racial issues have been portrayed in Brazilian film and culture, Stam raises some provocative notions that, in addition to shedding light on Brazilian society, suggest comparisons with the racial situation in the United States. He discusses Pan-Americanism, for example, as well as the films of Carmen Miranda and Orson Welles's keen interest in Brazil.

Stam, Robert, João Luiz Vieira, and Ismail Xavier. "The Shape of Brazilian Cinema in the Postmodern Age." *Brazilian Cinema.* Expanded ed. Ed. Randal Johnson and Robert Stam. New York: Columbia UP, 1995. 387–472.

This essay updates the 1982 edition of *Brazilian Cinema* and discusses the topic through the mid-1990s. Besides providing an excellent survey of Brazilian film from the late 1970s to about 1995, the authors establish a comparative framework that indicates how the Brazilian film industry has evolved and how it stands in relation to film production elsewhere.

Szoka, Elzbieta, and Joe W. Bratcher III, eds. *Three Contemporary Brazilian Plays in Bilingual Edition.* Austin: Host, 1988.

Featuring plays by Plínio Marcos, Leilah Assunção, and Consuelo de Castro, this anthology includes a concise history of the Brazilian stage by Margo Milleret. Each play is preceded by a short critical commentary.

Tolman, Jon M. "About the Author" and introduction. *Snakes' Nest; or, A Tale Badly Told.* By Lêdo Ivo. Trans. Kern Krapohl. New York: New Directions, 1981.

Tolman presents two short, useful articles that explore the novel that and the influences on its author.

Torres-Ríoseco, Arturo. *The Epic of Latin American Literature.* Rev. ed. New York: Oxford UP, 1946.

This famous study was perhaps the first to contain a chapter on Brazilian literature. Chapter 6, "Brazilian Literature," includes the sections "The Portuguese Colonial Pattern," "Colonial Literature," "Independence: The Birth of Brazilian Literature," "Brazilian Poetry," "Brazilian Prose Fiction," and "The Contemporary Novel" (the late 1930s and early 1940s). Reading these sections in sequence provides a view of Brazilian literature in comparison with that of Spanish America and the United States, as well as an understanding of European influences.

Unruh, Vicky. *Latin American Vanguards: The Art of Contentious Encounters.* Berkeley: U of California P, 1994.

Unruh examines the aesthetic and ideological development of the vanguard movements in Spanish America and Brazil during the 1920s and 1930s. European and North American concepts of the avant-garde are compared and contrasted with those in Latin America, as are the differences between the Brazilian *modernistas* and their Spanish American counterparts. From Brazil, Mário de Andrade and Oswald de Andrade receive the most attention.

Valente, Luiz F. "Marriages of Speaking and Hearing: Mediation and Response in

Absalom, Absalom! and *Grande Sertão: Veredas.*" *A Latin American Faulkner.*
Guest ed. Beatriz Vegh. Spec. issue of *Faulkner Journal* 11.1 and 2 (1995–96): 149–64.

In this engaging comparison of Faulkner's novel and Rosa's *The Devil to Pay in the Backlands*, two works that "occupy a pivotal position in the development of twentieth century fiction" (162), Valente, focusing on "the role played by the reader . . . in the construction of meaning" (150), concludes that these New World masterpieces "can be placed at the crossroads of modernism and post-modernism." He also finds that they exhibit "a growing suspicion of totalizing explanations" and reveal "an increasing self-consciousness about the status of the literary text and the nature of interpretation itself" (162).

Veloso, Caetano. "An Orpheus, Rising fron Caricature." Trans. Ana Maria Bahiana. *New York Times on the Web*, Arts and Leisure, 20 Aug. 2000.

Veloso, a prominent singer, musician, and songwriter, discusses the Carlos Diegues film *Orfeu* and its relation to its famous 1959 predecessor, *Black Orpheus* (Marcel Camus, director) as well as to the 1956 play *Orfeu da conceição*, by Vinícius de Moraes, on which *Black Orpheus* was based. Veloso comments on the popularity of the de Moraes play, on the unpopularity of the Camus film in Brazil (*Black Orpheus* was venerated abroad but was regarded with contempt by Brazilians, who thought the work depicts them as "exotics"), and, finally, on the success that Diegues's *Orfeu* has enjoyed in Brazil. As Veloso notes, this film utilizes rap music and takes a realistic look at Brazil's racial problems. *Orfeu* opened in the United States in August 2000.

———. *Tropical Truths: A Story of Music and Revolution in Brazil.* Trans. Isabel de Sena. New York: Knopf, 2003.

In this book, originally published as *Verdade tropical* (São Paulo: Cidade de Letras, 1997), Veloso shows us why he has become not only an internationally acclaimed musical celebrity, one hailed by such artists as Beck and David Byrne, but an astute social critic as well, one who clearly understands the vital role that music plays in Brazilian culture and, indeed, all cultures. At the heart of the book, however, is Veloso's discussion of *tropicalismo*, the eclectic and invigorating musical movement of the late 1960s that sought to merge Brazil and its culture with the rest of world culture and, in so doing, to help shape "a universal and international urban cultural reality" (6).

Versiani, Ivana. "The New-World's First Novelist." *The Brazilian Novel.* Ed. Heitor Martins. Bloomington: Indiana U. Dept. of Spanish and Portuguese, Research Center for Language and Semiotic Studies, 1976. 15–27.

Versiani discusses the life of Teresa Margarida da Silva e Orta, the author of what may be Brazil's first novel (to Versiani, perhaps the New World's), *As aventuras de Diófanes* (1752). She examines the style ("verbose, tangled, monotonous" [26]) and structure of the work and, terming it "a didactic novel" (16), compares it with Fénelon's *Les aventures de Télemaque*. An engaging part of the essay is Versiani's interpretation of Silva e Orta's "feminist ideas"—for Versiani, the book is "obsessed with feminine problems" (26).

Vianna, Oliveira. *Populações meridionais do Brasil*. Vols. 1 and 2. São Paulo: Monteiro Lobato, 1922.

In this work, Vianna—long concerned with the issue of race in Brazilian culture and its importance to national identity—discusses his belief that, to become a modern nation, Brazil needed a strong central government to offset the ineffective political institutions it had inherited from Portugal.

Wagley, Charles. *An Introduction to Brazil*. Rev. ed. New York: Columbia UP, 1963.

One of the most influential texts on Brazil to appear in the early 1960s, Wagley's study remains a useful overview. Illustrating the many comparisons he makes between Brazil and the United States, Wagley (quoting another Brazilianist, Tulio Ascarelli) writes that "an American country, yet fully participant in Latin culture, very young and yet old, Brazil finds itself between the United States and Europe, intermediary between one and the other. It is tied to the former by the direction of social change in its way of life, and to the latter by its cultural tradition" (301).

Wasserman, Renata R. Mautner. *Exotic Nations: Literature and Cultural Identity in the United States and Brazil, 1830–1930*. Ithaca: Cornell UP, 1994.

By utilizing the subtle "connection between exoticism and power" (33), this meticulously researched book examines the process by which two distinctive but culturally and historically related societies differentiated themselves from European modes of thought and established themselves as identifiable New World nations. Besides considering the influence of such French thinkers as Rousseau, Bernardin de Saint-Pierre, and Chateaubriand on New World literary development, Wasserman compares James Fenimore Cooper and his Brazilian counterpart, José de Alencar. A provocative chapter discusses Mário de Andrade's *Macunaíma* and its significance for Brazilian national identity.

———. "Mario Vargas Llosa, Euclides da Cunha, and the Strategy of Intertextuality." *PMLA* 108 (1993): 460–73.

Wasserman examines the close relation between Vargas Llosa's novel *The War of the End of the World* and da Cunha's *Rebellion in the Backlands* and shows how both texts confront the questions of cultural power and identity (460). Wasserman illuminates not only the direct influence of the Brazilian text on the Peruvian novel but also the conflicts that have risen in Brazil, and in Latin America generally, over attempts to graft European cultural mores onto societies that differ considerably from those on the Continent (470).

———. "Re-inventing the New World: Cooper and Alencar." *Comparative Literature* 36 (1984): 183–200.

The discussion in this excellent article, a narrowly focused version of the author's *Exotic Nations*, centers on the Indianist novels of Cooper and Alencar and shows their relevance to the formation of a national identity in both Brazil and the United States.

———. "The Theater of José de Anchieta and the Definition of Brazilian Literature." *Luso-Brazilian Review* 36.1 (1999): 71–86.

Wasserman explains the significance of Anchieta, a Jesuit priest, to the foundations of Brazilian literature. His multilingual theater (in Portuguese, Spanish, and Tupi) suggests to Wasserman that Anchieta helped create the image of Brazil as not only tolerant of but incorporating material from diverse origins. She discusses, in a way that invites comparison with the religious foundations of colonial North America, the intellectual importance of Anchieta's Jesuit training and sense of duty: "Seeking out controversy from its inception, and from the beginning pulling the colonial enterprise into the moral maelstrom of reformation and counter-reformation, the Society of Jesus constituted one of the forks on the road of development through and out of colonization in the Americas" (71).

Williams, Stanley T. *The Spanish Background of American Literature*. New Haven: Yale UP, 1955.

Williams, in contrasting the English Puritan heritage with the Spanish Catholic heritage of Latin America, examines the tensions at play in the colonial period. He does not deal with Brazil, although several issues he discusses are pertinent to its development.

Woodall, James. *A Simple Brazilian Song: Journeys through the Rio Sound*. New York: Little, Brown, 1997.

Focusing on the music and lyrics (several songs have English translations) of Caetano Veloso and Chico Buarque, Woodall discusses his enchantment with Brazilian music and Rio de Janeiro. Chico's 1992 novel, *Estorvo* (*Turbulence*), is also touched on. Of Chico's famous protest song, "Apesar de você" ("In Spite of You"), Woodall observes that it "remains one of the most infectious and defiant pop songs ever written," and he paraphrases Chico's assertion that "Brazilians don't make a distinction between 'pop' and 'serious' music" (15).

Woodyard, George, ed. *The Modern Stage in Latin America: Six Plays*. New York: Dutton, 1971.

Although it contains only one Brazilian play (Dias Gomes's *Payment as Pledged*), this volume, in Woodyard's short, incisive introduction, situates Brazilian theater in the context of the Latin American theater. And while not developing extended comparisons, Woodyard notes the playwrights who have influenced Brazilian and Spanish American drama.

Wright, Lawrence. "One Drop of Blood." *New Yorker* 25 July 1994: 46–55.

After discussing the way that "Washington chooses to define the population [of the United States] in the 2000 census," Wright's essay takes up race relations, affirmative action, and racial mixing in the United States. Wright concludes by quoting Representative Tom Sawyer (Ohio), who says, "We act as if we know what we're talking about when we talk about race, and we don't" (55). This article clearly shows that the United States is more of a racially mixed society than it likes to think of itself as being and that, in consequence, it is more like Brazil than most of its citizens would have thought possible.

Xavier, Ismail. *Allegories of Underdevelopment: Aesthetics and Politics in Modern Brazilian Cinema.* Minneapolis: U of Minnesota P, 1997.

As he considers the films of the *cinema novo* and the "marginal cinema" movements, the author aims to "characterize, through the analysis of Brazilian films made between 1964 and 1970, the allegorical representation of national history and contemporary society developed by young filmmakers who deeply transformed film culture in Brazil" and to discuss the rise of "Brazilian auteur cinema, which tightened relations between culture and politics as never before in the country" (1).

Yúdice, George. "Postmodernism in the Periphery." *South Atlantic Quarterly* 92.3 (1993): 543–56.

The author discusses the applicability of the postmodern perspective to the Latin American cultural scene.

———. "Postmodernity and Transnational Capitalism in Latin America." *On Edge: the Crisis of Contemporary Latin American Culture.* Ed. Yúdice, Jean Franco, and Juan Flores. Minneapolis: U of Minnesota P, 1992. 1–28.

Stressing the links between cultural and economic development, Yúdice explores the wide range of implications that the postmodern optic possesses for Latin America.

The index does not cover the four appendixes, where listings are arranged alphabetically.